DARK SIDE OF THE DREAM

Other titles in the series

National Fictions
Literature, film and the construction of Australian narrative
Graeme Turner

Myths of Oz
Reading Australian Popular Culture
John Fiske, Bob Hodge, Graeme Turner

Australian Television
Programs, Pleasures and Politics
Edited by John Tulloch and Graeme Turner

Fashioning the Feminine
Girls, popular culture and schooling
Pam Gilbert and Sandra Taylor

Australian Cultural Studies
Editor: John Tulloch

DARK SIDE OF THE DREAM

Australian literature and the postcolonial mind

Bob Hodge and Vijay Mishra

ALLEN & UNWIN

© Bob Hodge and Vijay Mishra 1990
This book is copyright under the Berne Convention.
No reproduction without permission. All rights reserved.

First published in 1991
Allen & Unwin Pty Ltd
8 Napier Street, North Sydney NSW 2059 Australia

National Library of Australia
Cataloguing-in-publication entry:

Hodge, Bob, (Robert Ian Vere).
 Dark side of the dream : Australian literature and the postcolonial mind.

 Bibliography.
 ISBN 0 04 442346 2.

 1. Australian literature — History and criticism.
 2. National characteristics, Australian. I. Mishra, Vijay.
 II. Title.

A820.9

Typeset in 10/11pt Sabon by Adtype Graphics, North Sydney

Printed by Chong Moh Offset Printing Pte Ltd, Singapore

This publication was assisted by the Australia Council, the Federal Government's arts funding and advisory body.

General Editor's Foreword

Nowadays the social and anthropological definition of 'culture' is probably gaining as much public currency as the aesthetic one. Particularly in Australia, politicians are liable to speak of the vital need for a domestic film industry in 'promoting our cultural identity'—and they mean by 'cultural identity' some sense of Australianness, of our nationalism as a distinct form of social organisation. Notably, though, the emphasis tends to be on Australian *film* (not popular television); and not just *any* film, but those of 'quality'. So the aesthetic definition tends to be smuggled back in—on top of the kind of cultural nationalism which assumes that 'Australia' is a unified entity with certain essential features that distinguish it from 'Britain', the 'USA' or any other national entities which threaten us with 'cultural dependency'.

This series is titled 'Australian Cultural Studies', and I should say at the outset that my understanding of 'Australian' is not as an essentially unified category; and further, that my understanding of cultural is anthropological rather than aesthetic. By 'culture' I mean the social production of meaning and understanding, whether in the inter-personal and practical organisation of daily routines or in broader institutional and ideological structures. I am *not* thinking of 'culture' as some form of universal 'excellence', based on aesthetic 'discrimination' and embodied in a pantheon of 'great works'. Rather, I take this aesthetic definition of culture itself to be part of the *social mobilisation of discourse* to differentiate a cultural 'élite' from the 'mass' of society.

Unlike the cultural nationalism of our opinion leaders, 'Cultural Studies' focuses not on the essential unity of national cultures, but on the meanings attached to social difference (as in the distinction between 'élite' and 'mass' taste). It analyses the construction and mobilisation of these distinctions to maintain or challenge existing power differentials, such as those of gender, class, age, race and ethnicity. In this analysis, terms designed to socially differentiate people (like 'élite' and 'mass') become categories of discourse, communication and power. Hence our concern in this series is for an analytical understanding of the meanings attached to social difference within the *history* and *politics* of discourse.

It follows that the analysis of 'texts' needs to be united from a single-minded association with 'high' culture (marked by 'authorship'), but must include the 'popular' too—since these distinctions of 'high' and 'popular' culture themselves need to be analysed, not assumed.

All of the books published in the series so far reject the assumed distinction between 'high' and 'popular' culture, and Bob Hodge and Vijay Mishra put the case particularly clearly in *Dark Side of the Dream*:

> The central theme of our book...is Australia's attempts to construct a national identity, and the massive effects on this enterprise that arise from the nature of the foundation of the modern Australian state, as the unjust act of an imperial power...In saying this we are not suggesting that there is a single agreed object, 'Australian Literature'. The term refers to a body of genres and texts that has always been stratified along social and political lines, with different orientations to the dominant groups in the society...But while this ideological project was always part of the context in which Australian literary texts were produced, its force was intermittent and variable across the full range of production. For that reason we look at many texts that would not be conventionally regarded as 'great' or 'Australian' or even 'literature'.

Culture, as Fiske, Hodge and Turner say in *Myths of Oz*, grows out of the divisions of society, not its unity. 'It has to work to construct any unity that it has, rather than simply celebrate an achieved or natural harmony.' Australian culture is then no more than the temporary, embattled construction of 'unity' at any particular historical moment. The 'readings' in this series of 'Australian Cultural Studies' inevitably (and polemically) form part of the struggle to make and break the boundaries of meaning which, in conflict and collusion, dynamically define our culture.

JOHN TULLOCH

Contents

Foreword		v
Preface		ix
Acknowledgements		xx
1	**Australian literature and the problem of history**	**1**
	Australian literature and the history of the real	1
	Reading texts, reading culture	6
	Fragments and literary history	14
2	**The bastard complex**	**23**
	Aborigines and Australian identity	24
	The foundation event	30
	The genocidal phase	38
3	**Return of the repressed**	**50**
	The dilemma of romance	52
	The epic turn	59
	Aborigines and film	64
4	**Dark traditions**	**71**
	Reading Aboriginal culture	74
	The politics of mediation	77
	The functions of myth	86
5	**Aboriginal voices**	**91**
	Land as theme	92
	Transformations	97
	Versions of history	101
	Aboriginal polyphony	107
6	**Crimes and punishments**	**116**
	The convict system	118
	The spectacle of punishment	120
	The bushranger myth	131
	The uses of deviancy	136

7	Reading the country	143
	Negations of the real	144
	The meaning of distance	151
	Explorer as hero	157
8	The Australian legend	162
	A gendered land	163
	A classic text revisited	167
	The ugly Australian	172
9	Multiculturalism and the fragment society	178
	Hidden countries	182
	The assimilationist muse	188
	Forms of multiculturalism	196
10	Reading the dream	204
	Antilanguage, anticulture	205
	Happy families	211
	The paranoiac culture	216
Notes: sources and contexts		220
Bibliography		235
Index		250

Preface

This book is mainly about Australian literature, but from a particular point of view. We are primarily interested in the literature as a set of texts which, read in certain ways against a range of other texts and priorities, throw light on some recurring features of the Australian 'character', the Australian *mentalité*. By this we refer to characteristic patterns of thinking, feeling and behaving that arise out of the social and political conditions of Australian life, and which serve in their turn to help to sustain it. In this way we are concerned with the literature as itself a political and social fact, to be understood alongside other political and social facts.

Our starting point is the present, with issues and debates that agitate Australians today about the nature of their society, the foundations of their identity. A convenient encapsulation of some of these issues was provided by an event that got under way as we were planning this book, the celebration of what was called the Australian Bicentenary of 1988. These celebrations went on so long and so publicly that certain contradictions in the national psyche became more obtrusive than its euphoric organisers would have liked. The Bicentenary took as its starting date the first invasion by the British in 1788, not the founding of the state of Australia itself, which happened in 1901, only 87 years before the 'Bicentenary'. There is here a characteristic Australian move in regard to history. On the one hand time is stretched out, to give a longer history to the nation than it has. But then that double century was drastically shortened and emptied out in the celebration, reduced to two moments juxtaposed: the pioneering moment, in which heroic blue-coats gazed at the empty land, and the contemporary moment, filled with cheering spectators.

Underlying this new myth was a more persistent feature of Australian constructions of nation and identity. The decisive event was the act of invasion, not the gesture of independence. Inevitably a number of shadows fell on the facile and empty historical charade: the shadow of the many thousands of years when Aboriginal Australians possessed the land, the shadow of more than a century of covert though unsuccessful attempts at cultural genocide, and finally the shadows cast by the dark bodies of Aborigines signifying their dignified but implacable protest, immediately recorded by the attentive media and transmitted to every television set in the land. It was clear that underlying the jingoistic and premature celebration was an acute anxiety at the core of the national self-image, and an obsession with the issue of legitimacy.

The central theme of our book, then, is Australians' attempts to construct a national identity, and the massive effects on this enterprise that arise from the nature of the foundation of the modern Australian state, as the unjust act of an imperial power whose direct beneficiaries have still not acknowledged that injustice nor succeeded in constructing a viable alternative basis for their legitimacy. Our particular concern is with the roles that Australian literature has played in this unceasing and doomed quest for symbolic forms of legitimacy: Australian literature both as a set of texts and as an object constructed by various agencies attempting to prescribe what texts should be written, what they should be taken to mean, and what authors and texts should be deemed to count as the major landmarks in the national tradition. We argue against both the competing views of Australian literature: that its claims to greatness (or fatal defect) lay in its heroic (or unfortunate) break with the culture of the centre. On the contrary we see the culture and its literature as still determined massively by its complicity with an imperialist enterprise, coexisting in a necessary but compromised symbiosis with moments and forces of subversion and resistance from within the society.

In saying this we are not supposing that there is a single agreed object, 'Australian literature'. The term refers to a body of genres and texts that has always been stratified along social and political lines, with different orientations to the dominant groups in the society: and these lines have been drawn at significantly different places over Australia's short history. In the past the Australian obsession with legitimacy has been translated into the project of establishing a distinctively Australian tradition, complete with a Great Australian Writer and a Great Australian Novel, whose manifest greatness would at last prove the colonists' right to belong, both to the metropolitan centre and in the territory that they had invaded and colonised, Australia itself. But this search was doomed from the outset by a contradiction in the project itself, a double message at its core. The concept of 'greatness' was saturated with imperial connotations, with the value system emanating from and controlled

PREFACE

by the centre, while 'Australian' was defined as an opposition to these values.

But while this ideological project was always part of the context in which Australian literary texts were produced, its force was intermittent and variable across the full range of production. For that reason we look at many texts that would not be conventionally regarded as 'great' or 'Australian' or even 'literature'. While the early colony had anxiously begun to debate whether it did or could have its own 'literature' and culture, it was already and inevitably producing a rich fabric of texts that worked over the experiences of everyday life, making sense of the problems and possibilities of the new situation in the new land: being both interesting and 'Australian' without having to try. Texts of this kind did not necessarily carry a more subversive content, but they were still positioned differently in relation to the dominant regimes of reading, less consistently subject to the scrutiny of various agents of control.

The framework that we have developed owes much to the work of many theorists of 'postcolonialism', such as are usefully surveyed in Ashcroft, Griffiths and Tiffin's recent introduction *The Empire Writes Back* (1989). This important and timely book proposes a definition of postcolonialism that is a convenient reference point for our own understanding of this complex phenomenon (1989:2):

> We use the term 'post-colonial', however, to cover all the culture affected by the imperial process from the moment of colonisation to the present day. This is because there is a continuity of preoccupations throughout the historical process initiated by European imperial aggression.

This definition has an exemplary scope, positioned around a single political–cultural category. That said, we need to insist on the differences that constitute the category at every level, to restore the heterogeneity that is intrinsic to the postcolonial complex. Firstly we note the equivocation with history contained in the prefix 'post'. As with other fashionable combinations such as 'postmodernism', the prefix seems to construct a simple version of history in which the 'modern' or the 'colonial' is totally superseded. However, within this field it is useful to distinguish between the postcolonial as an historical moment, and something broadly akin to Lyotard's postmodernism, a postcolonialism (like postmulticulturalism) in which certain tendencies are always inherently present. Postcolonialism in this second sense is the underside of any colonialism, and it can appear almost fully formed in colonial societies before they have formally achieved independence. Conversely, 'postcolonialism' as the period that follows a stage of colonisation is not necessarily subversive, and in most cases it incorporates much from its colonial past. By not distinguishing between oppositional postcolonialism and complicit postcolonialism, Ashcroft et al create a misleading impression that subversion reigns equally everywhere in all 'postcolonial' societies.

There is another fissure within the unity of the 'postcolonial' that we feel that Ashcroft et al and many others do not sufficiently recognise: the differences between 'settler' colonies such as Australia, and colonies like India which were colonised by a foreign power. We argue in this book that 'postcolonial' literatures like those of India and Australia are not more or less identical. There is the shadow of a new imperialism in claims that all sectors of all such societies have or should have a single position and a single cultural strategy, especially one that is characterised by subversion and resistance. Texts from both kinds of 'postcolonial' situation do have some potential for subversion. Agonistic confrontations tend to arise between a metropolitan centre and all those societies on its periphery, the 'postcolonial societies', but the issue of how and how far they realise this potential is not something to take for granted.

In exploring these issues we have found it salutary to refer extensively to the theories of the American historian Louis Hartz, as encapsulated in what has been termed the 'Hartz thesis' (Hartz 1964). Hartz produced his ideas over 25 years ago, and is no longer fashionable amongst Australianists. From our perspective on 'postcolonialism' we have serious reservations about many aspects of his thesis and its application to Australia. But the thesis is still salutary in its scope: the colonial process as constructed from the point of view of the heirs of European colonialism. Hartz proposed that all the colonies established by European powers had important structural features in common, arising out of the conditions of their foundation. He argued that each was a fragment of a metropolitan complex, and that this factor played a decisive role in the pattern of development that these different colonies then followed.

Hartz's analysis of Australia we will argue was 180° wrong: he accepted the egalitarian rhetoric of Australian nationalism at its face value and proposed that Australia is the classic instance of how a radical fragment evolves. But what is still of value in his approach is that he took it for granted that the Australian pattern is an instance of a wider pattern: the way the dispersed colonies of European powers worked out their new roles in their territorial base and in the geopolitical order. Australian commentators are typically so obsessed with minute signs of Australia's differences from British models that they do not look to other instances of the colonial phenomenon, not only AngloSaxon colonies like Canada and the US but imperial enclaves as in India and Africa, and the analogous experience of Spanish colonies in the Americas or French colonies in Africa. In such a framework, Australian literature becomes not just an anxiously inflated footnote to the English literary tradition, but a distinct instance of what is one of the most important political-cultural phenomena of the past 500 years, which has affected the cultural landscape of more than half the world's people.

PREFACE

This perspective leads us to recognise (as Hartz himself did not) that Australia is still thoroughly marked by its role as an agent of imperialism. Not only did Australia become in its own small way a colonising power in the Pacific region, where its behaviour was modelled exactly on current British practices, but more structurally in its formation it adopted the classic attitudes of imperialism in its treatment of the Aboriginal people of Australia. Moreover, this crucial imperialist enterprise was not incorporated at all into the national myth, which could accommodate this major threat to national legitimacy only by not mentioning the matter.

At this point we draw on the work of Edward Said and others on what Said has termed 'Orientalism', a class of strategies that colonial powers have adopted to construct the colonised Other. In the classic form of Orientalism as studied by Said, the Other is reduced to silence and is then fetishised and controlled, becoming an endlessly fascinating object of discourse. The Australian version of Orientalism has its own distinctive features but by and large it conforms closely to the basic pattern. All of its forms are distinct from those that cluster around the fragment ideology, and they seem unassimilable to it. Usually no attempt is made to assimilate the two. But the very depth of this fissure is evidence of the importance of the division. The Australian psyche is not a unitary phenomenon, which has an Orientalist piece of ideological baggage attached somehow to it. On the contrary it is organised around this fissure, it *is* this contradiction, and typically it projects an inarticulate, egalitarian Orientalist, a racist republican.

We do not wish to simplify the context of Australian literature by reducing it to a single opposition. The egalitarian ideology that deceived Hartz is undoubtedly present, alongside other elements, and its presence needs to be understood, not explained away. By virtue of this egalitarian ideology Australian literature can seem to be akin to that of postcolonial societies which had to fight free of the imperial power. We need to insist that this impression is profoundly misleading: Australia had no need to fight any war of independence, and has not done so. Australians may be able to convince themselves that Australia is more or less like India or Kenya or Fiji as a postcolonial nation, but people in those countries will not be deceived. But it is significant that even today middle-class Australians accept a definition of their national identity represented in terms that derive from radical working-class ideals.

In our modified version of the Hartz thesis, we see the early colonists not as a working-class fragment but as a displaced complex abstracted from the metropolitan culture. It transported its conflicts and antagonisms but in different circumstances, allied to a different mission, the colonial function. The ambiguities of this function introduced confusions into the initial fragment, since its mission required both autonomy and dependence, in proportions that had to be established afresh. So new alliances between the ruling group and former class enemies did become possible, against the distant power at the metropolitan centre, and against the common enemy, the lawful owners of Australia who first had to be dispossessed. These contradictions were reflected in everyday experience as well as in ideological forms, and they entered into text under both guises.

After 200 years, the situation is linked inexorably by a series of transformations back to the initial situation, and it is one of the strengths of the Hartz thesis that it recognises this kind of linkage, even if it does not look equally carefully at the forces which sustain the successive patterns. The continent of Australia is still occupied by the two distinct groups, one descended from Aboriginal people, the other from the invaders and their allies. Although Aboriginal people are numerically a small proportion of Australia's population, their importance in the construction of Australian identity is disproportionate precisely because these issues have not yet been resolved.

Until recently, in a referendum in 1967, Aborigines were not classified as citizens of Australia. Up till this time it was taken for granted that 'Australian literature' did not include Aboriginal texts, and Aboriginal art was confined to museums not displayed in art galleries. The study of Australian history and literature in schools and universities was able to marginalise Aboriginal history and silence Aboriginal voices, acting in parallel to the repressive government policies that attempted to 'eliminate' the 'Aboriginal problem'. This pattern has now been broken. Aborigines are at last being written back into the history of Australia. In literature and art, Aboriginal creativity is being recognised and valued as a major component of Australian cultural production. Recent histories of Australian literature can now be expected to have a (small) section at the end devoted to Aboriginal writers. Cultural justice, however belated, now seems to have come.

Our book initially may seem overbalanced in the other direction. Nearly half of it deals with Aboriginal literary production or texts that in some way touch on Aboriginal themes. This does not correspond at all to the balance of the texts that have survived in print, as 'literature'. However it is the only way we could do justice to our conception of Australian society as split around this particular fissure. It is a lapsed colonial power locked in an unresolved and undeclared struggle with the original possessors for legitimacy and land, producing a neocolonial form of literature from a neocolonial mentality that is still obsessed with the exploited Other. Into this complex is embedded a flourishing oppositional postcolonial development in politics, culture and literature. Unless this new symbiotic form is recognised to exist, the contradictions in it can hardly be understood, much less resolved in any fruitful way.

There is one important consequence of a doubled form of consciousness of this kind. Systematic double messages produce a schizoid nation,

PREFACE

in the classic terms proposed by Gregory Bateson (1973). This quality of the Australian mind is hardly recognised, concealed as it is by the Australian stereotype of the feckless, simple-minded inhabitant of what Donald Horne in 1964 ironically called 'the lucky country'. But this stereotype is itself part of the symptomology of the schizoid nation. Bateson refers to two kinds of schizophrenic, the paranoiac who is deeply suspicious of everything and sees hidden messages behind every event and every text, and the hebephrenic who relentlessly ignores anything but the most overt and literal meaning. The 'typical Australian' is a hebephrenic construct, but he is the product of a paranoiac vision, the other half of a single coin.

We can see the characteristic double vision of Australians in the complexities of the Australian stereotype, the so-called 'typical Australian', and the 'typical' space that he occupies, the Australian Bush, or 'outback'. This figure is a Caucasian adult male, an itinerant rural worker of no fixed address. His values and forms of language and thought are widely claimed to represent Australian authenticity, as a touchstone of Australian identity. In this capacity he has been used as a yard-stick of Australianness in literature and other arts, as though truly Australian literature should be written by, for and about this character.

One of the paradoxes of this character that has been noticed yet strangely discounted is the fact that neither this character nor his setting is or has been 'typical' in any useful sense. Australia is one of the most urbanised countries in the world, and this type would now constitute a small proportion of the populace that claims to find its true identity embodied by him. Even the belief that he was the norm at some time in the past is without foundations. At an optimistic estimate he could never have been much more than 15 per cent of the population. Most Australians are left with the paradox that they are not 'typical Australians' at all.

This contradiction is not at all simple or crude in its meanings and effects. At the most surface level, this figure exists to suppress from the national image recognition of what he isn't. He encodes a class, race and gender identity which classifies women, Aborigines and new migrants as 'unAustralian', a potent fact which is immediately recognised by all those who are subjected to this symbolic annihilation. But even at this level the figure has his ambiguities. Bank managers, real estate agents and many other successful middle-class Australians could equally object that they are excluded by the stereotype, but they do not protest. On the contrary they are voracious consumers of images of the stereotype. It is clear that this figure has a double inflection, able to disconfirm the Australianness of some kinds of people while leaving others unaffected.

There is another contradiction involving this figure: the valuations of him that seem to be proclaimed by the myth, in contrast to the common judgment on this type in the mundane world. There he inhabits the margins of social life, arousing anxiety and fear in solid citizens. He is a male who has acute problems with women and with all other intimate relationships. He is a worker who barely works, fleeing the cities in which other Australians live because he cannot survive in them, not because he loves nature or the land. He expresses the opposition between labour and capital, but in an individualistic and impotent form. He is excluded by the two major institutions that in practice organise Australian social life: the nuclear family and the world of work.

From this position, asserting his egalitarian ethos from near the bottom of the hierarchically organised heap, he is uncomfortably close to other kinds of marginalised Australians: the mad, the criminals, the dispossessed. Refractions of this core figure appear in literary and artistic texts, often glamorised as the convict, the bushranger, the explorer, but his aberrations are always remarked and always critiqued. Paradoxically his marginality allies him with two other types his surface meanings seemed designed to oppose: the old Australian, the Aborigines whom he helped to dispossess, and the new Australian, recent migrants whose newness both threatens his own marginal existence yet confirms the basis of his tenure of the land which he does not own.

This figure, then, masks an unlimited ambiguity under his excessive simplicities, in the shadows that he casts, in the exclusions that he makes and unmakes, in the contradictory valuations that complicate and refract his one-dimensional existence. If he is read for his surface value, as Australians loudly insist he should be read, he is an incomprehensible carrier of Australian identity. He only makes sense when he is read with the schizoid consciousness that is in practice the primary marker of Australianness. In this way Australian identity is constructed and maintained around a typical way of reading, not around the atypical representation on its own.

This is itself a dark secret of Australian consciousness, not spoken of to outsiders in case Australians themselves should acknowledge it in public. Yet it still has to enter into texts, otherwise it could not be known and transmitted to succeeding generations. This is where literary texts and other similar genres become so important. These texts have something of the structure and function of dreams, as in Freud's theories: dreams as the 'royal road to the unconscious'. Like dreams, many of these texts encode the deepest desires and fears of individuals and groups. And like dreams, the seeming unity of these texts decomposes into different levels and unmediated contradictions, layered over with disguise upon disguise yet repetitiously insisting on flaunting its secrets before the public gaze, sprinkling its truths in the pleasure of the text as well as in its hidden recesses. These are not easy texts to read, for a critic of the culture, but nor can they be ignored.

But it is equally important that their meanings must also be easily accessible in some respects, carried through a multitude of texts in general circulation, otherwise they could not have their massive reach and representative force. We are concerned with a social phenomenon of great tenacity, not with the contents of a purely individual and psychological unconscious. This set of texts express and exemplify the major conflicts and contradictions of Australian life, and they do so actively, as an unofficial tradition of commentary and critique that in many respects was more diverse and penetrating than official culture was allowed to be. We take Australian literature to be a crucial set of documents for an exploration of the contradictions in Australian social life, as these are realised in the dark side of the Australian dream.

The approach that we have adopted for this book reflects our theme and purpose. Our project requires an extensive reading of Australian literature and history, but our object is more general and of wider concern. So we wanted to write in a way that did not exclude readers by demanding a specialist historical or literary background, while indicating sufficiently the bases of our particular studies, so that our argument would be open to critique by specialists and nonspecialists alike. The notes to each chapter give background and context for our argument. In the main text we try to avoid the conventional practice of literary histories, which normally give rapid summaries and judgments on a large number of authors and texts which could not be adequately assessed by most other readers who did not know those texts. We have limited our discussion to a much smaller sample of instances, which we try to summarise sufficiently fully as a context for our discussion. We then develop our argument through a detailed examination of a specific portion of a text, which is normally represented through extensive quotations. That is because the argument often hinges on claims that important dimensions of the meaning and significance of a text can be best seen in patterns of language or theme, in displacements or deletions of other significant objects, texts or genres, in qualities that would be the first to disappear from a straightforward summary.

We assume that major social meanings will recur with massive redundancy throughout particular texts, and across different genres and media. So we include less extensive studies of various visual media, paintings, photographs, and films, as complementary texts for the study of key themes, supposing that the social functions of 'literature' are equally carried by these other genres, and that a more comprehensive definition of 'literature' that includes visual media allows for a more adequate object of study. We assume that the meanings and effects of these texts must always be interpreted by reference to relevant aspects of material and social reality, but that the construction of 'reality' is itself always problematic. We assume that the kind of meaning that we are interested in is importantly located in the conditions of the production, reception and circulation of texts, and in patterns of form, grammar and style, as well as in the 'content' (what they represent, and what their authors or characters say). And finally we assume that meaning is always actively negotiated and constructed in specific social contexts by specific participants, working over and transforming both the world that they are engaged with and the prior sets of texts and categorisations that converge in that instance. But these shifts and indeterminacies of meaning by no means lead to a paralysis of interpretation. On the contrary, ambiguity and difficulty are always themselves meaningful since they always proceed from the play of social forces, and provide evidence of the most important of meanings: the meanings that constitute the society itself.

In writing this book we have drawn extensively on the work of many historians, but we did not want to weigh the main text down with too many references or too much detail, beyond some uncontroversial statements of fact such as dates and the identity of the participants in any particular event. The historians we have quoted extensively tend not to be consensus thinkers, but ones who made their mark by generating provocative ideas. Among those whom we have found most stimulating have been Humphrey McQueen, Russel Ward, Geoffrey Blainey, Richard White, C. D. Rowley, Henry Reynolds, Miriam Dixson and Anne Summers. These historians have provoked many particular studies that have tested and modified some of their more sweeping generalisations. Our use of their work reflects this situation. We do not draw on them as the speakers of incontestable truths, for we recognise these as 'inventive' histories expressing their own polemical ends. Nonetheless they are producers of something that is rarer and more valuable: exciting and challenging ideas about the formation of Australian society that deserve to be known and debated in Australian society at large, beyond the confines of the academic discipline of history.

Our collaboration on a book on Australian literature began in 1979 when we worked briefly on a microfilm copy of Charles Harpur's *Discourse on Poetry* (Mitchell Library, C386). Our annotations remain incomplete to this day as pressure of work and the educational needs of a new university took us to other areas of research. We also collaborated on a course on Epic which provided a useful opportunity to explore a range of relevant frames. The core of the book developed in two sets of courses. One was on 'Australian literature' coordinated by Vijay Mishra, which worked increasingly uneasily within a framework of 'Commonwealth literature'. Many of the chapters of the present book are critical revisions of lectures originally devised for that course and that framework. We have also drawn on work that emerged in Murdoch University's courses on contemporary and traditional Aboriginal literature. For years Murdoch was the only university which offered these courses, set up by Bob Hodge with a decisive input from the Aboriginal writers Jack Davis and Mudrooroo Narogin (Colin Johnson), whose influence on the present book we acknowledge with profound gratitude.

PREFACE

The issues that we discuss have also been developed in a course on popular culture co-ordinated by Bob Hodge, which fed into work in collaboration with Graeme Turner and John Fiske that was published in 1987 as *Myths of Oz*. Amongst other colleagues whose ideas have been a valuable part of the context in which we worked, special mention should be made of Hugh Webb, Peter Jeffery, Kateryna Longley, Horst Ruthrof, John Frow, Pam Cox, Rae Frances, Bruce Scates, Lenore Layman, and the members of the Centre for Critical and Cultural Theory, University of Wales College of Cardiff. In addition we would like to thank our teachers, John Barnes, Thea Astley, Brian Kiernan, Elizabeth Webby, Leonie Kramer among them, who introduced us to Australian literature so many years ago.

Beyond this immediate teaching context, the book is a natural extension of work we have produced independently of each other over the past fifteen years. We arrived at a similar position after two years of intense debate, re-writing, disagreements and further reading. Our theoretical enterprise was sharpened by a strong sense of absence in Australian culture of its repressed side, marked most dramatically by the massive silence surrounding Aboriginal history and culture. In this way we hope that the book will make a contribution to debates about Australian literary culture and the ways in which its history might be told.

We would like to thank Elizabeth Horne for typing parts of the manuscript and Tom O'Regan for an exceptionally rigorous and informed commentary on the text. We regret that, in the final analysis, we have not been able to do full justice to the many points to which our attention was drawn. Pam and Nalini gave us enormous encouragement and support throughout, especially during periods when we were working under considerable stress. For any error in judgment, and omissions, we alone are responsible.

Acknowledgements

The authors gratefully acknowledge the following for permission to reproduce material in this book: Duncan Kentish and Peter Skipper for *Jila Japinga II*, 1987; Robert Treborlang and Major Mitchell Press for extract from *How to Survive in Australia*, 1986; Sally Morgan and Fremantle Arts Centre Press for cover of *My Place*, 1987; McPhee Gribble and Gabrielle Carey for extract from *Just Us*, 1984; David Malouf and Currency Press for extract from *Blood Relations*, 1989; The Mitchell Library, State Library of New South Wales, for reproduction of W. Bradley's 'First Interview' and Oscar Fristrom's 'Portrait of an Aboriginal'; Art Gallery of New South Wales for reproduction of Tom Roberts' 'Aboriginal Head—Charlie Turner'; Penguin Books for reproduction of cover of C.D. Rowley's *The Destruction of Aboriginal Society*, 1972; Judith Wright and Angus and Robertson for extracts from 'Old House' and 'Fire Sermon' from *Collected Poems 1942–1970*, 1971; Estate of Michael Dransfield and The University of Queensland Press for extracts from 'Bum's Rush', 1972; A.D. Hope and Angus and Robertson for extracts from 'Australia', 1972; Jack Davis and Currency Press for an extract from 'The Dreamers', 1982; Paddy Roe, Stephen Muecke and Fremantle Arts Centre Press for extract from *Gularabulu*, 1983; Ania Walwicz for extracts from 'Picture', 'Australia' and 'Wogs', 1988, 1989; Thomas Keneally and Angus and Robertson for extracts from *The Chant of Jimmie Blacksmith*, 1972; Mudrooroo Narogin for extracts from *Wildcat Falling*, 1969 and *Doin Wildcat*, 1988; Estate of Patrick White and Eyre and Spottiswoode for extracts from *Voss*, 1957 and *Riders in the Chariot*, 1961; Estate of Dorothea MacKellar and Lloyd O'Neil for extracts from 'My Country', 1982; Estate of Charles Chauvel for frame from *Jedda*, 1954; John O'Grady and Ure Smith for

ACKNOWLEDGEMENTS

extract from *They're a Weird Mob*, 1957; Bruce Dawe and Longman Cheshire Pty Ltd for 'Homecoming' from *Sometimes Gladness: Collected Poems 1954-1982*, 1983; The Museum of Victoria Council for reproduction of Baldwin Spencer's photograph of Aranda Boy; P. Lucich for extract from *Children's Stories from the Worora*, 1969; Peter Skipper and Joyce Hudson for extract from *The Walmatjari*, 1978.

1 Australian literature and the problem of history

Our concern in this book is with the evolution of the deep-seated forms of thought and belief, the habits of mind that have come to characterise the 'Australian character' and Australian society. These have arisen out of the basic conditions of material life and the play of social forces, where they in turn provide the ideological background for social and political action, in a process that connects the contradictions of a colonial past with the conditions of Australia's postcolonial present. Our study focuses primarily on the dialectic between material conditions and forces, and forms of consciousness, as these are mediated in texts—especially the texts of the literary tradition. In this chapter we will try to sketch in some of the preconditions of our project. We will illustrate the reading strategy which makes the enterprise possible in the first place, as it can be deployed on both literary and nonliterary texts. We will look at competing versions of history and the historical enterprise. And we will look at the Australian critical establishment, at the role that it has played historically and at the versions of history with which it plays.

AUSTRALIAN LITERATURE AND THE HISTORY OF THE REAL

1981 saw an event of some significance in the Australian cultural scene: the publication of the *Oxford History of Australian Literature (OHAL)*. This was edited by Dame Leonie Kramer, then Professor of Australian Literature at Sydney University, and it carried the weight of that kind of official endorsement. Its significance did not lie in its status as the definitive history for its time. In fact it received reviews that fell short of total deference. Its interest lies in this very ambiguity of status: a definitive history that defines nothing, a declaration of authority whose hollowness manifests the erosion of its legitimacy. It has become a symptomatic text, and that is how we will read it.

The title itself contains a fine compendium of categories which at another time would have seemed the self-evident basis for a self-contained enterprise, but which now provoke questions. What is literature? What is Australianness? What is history? And finally, where does Oxford fit in? If the book is to perform its task of legitimating and defining a field of study (a set of texts) and an ideological prime (the concept of Australia) the answers need to be so obvious that the questions can hardly be asked. But the 509 uneasy pages of this history, supplemented by another 589 pages of the companion *Oxford Anthology of Australian Literature* (*OAAL*) published in 1985, have proved insufficient to close off these questions and enforce the inevitability of these answers.

A government-commissioned report published in 1987 allows us to see something of the wider context within which *OHAL* has had to operate. The ACRASTE (Australian Committee of Review of Australian Studies in Tertiary Education) report found that Australian studies, including Australian literature, were marginalised in academic institutions. Australian literature is normally studied in departments called 'English', the very name signalling the anomalous status of 'Australian' literature within it. There is no English department where Australian literature is other than a minority subject, and the vested interests of English departments are committed to keeping it that way. This has been the case for many years, and could have remained a comfortable consensus view, except for the pressures that the ACRASTE report reflects. Outside university departments, in the community that funds them, on the other hand, the imbalance is just as strong in favour of Australianness.

Reflecting these two kinds of pressure there are two main models for the construction of Australian literary history. One can be termed the Nationalist model, which emphasises what is unique in Australian literature, its direct reflection of an Australian ethos growing out of Australian history and society. The other can be called the Eternalist model. This emphasises instead the 'eternal' values of literature, which are occasionally if faintly found in works by Australian writers. The Eternalist model is clearly very congenial to the institutional context of a university 'English' department, since it legitimates the centrality of the existing curriculum (assumed to contain 'eternal' values) along with the perpetual client status of Australian literature. However, for the same reason it has a weak justification for including Australian texts and it cannot provide a clear rationale for the study of their history.

This explains the contradiction at the core of *OHAL*'s enterprise. Kramer in her introduction roundly attacks the proponents of the

THE PROBLEM OF HISTORY

Nationalist position for their ignorance of both the literary process and historical reality. (These figures, writers like A. A. Phillips and Vance Palmer, Russel Ward and Judith Wright, significantly do not include a single professor of Literature. Ironically they do include two distinguished writers, plus one professor of History.) But an 'Eternalist' history is neither possible nor would it serve the point. The *OHAL* project can only be built around a complex reaction to the Nationalist position, since it has no means or incentive to establish another.

The strength as well as the weakness of the Nationalist position is the power of its model of history and society. It pivots around an event of unparalleled importance, no less than the foundation of the nation itself, and it prioritises literature whose function was perceived to be the construction of national identity. But that event is now in the past, and even in the past it had a complex meaning. And the literature that constructed the national identity was always in a minority. Faced with these problems, the Nationalist strategy had to delegitimate most writing done by Australians as not really Australian. And to establish the potent truth of its favoured canon it had to adopt a realist orientation, preferring either realist texts or realist readings of those texts, so that those texts could be claimed as representing directly the otherwise obscured truth about the national essence.

The Eternalist tradition, in spite of its power in the academies and its support among Australian writers, can still not totally rewrite history, or write or uncover sufficient texts of its own to form a convincing alternative canon. What it is in a better position to control is the official version of the reading process, through selection (what genres and periods, what authors and what texts are established as worthy of study) and interpretation (how texts are to be read, what readings are to be counted as valid). To achieve the first *OHAL* emphasises the notion of 'evaluation' as against 'description' or even 'analysis' (as Kramer stresses in her introduction, p. 5). 'Evaluation' justifies the wholesale omission of categories of text (e.g. 'popular literature', Aboriginal literature) and also attaches negative labels to other categories of text and to incontestably 'major' authors that cannot be so easily eliminated from the history (e.g. 'social realism', Xavier Herbert). A key reading strategy for Eternalists, then, is to disvalue realist readings and realist texts, in favour of texts and readings where the relations with social reality can be more easily ignored.

But *OHAL* cannot simply disrupt the Nationalist strategy. It has to yoke Eternalist values to a historical project, since it is committed to providing the 'history' that the institution still requires. It draws on three ways of fulfilling this function, all of which are common enough. Firstly, it writes as though literary historians can assume that what happened in the past is fully knowable and fully known, and doesn't need to be mentioned in a literary history. This allows an almost total division of labour with historians proper, only three of whom make it into the bibliography. Historians if asked will normally claim that knowing about the past is difficult and laborious and should be left to the professionals (themselves), but here they are not asked. OAAL also includes substantial numbers of texts that it regards as of 'historical interest' not 'literary value' (never 'historical value' or 'literary interest'), but these items are always carefully labelled as such. And finally, most historically, it orders its material chronologically. In the process it inevitably implies its own theory of history, inscribed into the period categories that it uses.

In the two books, *OHAL* and *OAAL*, there are in fact four schemas, not just one. *OHAL* has three sections for the genres of poetry, fiction and drama, each with a slightly different chronological principle organising the material, each time however except for drama dividing it into four parts. We can see the pattern from the following:

Category	Part 1	Part 2	Part 3	Part 4
Fiction	1788–1880s	1890–1920	1920s–1930s	Post-war
Drama	1788–1900	1900–1960	1960 on	
Poetry	Colonial	1880–1920	1920–1960	Recent
Anthology	1788–1918	1920–1940	1940–1960	Contemporary

The differences suggest that literary history has a trajectory distinct from that of other histories, and that even individual genres are distinct categories, with their own histories. If even literature as such does not have a single chronological pattern, then it would seem even more pointless to look for any consistent relation with chronologies developed by other historians. The mode of organisation, then, partly functions to rule out the possibility of connections with a broader theory of history, though terms like 'colonial' and 'post-war' hint at extra-literary points of anchorage.

But we can be a little suspicious of one effect of this multiplicity of chronologies. Where the Nationalist history pivots around the decisive years of the 1890s, its lead-up and its aftermath, *OHAL*'s scattering of boundaries seems designed to obscure the primacy of this constitutive event. It cannot remove it from the history, because of its pivotal role in the construction of Australian identity, but it tries to treat it as just another couple of decades, containing writers and works that can simply be added to the list that is 'Australian literature'. It then surreptitiously establishes its own golden age: the period from the 40s to the 50s, especially its poetry. Two hundred and forty-four pages of the anthology are devoted to these two decades, nearly half the book, and these are the years most extensively covered by *OHAL* in all genres.

Underlying this set of manoeuvres we can detect an implicit scheme which in practice corresponds to the basic pattern for the Nationalist history. The Eternalist historical scheme recognises a progression from a colonial stage through to a 'nationalist' stage, followed by a reactionary stage which we will term conservative, followed by a more recent phase that we will label modernist. The movement from the first to the second stage is common to both Eternalists and Nationalists, since it was so strongly articulated at the time. However, Nationalist writers and ideologues particularly emphasise the opposition between these two stages, proclaiming Australia's need to repudiate its colonial phase in order to progress to its status as a 'free' nation.

The Nationalist program foregrounds a political event of the first importance in the history of the nation, its constitution as a nation state, something which the Eternalist version of history wishes to minimise or ignore. But the Nationalist move is not ideologically innocent. It constructs the preceding 100 years of Australian history as though it was somehow the history of some other entity, a colonial pre-Australia. It is thus able to construct the essential Australia not as a continuation of a colonial enterprise but as a radical break. This mystification is ideologically so valuable that it can't after all be dispensed with by later ideologues of the nation state. But because the Nationalist history downplays Australia's colonial past it has to minimise Australia's continuing colonial future, as though the 90 years since federation are an inexplicable postscript to a beautifully completed history. The Nationalist form of history is unable to have a consistent historical account of 20th century Australian social and political developments.

The further segmentation of Australian literary history, then, has to be a post-nationalist move. The post-federation period, whenever it is supposed to end, was a xenophobic and conservative mirror image of the radical nationalist ethos, orientated to the consolidation of the new nation, not to its separation from the old. The negation of this phase, whether it is dated immediately after the second world war or after the traumatic decade of the 1960s, repudiates both the conservatism and the nationalism of the conservative phase. Thus it becomes possible to acknowledge the forces and themes that had been suppressed: ethnic and racial diversity, gender differences, and the interconnections between Australia and a complex world of different nations and cultures outside its borders. The 'modernist' phase, as we have described it, is not a homogeneous or autonomous formation. It is more a disruption of the previously dominant conservative discursive regime, whose forms still continue to have wide currency. In fact this is a general pattern: the successive stages can be tracked and the moments of transition located, but along with this neat division into stages there are all kinds of continuities that are just as important to account for.

The two models for Australian history, then, in practice represent two kinds of intervention in the rewriting of this complex and tangled history of discursive forms, this dialectic of control and resistance. There is much at stake in the struggle, whose outcomes are so important yet so difficult to read. We have described *OHAL* for instance as a self-contradictory ideological enterprise, trying unavailingly to impose its ahistorical history, its unAustralian Australianness on an unconvinced and increasingly suspicious community. At the same time it must be said that the professoriat of Australian literature is dominated by Eternalists, and that the institutional hold of English departments and their ideology over the study of Australian literature appears to be weakened not a jot. In spite of its egalitarian image and ethos Australia mostly elects conservative governments and votes No in referendums. This paradox is expressed directly in the ambiguities about the Australianness of Australian literature, why it should be studied, how it should be studied, and what exactly it is that is being studied.

READING TEXTS, READING CULTURE

Literary history in the style of *OHAL* is primarily an ideological enterprise, without a comprehensive or explicit theory of history and (less obviously) without a productive practice of close reading (for that kind of thing, Australian literary critics make use of variants of American 'New Criticism'). What we propose in this book is a form of disciplinary double-vision. We read texts as we read political and social forces, drawing on the methods, priorities and documents of two disciplines, literature and history, within an overall framework of social semiotics. For our purposes it would be possible to start from either end, going from literary texts to the issues that they deal with or from issues to texts that deal with them. To some extent these moves are complementary, and we adopt both at different times. But for our enterprise there is no doubt which has the priority. Our agenda arises out of the present as it interrogates the past, shaped by our understandings of current issues and debates about the social and political forces that have converged in the making of Australia.

To illustrate this strategy we will take Australia's involvement in the Vietnam war as a focal point. As we survey the four decades of Australian history since the second world war this seems to us a symptomatic and decisive event. Initially the Australian government enthusiastically supported the US: 'All the way with LBJ' was the catch-cry of Australian Prime Minister Harold Holt, a cringe so fulsome that it returned to haunt the pro-war movement. In the context of Australian history, this commitment signalled one extreme development in Australia's relationship to imperialism, its shift from Britain to the US as its guarantor: a deferential, client status no less abject than before, but hailed as marking a new national self-confidence.

The Vietnam experience also bears on another recurring theme of Australian history: Australia's involvement in the Asian region and its consciousness of its ambiguous but inescapable role in Asia's political and economic destiny. The foundation of the nation state in 1901 was

THE PROBLEM OF HISTORY

followed not coincidentally by the infamous 'White Australia' restricted immigration policy, which attempted to establish an Anglo-Celtic ghetto in the continent. The 40 years after federation saw Asians virtually (but not completely) purged from the land, banished into the cultural unconscious, from where they emerged with traumatic force in the guise of the Japanese. This enemy was charged with such ideological potency that it invested the Americans unassailably as saviours. So support for American adventurism in the region had powerful roots in the popular mind: 'egalitarian' Australia was well prepared for its role as the docile ally of a colonial superpower.

But the Vietnam experience was a major event in Australian history for another reason. On the world stage this war came to focus as a crisis for postcolonialism itself, as a highly public instance when the superior technology and resources of a colonial superpower were defeated by the ingenuity and resolve of a colonised people, aided by the effective radicalisation of a large segment of the population at home. The phenomenon had a double centre, in the US and in Vietnam itself, and what happened in Australia as in many other countries in the rest of the world was affected and conditioned by events outside its sphere of control. The period between 1965 and 1972 in Australia saw a transformation of attitudes that was no less momentous for being similar to what was happening elsewhere. At the beginning of this period, Australia's military involvement had massive popular support. By the end the antiwar movement had won the battle for Australian minds. In this change what is most in need of explanation is not so much the move to withdraw from a war that was by then obviously unwinnable, but the early support for the policy, which was always foolish in terms of the interests of the majority of Australians. Before Vietnam, Australian radicalism was channelled by nationalism, unable to produce an effective critique of Australian imperialism. For Australian radicalism after Vietnam an international and postcolonial model was more readily available.

The literary text that we have chosen for illustrative purposes is a single poem, 'Homecoming' by Bruce Dawe (1983:92). Dawe's poem was written in 1968, at a transition point in Australian attitudes to the war. As an antiwar poem it was to some extent in advance of the movement of mind of the populace, though that movement was already gaining momentum on its way to becoming the dominant attitude. Dawe himself has been described as one of the two most popular Australian poets of the post-war period, and this text gained the *OHAL* seal of approval as the 'one outstanding poem' that the Vietnam war produced (*OHAL* 425). The poem is as follows:

Homecoming

All day, day after day, they're bringing them home,
they're picking them up, those they can find, and bringing
them home,

7

>   they're bringing them in, piled on the hulls of Grants, in trucks,
>   in convoys,
>   they're zipping them up in green plastic bags,
>   they're tagging them now in Saigon, in the mortuary coolness
>   they're giving them names, they're rolling them out of
>   the deep-freeze lockers—on the tarmac at Tan Son Nhut
>   the noble jets are whining like hounds,
>   they are bringing them home
>   —curly-heads, kinky-hairs, crew-cuts, balding non-coms
>   —they're high, now, high and higher, over the land, the
>   steaming chow mein
>   their shadows are tracing the blue curve of the Pacific
>   with sorrowful quick fingers, heading south, heading east,
>   home, home, home—and the coasts swing upward, the old
>   ridiculous curvatures
>   of earth, the knuckled hills, the mangrove-swamps, the desert
>   emptiness . . .
>   in their sterile housing they tilt towards these like skiers
>   —taxiing in, on the long runways, the howl of their
>   homecoming rises
>   surrounding them like their last moments (the mash, the
>   splendour)
>   then fading at length as they move
>   on to small towns where dogs in the frozen sunset
>   raise muzzles in mute salute,
>   and on to cities in whose wide web of suburbs
>   telegrams tremble like leaves from a wintering tree
>   and the spider grief swings in his bitter geometry
>   —they're bringing them home, now, too late, too early.

If we try to read this as a document, as a historian might, its meaning would seem transparent enough, though not particularly illuminating about the attitudes that led to or opposed the war. It mainly records grief for the dead rather than opposition to the war. There's a hint of criticism in the excessive number of bodies being transported and in the lack of a counterbalancing number of heroic victories, but there is no direct call to arms, for or against the war. The punchline 'too late, or too early' points to an excess, but on closer inspection this too becomes puzzling and equivocal. 'Too late', yes, because they're dead, but why too early? Is it too early for the jingoistic nation, which cannot cope with dead victims now, rather than victorious troops in the future? Is Dawe endorsing the nation's commitment, expressed by its elected leaders, to stay in Vietnam until victory has been won? Or has this homecoming which is death come too early in the life cycle of these young men, or too early in their tour of duty? The poem is a curious mix: it has a didactic intent but doesn't quite say what the message is.

This uncertainty, this self-cancelling ambiguity, is an endemic meaning in the poem, inscribed in qualities of form as well as in its content.

THE PROBLEM OF HISTORY

Form always carries meanings, often the most important meanings precisely because they are normally not unique to a specific work, but summon up a whole set of intertextual meanings. In this case, it is important to recognise that this is a poem which is trying not to seem one. Its left hand margin declares it to be prose, while its right-hand margin acknowledges that it is a kind of poetry. It works with this opposition in other ways. Sometimes its diction is poetic ('spider grief') while at other times it is antipoetic ('green plastic bags'). It also has a double evaluation of both kinds of diction. Sometimes the poetic diction is given a parodic value by juxtaposition ('noble jets') whereas at other times the poetic is endorsed ('bitter geometry'). Sometimes the colloquial form guarantees authenticity ('those they can find') while at other times it implies triviality ('zipping them up').

These qualities are not specific to this poem, but that fact is precisely what allows us to read this text as a site for the play of meanings, rather than as a receptacle or container of specific meanings. Dawe reflected on an opposition of this kind as the proper context for seeing the social value of his poetry:

> To confront our private selves in public was, for generations, considered not 'on' for many Australians who skittered nervously away from that kind of confrontation as a threat to their sense of identity. This is changing; we can no longer afford (could we ever?) this gawkiness about our feelings, this national awkwardness.' (1983:xv)

Dawe here is repeating a widely held diagnosis of the Australian national character, and proposing poetry, his own included, as part of the cure. But symptomatically, even this statement retreats into a colloquial refusal of emotion ('not "on"') at the point of his attack on the Australian emotional inadequacy, and 'Homecoming' displays an acute form of the national inadequacy. It is a public poem whose persona is split (in public) in at least four ways, in a complex structure of repudiations and refusals. He cannot write a conventional elegy for the dead because he profoundly distrusts the rhetoric of that genre, though in many respects this poem is a tribute of this kind. But nor can he express passionate indignation in richly expressive language, though that too is implied. Similarly his use of the colloquial exploits both a snobbish rejection of the everyday and a belief in its authenticity as a bedrock of common values. A persona pointing in four ways simultaneously like this is well placed to speak on behalf of a divided totality, to be representative in his incapacity to speak with a single voice; but for this very reason he would be unable to mobilise anyone on behalf of a single course of action.

These qualities, as we have said, are very widespread indeed in Australian literary and cultural life. What the poem allows us to trace is the intersection of this set of attitudes and values with the complex meanings posed by the Vietnam war at this particular time, so that we can understand both the relative paralysis of the opposition, and its ultimate triumph. But the poem functions dialogically, and we need to set its forms against the dominant discourse, the discourse of the dominant, which was both non-literary and pro-war. As an instance of this discourse at its most effective, here is an extract from Paul Hasluck's ministerial speech of 23 March 1965, announcing Australia's commitment to the war:

> In the circumstances that now exist, the United States could not withdraw from South Vietnam without abandoning the responsibilities that belong to power or the principles they are trying to uphold. The United States could not withdraw without necessarily considering the world-wide impact of such a withdrawal on the broader stategies of world politics.
> If the United States did withdraw, the same conflict would be renewed somewhere else. Within a brief period the struggle now taking place in South Vietnam would be shifted to Thailand. If in turn there was abandonment of Thailand, it would shift to Malaysia, to Indonesia, to Burma, to India and further. Nothing would be achieved by yielding in South Vietnam. (Hansard 23 Mar 1965)

Whatever criticisms may be made of the wisdom of Australia's involvement in the war, there can be no dispute about the effectiveness of Hasluck's advocacy, which in 1966 helped to sweep the conservative coalition to a large majority in an election in which the Vietnam issue played a major role. To read the Australian consciousness of this time we must be able to interpret a Hasluck as well as a Dawe (and vice versa).

Hasluck's text represents a different genre, that of parliamentary discourse, which aspires to be 'Australian' in a different sense to that of nationalistic literary programs. Hasluck aims to speak on behalf of Australia itself as a single political entity. In this speech he projects authority without grandiloquence, working in a space that avoids the flights that a Churchill or a Kennedy could deploy. In 'power or the principles that they are trying to uphold', for instance, he acknowledges the interests of power as a motive, linking it with 'principles' through the off-hand ambiguity of 'or', immediately qualifying this with the more low key 'they are trying to uphold'. He is thus able to appeal to principle without making 'unAustralian' claims to high moral ground. His is a public voice with every trace of individuality removed, a unitary metaself whose unity constructs the unity of his audience, where Dawe's tone constructs the impossibility of such a unity or such a relation. Dawe's qualities can be seen as 'typical' of Australian literature precisely because they are endemic in Australian social life, but they are by no means universal. They are immediately political insofar as they rule out a specific kind of discourse and a specific political program: precisely the one pursued so effectively by Hasluck.

THE PROBLEM OF HISTORY

One thing that is common to Dawe's and Hasluck's texts is so obvious that it can easily be ignored: both texts draw on the resources of a common language, Australian English. In spite of its ubiquity a language is not a transparent medium for thought. Language carries the traces of its social use, in grooves that organise and constrain expression and thought itself. In this way qualities of language and form function like statements, of a particularly representative kind: and that is how we will treat them. A minute attention to the specificities of language, to details of syntax and choice of words, can illuminate a level of meaning that is as important to historians and political scientists as it is to literary critics.

In this case, Hasluck's words state clearly the basic premise that underpinned the pro-war case, what is called the domino theory. This theory did not originate in Australia, so it cannot be said to be uniquely Australian, but as an argument it penetrated so rapidly and so deeply into the Australian political and ideological consciousness that it becomes a crucial phenomenon in any attempt to define Australianness. What we want to isolate here is what can be called the linguistic correlates of the domino theory. These are the patterns of language which make the propositions of the theory seem natural and inevitable, patterns which in this way powerfully prepare the way for the ideology.

In these terms the first pattern to look at is the syntactic frame that encodes the domino theory itself. This is realised with exemplary directness in the clause 'it would shift to Malaysia, to Indonesia, to India and further'. In this form it seems so transparent that no alternative mode of thought or expression seems possible. But on closer inspection we can see how the trick is worked. First there is the vagueness of reference: 'it would shift'. What is 'it'? The innocent-seeming pronoun collapses all the liberation movements in the different countries into a self-evident unity which is precisely what is in question. Why would it 'shift'? By what mechanism is this unexamined event transmitted from location to location?

The answer is, in the forms of language itself. The proposition becomes thinkable because it is speakable, enabled by a process of addition of the names of places. But for this to occur, those places must be emptied of significance, so that they can take their place in this otherwise unmotivated string. We can observe a consistent difference in Hasluck's use of 'the United States' as against these names for Asian countries. The United States functions as a quasi-human agent, who feels (his) responsibilities heavily. The Asian countries, even South Vietnam, indicate only a location, from which the metahuman entities like Australia, the United States and 'Asian Communism' might or might not withdraw. Hasluck's classification system lumps together these countries

11

as mere places, emptied of human beings with their own cultures, histories and politics, and concentrates their essence into a single homogeneous and malign being, locked in struggle with another equally homogeneous but benign being. His political 'realism' is made plausible through a language device that deprives all Asian peoples of their own reality.

In contrast to the hypothetical nightmare constructed by domino syntax, the normalising vision is presented in a very different kind of syntax, not a series of clauses or verbs, but a single phrase without a verb and therefore without markers of tense: 'broader strategies of world politics'. This refers to a state of affairs without a past or a future, whose timeless existence, however, needs to be protected from the 'impact' of actions by others, while not itself being a set of actions that will have their own impact on others.

Most of Dawe's poem is constructed by a single repeated syntactic formula with many of the features of domino syntax: 'they're bringing them (X) in from (Y) to (Z)'. As in the Hasluck formula it is not made clear who are doing the bringing or why. The 'them' who are brought are classified in a parody-list, in terms of the length of their hair (whose characteristics suggest that many of these may be American dead, no longer otherwise distinguishable). But the main elaboration is the set of containers and the set of places, strung together in a chain exactly as in the domino theory.

The set of containers is deliberately heterogeneous, with a unity that comes only from being included in the same list. There are two such lists, ordered by a simple underlying dichotomy, the opposition between home and not-home. 'Home' is the potent term here, giving unity to the diverse destinations of these soldiers' bodies, standing in for and functioning like the category 'Australia'. But in this construction, home/Australia does not give any higher order unity to the items it organises. The unity of Australia is simply the collapse of excessive difference under the weight of the subsuming category. By the same mechanism and in response to the same pressure the heterogeneous items of non-home acquire a necessary unity, the unity of the Other. This unity cannot be challenged by pointing to any actual diversity, because it is precisely this diversity, felt as unmanageable, that creates the need for the unity.

Dawe does not have the complex hypothetical structures that are marked in Hasluck's text. He appears to employ an exactly opposite form, an endlessly repeated continuous present. But the opening words force us to construct this continuous present in a complex way. 'All day' blocks out a continuous stretch of time, but as a generalised description (normally we would expect the simple present 'they bring' or perhaps the simple past, 'they brought'). 'Day after day' however constructs this as a sequence of actions, again with the expectation of a simple present, not a continuous present. The effect of Dawe's use of tense here is to collapse a real time which has a past, a present and a future into a frozen moment which is forced to contain an unlimited amount of carnage, more than any moment can bear.

In this context we can see a new significance in the poem's puzzling conclusion: 'now, too late, too early'. This is a juxtaposition of three incompatible time schemes: the now of this endless present which exists outside of time; another time scheme in terms of which this return is too late; and another time scheme or set of time schemes which has the opposite valuation. Whatever histories are constructed to make sense of the final four words of the poem, they mark the irruption of history into a world whose incomprehensibility derives from the suppression of history.

Dawe's poem like Hasluck's speech contains two principles of order, two forms of syntax: the linear forms of domino syntax, and another more complex order. In his poem the 'solution' lies in a muffled appeal to nonlinear modes, from a world whose madness is constructed primarily in linear terms. To show other ways these two principles could be mobilised within Australian discourse, we will look more briefly at a poem about Vietnam by another poet who is rated even more highly than Dawe by *OHAL*: Judith Wright's 'Fire Sermon', first published in 1970. Wright begins her poem with an image from the mass media, an interview with what seems to be a representative of South Vietnam. (1971:279):

> *'Sinister powers,' the ambassador said, 'are moving*
> *into our ricefields. We are a little people*
> *and all we want is to live.'*

To this Hasluckian discourse she juxtaposes another image from the mass media, 'the newsreel child/ crying, crying quite silently, here in my house'. This refers to what was arguably the most potent single image around which antiwar feeling crystallised in Australia as in the US, the image of a naked young Vietnamese girl, her body alight, running towards the camera, screaming in terror—a 'fire sermon' indeed. Wright then superimposes on these disjunctive images from the mass media a set of images from a different source:

> *In the temple the great gold Buddha*
> *smiles inward with half-closed eyes.*
> *All is Maya, the dance, the veil,*
> *Shiva's violent dream.*

This image comes from a convergence of touristic discourse and what Said has critiqued as 'Orientalism', an appropriation of the discourse of the Other as a mysterious essence. But Wright draws on this trope of Eastern wisdom in a way that draws attention to its usefulness for

Western ideological purposes, as a way of neutralising a critique of colonial policies from within the colonising power. Her poem ends:

> Let me out of this dream, I cry,
> but the great gold Buddha
> smiles in the temple
> under a napalm rain.

Like Dawe, Wright constructs a poem out of meretricious fragments, and like him she finishes her poem with a juxtaposition of linear and eternalist modes, seemingly poising her world between the two. But the trajectory of the two poems is exactly opposite. The nonlinear is Dawe's desired destination, whose complexity will make all action seem simplistic and inadequate. Wright's words announce her inability to escape from the dream into activity and protest, but the eternal present of the Buddha's smile is threatened by the inexorable linearity of the 'napalm rain' which closes the poem, and points unequivocally towards the world of action and protest outside the poem. Her fragments do not defeat her critical powers, but on the contrary are the materials for her critique of paralysing contradictions in the ideological forms.

These two poems were written at essentially the same conjuncture in Australian history, with seemingly similar sentiments. Both are equally 'Australian', equally poetic. If we add Hasluck what we have is a repertoire of positions that map the field of available responses. The oppositions between poet and politician, radical and conservative, activist and quietist are all important at some levels, but each text contains a common set of oppositions and contradictions, in an unstable equilibrium. The 'typical Australian' is not to be seen in one term from any of these oppositions, but in the complex itself. From these analyses we can see more clearly what historians might be interested in: evidence of the multiplicity of responses to the problem posed to the 'Australian people' by this particular war. And we can also see the political dimensions of a style of thought that is often seen as about 'character' and not about politics: a style which both expresses and defuses dissent, which has affinities with a neocolonial ideology that has constructed the Asian world as a usefully terrifying Other in order to hold that potential dissent in check.

FRAGMENTS AND LITERARY HISTORY

The category of history has a crucial but problematic role to play in constructions of Australian identity. If amnesia is a defining quality of the Australian mind, then the proper history of that mind should be the history of an absence of history, and the writing of that history would itself seem an unAustralian activity: which of course is why Australians do it so obsessively. The history of Australian literature is determined and deformed by precisely this problem. Australian literature from the outset was inevitably a set of transformations of other texts, other genres, other stages of other cultures. But the hebephrenic search for what was purely and uniquely 'Australian' ignored this essential intertextuality, and instead tried to isolate Australianness as the autonomous residue left after all alien elements had been subtracted. This approach made the earlier texts seem impoverished to the point of incomprehensibility, condemned as 'derivative': and even later texts were required to limit their intertextual connections to the Australian tradition. The result was a recipe for one-dimensional writing, and (for the many texts that did not conform) a resolutely one-dimensional form of reading. This position never adequately described the reading and writing practices that constituted Australian literature, yet it retains its status as a consensus view. In order to criticise it, then, we need a transformational framework, one that recognises that social forms always grow out of other social forms, and that texts likewise grow out of other texts.

It is here that we draw on the ideas of the American historian Louis Hartz, whose work offers a transformational model to describe typical patterns of development of the European settler colonies in Africa, Australia and the Americas. We will summarise his argument first, before going on to indicate some qualifications to his views. His starting point was the claim that typically these colonies were founded by a group which was only a part or fragment of the structure of oppositions that made up the metropolitan society. Because they were detached from the structure of oppositions, they lost the dynamic principle of growth of that society, which lay precisely in the conflicts and contradictions from which they had escaped. This now-dominant group jettisoned their European past and in the process they jettisoned their chance of a future, and their culture ossified, just as languages cease to develop when they have been provincialised and cut off from the centre.

In this way Hartz accounted for the strange conservatism of all these colonies, even those (like Australia) which prided themselves on being progressive. But he also noted a surge of energy in these colonies, especially in their earlier years, an energy that provided the momentum for a highly developed idea of the 'nation' and national identity. At the same time, to compensate for the structural absences that arose from their status as fragment, they constructed ghostly enemies, phantoms that generated a sense of threat and maintained the need for unity in the growing state. This pattern he saw as common to all the former colonies. Differences arose from two main sources. One was the location of the fragment in relation to the metropolitan complex: whether aristocratic as in the Spanish colonies, bourgeois like the American puritans or working-class as he saw the Australian fragment. The other was the more fundamental polarity between Catholicism as in Latin America and Protestantism as in the US.

Hartz's thesis is illuminating insofar as it encourages us to look for vertical transformations (prior stages and structures in the originating culture, later stages in the evolution of the new state) and lateral transformations (analogous developments elsewhere from similar originating structures). It also foregrounds two aspects of that transformational process: the moment of colonisation as a decisive site of transformations, and the importance of processes or mechanisms that specifically limit further change, without which the founding moment would soon cease to have much importance as an explanatory principle.

When we apply this broad scheme to the ways Australia actually developed we can see many aspects of the thesis which need to be modified: in particular the structure of the fragment itself, as it was constituted from the outset as a component of a fuller structure which included the original inhabitants of the land. We will illustrate this point by looking at one concrete instance, the case of George Grey, one of the early explorers, who later became the governor of South Australia and New Zealand; and in particular one moment from his journal of the expedition that set him off on his illustrious career.

Grey's journey, down the coast of Western Australia from the Murchison district to Perth in 1837, was typical of the early explorations. He lost most of his equipment when the two boats that landed him on the coast were wrecked. Major divisions emerged in the group under his command, most of whom perished on the journey. He followed the coast line for about 600 kilometres till he staggered into Perth and civilisation, nearly dead from starvation, to become a hero who had 'opened up' the land to future settlement. Such futility and incompetence was no bar to his rapid rise to the rank of governor of a colony.

His journal describes one incident that throws some light on the Hartz thesis, as it applies to the actions and consciousness of the agents of Australian colonialism. He recorded with a note of puzzlement a curious piece of behaviour by many of his men, the representatives of the lower-class fragment that was to inherit the land according to Hartz. After the boats were wrecked, these men salvaged items from the wreckage, such as pieces of canvas, which they insisted on carrying with them to Perth, even though Grey ordered them to leave them, and the extra burden was a threat to their very lives. He was amazed at their irrational insistence but confident of his own rationality, not seeing that the items that he had them carry on his behalf (he mentions books and scientific equipment and no doubt there were other personal effects) had a similar function: fragments from the old land used as counters in the continuing struggles in the new.

The incident illustrates a number of things. One can be seen in the fact that the expedition was under the control of Grey, not any of the members of the lower-class fragment. In this way the expedition constituted a microcosm of the new colony as replicating the structures of the metropolitan centre. It was led by a member of the ruling elite, for purposes approved by the British administration, and was recorded for posterity by Grey as leader. In the new situation Grey's authority was more open to challenge, but it survived intact. Each section in his party derived its sense of identity from signifiers of the distant centre, and each had a vested interest in reproducing those originating structures. Far from being a free-floating amnesiac fragment, they joined in a common endeavour to reconstitute the centre in an ideal form, precisely in order to continue its struggles and conflicts to their best advantage.

It is interesting, then, to look at how this situation is refracted in Grey's journal. We quote from a point in the narrative when Grey and his party are at a low point, weak from starvation in what to them seemed an inhospitable land. Grey's party by this stage consisted of himself, four whites, and Kaiber his Aboriginal guide.

> Poor Kaiber alone lay crouching by my fire, occasionally feeding it with fresh fuel, and chanting to himself these two songs, in his own language.
>
> *Thither, mother oh, I return again,*
> *Thither oh, I return again.*
>
> The other had been sung by the mother of Miago, a native who had accompanied Captain Wickham in the Beagle from the Swan River, and it had made a great impression on the natives.
>
> *Whither does that lone ship wander,*
> *My young son I shall never see again.*
> *Whither does that lone ship wander.*
>
> (Grey 1841:70)

The immediately striking thing about this text is the importance of the Aborigine, Kaiber, in it. The other Whites are not even mentioned here. When they are, they are referred to as 'the men' or 'the others', only individuated when they are problems to their leader. 'Poor' Kaiber alone is the object of intense affection and concern. It's certainly the case that without Kaiber the party would have perished many times over, but it is not his usefulness that is foregrounded in Grey's narrative. It is his feelings and the cultural forms through which they are expressed that Grey records, in a way that he does not do for his 'men'.

The texts of the songs are translated, but their features can be paralleled closely in many surviving *tabi*, Aboriginal song forms. We can be reasonably sure that these are fair translations of two songs sung by Kaiber in his own language, and thus are among the earliest published texts of Aboriginal literature. This, we must remember, is an event that occurred within ten years of the founding of the Swan River colony, and within only a few years of Grey's arriving there. It shows therefore a surprising level of understanding of Aboriginal language and culture for so early a stage in the colonial period: surprising, that is, in terms of the dominant view of this history. Far from Aboriginality being an alien and uncomprehended form for the early period of the colony, this and other instances show an explosion of receptivity which only later on seemed to disappear into ignorance, hostility and disinterest.

Grey's interest in Aboriginal culture it should be stressed was not just a personal idiosyncrasy. Shortly after this period, in 1841, he became Governor of South Australia, where his positive policy towards Aborigines impressed the British Colonial Office, so much so that he was appointed Governor of New Zealand from 1845 to 1853, primarily as a response to the Maori war, and again he developed an impressive interest in and understanding of the indigenous culture, which played a significant role in his capacity to establish peace and British supremacy. From this position he went as Governor to the Cape Colony in South Africa, where this time it was the war between the Kaffirs and the colonial power that he had to resolve with his blend of scholarly empathy and military effectiveness. His career demonstrates unmistakeably the political dimensions of his role as cultural mediator, and the extent to which the need he fulfilled was highly regarded at the centre itself.

We need therefore to supplement the Hartz theory of fragments by recognising that in all these cases the metropolitan fragment was also a splinter in the side of an existing indigenous cultural system. The new order at its formative moment was as strongly determined by the obstructing or hostile presence of these competing systems, immigrant and indigenous, as by any absence of components from the metropolitan centre. The new structure had to find a place for these disturbing elements, the system of the dispossessed, at the same time as it tried to deny that dispossession had occurred. They had to be incorporated, but in a masked form. Grey's translation records Kaiber's songs, but at the same time makes them 'decent' in a poetic discourse that was archaic when he was writing it. The radically new has to be inserted into a place that already exists in the history of the culture, not as new but as familiar and safe: just as pieces of torn canvas provided remarkable comfort to Grey's men in the new terrain.

Grey's text helps us to see the reason for one paradox of the early colony: that members of the ruling elite were often more sympathetic to Aborigines than were other colonists. Grey clearly found the White members of his party insufficiently deferential and obedient. This may have been exacerbated by the new conditions, but it derived from the conflicts at the centre. Grey's solution to the problem of disorder that he had brought with him to the new country was to construct an alliance with Aborigines as faithful feudal retainers. His affirmation of Kaiber and Aboriginality, which in some respects was progressive, was at the same time a conservative and reactionary response. It involved genuine

THE PROBLEM OF HISTORY

understanding of Aboriginal people and their language and culture, and also the attempt to reconstruct an ideological schema that was no longer viable at the centre.

With this in mind we need to look again at the literary texts produced during the foundation moment, and at the consensus account of this early literature. About this period at least, the Nationalists and the Eternalists agree: colonial writing was not very interesting, and not very Australian. As Judith Wright wrote, in a sensitive defence of the poet Charles Harpur:

> The landscape of this country was difficult both to love and to absorb, as a glance at early painters' attempts to render it will attest. Only after generations of living in it has it finally become part of our vision; and this has come about precisely through the efforts of earlier artists and writers such as Harpur, to grasp and render its qualities.   (Dutton 1964:63)

Much of this early work has been seen as either derivative and incompetent (by the standards of the metropolitan centre, as judged by Eternalists) or derivative and inauthentic (by Nationalists like Wright). Australian writers, it seems, could not see well, nor write well. To use the formula from *OHAL,* they are of 'historical significance' but without 'literary value'.

The Hartz thesis provides a useful model for looking again at this version of literary history. Such extraordinary incompetence and blindness have a homeostatic function in the processes through which the colonial fragment is constituted, with clear political motives and rationale. We don't have to invent a new pathology for these early settlers, as though they could only wait passively for Australia to happen by some mysterious process of osmosis. The process needed conscious and effective agents whose endeavours are likely to have left traces in texts: including the texts of the despised literary tradition.

There are two obvious places to look for such traces. One is amongst the texts that survive from the popular tradition, including ballads such as those collected diligently by Russel Ward, which provided some of the rationale for his Nationalist history in *The Australian Legend* (1958). The other place is amongst the writers in the recognised literary tradition, where we need to reassess the scale of their 'failure' in the light of the complex and successful strategies of the triumphant fragment.

As an illustration of popular traditions we will take a poem written in 1824 by John Dunmore Lang, later a radical political voice in the colony. Lang's target at this time was Governor Macquarie, governor from 1809 till 1821: himself a reformist, with relatively humane policies towards convicts and Aborigines. Lang's poem begins:

> *'Twas said of Greece two thousand years ago,*
> *That every stone i' the land had got a name.*
> *Of New South Wales too, men will soon say so too;*

> *But every stone there seems to get the same.*
> *'Macquarie' for a name is all the go:*

There is no doubt that his poetic technique is crude. But his 'lapses' are clearly intended to be outrageous, carrying their own unmistakeable point. By rhyming 'ago' with 'too' he is aggressively inserting his own Scottish accent into the poem's rhyme scheme. He then compounds this assault on both standard English pronunciation and poetic diction by including the colloquial '*the go*' (pronounced 'goo'). The clash of kinds of language is the same strategy Dawe was to use 150 years later, and in both instances it declares the refusal of fragments to be assimilated into a single whole.

Lang's points are clear and surprisingly 'modern'. He satirises the way the colonial power anxiously attempts to appropriate the new land by casting over it a network of reassuring names—a point that would be made with greater sophistication but no more clearly by Paul Carter in his recent book *The Road to Botany Bay* (1987). Lang sees that a central premise of this strategy is the attempt to rewrite history and thus to preempt the future's version of the past. He counters this by invoking other kinds of history, of far greater antiquity and prestige. But he also notes the way that Aboriginal culture has been recognised and displaced onto names, and he mobilises their ideological force:

> *I like the native names, as Parramatta,*
> *And Illawarra, and Woolloomooloo;*

Where Grey wished to construct an Aboriginal alliance on behalf of the rulers, to recover a vanished feudal order, Lang invokes an alliance of the oppressed, and defers to a very different history. For both, Aboriginality appears in a preexisting place in a structure of oppositions, which they have brought with them to the new land. Yet for both, in different ways, the prior rights of Aborigines to the land is tacitly recognised, as another structure that must itself be accommodated.

To illustrate the ambiguous qualities of the fragment literary tradition, the obvious case to look at is the poetry of Charles Harpur. His Nationalist credentials were impeccable: born in 1813 in Australia to ex-convict parents, he espoused a radical politics, and wrote intricate verse that was briefly hailed as the first authentic native poetry: 'Australia has now produced a poet all her own, to atone for the indiscretions of poetasters among her adopted sons' wrote Henry Parkes (later to become a founding father of the Australian Commonwealth) in his enthusiastic review of Harpur's first volume of poetry in 1845.

Later critics have been less enthusiastic, finding his work quite poetic but awkward and uneven, and not only rather derivative but out of date by the standards of the metropolitan centre of the time: a worthy trier in the circumstances, but no more. But the qualities in his poetry that give

THE PROBLEM OF HISTORY

rise to such judgments can be interpreted differently in the context of the characteristic tensions and contradictions of a fragment writer in the colonising phase. His early verse, for instance, enthusiastically adopted English lyric modes that were 50 years old by Harpur's time: ships to Australia were indeed slow. But worse was to come. Instead of trying to catch up, Harpur sank even further back, so disconcerted was he (or so the case goes) by the unspeakable novelty of the landscape in which he had grown up. Here for instance is his description of a 'Dragon-hornet', in his 'A Mid-summer Noon in the Australian Forest':

> *Only there's a drowsy humming*
> *From yon warm lagoon slow coming:*
> *'Tis the dragon-hornet—see!*
> *All bedaubed resplendently*
> *With yellow on a tawny ground—*
> *Each rich spot nor square nor round,*
> *But rudely heart-shaped, as it were*
> *The blurred and hasty impress there,*
> *Of a vermeil-crusted seal*
> *Dusted o'er with golden meal*

The style and diction of the poem seem to be going to the opposite extreme from Lang, as far away as possible from contemporary colloquial forms. Its diction is reminiscent of Pope of *Windsor Forest* of the early 18th century, while its metre is reminiscent of even earlier poetry— perhaps Milton's 'Il Penseroso' or Marvell's 'The Garden' and 'Upon Appleton House' of the mid-17th century, with their fanciful allegorisation of the landscape in free-running octosyllabic couplets.

But Harpur's diction is not only archaic, it is curiously obscure and apparently imprecise as well as being insistently elaborate. It is hard to doubt that he had a specific insect in view, so why did he not describe it more precisely? In this case it isn't plausible to suggest that the phenomenon was too strange for him to be able to 'see' it, because Australian hornets or wasps are physically similar to British ones: members of the family of Hymenoptera, solitary flying insects equipped with a painful sting. Nor is there a problem of language; 'yellow' and 'black' for the stripes of a wasp or hornet were standard English then as now. The site of the disturbance is the word 'tawny'. 'Tawny' is an imprecise colour, ranging from dull yellow to dark brown, it derives from 'tanned', as applied to skin, and this is part of its field of connotations (gypsies and lions are tawny: mud or wood isn't). In the Australian context, it is the skin of Aborigines which is 'tawny', skin which they daubed with yellow and white ochres. In the poem, this hornet represents the one discordant, threatening note in the otherwise tranquil landscape. If Harpur's elaborate description had an allegorical target in mind, the most likely candidate is the Aboriginal people: Aborigines as a latent threat in this otherwise paradisiacal environment. In this text, the threat is unspeakable, though in other poems Harpur was able to write at length about the dangers posed by Aboriginal hostility.

Harpur's seeming archaism has another function which has much in common with Lang's seemingly different style. Both repudiate the current standards of the centre, Lang by his crudity and Harpur by obscure erudition. Both men in different ways appeal to a version of history, thus countering the amnesia that Hartz saw as characteristic of a fragment society but which Lang saw so clearly was an effect of the colonial power's typical practice of rewriting history. Lang's crude clarity contrasts with Harpur's obliqueness, but Harpur wrote from a less secure social position, and attached greater weight to the meanings that he encoded in poetry. We don't need to propose some strange and massive visual defect afflicting Harpur and his readers, or any failure in language as such to cope with the new. Harpur and Lang in different ways reached out for alternative histories, alternative structures of meaning, in which to position a contemporary critical perspective. Within this perspective a major site of disturbance was the presence of Aboriginal people in the new totality, as a fragment incorporated within this fragment. At the interface of the colonial with the non-colonial, it is misleading to suppose that a homogeneous fragment encountered an empty land, and proceeded to work out its unique destiny. These early texts cannot be understood as empty forms waiting for a language in order for Australians to see, or for history to begin in order to be filled with Australianness. Rather they were always full forms, inserted in one kind of history and trying to construct others, escapee fragments in search of a whole to call their own.

2 The bastard complex

The role of Aboriginal Australians in the dominant constructions of Australian identity is at first sight contradictory and ambiguous. The 'typical Australian' is all White and he occupies a landscape from which all Aboriginal traces have been removed. But the iconography of Australia that is packaged for the tourist industry is full of Aboriginal motifs. These two traditions of representation are normally kept quite distinct. Paul Hogan's highly successful *Crocodile Dundee* films broke with this general rule, that the two kinds of definition of Australian identity should never be represented in the same space, but these texts were innovative, responding to new trends in the overall system of representations. The normal schema works with a double image and an enforced split between them, signifying the schizoid quality of the Australian mind.

The complexities of what is at issue here can be seen in the curious use of the word 'bastard' in Australian male colloquial speech. It has two opposed uses. It is often a term of abuse ('Get lost you bastard') but it can also express high solidarity between male 'mates' ('Howya goin you old bastard'). It is the solidary meaning which is most worthy of note, because it is this usage that is definitionally Australian: only the true Australian can call his 'mate' a 'bastard'. This quirk of the language foregrounds the issue of legitimacy as crucial in the Australian definition of identity. And paradoxically the basis of identity that it constructs is a sense of shared illegitimacy: a sense that can only be acknowledged however among (male) friends.

This colloquial usage does not point directly to the source of this anxiety about legitimacy in the national psyche. On the contrary it affirms illegitimacy in order to evade an anxiety about origins. It is the other tradition in the iconography of Australia that gestures at the secret of the Australian obsession with legitimacy: the occluded but central and problematic place of Aboriginal Australians in the foundation of the contemporary Australian state and in the construction of the national identity.

Legitimacy is a raw and buried issue in the contemporary Australian consciousness for good reasons. The current system of government, law and property derives from a chain of juridical acts which leads inexorably back to the founding event itself: an act of invasion by which the Aboriginal owners of the land were dispossessed with some cruelty and without compensation. Many White Australians try to minimise the importance of this history, claiming that it is something that happened to other people a long time ago, only of interest to Aboriginal activists and a minority of neurotics indulging in White liberal guilt. But the chain that links the present to this past is fundamental and structural in the current order, not mere nostalgia or sentimentality. This is clear to Aborigines, even if Whites seek to ignore the fact. In the words of Yami Lester, Chairman of the Anangu Pitjantjatjara in 1988, 'Until a real settlement is worked out, until a real treaty is agreed, we will continue to be surrounded by invaders, and you can't really call this land your home' (*West Australian* 31 October 1988).

ABORIGINES AND AUSTRALIAN IDENTITY

Australian Aborigines have much in common with other indigenous peoples who suffered under the impact of European colonisation. But there are a number of distinctive features about the Australian Aborigines and the formation of the Australian colony that need to be recognised, in order for us to understand the particular forms of their history and the distinctive features of the representational complex which was constructed on their behalf.

The Aboriginal people for most of the last 200 years lacked the numbers, technology and military organisation to pose a serious threat to the dominance of the European power. Recently it has been recognised that Aboriginal resistance was more continuous and effective than had been previously acknowledged, but it is still the case that with Aborigines the war was able to be won without having to be declared, so that it could end without ratification in a form of treaty that at least could acknowledge the scale of the defeat. The experience of American Indians or closer to hand the Maori people of New Zealand shows that the existence of a treaty is no guarantee that its terms will be observed, but there is a crucial difference between being the victim of illegality in terms of an accepted framework of law, and lacking that framework itself.

THE BASTARD COMPLEX

Aborigines in contemporary Australia are a small minority: less than 2 per cent of the overall population, a figure which includes persons of mixed descent. This is slightly greater than the proportion of American Indians within the US but of the same order. It is different to the proportion of Maoris in New Zealand, who are still a minority but a more significant one. This situation in turn is different from a nation like Mexico, where Indians and Mestizos combined constitute the overwhelming majority, or the situation in many European colonies in Asia and Africa where the colonised peoples had a numerical superiority over their colonisers. Because of this small figure, Aborigines do not represent a serious threat, politically or economically, to the majority of Australians, even if they were to be freed from the massive discrimination which currently affects them.

Finally, Australian Aborigines have an exceptionally persuasive claim to the territories in dispute against the claims of the colonising power. This claim can be sustained by appeal to archeology, which currently recognises evidence of their continuous occupation of Australia for over 40 000 years, but more to the point is the tacit recognition of an absolute legitimacy which is inscribed in the name that the colonisers give to these people: Aborigines, from the latin *ab origine*, 'from the origin'. Other indigenous groups tend to be referred to as 'indigenes', from the latin *indigenus*, 'born in', 'native to'. 'Aborigine' tends elsewhere to refer to small enclaves of very early and primitive peoples, whose subordination by another indigenous majority occurred long ago. Many Aborigines prefer one of the names from their own languages, Koori, Murri, Nyoongar, names which signify the plurality of nations of the Aboriginal people. In Australia the coloniser's name concedes the whole case: the White 'bastards' do not after all try to deny the priority of Aboriginal rights.

In other colonial and post-colonial situations, the Other is constructed out of a double impulse: fear of revenge and desire for the security of legitimacy. In this respect Aborigines in Australia are a kind of limit case. They posed the minimal material threat and the maximal threat to legitimacy. For most of the history of European–Aboriginal relations, colonial policy has been driven more by ideological than by material considerations. After the initial dispossession was achieved, and allowing for continual Aboriginal attempts at subversion, the main thrust of policy was in effect to dispose of Aboriginal peoples in such a way that they did not interfere with the processes by which national identity was being constructed. In practice this meant that alongside the images of Aborigines that were being constructed, other meanings were also being inscribed on Aboriginal bodies and Aboriginal lives, and these two processes were two aspects of a single ideological program. Aboriginal people were subjected to suffering and indignity, their families broken up, their traditions threatened, even when this meant no great

25

economic benefits to the colonial masters. It was as though all this was done so that White Australians could feel more comfortable about being Australian.

The colonial strategy of legitimation had a double form, as we have said. On the one hand it had to construct a foundation myth that pivoted around a moment and an event in the past which unequivocally and irreversibly established the right of the group to transmit its pattern of ownership from generation to generation. NonAboriginal Australians try to build their foundation myth around the sufferings and achievements of the pioneers and early settlers, but that is not enough. In spite of what some may claim, neither myth nor history is totally malleable, because the need for real legitimation is so strong that it breaks through the too obviously specious. So White Australians have had a continuous need to generate new forms of the foundation myth, which exists to annul, defuse, displace and negate the intractable conditions of the foundation event.

The other aspect of this legitimation enterprise was the development of strategies to resolve the 'Aboriginal problem', which from the outset was a problem for European Australians not for Aborigines themselves. Aborigines had to be discursively constructed and symbolically managed by specific discursive regimes. In the sense in which we will use it, a discursive regime prescribes who can speak about what in what way (where, when and how) and with what authority. Discursive regimes are political and social facts which profoundly affect what is commonly said or communicated, and what is recognised to be a legitimate meaning. Discursive regimes reinforce particular pictures of the world and give them official currency. But precisely because they operate to constrain what otherwise would be said and thought they cannot correspond even approximately to the full content of what is known to exist. In order to operate with a discursive regime speakers must also know what lies outside its scope, so that that can be recognised and dealt with in appropriate ways. This outside of a discursive regime, that is to say, is unspeakable but not unconscious, and those who deploy it are never 'innocent'.

Most White representations and constructions of Aborigines take place within terms of what is ultimately a single discursive regime, whose primary function is to sustain the foundation myth. This discursive regime consists of a number of specific moves which at first seem so different as to be part of different systems, but on closer inspection we can see the ways that the differences interlock into a single functional whole.

One major strategy is total suppression: suppression of the existence of Aborigines from major domains of discourse, and elimination of Aborigines as acceptable speakers on any topic. So Aboriginal history almost disappeared from the dominant White histories of Australia.

Until recently, Aboriginal literature was treated as not even 'literature', much less part of Australian literature, and Aborigines appeared only on the margins of works in the mainstream of White literature. But total suppression is too crude to meet all the aims of control, because those who are controlled by the regime are Whites as much as Aborigines. Alongside the system of suppressions must be another system of controls on permissible forms of representation. Otherwise, leakage may occur, and uncontested accounts of the supposedly non-existent may circulate and acquire force.

There is another reason why Aborigines cannot be completely effaced from the record. They still have a crucial role to play in the process of the foundation myth: to confer legitimacy on those who raped, pillaged, poisoned and dispossessed them. So they cannot be silenced: or more precisely, a voice that is labelled as theirs must have a place, legitimated as theirs yet not disrupting the fine balance of contradictions in the foundation myth.

As we have said, the discursive regime at issue has affinities with others that have been deployed to legitimate imperialist rule. We see it as a type of what Edward Said has theorised as 'Orientalism'. Orientalism in his account has a double movement, a fascination with the culture of the colonised along with a suppression of their capacity to speak or truly know it. One of its great themes, writes Said (1985:7) is that since they (the Other) cannot represent themselves, 'they must therefore be represented by others' who know more about them than they know about themselves. Within Australian culture a similar phenomenon can be labelled 'Aboriginalism'. As Said argues, this kind of regime should not be allowed to go unchallenged, because the contradiction at its core is not symmetrical. It is no accident that its vague positivities commonly are cancelled out by the negative meanings that are strongly encoded in it: smugness and sense of superiority, racist stereotypes, and assertion of rights of ownership in the intellectual and cultural sphere to match power in the political and economic spheres.

Within Indian Orientalism, a crucial argument has been that of Hegel, which has intriguingly close parallels in the Australian intellectual tradition. In *The Philosophy of Fine Art* (1835-38) Hegel reduced Hindu thought to what he called 'fantastic symbolism', a term that he believed reflected the absence of an historical consciousness in the Hindu. The corresponding premise in Aboriginalism is the concept of 'the Dreaming', which refers to a complex of aspects of traditional Aboriginal belief, including mythology, law and history. All commentators agree that it is untranslateable and incomprehensible to (other) Europeans, and celebrate this as proving the intricate and mystical incapacity of Aborigines to comprehend linear history in the European mode. As in Orientalism a warm positivity about this mystical incapacity masks the political function and meaning of the move, one of whose most direct effects is to deny Aborigines the ability (as Aborigines) to establish an alternative account of the foundation event and its aftermath, an account which might refuse to contain the violence and illegalities within the moment of innocence.

The place of the concept of 'the Dreamtime' or 'the Dreaming' in contemporary Australian discourse is now a complex product of the conflicting forces involved. It is a widely accepted shorthand to refer to the whole of the traditional Aboriginal culture that has been threatened by a variety of attacks from nonAboriginal agents of cultural policy. It has been authorised by anthropology, the discipline that has been assigned the task of understanding and mediating Aboriginal culture to the rest of Australia and to the world.

Those who use the term use it to signify not simply an object (traditional texts and beliefs) but also their own very positive orientation to that object. The term is also part of Aboriginal English, used by many traditional people to refer to such texts. However, the many Aboriginal words in different languages that are now automatically translated as 'the Dreaming' normally have no semantic connection to 'dreams' or 'dreaming'. The unusual syntax of the word (combining a definite article with a gerund, with no agent presumed to be doing the dreaming, and no object that is being dreamt) is a product of the grammar of English, a grammar deformed by certain English speakers for their own purposes to create a specific form of discourse which renounces the standard language and the dominant rationality. So although it now seems to be part of Aboriginal English, in fact it represents the insertion there of a fragment of a subdialect of standard English, anthropologese. Those in the wider Australian community who use it do so without any clear sense of what it might 'mean' (refer to), but with a strong feeling of identity with those who are supposed to know (Aboriginal people and their anthropological interpreters). Meanwhile Aborigines themselves negotiate the word with their customary linguistic tact and flexibility. As one Aborigine said recently in an ABC radio broadcast, in response to the question, Is English a very inadequate sort of tool to describe Aboriginal Dreamings and lifestyles and that sort of thing?: 'I think so, because I think that the word dreaming in English is sleeping—you know, sleeping what you dream about. But for us it's got nothing to do with that whatsoever' (Bowden and Bunbury 1990: 33).

Aboriginalism and notions of the primitive Aboriginal mentality have played an equivocal role in Australian history and in the political significance of representations of Aborigines in literature and art. Although Aboriginalism has the effect of silencing actual Aborigines and negating their right to speak on their own behalf, it has also been mobilised positively for and by Aboriginal people, whose struggles would have been even more difficult without Aboriginalist allies. In this respect it has played a similar role to the concept of Negritude, though no Aboriginal writer has espoused this term as militantly as did Aimé Césaire, Leopold Senghor, Frantz Fanon and other Black writers in the 1940s and 1950s. Aboriginalism does not have a single value or a single position. On the contrary it is a set of representations whose final value derives from the role they play in particular struggles and debates.

To show the complex uses of Aboriginalism as it can be deployed in particular struggles, we will look briefly at an essay entitled 'Literature and the Aborigine' written by Frederick Macartney (1957). The polemical point of this essay was to exclude Aboriginal culture from Australian literature, and its main premise was its denial of any intellectual or imaginative ability to the Aborigines. Macartney is especially harsh on A.P. Elkin, a Sydney University anthropologist, for daring to suggest that Aborigines are 'native philosophers'. Elkin's argument was a classic form of Aboriginalism, intended to defend the intrinsic value of traditional Aboriginal culture as he saw it. Macartney's fury takes on a mean and racist tone. How dare he, Elkin, suggest that a primitive race can produce philosophers and 'native' (i.e. natural) ones at that? Isn't philosophy the intellectual analysis of ideas and phenomena? And of course, in the final analysis, how could any of this be possible when they, the Aborigines, blur 'the distinction between self and external objects'? (1957: 117)

This is precisely what Hegel too was talking about. Armed with this kind of 'Orientalist' ammunition, Macartney can then deny this race the ability to produce its grandest cultural artefact, that is, the literary text. He refuses to use the word 'literature' when discussing Aboriginal narratives, which he judges to be either 'tediously discursive and inchoate' or incapable of 'critical reflectiveness' (if that is different). He then turns with equal scorn to Aboriginalism in literary works, and claims not to understand how Eleanor Dark's Aboriginal character Booron in *The Timeless Land* could say 'A Law, if it was anything at all, was surely something to live by, something to which one might anchor one's spiritual life' (1966: 252).

There is nothing inherently incomprehensible in this statement. Presumably it is only its attribution to an Aboriginal speaker that arouses his incredulity. But worse was to follow in Dark's text, which he did not quote either out of respect for Dark's reputation amongst commonsensical Australians, or for some other less benign reason. The passage concludes with the words '(the law) was so intricately interwoven not only with their own physical and spiritual needs, but with the peculiarities of the land itself, that all three became one, a mystical trinity functioning in harmony—the Law, the Land, the People' (Dark 1966: 252).

Macartney was an early defender of Australian literature, and is perhaps best known as one of the first Commonwealth Literary Fund lecturers of the 1940s (at the universities of Queensland, Tasmania,

Melbourne and Sydney). It may seem surprising that he should have been so militantly insensitive towards Aboriginal culture, and oblivious of the many ways in which that culture has interacted with White Australian literature. The Aboriginalist tradition in Australian literature had some significant names in it by the 1950s when his essay was first written, going at least as far back as Dame Mary Gilmore in 1910 and including the highly publicised 'Jindyworobak' school of the 1930s and 1940s as well as Dark. Macartney's polemic shows the tension that existed in practice between the two basic strategies of legitimation in Australian cultural life: the celebration of the 'typical Australian' and the Aboriginalist theme.

But for all his aggression and hostility towards Aboriginalism it is important to realise that he is not proposing a different construction of Aboriginality from Elkin or Dark, so much as giving a hostile materialist reading of their version of Aboriginalism. If he is trying to remove Aborigines from literature, Dark's 'timeless land' in effect removes them from history. However positive she is about the value and validity of Aboriginal beliefs, she has situated them in a kind of 'dreamtime' which exists outside the material world and physical space and time. Some kind of materialism is needed if the mystical premises of an Elkin or a Dark are to be translated into a genuine political or social program—though Macartney himself is not looking very hard in this direction.

We can see from this exchange how both approaches could coexist in a paradoxical unity in constructing what Rowley (1978:14) called an 'Aboriginal Archipelago' (by analogy with Solzhenitsyn's 'Gulag Archipelago'). This domain was constructed on a double premise, of exclusion (by refusing to acknowledge the Aboriginal presence in society) and ubiquitous presence (so that land rights already exist in some spiritual plane, and do not need to be denied). If Macartney's position tends toward the first, Dark and Elkin's position provides support for the second. But here as elsewhere it is important to recognise that although the two kinds of move, the materialist and the idealist, have more in common than may initially appear, that is not to say that Dark and Elkin are no different from Macartney after all. The two strands of Aboriginalism were complementary but they were also opposed, and it was out of that opposition that genuine changes were to come for Aboriginal people.

THE FOUNDATION EVENT

The foundation event has a double role in the discursive history that we are concerned with. It is both the ostensible object of all subsequent versions of the foundation myth, and was itself the privileged site where the first set of versions of that myth emerged. What we want to define here is a structure that is more or less repeated on many different occasions, rather than a single once-for-all event. As the Hartz thesis insists, the foundation event is always a transformation of a previous situation and structure, transposed to the new colonial setting. That situation of risk, at the interface between old and new, typically has unique properties that distinguish it from all subsequent transformations, in spite of the deference that is paid to it as the ancestral form.

What is most important about this stage is that at this point the power and the legitimacy of the invaders were most at risk. Correspondingly, this was the time when the power and knowledge of Aborigines were held in most respect, though the degree to which this was so varied from place to place. In this situation, in spite of widely held views to the contrary, White knowledge of Aborigines like Aboriginal knowledge of Whites advanced at a rapid pace. The knowledge may have been pragmatic, partial and superficial but as far as it went it was reasonably accurate. There was survival value in accurate knowledge and representation, at this point: only later could that be taken for granted, and the massive investment in legitimation could take over.

The foundation event, then, is a crucial discursive site for us to study in order to understand later moves in the legitimation strategy. For this reason we need to distinguish meticulously between the core narrative of the event and the rapid sequence of revisions and versions of this narrative which then fed into later versions of the foundation myth. The importance of these subtle distinctions can be seen from a close reading of the following statement, from the classic study of Aboriginal history by C.D. Rowley:

> What the colonists everywhere thought of the Aborigines is easy enough to learn: what we now know shows how great was the misunderstanding. But the moral question of dispossession was probably as clear then as it is now; and though it was blurred by self-interested discussion of what 'occupation' meant, and by stated good intentions of compensation and uplift, the question of justice has been raised in every generation from then till now. (Rowley 1970:27)

What Rowley calls 'moral' here is more properly called legal, since what is at issue is the basis of the system of land ownership which underpins the property rights by which all citizens of Australia are required to live. So we can begin by rephrasing Rowley to note that no generation of Australians has been able to be unaware, 'innocent', of the fact that the dominant White economic and political system rests on a series of illegitimate acts by which the 'rightful' owners were dispossessed. However, we still need to be sceptical of the implications of Rowley's opening comment. It is not after all 'easy enough to learn' what the early colonists thought about Aborigines. What survives in the historical record is only what they said, which is a rather different matter.

With the discourse of people so directly self-interested it would be unwise to trust their words at their face value. Rowley contrasts 'what we now know' with what was known and understood then, as though at the crucial moment of the foundation event the invaders 'did not know' and therefore in some quasi-legal sense were not responsible for their actions.

This argument is a crucial component of the foundation myth, and is very widespread in accounts of the early settlement, even amongst writers who are critical of the repressive policies of the early settlers. Here as another instance is a pronouncement by W.E.H. Stanner, an anthropologist whose own description of 'the Dreaming' was an influential contribution to the development of Aboriginalism: 'In the early years of settlement insensibility towards the Aborigines' human status hardened into contempt, derision and indifference. The romantic idealism, unable to stand the shock of experience drifted through dismay into pessimism about the capacity for civilisation' (1979:145).

The idea that in the beginning there were only two alternative positions, either 'insensibility' and contempt, or sentimental idealism, with the latter helpless before the power of 'experience', is not supported by a study of early accounts and representations. Tench's journal, with its wealth of sharp observations of Aboriginal life, was not only written but published in the early days of the colony. We have mentioned Grey's close study of Aboriginal language and culture, again published and again emanating from an authoritative position within colonial life, and there are many more such instances.

'Experience' was not after all so overwhelming, and accurate knowledge neither so difficult nor rare as is claimed. There must be some other explanation, and it is to be found in discursive regimes, not in brute reality. Coming from the two contradictory demands on representation came two distinct generic types or modalities which were to recur in some form or another for the next two centuries. One we can term the 'realist' mode, concerned above all with accurate representation on behalf of those who needed to know. The other took many different forms, but underlying all of them was a strategy of displacement, which we will call the 'subjectivist' mode, since it foregrounds the subject who is constructing the images and meanings, whose thoughts and feelings are an intrinsic component of what is represented.

Texts from the founding event itself are rare and precious documents, demanding intense scrutiny if we are to catch the nascent forms of the future myth coexisting with other forces and meanings at this eye of the ideological storm. To illustrate the process of reading at issue we will begin with the following passage, taken from the journal of Philip Gidley King, then a trusted lieutenant to Governor Phillip, later to be Governor himself:

They wanted to know what sex we were, which they explained by pointing to where it was distinguishable. As they took us for women, not having our beard grown, I ordered one of the people to undeceive them in this particular, when they made a great shout of admiration, and pointing to the shore, which was but ten yards from us, we saw a great number of Women & Girls, with infant children on their shoulders, make their appearance on the beach—all in *puris naturalibus, pas même la feuille de figueur*. Those natives who were round the boats made signs for us to go to them and made us to understand their persons were at our service. However, I declined this mark of their hospitality but shewed a handkerchief, which I offered to one of the women, pointing her out. She immediately put her child down and came alongside the boat and suffered me to apply the handkerchief where Eve did the Fig leaf; the natives then set up another very great shout and my female visitor returned on shore. (King, in Berzins 1988:19-20)

The event recorded by King is a significant political encounter, an early confrontation between the two nations, but his version transforms this in two ways. On the one hand the Aborigines' offer of their wives functions like a kind of phantom treaty, a formal renunciation of the only property they are recognised to possess, a confirmation therefore that the other renunciation (of their rights to their own land) can be taken for granted. In King's description he symbolically takes possession of an offered woman, while also affirming the superior morality that is another guarantee of the fitness of Whites to possess and rule. In practice the massive exploitation of Aboriginal women by White men was to be a scandal to Whites and a lethal source of disease to Aborigines.

But King also reads the event through two other frames: as an erotic encounter and as a form of myth. The erotic encounter consists of the mutual voyeurism of the males, in which the Whites won a 'great shout' when they displayed their manhood, and the ambiguous offer of the Aboriginal women. In this exchange King presses a handkerchief to the naked genitals of a selected Aboriginal woman, in a 'joke' that neatly expresses both salaciousness and its renunciation in favour of (on this occasion) high morality.

But his renunciation is not mere asceticism. By invoking the myth of Eden he inserts the exchange into a potent structure of meanings which at first glance seem to attach importance and positive value to the woman, and thus to Aborigines. If she is Eve then her husband is Adam. But King himself is God, a god who is also a sexually active male at the very moment that he administers the rebuke. So the Aboriginal woman has a double value as Eve. She is a symbol of prelapsarian innocence (not noticing that she is naked was a sign of her virtue, in the Biblical narrative), but she was the cause of the Fall and the reason for the expulsion from Eden—even though it is King and his men who are more thoroughly fallen, in terms of this scene.

Because she is Eve in both aspects her innocence (which connects with notions of the 'noble savage') is inseparable not simply from her status as fallen but also from her role in the fall: as though innocence and femininity are primarily to blame, and justify a punishment such as expulsion from Eden (Australia). Conversely, King is both puritanical god and bastard (or symbolic begetter of bastards), and both parts of the contradiction are functional for him in his role in the foundation event and the myth he is constructing.

These meanings—the attraction of the innocence/nakedness and the condemnation of it as justification for a punitive response—are present, but they are only lightly touched on, and we need to recognise the tone and how it affects our reading of the text. King's manner is that of a man of the world conveying to others like himself his own nuanced sense of the meaning of the scene. The whole business of the handkerchief reads like a joke between himself and others in an all-male gathering back in London, as though that civilised company was more real for him than the Aborigines in front of him, for whom the 'joke' may have been read as a calculated insult (the 'very great shout' they gave may not have expressed humour or approval). The construction of this persona and this audience is not only part of the pleasure of the text (for such an audience), it is itself part of a strategy of legitimation, since this persona with his breadth of culture (French and Latin) moral strength (knowledge of the Bible, resistance to temptation) and flexibility (tolerance of human sexuality) has all the credentials for sound judgment and humane rule. If Aborigines do not recognise this, the unstated argument goes, then they need this kind of ruler the more.

We will now look at a visual text, a sketch that was executed probably early in 1788 by Lt William Bradley, a significant figure in the first fleet. It was part of the record of his journal, serving a practical purpose in recording a specific incident. It does not attempt to construct a glamorised image, so that in spite of the simple drawing technique we can label it 'realistic'. Bradley was a drawer of maps, and we can see the cartographic precision of his record of the configuration of the bay.

Bradley's sketch would not count as art, any more than King's text would count as 'literature' but nonetheless they are examples of two significant genres from the early settlement period: the journal and the topographical sketch. In spite of apparent differences, both record a response to a similar incident, from a similar position within the colonial power structure. The differences, then, subsist within a broader unity.

The first difference concerns medium, visual as against verbal. In some discussions of these early pictorial representations, there is a naive assumption that pictures faithfully represent what people see (though not what is actually there to be seen), so that a painting like Bradley's records the limits of his perception, faced with the 'shock of the new'. There is a similar naive assumption that a text like King's records what he thought. Both assumptions are untenable, for the same common

W. Bradley: *First Interview with the Native Women at Port Jackson.* (Picture courtesy of Mitchell Library, the State Library of New South Wales)

sense reason. It strains belief to suppose that a skilful navigator and cartographer like Bradley really 'saw' the Aborigines in boats to the right as midgets, and the Aborigines on the rock as giants, as compared to the Europeans in the centre. And as we have seen, King's text has a complex set of indications of what he was actually 'thinking'.

Bradley's text basically works with what we have called the realist strategy, whereas King's text, with its biblical reference and cultured tone, falls into the other broad category which we call the subjectivist mode. In contrast to King's text, Bradley's little sketch is much more literal, seemingly more concerned with the picture in front of him than with the status of the observer. But the title of the picture would not be easy to guess from the drawing itself: *First Interview with the Native Women at Port Jackson.* The gender of the stick-like natives is not easy to determine, as though contact-astigmatism has prevented Bradley from noticing black breasts and buttocks as well as gum-trees and kangaroos. The painting as a whole has a number of qualities that are typical of the genre. Human beings, both Aboriginal and British, are deindividuated, and they are represented as aggregates, as are the trees and landscape, whose disposition is important, not the details. Another way of putting it is to see this painting as concerned with the strategic rather than the sensual, reporting with sufficient accuracy for practical purposes only.

That is why the information coded in the title, together with King's account, is so useful in reading this text, because it acknowledges that this was an erotic as well as a strategic encounter. The Aborigine in the boat is desexed by the style of drawing, but presumably must be a naked female, leaning (or being pulled) toward the seated male in front of her and presenting her naked bottom to the seaman behind. Bradley's title shows that he recognised the erotic significance of the scene, but the term 'interview' is a euphemism that does not give much away.

Again we see that words and picture suppress much of what we can confidently assume that Bradley both saw and thought, and was fully conscious of. What Bradley is concerned to be accurate about is the military implications of the situation (he is meticulous in drawing guns and spears, where all other details are rendered impressionistically). King obscures this dimension (we are given no idea of whether his party were confident of their military superiority or not). But there is no reason to suppose that King was unaware of the strategic situation, or did not take it into account when he planned his 'joke'. The two texts are highly complementary, in spite of the fact that the different modes (realist and subjectivist) construct consistently different versions of a common experience.

At the time they produced these texts, Bradley and King seemed barely distinguishable, but their later careers diverged interestingly. King became Governor in his turn. Bradley's career nearly brought him back to the colony under very different circumstances. In 1812 he engaged in some odd and criminal behaviour which was excused on the grounds of insanity. To prevent a scandal he was promoted to the rank of rear-admiral and cashiered. In 1814 the eccentricity persisted, and this time he was found guilty of 'meaningless fraud against the post office', and sentenced to death. This was then commuted to transportation, and this in turn was commuted to exile abroad, at a place of his choosing. He finally received a free pardon in 1822, thus missing the heights that King reached in the colony and the depths of the ordinary class of criminal.

Bradley's later instability seems to contrast with the mathematical precision of his drawing style, with its sense of rationality and control. Bradley's journal similarly implies a kind of split sensibility. Describing the events of the 'first interview' he begins by giving the official rationale: 'The Governor's plan with respect to the Natives, was, if possible to cultivate an acquaintance with them without their having an idea of our great superiority over them'. But Bradley's version of this plan was more specific: to induce the women to come into the boat. At first men and even children thronged around, but Bradley was insistent: 'We did not give them anything in hopes of bringing the Women among us by keeping what articles we had to give them & signified to the Men that we would give all to the Women if they would come from the woods where they were sitting looking at us'.

The deep policy reasons behind this obsession with the women are never explained, but the triumphant moment when one Aboriginal woman did approach is described in these terms: 'We ornamented this naked Beauty with strings of Beads and Buttons, round her neck, arms and waist she appear'd rather frightened at tho' she affected a laugh & seem'd pleas'd with her presents'. But at this moment of politically motivated seduction of the Aboriginal woman, Bradley's strategic sense was alert: 'We counted 72 besides women and children, this was more than twice the number yet seen together' (we note that it is only the men who are thought worthy of being counted). Nor was the pleasure in seduction allowed to be unchecked for long. Within two days of this incident, Bradley's journal carries the following moralistic commentary on the character of a people whom he has only known for just over a week: 'If they ever deign to come near you to take a present they appear as coy, shy and timorous as a maid on her wedding night. But when they are, as they think, out of your reach, they holler and chatter to you, and frisk and flirt and play a hundred wanton pranks, equally as significant as the solicitations of a Covent Garden strumpet.'

The hypocrisy of this is blatant enough to need no commentary. The split in Bradley which he projects on to the Aboriginal women is the same as in King's text, only more extreme. Both attempt to ensure moral superiority and the right of the founding fathers to beget bastards without responsibility and without guilt. For both, economic, political and erotic motives interweave, each masking the others at particular textual moments so that the full bastard-complex is never fully available for inspection.

It is easy to see why the meanings of Aborigines have to be preempted, because it is their effective complicity that is crucial in this one-sided and specious 'treaty'. So the Aboriginal meanings are constructed as sufficiently transparent as to be unambiguous, while the processes by which the English officers constructed those meanings are kept as much as possible from view. After 200 years it is difficult to reconstruct contemporary Aborigines as they tried to understand the events that were unfolding and the motives of the invaders. But the materiality of the texts by people like King and Bradley remain, not well-known by nonAboriginal Australians but still waiting to be scrutinised and deconstructed. In 1987 the Aboriginal film-maker Tracey Moffat produced an experimental film, *Nice Coloured Girls*, set primarily in Sydney in the 1980s showing a group of 'nice coloured girls' who lure some randy White men with the prospect of easy sex and then mug them. But the text intercuts with the foundation moment, represented through Lt Bradley's 'strumpet' text that we have quoted above. Its centuries old hypocrisy is at last answered by Black females, who give him back the stereotype that he constructed, but as part of the undeclared and continuing war that he refused to acknowledge that he was involved in starting.

THE GENOCIDAL PHASE

The texts that we have looked at so far come from the foundation moment, yet they lay down tracks that lead directly into the genocide phase and beyond. 'Genocide' is an emotive term, but it is not inappropriate for a pattern that saw the Aboriginal population of perhaps 300 000 in 1788 reduced to 66 000 by 1901, to reach a low point of 60 000 by 1921 (Rowley 1970:384–5). Rowley's work documents a process with two phases. The frontier stage is characterised by forced dispossession of Aborigines, with Aboriginal resistance crushed brutally and outside due legal process. This was followed by a phase in which Aborigines were constrained by restrictive laws and controlled through institutionalisation. Rowley notes wryly of this second phase: 'To match such a tradition of management, one may look to institutions used to confine enemy aliens in war time' (1970:2).

Because the frontier was continually moving, these two stages coexisted in different parts of Australia until the 1930s. By then, according to Rowley, the frontier ethos that condoned White violence against Aborigines became an official embarrassment. From this date the frontier was declared closed, because the walls around Aborigines in their enclaves were considered high enough to contain them and 'protect them' from the dangers of being Australian. This double policy (unofficial brutality and official 'protection') for a long time allowed a double-stranded discursive strategy. This resolved the problem of legitimacy by constructing the government policy as a benign but doomed attempt to save Aborigines from their inability to survive as a people.

This long period was marked by the dominance of what can be seen as a single discursive regime, which took two forms and followed two strategies distinguished by their reliance on the two modes that we have identified: realism and subjectivism. This is a pattern whose single functional system organised all genres, visual and verbal, popular and high culture, whether positive or negative towards Aboriginal people. But though this over-riding unity can be missed by those who attend too closely to dramatic surface differences in texts, it is equally important to recognise that the contradictions were never fully contained. We need to understand how this regime operated for so long with such apparent success. We also need to trace the fissures that were to lead inexorably to its final collapse. The subjectivist mode allowed an apparent positivity towards Aborigines to function as one wing of the overall strategy of legitimation. However, it also functioned as a carrier of resistance, how-

THE BASTARD COMPLEX

ever contained, to the dominant construction of Aborigines. The differences were not only in qualities of texts, but also in regimes of reading. A form of the 'romantic' at least established some distance from the crushing weight of the officially 'real'. And conversely, effective changes could only come from a recognition of the real material and social conditions of Aborigines, so that versions of 'realist' texts, sustained by a realist reading regime, were indispensible to the struggle that was ultimately successful in transforming the basis for Aboriginal participation in Australian political and cultural life.

The distinctive attribute of the realist mode is its persuasive claim to represent things as they 'really' are. The subjectivist mode (romance, fantasy, modernism, the artistic) makes less insistent claims. By the laws of literary modality, the less an image is claimed to be true the more its truth is inverted, to become an image of the untrue. For this reason the discursive regime that was employed to control the construction of Aborigines made use of two apparently opposed forms, in the two modes. One was a 'subjectivist' form, which represented Aborigines in a positive light, but with subtle but unmistakeable indicators of untruth to invert its force ('If only they were like that . . . '). The other was a 'realist' form, which presented a negative image of Aborigines and then attached markers of strong truth ('We've smashed them, whatever you bleeding hearts may say . . . ').

We can see something of this double strategy already in the King and the Bradley texts. Bradley's more realist text foregrounded power as the primary link between Aborigines and Whites. King's whimsy obscured power in order to construct a positive fantasy, but one which could not easily be connected to specific actions to recognise Aboriginal interests or rights. But neither of these texts was intended as a public text, a work of art, and they were too close to the insecurities of the foundation moment to provide secure models. Literary genres, especially poetry as the most prestigious of genres, were soon drafted to the legitimation project. Unsurprisingly, most of these early poems took the safer path of eliminating all mention of Aborigines (though the aptly named Barron Field, a future judge in the colony, was able to rise to wit at the expense of kangaroos). Charles Tompson's 'Black Town' of 1826 was the most significant early poetic text dealing primarily with Aborigines, showing the main features of the discursive strategies that were to remain in place for more than a century. Tompson himself carefully explained the context for the poem:

> Written in the Verandah of the Chapel at the deserted hamlet of 'Black Town', an Establishment formed by Government some years since, for the purpose of civilizing the aboriginal Natives of Australia, and teaching them the art of agriculture, &c. on the new Richmond-road, about 28 miles distant

39

from the metropolis. It is much to be lamented that the poor heathen possessors were allowed to desert the Establishment, as much good emanated from the Rules first adopted there. (Tompson, in Wilkes 1974:9)

This has the precision and cartographic accuracy of the realist mode, and its position as preface declares that this account gives the 'truth' of the situation. The poetic account that is to follow is therefore marked as having only 'poetic' truth. The first sentence spells out the position, aims and funding body behind the institution. With the second, objectivity gives way to strong feeling: 'much to be lamented' demonstrates the strength of the poet's compassion. This then becomes the basis for criticism of an error of administrative judgment, committed by those who 'allowed' the Aborigines to 'desert'. White benevolence is cancelled out by Aboriginal incapacity, and the Aborigines' claims as 'possessors' (by due grant from government) lapse owing to their 'desertion'. In effect this authorises the government's rights to possession twice over: they possessed the land first in order to hand it over, and they have now repossessed it, and the Aborigines' actions in both instances tacitly acknowledge that right.

The poem itself seems less censorious of the Aborigines, attempting to understand the different values of a nomadic people:

> *Ill-fated Hamlet! from each tott'ring shed,*
> *Thy sable inmates perhaps for ever fled,*
> *(Poor restless wand'rers of the woody plain!*
> *The skies their covert—nature their domain)*
> *Seek, with the birds, the casual dole of heav'n,*
> *Pleas'd with their lot—content with what is giv'n.*
> (lines 11–16)

Here the Aborigines 'flee', they do not 'desert'. They have chosen their natural way of life, so the pity is balanced by a claim that they are 'pleas'd' with this lot, and 'content with what is giv'n'—leaving aside the crucial issue of whether the lot that they are now given is the same as what they believed they once laid claim to. Woven into a celebration of their 'naturalness', a form of the 'noble savage' myth, goes another construction of nature as an absence of specifically human rights and characteristics. A few lines later these primitives are offered training in the basics of social life:

> *The lordling tenant and his sable wife*
> *Were taught to prize the sweets of social life,*
> (lines 21–22)

The incredibly patronising tone of this doesn't need emphasising. What does need to be stressed, however, is the ideological function of the assumption. By placing such a low value on what Aborigines had and want (and commending them for having and wanting so little) the level of

White offering that will count as generosity can be set very low indeed. The likelihood of Aborigines spurning such irrelevant or obnoxious 'gifts' then becomes greater, thus resolving the debt another way. This is the kind of ignorance or misunderstanding of Aboriginal life that Rowley and Stanner accepted as genuine. It is worth pointing out at the least just how convenient these 'misunderstandings' were, and how often they were to be found precisely amongst those who were White Australia's official agents of benevolence for the next 100 years, as though such beliefs were the precondition for carrying out those functions.

There is another way that a poem like Tompson's is commonly read, that needs to be contested. The poem is clearly reminiscent of two very famous English poems: Gray's 'Elegy' and even more strongly, Goldsmith's 'The Deserted Village', whose form and sentiments are often very close to this poem. This close relationship is often interpreted as a mark of the early inability of the invaders to 'see' the scene that was in front of them. Instead, this kind of reading argues, the set of generic expectations acts like a template, a machine which virtually writes the poem: in this case, only changing a few of the names and details to preserve the feelings.

This view does much less than justice to Tompson's intelligence and rhetorical skill. For instance, here is his peroration, seemingly cast in poetic vacuities:

> *Ill-fated Hamlet! round thy dull domain*
> *Lone Silence holds her melancholy reign;*
> *This lowly structure, where each Sabbath press'd*
> *A pious group, by strangers is possess'd.*
> (lines 81–84)

This mood of general melancholy and nostalgia for a vanished past is similar to what is found in the two English poems, and terms like 'Hamlet' seem quite inappropriate to whatever 'Black Town' looked like. But this is not just any kind of mismatch. When we note that this poem was published in 1826, only 38 years after the founding of the colony, and that the buildings whose ruin Tompson laments were built in 1814, only twelve years before, we must suspect something more than an inattentive choice of models. What Goldsmith and Gray provide is instant history, a history long enough to accommodate both a golden age (or perhaps two golden ages: the Aboriginal state of nature, and the age of heroic benevolence under Governor Macquarie) and its sad decline. This is a time long enough for everything possible to have been done for the 'natives', but to no avail. It expresses not a single sentiment which is not benign, yet it serves to legitimate an end to all further efforts to try. It announces the definitive failure of what Stanner called 'romantic idealism', but the experience that forces it to do so is not exactly irresistible. The potent mood of melancholy, which it seems to take from Goldsmith's village, is in practice a premature elegy for a people who have not yet died. The mood of the premature elegy was to be a frequent one in well-meaning people for the next hundred years, where it served important ideological functions. It predicted the desired end to the 'Aboriginal problem', while expressing a regret that absolved the feeling person from complicity or responsibility. On the contrary, and this is a function that links this strategy with that of King's seemingly dissimilar text, the primary work done by the author in the subjectivist mode is to construct an admirable and nuanced response that guarantees the worth of both writer and reader.

Deeper into the genocidal phase we can see the contradictions of Tompson's poem distributed out across a range of genres and media in both elite and popular forms. Tompson's sentiments seem so sincerely if misguidedly benign towards Aborigines that it is important to recognise their role in an overall ideological strategy. But that is not to say that there is no difference between promoting speciously benevolent projects and poisoning flour. The entry of positive views of Aborigines into public discourse, even in this form, showed the existence of a recognition of the rights and value of Aborigines, and enabled it to be carried on to succeeding generations. And a romantic frame and a literary form did not always neutralise a clear perception of Aborigines' position. An early anonymous poem, 'The Gin', for instance, started ostensibly inside the consciousness of an Aboriginal woman but used diction a long way removed from an authentic Aboriginal voice:

> 'Where spreads the sloping shaded turf
> By Coodgee's smooth and sandy bay,
> And roars the ever-ceaseless surf,
> I've built my gunya for today.'

But the poem finishes in a more direct and realist mode:

> Their health destroyed—their sense depraved—
> The game, their food, for ever gone;
> Let me invoke religion's aid
> To shield them from this double storm
>
> Of physical and moral ill;
> We owe them all that we possess—
> The forest, plain, the glen, the hill,
> Were theirs;—to slight is to oppress.
> (In Dutton 1976:17, 19)

Outside literature we can see a similar complex pattern over the genocidal phase. In art too, forms of subjectivism predominate. Maynard's significant study 'Projections of Melancholy' (1983) focuses on a dominant iconography from the 1880s to the early years of the

20th century which offers a 'romantic' image of Aborigines, suffused with a melancholy tonality that she diagnoses as an expression of the expectation that Aborigines were a dying race: essentially the same ideology that we saw organising Tompson's earlier text. From an important study of postcards during the same period (Peterson 1983) it appears that realist modes were more dominant in popular forms. Peterson studied representations of Aborigines in postcards between 1900 and 1920. He classified these basically into two categories, 'realist' and 'romantic', along the same lines as we have done, and found that 'realist' forms outnumbered 'romantic' forms by 4 to 1.

But the ideology of 'realism' as described by Peterson is no more positive towards Aborigines than the ideology of high art. He sets out in tabular form the main differences that he observed:

Romantic framework	Realistic framework
Decontextualisation: blank backgrounds Recontextualisation: bush settings	Contextualisation in contemporary living situation
Naked or in traditional attire	Clothed more or less completely in European attire
Considered posing, rarely front-on	Front-on artless posing
Absence of European artefacts (Peterson 1983:179)	Presence of European artefacts

Peterson's schema is a powerful one which applies to many other forms of discourse of the period. Photographs produced in the two modes that he isolates circulated in two other forms of discourse that played an important role in the construction of Aborigines: the discourse of anthropology and the discourse of history. The subjectivist discourse of anthropology played a key role in the formation of Aboriginalism, while the realist discourse of history presided over the 'truth' of Aboriginal–White interactions during real time and in real history.

In order to illustrate the role of the two modes in the construction of disciplinary truth we will look at the photograph of an Aranda boy, taken from Spencer and Gillen's photographic record of Aborigines. Their photographs, taken between 1894 and 1927, are classics of anthropology, mainly taken to preserve images of traditional life before they disappeared. They conform to the Peterson specifications for 'romanticism' except that the context was insistently present, making strong claims for the objective truth of their picture of Aboriginal life. This photograph is unusual in that it shows the conjunction of Aboriginality and Europeanness, inscribed on an Aboriginal body. Spencer spells out the meaning of the conjunction, for him: 'The natural result is that, no sooner do the natives come into contact with white men, than phthisis and other diseases soon make their appearance, and, after a comparatively short time, all that can be done is to gather the few remnants of the tribe into some mission station where the path to final extinction may be made as pleasant as possible' (Spencer 1982:26).

From this we can see that the same meaning as is encoded in melancholy romanticism can be equally strongly coded into realism: romanticism legitimates the policy of 'protective' incarceration. The meanings of the patterns described by Peterson pivot around this primary meaning. The conjunction of Aboriginal and European, in clothes, artefacts, settings, is the repeated message of the overwhelming and destructive presence of White power inscribed on Aboriginal bodies. What Peterson calls an 'artless' front-on gaze is better described as total if sullen submission to the White gaze, whose power is expressed through the brutal and unvarying centrality of the (White) camera and the White viewer.

But the photograph taken from the cover of C.D. Rowley's book, *The Destruction of Aboriginal Society*, is even more typical of the realist genre as described by Peterson. The message of White clothes and White chains on the two Aboriginal bodies is brutally explicit and unequivocal. But this kind of image inserted into a different reading regime had its own kind of ambiguity. Rowley was able to use it as the cover of a polemical text which mobilised the photograph's persuasive claims to truth on behalf of his own project to contest official history. Neither realist nor subjectivist modes are tied irremoveably to particular ideological positions.

There is a similar ambiguity and instability in high art. In the popular form as described by Peterson the 'romantic' is not only less common than the realist, it is clearly derivative and marked as such. It represents the same reality, and softens and idealises its meanings without contesting its authority. The same relationship between realist and romantic representations can be seen in paintings which were based on photographic models. The one that we have reproduced was painted by Oscar Fristrom, following his normal practice of drawing from a photograph and adding a spiritualising background. Here the head is superimposed on a cloth background on which it floats like the face of Christ on the Turin shroud. It seems like a glorification of Aboriginal spirituality, outdoing King's comparisons with Adam and Eve, but the regime of photography not only underpins the Aborigine's reality (as opposed to his sprituality), it has determined his position within the gaze, as controlled now by the eye behind the camera as he was in the original form. The precondition for the Aborigine's immortality and transcendence is to be photographed and decapitated—not unlike the obsession with Aboriginal skulls of the period, which led to huge quantities of them being transported to England, to be studied by science and fitted into its ideological history of the human race.

THE BASTARD COMPLEX

B. Spencer: photograph of Aranda Boy. (*Photograph courtesy of the Museum of Victoria Council*)

Tom Roberts' apparently similar formula, as evidenced in his *Aboriginal head—Charlie Turner*, in practice has a number of significant differences. Undoubtedly it has the same macabre fascination with the

C.D. Rowley: Cover of *The Destruction of Aboriginal Society.* (*Picture courtesy of Penguin Books*)

conjunction of death and life, the anatomist's record of an interesting skull. However, Turner doesn't have the features that fuelled that obsession—the marks of the primitive, the archaic, the pre-human. On the contrary, Charlie Turner is rendered with naturalistic precision, from life not from a photograph, and the realism of the draughtsmanship gives a power and authenticity to the image. The contemporary response to this painting recognised the presence in it of potent contradictions. In the words of the *Sydney Morning Herald* it was painted with 'so much

THE BASTARD COMPLEX

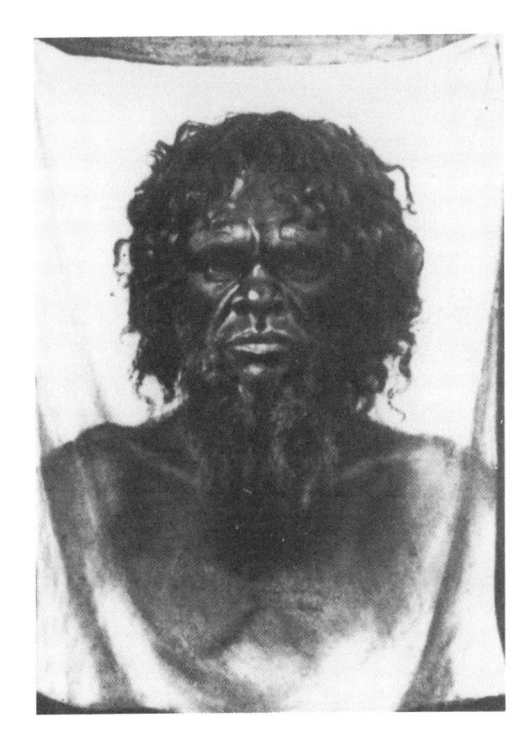

Tom Roberts: *Aboriginal Head—Charlie Turner*. (*Picture courtesy of Art Gallery of New South Wales*)

strength and fidelity, that its value will grow year by year with the gradual disappearance from our midst of the original possessors of the soil. Thus it has a permanent, if melancholy interest, which justifies its inclusion in our national collection' (*SMH* 2 Sept 1892. Quoted Maynard 1983:93).

This commentary states unequivocally that the 'value' of this painting is directly proportional to the extent to which Aborigines disappear from Australia, and Maynard uses this comment to reinforce her claim that Aboriginal self-elimination was the covert content of this form of romanticism. But the strength also has another source and another value. It is a powerful painting because Charlie Turner is manifestly not yet dead (as all Fristrom's portraits are made to seem), and Roberts' skill has been deployed on representing Charlie Turner's self-originating response to the assaults of White power on his own existence, ignoring the way in which material markers of White power (e.g. ill-fitting European clothes, poverty, disease) were stamped onto a sullen but passive and unresisting Aboriginal body.

In art and literature it is important to insist that not all texts produced in the two modes during the genocidal phase had the same degree of complicity with the dominant racist ideology and the same message

Oscar Fristrom: *Portrait of an Aboriginal.* (*Picture courtesy of Mitchell Library, State Library of New South Wales*) *The fine details of this image have been unavoidably lost in reproduction.*

about Aborigines and White society. The problem of legitimacy was contained within a structure of contradictions that was inherently unstable, held in place by a complex double regime of reading. It is hard to estimate the scale of resistance and subversion against this dominant ideological structure, but Aboriginal endurance and persistence is a guarantee that these possibilities always existed systemically. We do not want to exaggerate the extent of counter-readings and counter-meanings during this dark phase in Australia's social history. But in our archeology of this phase we believe that the evidence justifies our projecting the existence of systematic strategies of resistance operating against the official ideology along specific lines of cleavage. Reading against the grain as we have done has its problems, but they are no worse than an uncritical acceptance of the normative texts and readings that bulk so large in the received version of Australian history. The 'bastard' nation never forgot its dubious origins, and never lost the need for its bastardly ways of reading.

3 Return of the repressed

The first phase in Aboriginal–White relations was followed closely by the genocidal phase, whose excessively long dominance has been so massively documented by Rowley and others, driven by racist values that are still potent today. But it is important to recognise that the genocidal phase was also a time of Aboriginal resistance, as argued by Reynolds (1978). And our account must recognise that we are now in a third phase, which can be termed Aboriginal resurgence. It is a relatively late and still threatened movement, and the grim statistics for Aboriginal health and incarceration rates show that no golden age has yet arrived for Aboriginal people in Australia. But there is now a new political and discursive situation, one in which some of the previously dominant discursive strategies are no longer tenable. The marker for this transformation is the referendum of 1967, in which an overwhelming majority of nonAboriginal Australians officially acknowledged the rights of Aborigines as Australian citizens. In 1976 a limited recognition of Aboriginal land rights was enshrined in legislation in the Commonwealth *Aboriginal Land Rights Act (Northern Territory)*. This at last is a situation in which Aboriginal demands for a treaty may become politically feasible, recognised even by nonAboriginal Australians as intrinsic to their own identity, just as Yami Lester insisted.

We do not wish to overstate the scale of the change, but it would be equally wrong to ignore it and to fail to understand how and when and why it has happened. The discursive construction of Aborigines seemed so overwhelmingly successful before the 1970s that it would not have seemed worthwhile to scrutinise the textual record for signs of subversion, instability and deep-seated change. Now with hindsight this task has a high priority, since the new discursive situation must have had roots in the past, in the minds and attitudes of the White majority. In this chapter we will contribute to this enterprise, re-examining the neglected site of the emergence of this new set of possibilities.

It is not in dispute that Australian government policy towards Aboriginal people was built on the kind of racism that was found in all the European settler colonies. But we need to look again at the structure of the racist complex, to locate its point of weakness and insecurity and deconstruct its obsessive claims to monolithic unity. This point of weakness is also the site of its most massive investment of energies: the role of the concept of purity in an impossible enterprise of legitimation. This concept applied to both the macro level (race relations) and the micro level (gender and family relations), mobilising energies and ideological investments at the micro level on behalf of policies at the macro level so that the needs of the patriarchal family provided much of the motive force for White Australian racism.

The Protestant settler colonies (Australia, the US, British Canada, South Africa) deployed a distinctive form of the racist complex, marked by more rigid categories and stronger boundaries than Catholic settler colonies. Structuralism in the tradition of Lévi-Strauss and Douglas has alerted us to the typical consequences of this kind of structure as applied to a shifting and unstable reality. The price of purity is that the anomolous becomes the focus of energy in the system, which seeks to contain and deny the impurity that would destroy its constitutive principles. The impure, the hybrid, the bastard are such threats to the system that they become taboo, objects of excessive hatred and disgust. But at the same time they are disturbingly attractive, the locus of pleasure and power, where change and growth are still possible.

For this reason, the main thrust of government policy during the genocidal phase was always shadowed by its opposite. The policy options consisted of a form of apartheid, separating Aboriginal people from each other and from White society (under conditions which threatened their physical survival) and 'assimilation', the integration of Aboriginal people into the dominant society on that society's terms. 'Assimilation' sounds like a recognition of an Aboriginal contribution to the dominant society but what it aimed at was the total transformation of Aborigine to White, preserving the principle of purity by dividing Aborigines into the two categories of black and white Aborigines, with nothing in between.

But in practice, all Aboriginal people in some respect occupy an intermediate space between the pure forms of the categories, the space of impurity and dirt, of taboo and power. In 200 years of contact Aboriginal society has undergone a transformation that has been both desired and deplored by official policy. The option of continuing with traditional ways of life under the conditions that existed before 1788 is no longer available. Aboriginalism may pretend to value and defend traditional life in its pure form but Aborigines know that history has moved on. 'Self-determination' as their slogan refers to their right to choose how they will relate to the dominant society, not to a right to suppose that that dominance does not exist.

One consequence of the rigid structures of classic Australian racism is the way that part Aborigines have been classified. The rigid application of the binary categories meant that the presence of European blood could not allow part Aborigines to be seen as 'real Aborigines', whose Aboriginality represented a threat to White legitimacy. Nor were they real Whites. But nor could they be acknowledged to exist as their own category, like the Mestizos of Catholic Mexico. So they had to be classified as one or the other after all, and in practice they were mostly classified and discriminated against as Aborigines, while also being despised as 'half castes' or 'half-breeds'. Estimates of the proportion of 'full blood' to 'part Aborigines' at different times have fluctuated wildly, owing among other things to conflicting definitions of each and arbitrary methods of assembling the data, but throughout this century 'part Aborigines' have probably constituted a large proportion of the group that is treated by White Australia as Aborigines. The current policy of the Commonwealth government is a recognition of this fact: an Aborigine is a person of some Aboriginal descent who identifies as an Aborigine.

The effect of this is that Aboriginal people have been assigned the task by the majority of Australians of constructing the terms of a single Australian identity that resolves the opposition between Aborigines and Whites: the only identity that can constitute a secure basis for the legitimation of Australian society. This task and those who carry it out have paradoxically been declared doubly illegitimate, presumed (by White society at least) to have been disinherited by both groups, but this double message is itself a characteristic of the ideological system and its mode of operation. The referendum of 1967 officially affirmed that the Australian nation included the Aboriginal people, and this recognition existed unofficially for many years before. Aborigines were important to White Australians out of all proportion to their numbers for this ideological work that they alone could do. They have always been 'goods to think with', to use Lévi-Strauss's graphic phrase: and one of the most highly prized goods that they make thinkable is the possibility of a new identity, based on a new justice and a new scope. But the necessary price for this is a different valuation of purity, to give high status to cultural mediators, Aboriginal and White, and to miscegenation of all kinds, cultural and physical.

THE DILEMMA OF ROMANCE

We will turn now to some of the sites where this emerging consciousness was articulated in a public form, especially in the literature before the second world war. This period saw increasingly articulate criticism of government policies and of injustice towards Aborigines. Government reports such as the Bleakley Report of 1929 showed the abject failure of government policies even by their own paternalistic standards, though the aspect that received most attention in practice was the problem of miscegenation, with a tightening up of controls on mixed marriages and more punitive treatment of 'half castes'. Attitudes towards frontier justice were also changing. Rowley (1970:288) sees the Brooks case of 1928 as one marker of this change. This was first reported as an incident in which police had shot eight Aborigines suspected of killing a white man, Brooks. By the next day this had become seventeen. A subsequent inquiry increased this number to 31. What was significant was not the massacre but the public outcry it aroused in urban Australia. For Rowley this marked the beginning of the end of the frontier system of 'justice' against Aboriginal people. Though that end has been a long time coming, the 1930s did herald a discursive change: such practices were no longer spoken for by the White community.

It is no coincidence that two of the most influential works of literature dealing with Aborigines appeared during this period: Katharine Susannah Prichard's *Coonardoo*, and Xavier Herbert's *Capricornia*. These two books were written from within the genocidal phase, but at a site of transition. Inevitably they both incorporated compromise and contradiction into their literary strategy, yet each broke new ground, and they both need to be read against the shifting conditions of the period if we are to do them justice.

Katharine Susannah Prichard's *Coonardoo* was written in 1929, Xavier Herbert's *Capricornia* in 1937. Both were immensely popular, at the same time as they were recognised to have a polemical and radical intent. And both were novels, drawing inevitably on the traditions and resources of that form, heirs to its authority and its broad appeal at the same time as they complied with its prescriptions. But the modern novel at the time that they were writing was not a monolithic form. It was determined by its own forms of the two modes, realist and subjectivist. And behind these lay the confluence of two earlier major generic forms, the epic and the romance, whose primary structures and meanings are still visible in modern works.

As a number of major theorists have pointed out, the epic was a totalising and realist mode, whereas the romance was partial and subjective. But the two genres have distinctive underlying ideologies at their core. The epic has typically been a masculine genre, and romance a feminine one, and they have pivoted around a common problematic, the problematic of legitimacy, from an opposite point of view. The epic genre places power in the heroic male and grants him public success, but denies him love. The romance genre places love in the domain of the woman but denies her power. So epic offers a continual critique of the cost of power, while romance constructs a sphere where the operations of power can cease, briefly, to apply.

Both genres are acutely concerned with the problem of difference as it disturbs legitimacy. For both, the problem of legitimacy is resolved through appeal to genealogy. The right of the epic hero is based on his impeccable genealogy as well as on his military might, and the couple formation that crowns the romance is an image of the resolution of the oppositions that are destroying the nation. So the epic constructs society and history on a grand scale, as the meaning of the action of its individual characters, whereas romance compresses and mystifies society and history, making the extent of its own claims difficult to determine. Epic is typically the product of a social group that is confident of its power but insecure about the basis of that power, whereas romance is more indirect, more defensive. It is unsurprising, then, that both *Coonardoo* and *Capricornia* are closer to romance than epic, coming as they did at a time when the genocidal phase was still dominant but soon to be successfully challenged.

Prichard stressed the realist nature of her writing, but the power and safety of her work derived like Roberts' from a skilful blend of realism and subjectivism. She proclaimed an allegiance to Marxist theories and was an active member of the Communist Party. In her preface to the book she emphasised the factual basis of the novel, its grounding in first-hand knowledge and research in the field. But surprisingly her preface appeals to the authority of no less than Ernest Mitchell, then Chief Inspector of Aborigines for Western Australia, ('no one in this country has wider knowledge and more sympathetic understanding of the Western and No'-West tribes'), who 'could not fault the drawing of aborigines and conditions, in *Coonardoo*, as he knew them' (1956:v). A version which could not be faulted by such a source must be extremely devious, or else complicit with the dominant regime.

In practice the novel does not demonstrate a fresh or original grasp of Aboriginal life. Its heroine, Coonardoo, an Aboriginal woman born on a White station in Western Australia, is represented as capable and even reliable in performing domestic duties, but otherwise is shown as without powers of thought or conceptualisation. She is passionate, intense, loving and loyal to the White station owner, Hugh, beyond his merits—but intellectually she is not far above a faithful horse or dog. What is original about the novel is its grasp of the intrinsic connection of Aborigines (however superficially understood) with crucial problems of legitimacy. What Prichard did grasp, at the same time as she was failing to understand the Aborigines of the north-west, was the complex patterns of ownership in the frontier situation. As a result her novel was able to lay down the outlines of a new foundation myth for the European invaders.

RETURN OF THE REPRESSED

The novel traces the pattern of ownership of Wytaliba station, in the north-west of Western Australia. The station was established as a successful enterprise by a capable and energetic woman, Bessie, whose husband, Ted Watts, was an amiable drifter who would never have been able to purchase or manage it on his own. Their one son, Hughie, inherits the station and its loyal Aborigines, including Coonardoo, who has a lifelong devotion for him. He in turn has a deep love for her which he refuses to acknowledge. He marries Molly, a White girl, who bears him five children, all daughters. Molly eventually leaves the station, ostensibly indignant at learning that Hughie (while unconscious) had fathered a boy by Coonardoo. Alone on the station and full of love for both Coonardoo and Winni his son, Hughie still refuses to sleep with her, although he accepts her as 'his woman'.

A ratbag White named Sam Geary has always coveted both Wytaliba and Coonardoo. One night when Hughie is absent he coerces Coonardoo, who is brutally repudiated by Hughie, and banished from the station, when he finds out. Hughie struggles on, against droughts and bad times and emotional desolation, supported for a while by the return of Phyllis, one of his daughters. However, Phyllis marries Billy Gale, a restless young White, and is clearly going to transform him as Bessie transformed Ted. Hughie finally loses the battle to save Wytaliba, and is forced to sell it to Sam Geary. Coonardoo lapses into desperate promiscuity after her banishment, but at the end of the novel, ravaged by diseases (mostly sexually transmitted) she returns to Wytaliba to die.

In the scheme of the novel, marriage is the signifier of political and economic union, conferring legitimacy on the transfer of property to the next generation. There are a number of principles affecting the tortuous passage of the land, Wytaliba. The foundation act sees the property as essentially that of a matriarch, transmitting it matrilinearly to her son. Hughie inherits, but his tenureship fails, as do his alliances with women. The most important failure is with Coonardoo, which the novel presents unmistakeably as a moral and emotional failure, masquerading as strength of character. Out of his repudiation of Coonardoo comes his second failure, with his White wife Mollie. As a White he is unable to recognise the reality and importance of his alliance with Coonardoo, or the legitimacy of his half-Aboriginal son as a worthy heir. As a male he is unable to recognise the merits of his daughter Phyllis, so that she like her grandmother has to work through another male, to establish another line of inheritance. The repulsive Geary is the eventual possessor, but one whose possession lack any pretensions to legitimacy. Because of the focus of the analysis and what is implied by it, it doesn't matter that Prichard hasn't risen above the stock-in-trade of White misrepresentations of Aborigines' abilities and understandings, because these abilities do not act as a crucial premise in the logic of legitimation here, as they do in the dominant discursive regime. Irrespective of Prichard's two-dimensional portrayal of Coonardoo, the author shows her to be necessary to Hughie's survival. Similarly, Phyllis did not have to be a man in order to be worthy to inherit, nor did Winni have to be White. The novel takes for granted that the only genealogy that can confer legitimacy is the willing and equal union of Whites and Aborigines—at exactly the same time as the Bleakley Report was deploring this development, and Australian laws were attempting to stamp it out. In Coonardoo's fate, after she has been repudiated by Hughie and turned off her own land, there is a rapid shift to the realist mode by Prichard, but this indicates not the inherent inability of Coonardoo and her race to survive contact with Whites, but an angry and self-destructive response to dispossession. The two alternatives for Whites, immoral and illegitimate possession (Geary) and moralistic but still illegitimate dispossession (Hughie), together add up to a double condemnation of the rule of the invaders. At the same time Prichard projects, if in a veiled and allegorical form, a radical new basis of legitimacy for the Australian nation.

Xavier Herbert's *Capricornia*, first published in 1937, is the other major novel of the pre-war period to attempt to construct a new image of Aborigines. We have classified it as romance, but that is not to say that it is a pure example of the genre. On the contrary, impurity and miscegenation are characteristic of its form as well as its content. Herbert himself called it affectionately 'that old botch' (1960:32). The publisher's blurb called it a 'best-selling epic novel', and it does sprawl over the space and time of the classic epic. Its central character, Norman Shillingworth, half-caste son of a dissolute White and a traditional Aborigine, engages in a redemptive search for personal identity and a secure inheritance, a modern Odysseus ('Norman' derives from 'No-name', not so far from the Odyssean 'No-man'). Along with epic and romance, picaresque and satire it includes chunks of polemical prose, set pieces on the Aboriginal problem put unconvincingly but passionately in the mouths of various characters. But at the core of the novel is a version of the classic form of the romance genre, an elaboration of genealogies as the image for the solution of the problems of legitimacy.

The most obvious signifier of illegitimacy in the novel is the set of mixed unions and half-caste offspring with which the novel abounds. In most of the unions of Black and White depicted in the novel, the relationship is a strong and continuing one, with mutual loyalty between White husband and Black wife. Connie Differ, for instance, is the beloved half-caste daughter of Peter Differ and his Black wife. She is seduced by Humbolt Lace, who conceals his shame, but still tries to look after her and her daughter, Tocky, to the extent that his hypocrisy will allow. Tocky is brought up by Tim O'Cannon, husband of part-Aboriginal Blossom, another stable Black-White relationship. The ambiguous Tocky becomes the lover of Norman, and bears his child, and it is this relationship which carries the theme of the novel in its exemplary form.

In the novel the union of Black and White is typically fertile but remains on the fringes of society, producing a plenitude of heirs but nothing to inherit, while the White possessors have no-one to leave their possessions to. A cattle station, Red Ochre, has the same meaning in the novel as Wytaliba in *Coonardoo*, as the signifier of the land that has been won but is not yet owned. Where Prichard shrouds the foundation of Wytaliba in a hazy mist, Herbert uses the realist mode to sketch in the series of brutal acts of the White conquerors. Oscar Shillingworth, who becomes the owner of Red Ochre, struggles for many years to make a living on it, but like the archetypal White owner he has no son to bequeath it to. His son died in his infancy, his daughter is not a Phyllis, and his wife left him early on for a Portuguese sea captain. It is left to Norman, half-caste son of his brother, to inherit the place, and ultimately to make it thrive. It is Oscar's recognition of the possibility of this line of inheritance that allows inheritance to happen in a legitimate form, in contrast to Hugh's refusal to acknowledge the similar merits of his own half-caste son. The plot outcome is opposite, but the meaning of the two novels is the same: only the union of Black and White is worthy to inherit the land.

Into the romance structure of the potent but deferred union Herbert inserts the romance theme of the Guilty Secret. Norman's secret, for many years, is his own Aboriginal identity (we are required to believe that although he lived in a native camp until six years old, he was genuinely unaware that he was of Aboriginal descent, and he talks and thinks like a priggish middle-class urban White throughout the novel). His inheritance of Red Ochre is jeopardised at first by the court costs incurred for defending his father, Mark, from the charge of murdering a Chinese, an act that had Mark on the run for many years, believed dead. Then it is jeopardised by a second court case, Norman's own trial for the murder of a White man, Frank Lash. Norman was innocent: in fact Tocky had killed the man, defending her honour from his attack. But Tocky's sense of guilt, fuelled by Norman's concept of 'justice', kept her silent. So Norman is punished for the sins of his father and the sins of his wife. He wins both court cases, however, benefiting from the contentious coming of southern justice to the frontier north that marked the 1930s after the Brook case. In this way he acquired White man's legitimacy for his rights, and a fortunate turn-around in the Darwin economy leaves him at the end in secure possession of a solvent Red Ochre. But Tocky has disappeared. On the last page she is discovered, a corpse with a dead child, Norman's heir, in an empty tank: victim of her fear of the irrational processes of White justice. Norman's capacity to own the land and pass it on is after all a tenuous one. It is his continuing endorsement of his White mentality over his Aboriginal identity that is the source of his inhumanity and the failure of his line.

The genealogical core of the novel is an ideologically impeccable argument for the co-ownership of the land, as the only possible basis for legitimacy. Herbert paints a scathing picture of the brutal, stupid and unjust frontier society of Darwin in the early 20th century, as an exemplary instance of the foundation moment of Australian society. Herbert's passionate indignation masks real limitations in his capacity to understand Aboriginal society and forms of consciousness, but in the context of its time it was both proper and effective.

Mainstream literary criticism has tried to rewrite the meaning of *Capricornia* to neutralise its importance. The best-known instance of this strategy is Vincent Buckley's pronouncement that 'The book is about the universe which ... Herbert seems not to accept' (1960:13). The text does offer the author's refusal to accept a world in which anarchy and ungodliness reign supreme. There is an over-riding sense of fate which plays 'dingo to all men', Black and White. But Buckley's attempt to transfer the struggle from Darwin and Australia to the cosmos misses the cumulative weight of Herbert's satiric grasp of a particular society and a particular time. It is not universal injustice that is Herbert's continual theme, but the specific set of injustices that lie at the basis of the foundation moment, that still threatens the possibility of a secure Australian identity. And Buckley's strategy of implying that Herbert's refusal to accept this injustice can be no more than a childish and futile gesture is not a definitive put-down but an obvious and resistible eternalist ploy.

That is not to say that Herbert's work is beyond criticism, or without its own profound fissures and confusions. Just as Prichard the Communist could defer to the Chief Protector of Aborigines in her preface, so Herbert's text is seemingly problematised by its relationship to P.R. Stephensen, its original editor, who indeed claimed co-authorship on the basis of his editorial work on the text. Stephensen's ambivalent politics—he endorsed neo-Nazism, was defiantly anti-Semitic and pro-Japanese—was able also to accommodate a strong claim that Australian Aborigines were essential to Australian nationalism (Stephensen 1935). On this point he may be loosely associated with the Australia First Movement and, ironically enough, with the pro-Aboriginal poetic movement of the late 1930s, the Jindyworobaks (Elliott 1979), especially insofar as his utopian vision of Australian culture required a positive acknowledgement of the Aboriginal past. We invoke Stephensen because he is symptomatic of the complex and contradictory ways in which 'historically' 'Aboriginalism' has been articulated and has performed its functions. Both *Coonardoo* and *Capricornia* were immensely popular, both of them going through many editions, and this popularity undoubtedly owed much to Aboriginalism. Inevitably these books must have been read in different ways by their many readers, incorporating the dominant contradictions as well as situating them in a new or emerging ideological and literary terrain.

THE EPIC TURN

It is only in the third phase, the period of Aboriginal resurgence, that the epic becomes a possible genre for representing Aboriginal society, as Whites begin to acknowledge the scale and longevity of the struggle. But it must be added that this possibility exists more strongly for Aboriginal writers. It is no accident that the major Aboriginal dramatist writing today, Jack Davis, has organised his three most important plays as a trilogy of epic scope, stretching from the first founding of the colony to the present, and Mudrooroo Narogin's (Colin Johnson's) novels also address this major conflict in a version of the epic. But epic classically has been the form used to claim legitimacy through heroic struggle, and that is not the form of legitimacy that White Australians need. Instead, works of an epic scope have begun to emerge, but they are all in some way evasions of the epic, displacements, refractions, shadows of the form. And that is as it should be: Australians White and Black alike have no need for the pure epic.

There have been two main turns of the epic in post-war White Australian novels. One has been the ironic epic, which represents Aboriginal anger and resistance as filtered through an ironic frame, a double perspective which neutralises its force. The other has been the allegorical epic, which transposes the elements of the struggle onto a cosmic stage, where the battle is monumental but indecisive and irrelevant. The most significant instance of the first kind is Thomas Keneally's *The Chant of Jimmie Blacksmith*, with Patrick White's *Riders in the Chariot* the exemplary instance of the other.

Keneally's novel has to be taken seriously as a cultural phenomenon. It has been hugely successful, not only in sales to the general public, but in the way that it has penetrated the school curriculum, where it occupies the space of official truth-sayer about Aboriginal–White relations. The source of this authority is located in its depiction of violence, Aboriginal violence against Whites, a key truth that was suppressed during the genocide phase. Keneally's novel took a historical incident from the turn of the 19th century concerning Jimmy Governor, a part Aborigine who killed some white women with an axe and then escaped, with his brother, evading a huge man-hunt for many months. Keneally's Jimmie Blacksmith seems to speak a contemporary Aboriginal anger, juxtaposed to a foundation event of Australian political life, the coming of Federation at the turn of the century. His book was published in 1972, six years before Henry Reynolds' *The Other Side of the Frontier* established the significance of Aboriginal resistance as a major theme for historians.

But Keneally's book is not entirely what it seems or claims to be. The title refers to a 'chant', recalling the ancient singers of tales, Homer, the Irish bards, or the mediaeval singers of epic tales like the *Niebelungenlied* or the *Song of Roland*. The Aboriginal tradition contains songs too, but not of this militaristic genre, and in any case Jimmie does not really know how to sing in the Aboriginal way, in Keneally's story. What Keneally has written is a novel of an ambiguous kind (the relationship to 'real' history is never fully declared) not a 'song' of any kind, Aboriginal or White. To call it a 'chant' seems ironic, the juxtaposition of two incompatible points of view, but the Aboriginal perspective comes not from any Aboriginal voice, but from Aboriginalism and its myths. The claim that this episode will be refracted through the double prism of Aboriginal and White forms of consciousness and genres is not sustained by the novel that follows.

We can see the asymmetry of the irony in Keneally's tone in the following passage, describing Jimmie's birth:

> Half-breed Jimmie had resulted from a visit some white man had made to Brentwood blacks' camp in 1878. The missionaries—who had never been told the higher things of Wibbera—had made it clear that if you had pale children it was because you'd been rolled by white men. They had not been told that it was Emu-Wren, the tribal totem, who quickened the womb.
>
> Mrs Dulcie Blacksmith believed the missionaries more or less. They took such a low view of lying in other people that they were unlikely to lie themselves. And certainly, Mrs Blacksmith had been rolled by white men. For warmth in winter, she once said. For warmth in winter and for comfort in summer. But the deep truth was that Emu-Wren had quickened Jimmie Blacksmith (pale or not) in the womb and that Mungara owed him a woman. (Keneally 1976:1–2)

Keneally's irony here may seem so complex and even-handed that any criticism of his stance would miss the point. But the irony is not really symmetrical between Aboriginal and White forms of truth. The facts of biology are presented as beyond question ('had resulted') but this knowledge, it appears, is outside the comprehension of Aborigines, until they are told about it by missionaries. It may be ironic that missionaries are the vehicles of this secular knowledge, coded as it is in vulgar language ('rolled'). It's part of the same irony that these missionaries are ignorant of the 'higher things/deep truths' of Aboriginal religious beliefs, which are, however, so well-known to Keneally's narrator, who it seems has been 'told' them. This 'knowledge', which is not ironised here or elsewhere in the novel, turns out to be a hoary myth straight out of Aboriginalism, that Aboriginals did not understand the basic facts of human biology before the coming of White science, that they had only a childlike grasp of human sexuality and the role of the father.

It's worth comparing the consequences of Keneally's Aboriginalist reading of Aboriginal culture with Prichard's. In spite of Prichard's earnest efforts to become informed, her Coonardoo is in many ways an artefact of Aboriginalism: barely capable of reflection or abstract thought, capable only of intense loyalty and affection. But Coonardoo knows perfectly well who is the father of her child (it's Hugh who refuses to believe it for as long as he can). And Coonardoo's rights do not depend on her capacity for abstract thought. But Keneally's Aboriginalism is more structural. His label for Jimmie, 'half-breed', neither one thing nor the other, comes not out of anthropological or scientific nor even missionary discourse, but out of the popular racism which delegitimated any departure from an abstract form of pure Aboriginality.

Keneally's narrative endorses this Aboriginalist premise: in his account Jimmie is excluded in important ways from Aboriginality, to which only his fully Aboriginal half-brother Mort and his uncle Jackie Smolders have access. At the climax of the novel, Keneally makes Jimmie come to recognise this exclusion, when he and his brother and an Irish school teacher they have taken as a hostage rest at a desecrated sacred site. But 'ironically', both the Irish school teacher (and Keneally behind him) can perceive the Aboriginality of this sacred site, from which only Jimmie feels excluded. Mort and Jackie in contrast are effortlessly Aboriginal in the Aboriginalist way, showing a happy incomprehension of the motives of White, Black and half caste alike. It was the old double message: pure Aborigines are incapable of rationally understanding their own culture and civilisation, and can be allowed to disappear from sheer nonviability, while impure Aborigines are not real Aborigines, and have lost their rights, without being able to understand either White or Aboriginal culture. But in the novel, the double message was resolved in the good old way: Mort was shot still happy in his innocence, while Jimmie repented his ways and was hung.

If anyone is to write the story of Jimmy Governor in such a way as to represent the clash of cultures and the contradictions of experience that lay behind that episode, it will probably be an Aboriginal not a White writer: someone like Mudrooroo Narogin not Keneally. But that is not to say that this field of experience is incomprehensible to nonAborigines, so that Keneally can't really be criticised. In 1972 (as in earlier periods) it was possible to try to understand Aboriginal beliefs and problems by listening attentively to Aborigines themselves rather than to the dominant White construction of Aboriginality. In the 1990s it should at last be possible for White readers to recognise this.

Keneally does deploy his ironic vision on White pretensions as well. On the last page (p. 178), as he sets the framework for Jimmie's execution, he describes the revels of ordinary Australians:

> They knew they were good. They knew they were strong. They knew they were free and had a fury for equality. The *Bulletin*, after all its irony, kept saying so.
> It was happy Easter and open another bottle as the wild men pitched over the necks of crazy bulls from Wyalong.
> You couldn't hang blacks on such an occasion.

This irony attacks one of the foundation myths that legitimate White Australia. Keneally juxtaposes the claimed 'goodness' and 'strength' of these archetypal Australians with the hanging of Blacks. The goodness in fact works, deferring the executions ('on such an occasion'). But this goodness is not negated by the hanging of Blacks: it is negated by the contradiction between the sacred (Easter) and the profane (getting drunk and having sport with wild bulls). Keneally does have an unease with the right of Australians to their new Commonwealth, but more because of their vulgarity than their treatment of Aborigines. In literary terms his irony undercuts the possibility of epic for both Aborigines and Whites. In political terms the effect is to deprive both groups of the right of appeal to heroism to sustain its legitimacy: an even-handedness that still leaves Aborigines as the dispossessed, in a White-dominated status quo.

In contrast to the undercutting effect of Keneally's irony, Patrick White's *Riders in the Chariot* attributes cosmic stature to Alf Dubbo, the Aborigine who is one of the four 'riders' in his apocalyptic chariot. In spite of the metaphysical resonance, White is concerned to construct a specifically Australian identity, and his novel is built around the depiction of four characters, four 'riders' who represent the four strands that constitute an identity which is irreducibly compound: the Aboriginal Australian, the Australian born, the immigrant from the Mother Country, and the refugee. The chosen instances are all socially marginal individuals, on the fringes of the society that they represent and validate, incorporating marginality therefore into the core of the definitive identity. But epic heroes are never like the society that they validate and save. The epic hero is expendable, with qualities that are an embarrassment in the new society, to be admired but not imitated. So White's riders perform the characteristic function of the epic hero, at a symbolic level. Their existence, their suffering, and finally their irrelevance gives value to the society that reveres them. The fact that that society does not live by the same codes does not affect their redemptive function, since it is precisely that failure which proves their heroic and redemptive status. So White's kind of epic is the antidote to the ironic or degraded epic of Keneally. Where Keneally's diffused irony negated belief as the basis for commitment, White makes belief possible again by concentrating it in his carriers of pure negativity, mediated by the negative modality of the subjectivist mode.

In many respects, White is continuing the strategy which was dominant in the art of the late 1800s. Alf Dubbo is constructed as an archetype rather than as an Aborigine: like Fristrom's Aboriginal head superimposed on a shroud, Christlike but dead, potent but outside the domain of the real. But White like Roberts establishes a critical space within this subjectivist mode, by also drawing on realist techniques which qualify and intensify the meaning of the image. Dubbo is viewed from a double perspective, from the points of view of the metaphysical ideologue and the acute social observer. As a typical instance, here is one passage where Dubbo enters the sprawling discourse, seen through Himmelfarb's point of view:

> The blackfellow, or half-caste, he could have been, resumed possession of his broom, and pushed it ahead of him as he walked backwards and forwards between the benches. Some of the women lowered their eyes as he passed, others smiled knowingly, though not exactly at him. But the black man, involved in some incident of the inner life, ignored even the mechanical gestures of his own sweeping. But swept, and swept. (1961:223)

The text first emphasises his excessive thinness, a physical image which negates his physicality, establishing his nonmaterial solidity, in the same way that Fristrom's lean Aborigine floats on his shroud, and Roberts' Charlie Turner has become a two-dimensional smear on the canvas. The Elijah/Blake intertext which casts its long shadow over *Riders in the Chariot* has already warned us to be on the lookout for bony eccentrics involved, like this one, in 'some incident of inner life'. But Dubbo is also constructed as the object of the social gaze: 'Some of the women lowered their eyes as he passed, others smiled knowingly, though not exactly at him'. White here encapsulates the doubled gaze which constructs the Aborigine in White discourse: the averted eye that eliminates him from the visual field, to exist only as the taboo Other, or the smug and knowing look that affirms his right to exist, as it passes through and beyond him, en route for another space, another object for its gaze. White's realism here is focused on the ideological meanings of the discursive frame, which qualifies and corrects the meanings of his subjectivist idealism. Aborigines can rightly object to the authenticity of Dubbo as the carrier of their social meaning in White's fiction ('He's not a bloody Aborigine!' Mudrooroo Narogin remarked). White's concentration on his own construction of the Aborigine's 'inner life' carries on that strand of Aboriginalism into this third phase, the moment of Aboriginal regeneration. Now as always it is a profoundly ambiguous strategy, defending the value of Aborigines, celebrating their inner strength, acknowledging their centrality in the construction of Australianness, but attending only to White voices, White looks, White experience and White needs. But in spite of the metaphysical closure of the allegorical epic, it is still open to the question: What are Aborigines really like? In contrast the degraded epic as in Keneally clamps its premature answer over the possibility of the question.

ABORIGINES AND FILM

The forms that we have looked at so far have all had long histories, during which the dominant discursive regimes have had sufficient opportunity to preempt all forms of genuine resistance. It may be very difficult for nonAboriginal writers in the major genres to break free from the constraints of the dominant, insofar as these act as the precondition for their own discourse. It would be a foolish mistake to suppose that new media and new genres such as film emerge without history, innocent of prior determinations. Yet without claiming too much for these new forms, they do offer a sharper potential break with the past, a moment of risk, a moment of opportunity. Aborigines have welcomed the new media with an enthusiasm that contradicts the Aboriginalist belief that they should find them incomprehensible or antipathetic. In a later chapter we will consider Aboriginal uses of literary and other media. Here we will look at representations of Aborigines in the brief history of Australian film.

As with the literary tradition, the first point to note is that while filmic representations grow out of and are constrained by their social and ideological conditions, there is not a simple progress to be observed in the fullness or honesty of representations. The dialectic progression from the foundation moment through the genocidal phase to the phase of Aboriginal regeneration reads like a comfortable progression to contemporary enlightenment, but each of these phases was constituted out of the same basic set of oppositions, and at every point there was a range of available positions, not a single inevitably racist stance in the past. So the new conditions that allowed *The Chant of Jimmie Blacksmith* to emerge in the 1970s did not after all make redundant the two centuries of racist thought that it still drew on, or give it a privileged access to Aboriginal structures of meaning and experience, compared to the earlier *Coonardoo*. Similarly the most successful representation of Aborigines by Whites in Australian cinema is still Charles Chauvel's *Jedda* of 1954. We will make the point by contrasting this film with two later texts, the film version of *The Chant of Jimmie Blacksmith* (1978) and *Mangannnie* (1980).

Jedda concerns the relationship of Jedda, an Aboriginal girl carefully brought up in White ways on the Mungalla buffalo station in the Northern Territory, with Marbuk, a traditional Aborigine who seduces/abducts her back to the land. The couple are pursued throughout the film by the station owners eager to 'save' Jedda for civilisation, assisted by Aborigines for whom the marriage was 'wrong' by tribal law. The film

RETURN OF THE REPRESSED

was clearly framed within available discourses and generic limitations of its period—its high melodramatic note, mythic resonances and epic vistas are obvious even to the most casual viewer—but it has a strong authorial presence, an excitement and an awareness of the radical nature of its own experiment. For Charles Chauvel, who had already made a string of reasonably successful movies (*Sons of Matthew, Heritage, The Rats of Tobruk, Forty Thousand Horsemen*) the film was more than an acknowledgement of Australia's 'unsayable' past: it was a revolutionary act which enabled the return of the repressed, for both Whites and Aborigines (Cunningham 1986).

This surfacing of the repressed is articulated through a number of relatively distinct modes. The first mode is the dialogic. The film opens with the White couple, Doug and Sarah McMahon, discussing the relative merits and demerits of adopting an Aboriginal child, establishing the issue of genealogy as a focus which throws into high relief the clash of legitimating discourses. Doug is in favour of allowing the Aborigines to 'regain their pride of race' by basically leaving them alone ('Still trying to turn that wild little magpie into a tame canary' he expostulates with Sarah). She wants to 'bring them closer to our way of living'. The dialogue is self-conscious and contrived, schematically opposing the two recurring constructions of Aborigines that have lain behind Australian government policy from the beginning: romantic apartheid and realist assimilation. But against this speech we get snippets of Aboriginal discourse ('White baby fly out, black baby fly in,' exclaims one of the kitchen maids, or 'I think more better you do see her', as an Aboriginal stockman tells Felix). There is also a dominant voice-over, probably played by a White, who introduces himself 'My name is Joe, I am a half-caste son of an Afghan teamster and an Aboriginal woman'. The indifference to anything that an Aborigine would regard as a relevant genealogy here declares its nonAboriginal authorship.

The film opens with the relative serenity of the Mungalla buffalo station, showing a harmonious and stable mediation of White and Black on the peripheries of White settlement, but this peace is broken by the entry of Marbuk, played with extraordinary skill by Robert Tudewali, who has himself become a significant Aboriginal text in his own right. With Marbuk's entry, the text loses its reassuring ideological anchorage. He represents a threat to Jedda as nature to her recently acquired culture, as the challenge of Aboriginality to what in every other European text is represented as the irresistible and uncontested power of the White phallus. Even Prichard and Herbert had no doubts about the superior sex appeal of almost any White man for almost every Black woman. Marbuk thus signifies both sexual threat and that domain of the unconscious where mankind's histories are formed.

But this reading, in which Marbuk represents the challenge of Black solidarity and Black (re)generation to assimilationist policy, is only one level of meaning of the text. The conflict for Jedda is as multivalent as that in a dream text, and much of the time she is shown in a state of anxious stupor. Her ambivalence towards Marbuk is not dictated only by her veneer of White cultural conditioning. The alliance offends against Aboriginal sexual mores as well as White policy ('she's no good for you, she's wrong skin' pleads Joe to Marbuk before their cataclysmic end). The simple logic of White versus Black fails to have sufficient explanatory power, and a White audience is forced to reach out to another (Aboriginal) order of explanation, which overlaps bewilderingly with their own more familiar view.

We can see the subtle conjunction as it works at the level of image and frame, in a single still from the film. In narrative terms it shows Marbuk as heroic male above the supine Jedda. The Aboriginal novelist Mudrooroo Narogin compared the image to Tarzan in an adventure flick—a Black Tarzan with a Black Jane. At this level it is a neat inversion, which was satisfying enough to Aboriginal audiences of the time, though as satisfactions go it is not profound. The other generic feature of the shot is the relation of figures to background, with the rocks and the water in sharp focus, significant presences but dominated by the human beings. This is the quintessential Australian landscape, represented as continuous with the Aborigines who move easily within it, the two together expressing a single identity. Chauvel polemically insisted on a commitment to what he called 'locationism', a practice that established 'authentic' Australian exteriors as protagonists in his films, and this is here explicitly linked to Aborigines as the authenticating human presences in that landscape.

The long shot shows an active male and a supine female, a familiar White gender stereotype that runs throughout the film. But the composition within the frame makes sense in terms of another more Aboriginal set of principles. The verticality and linearity of Marbuk is a dominant feature of Aboriginal art, normally juxtaposed with structures of concentric circles: here formed by Jedda, the raft and the enclosing waters, surrounded by the land itself. Paintings of this kind in Aboriginal culture normally represent a landscape as it is made sense of by the journeys of 'mythic' creative spirits, ancestral beings whose wanderings are a mnemonic for basic political and social rights over land.

These figures from myth normally are not model Aboriginal citizens, acting out the ideal form of domestic life for their successors to follow. In this respect they do not perform a clearly ideological function, or at least not of the kind that is claimed (equally inappropriately) for the European fairy story. Rape and incest, forbidden unions and acts of immorality and violence are the staple ingredients of Aboriginal myths (as they are of Greek myths). Typically they record acts of transgression

Jedda and Marbuk: from *Jedda*. (*Picture courtesy of the Estate of Charles Chauvel*)

by marginal characters whose defiance of social sanctions provides the potency that is then attached to the genealogical claims that they also encode. In this respect the narrative of Marbuk and Jedda is typical of indigenous myth. The film begins by claiming that 'the story of Jedda is founded on fact', but the 'fact' at its base has already been worked over, to an extent that Chauvel himself may well not have realised, by Aboriginal narrative strategies. The result is a text that for a White audience is irrecoverably destablised, fractured, broken. It marks a significant contrast with Keneally's ironic vision, which claimed to be juxtaposing two modes of thought but in practice could only shift restlessly between two forms of White discourse. Chauvel's multilevel text does not need to be ironic: it achieves, for brief instances perhaps, a scope which incorporates unresolved parallels and contradictions, a scope which deserves to be called epic. It has the potency of the intermediary, and it is this rather than the 'authenticity' that has been claimed for it that marks it as a major text in the construction of Australian identity.

Fred Schepisi's film of *The Chant of Jimmie Blacksmith* of 1978 contrasts interestingly with both the novel it is based on and the film,

Jedda, which influenced it as it has done many other representations of Aborigines on film, in its historical role as a founding text. Schepisi's film has an integrity which Keneally's novel lacked, partly because it is a film. Keneally's ironic, smartly knowing commentary is largely eliminated. In fact for a film based on a novel the verbal dimension of the film is extremely sparse. The only sustained dialogue is between the Reverend Neville and his wife, the young Jimmie's White patrons, on the value of an assimilationist policy, which needless to say they endorse: the policy whose reality is the carnage that the film goes on to depict. (What an achievement it would be if Jimmie's children were only a quarter black! 'Scarcely black at all', suggests the Rev. Neville). The film skilfully establishes the ideological premise of the film, the contradictions within White discourse about Aborigines. It begins without the obligatory credit stills. The first shot is of a group of Aboriginal children playing games. This is broken by the words of Rev. Neville, 'Blasted blacks! At least they're likely to disappear at any time'. Before the title of the film is flashed on to the screen, we get no fewer than fourteen cuts which collectively establish the Aboriginal presence. The tactic mobilises the generic potential of cinema to marginalise the spoken and written word. It establishes this film as a relatively 'inarticulate' text, one that will deprive the viewer of the customary ideological anchors that can neutralise experience. By these means it has something of the inscrutability and sense of mystery of Chauvel's text, though it remains firmly within the conventions of realism, without the levels of meaning that Chauvel can also hint at.

Our point in this discussion is that the medium of film has certain possibilities that can open up levels and kinds of meaning that have been largely closed off by the regimes of mainstream literature. But to qualify this claim we will look at a final film, *Manganninie*, which shows the ideological effects that contemporary film, drawing on a long tradition of representation of Aborigines, can still achieve with a fair degree of commercial success. *Manganninie* like *Jedda* has a narrator, offered as a mediator to make sense of the otherness of the Aboriginal narratives and meanings. In this film, however, it is the White girl, Joanna, who recalls her relationship with Manganninie ('I remember as clearly as a dream') and continues to be the sole authority for the narrative that follows. Joanna's sense of herself as a fully adequate mediator and authority on Tasmanian Aborigines is never questioned throughout the film, which is based on the book written in later life by this character: 'founded in fact' like *Jedda*.

As a film it is seductive in a way that neither *Jedda* nor *The Chant of Jimmie Blacksmith* aspires to be, lingering on the beauty of the Tasmanian landscape and Manganninie's light brown skin, seeming to affirm the gentleness of the people and their kinship with the land. The narrative describes the adventures of the White girl, Joanna, who is abducted by a sorrowing Manganninie, who has lost her own child in a battle between Aborigines and Whites. Manganninie looks after her tenderly, and Joanna learns Aboriginal ways, and loves and respects her Aboriginal mother. But the trade is not entirely symmetrical. Joanna finally learns to chant in the native language, a signifier of her ability to assimilate this alien culture from the inside, but Manganninie learns no English, and the audience has no unmediated access to her thoughts and feelings. And at a crucial point in the film, Manganninie loses control over fire, and the young Joanna restores it to her as a gift. A basic premise of the film, taken from the same stock of anthropological wisdom that assures Whites that Aborigines did not understand about sexual reproduction, is that the Tasmanian Aborigines did not know how to make fire, and were reduced to carrying it around in fire sticks. When Manganninie's fire went out, Joanna rekindled it with a packet of matches that she had found. What the whole Aboriginal race of Tasmania could not do, a white child could effortlessly achieve.

Behind this simple narrative, with what seems like a charming message of love crossing boundaries of language and culture, is the genealogical subtext again. Two years before, in 1978, *The Last Tasmanian* and the controversy that it aroused had brought this subtext unmistakeably to the surface. This film by Tom Haydon and Rhys Jones had reconstructed the life of Truganinnie as the 'last Tasmanian', reputedly the last full blood Aborigine to die in the face of genocidal policies that were more brutally successful on the island of Tasmania than they were on the mainland. But the title of their film incorporated the purity premise of Australian racism, thus delegitimating today's Tasmanian Aborigines as no longer Tasmanians. A film that was intended to protest against the genocide of the 19th century Tasmanian Aborigines was read by their descendants such as Michael Mansell as announcing the complete success of that policy, thereby 'ignoring a fact of life' (their life) as Mansell indignantly objected.

Manganninie reworks this claim much more gently, avoiding the antagonism aroused by the Haydon/Jones film but retaining (partly from its source in Joanna's memoirs) the core belief, that the Tasmanian Aborigines are without legitimate heirs, so that Tasmanian Whites can rest happy in their possession of the land. Joanna represents herself as the adopted heir to the childless Manganninie. Her memory of their culture is all that survives, but she does not doubt its sufficiency. Their inability to make fire marked them as evolutionarily so primitive that sadly they could not survive, when faced with a superior technology—a minimally human technology, which even a (White) child can use. Joanna becomes like a goddess to these people, a benign goddess who gave them the gift of fire, which they were unable to receive.

As we look over this span of 200 years of representations of Aborigines we need to avoid two equally inappropriate conclusions. One that is suggested by a *Mangannine* is that nothing has changed. Certainly it is true that the primary ideological forms have remained remarkably constant, as a set of resources on which successive generations have been able to draw. It would be a misleading myth to suppose (as many do) that there has been slow and continuous progress in understanding between the two groups of people, accelerating over the last 20 years into something very close to a definitive harmony. In fundamental political terms, there has been no essential change in the formal legal position between the two peoples, and until a treaty is agreed, that will continue to be the case. This inequity will be an inexhaustible reservoir for the ideological tropes that we have seen so far, in all media. Yet at no time has the situation been without its contradictions, and these contradictions have ensured the instability of the dominant ideological structures. Changes have occurred, resistance has been effective, and progress has been real if never continuous or assured. It is not foolish to read the last two decades as a period of massive and fundamental change in the relations between Aboriginal and nonAboriginal Australians: though it would be foolish to suppose that texts like *Mangannine* will not be possible and popular for a long time to come.

4 Dark traditions

Australian culture is a composite, consisting of the dominant settler culture (with its own complex structure), with a colonised culture embedded within it. The two cultures together form a single dynamic system, with each part affecting the others in numerous obvious and unobvious ways. In the next two chapters we will look at this embedded culture of Australia's Aboriginal peoples, but not as a self-contained set of forms. On the contrary, contemporary Aboriginal culture can only be understood as a complex product of the Australian colonial process acting on earlier forms of life and culture. Conversely, the dominant society will remain incomprehensible to itself as long as it ignores or disregards Aboriginal culture, Aboriginal perspectives and Aboriginal understandings of Australian society.

For the past 200 years Aboriginal culture has been produced against the background of repressive policies which attacked Aboriginal people on two fronts: through overt racism and through the more devious methods of 'Aboriginalism'. But in understanding Aboriginal culture today it is equally important to recognise the facts of Aboriginal survival and cultural resilience. This could not have happened without a massive subterranean continuity across periods where mainstream commentators have seen only total disruption. Nor could it have happened without the continuing cultural dependency of other Australians on Aboriginal meanings, even at moments of greatest destructiveness.

It is a commonplace that throughout this period there has been seriously defective communication, an almost complete absence of dialogue and mutually sustaining cultural exchange. Clearly if there is no improvement in this area in the future this will impede the progress of the two groups towards harmonious interrelations in a just society. For this reason it is more important than ever to understand the dynamics of this aberrant communication. This means that we must recognise the complex role that has been played in it by Aboriginal forms of cultural production. White society has silenced Aborigines in a variety of ways, from overt suppression to the subtle stratagems of Aboriginalism, but Aborigines for their part have never been mere passive victims of White cultural practices.

Aboriginal culture is not a set of simple and transparent but neglected texts. On the contrary it is typically enigmatic and deceptive. The mystery of Aboriginal culture is the product of Aboriginal protectiveness as well as White indifference. Aboriginal people have always had their discursive regimes and systems of control which have been and still are bound up with the maintenance of their political and social identity. Traditional society was constituted as a series of groups within groups, with secret knowledges carefully encoded and protected from other Aborigines outside the inner circles of those with the right to know. These strategies were superbly suited to the primary task of Aboriginal people faced with a hostile occupying power. They maintained an invisible continuity between past and present, making sense of the new in terms of the old, holding a people together against all that the enemy could do while concealing from them that this was being done. The White rulers culpably ignored what Aboriginal people said quite clearly about their rights and needs, but Aboriginalism was able to flourish partly because Aborigines were so reticent about their own dark traditions: which in many cases were all that they could call their own.

It isn't the case that Aboriginal culture was ever entirely neglected or despised in Australian society at large. But within the discipline of English in its Australian colonial manifestation, in the long period when it was obsessed with the problem of judgment and the search for 'greatness' in Australian literature, there was no wish to propose that Aboriginal literature and culture (including traditional and post-traditional forms as parts of a single complex) was a major component of world literature and culture. Yet such a claim could be argued persuasively. This complex stands alongside a small number of similar complexes in the postcolonial world (e.g. African, American Indian) which incorporate texts and modes of thought from the extremes of a spectrum that runs from preliterate, preindustrial social forms to contemporary electronic, post-industrial mass societies. Because of this scope, such a cultural complex incorporates not simply the 'primitive' end of the spectrum, like a living museum, but the process of the transformation itself, as a phenomenon that has been dramatically accelerated to become part of the lived experience of the majority of the group.

The Social Darwinism that justified the elimination of these 'superseded' peoples in the name of 19th century progress also encoded the opposite evaluation: that these races and cultures were the ignorant

DARK TRADITIONS

carriers of the supreme mystery of origins, the origin of the species and of modern industrial society. So the secrets of the traditional forms have been seen, even by influential representatives of the developed world, as possessing a significance in world-historical terms that dwarfs anything that has been or is likely to be achieved by nonAboriginal Australian writers and artists. There is also a deeper secret: that the original possessors of the secret are alive and well and still own a vision that connects the past and the future of the dominant society itself.

The virtual suppression of this living body of culture and its records by White Australian society ranks alongside the destruction of the library at Alexandria or the assault of the eponymous Vandals on Rome as an offence against human culture. A small number of scholars and others have played a part in preserving some of these texts, but only the resourcefulness of Aboriginal people and the flexibility of their cultural system have kept enough of it alive for exegesis to still be an option, alongside the work of many Aborigines who in various ways are continuing to carry their cultural traditions forwards into new forms.

Aboriginalism played an equivocal role in this process. It arose because Aborigines were assigned the task of achieving cultural mediation on behalf of both peoples, but were then not trusted to carry it out properly (i.e. so as not to disturb the existing unequal distribution of property and other goods). For this reason Aboriginalism itself was always a radically impure enterprise, in spite of its stated obsession with purity: taking on the lonely burden of mediation on behalf of the whole community, so that Whites could remain as pure as they wanted to be without loss of potency, and Blacks could retain an imputed purity from which they had lapsed.

But there are some practical reasons why White Australians should want to learn to read these texts better, and why Aborigines are now more ready to help them to do so. Aborigines are still an oppressed minority group within Australia, but the issue of social justice is now firmly on the agenda, and the texts of Aboriginal literature and culture have an important role to play in the process of constructing policies that are sensitive to the needs and values of Aborigines. In this chapter we will propose that Aboriginal cultural forms have always had two crucial social functions: to interpret, reflect, report, and comment on social life, and to actively construct forms of social existence, ensuring social cohesion and flexibility in responding to the major problems facing Aboriginal people. These two functions were not rendered obsolete with the coming of the Whites. On the contrary, the demands made on these cultural forms intensified. The set of issues that conventionally make up the 'Aboriginal problem' all include both material and cultural dimensions. Dispossession, unemployment, imprisonment, poor health and infant mortality feed into and are exacerbated by the so-called 'culture of poverty', marked by alcoholism, suicide and social disintegration. Aboriginal cultural forms encode the specific meanings through which Aborigines make sense of what seems to outsiders to be the overwhelming meaninglessness of much of Aboriginal life. They also encode the kinds of solutions that have emerged from within Aboriginal society, solutions which are indispensible components of any viable Aboriginal policy.

READING ABORIGINAL CULTURE

The first obstacle in the way of establishing a new practice for reading Aboriginal texts and Aboriginal culture is the invisible power of the existing dominant way of reading, the reading regime that is organised through what we have called 'Aboriginalism'. Aboriginalism insists that Aborigines as the Other cannot (be allowed to) represent themselves, cannot even be supposed to know themselves as subjects or objects of discourse. This tactic deprives Aborigines of the possibility of authority, of being authors of their own meanings able to monitor and influence the meanings that circulate about and among Aborigines. Less obviously but equally drastically this tactic disables nonAborigines also. They cannot draw on their own social and cultural experience to guide their reading, since that has been totally discredited for these purposes, but nor can they make any appeal by any code to Aboriginal authorities. The result is a reading regime constituted by a set of contradictory prohibitions, giving a high cultural status to an almost complete inability to read Aboriginal meanings at all, in the name of Aboriginality. One of our main tasks, then, will be to disengage the energies that have been locked up in the mechanisms of suppression and displacement, and to dismantle the discursive regimes that have hitherto been given the task of control.

The discursive regime of Aboriginality has been built up around a series of false dichotomies, forced choices that have been imposed on Aborigines in a kind of strategy to divide and rule. At the base of all these dichotomies is the fundamental political issue that has exercised Aboriginal people for 200 years: the issue of accommodation or separate existence. Aborigines have objected at different times to government policies of 'integration' and 'assimilation'. They have also objected to policies that have separated Aboriginal people from White society, incarcerating them in camps in a form of apartheid. But Aborigines themselves sometimes emphasise relative separation, as in the Outstation movement, and sometimes the right to participate in mainstream White society, with many positions in between, so that they can be represented as both confused and not after all wanting anything distinct from what they are already being offered. But what is crucially different between what Aborigines want and what they are offered is their right to be discursive agents, able to declare in their own forms and terms which option it is that they want, and when and how they want it to be available.

In tracing the full set of forms that must count as Aboriginal, we need to allow the legitimacy of both strategies (separateness and integration) as fully Aboriginal, yet also be able to distinguish them from their mirror images that have been used as tactics of oppression. The distinction is both important yet not always easy to apply in practice. Some White critics have repudiated all forms of cultural adaptation by Aborigines as tainted compromises (e.g. Aboriginal novels or poetry, Aboriginal film, Papunya art) but this requirement that Aboriginal culture should not adapt is not applied to European culture and the virtues of 18th century clothes, art or plumbing. On the other hand Aborigines use the term 'coconut' (White on the inside) as a term of abuse for Aborigines who have, they feel, become too complicit with White forms of thought. Like all terms in political discourse this does not have a consistent meaning or application, but it does mark this as a problem within Aboriginal society, which does not have the luxury of a simple consistent position.

When we seek to define the range of forms that can count as Aboriginal discourse, we must posit not a single set of criteria that fixes a closed form, but a genealogical scheme which is still open, which is anchored to Aboriginality both in the past (through understood derivation from Aboriginal forms) and in the present (through Aboriginal ownership and agency). Traditional Aboriginal culture plays a crucial role in this process, even in genres that superficially seem to have very little in common with it. In order to understand the process as a whole we need to operate with a flexible transformational framework. But equally necessary is a grasp of the range of possibilities of traditional Aboriginal culture itself.

Aboriginal culture was a distinctively *oral* culture. This means that it possessed a set of qualities that have been disvalued in the post-Gutenberg regime of literary discourse: absence of closure, generic fluidity, the dimension of performance, and a specific attitude to the potency of the spoken word. As Bruce Shaw has pointed out, many of these are also features of 'Aboriginal English', as unappreciated resources of verbal art: 'non-verbal and semi-verbal markers, repetition, reversals, standard substantives, a vocabulary of special terms, scatology, dialogue, interrogatives, verbal punctuation, mythological allusions, onomatopoeia, similes and the maintenance of suspense' (Shaw 1981:4).

But although modern 'readers' are trained by the discursive regimes of literate culture to disvalue the specific forms of oral discourse, a genealogical link with oral modes is still a marker of exceptionally high status within literary culture. The most prized of the ancient written epics still show the marks of their preliterary origin: retarding narratives, prolepsis, bricolage, the surfacing of residual matter, in fact all the characteristics of the palimpsest. Poetry and drama are realised in the oral mode, though they circulate in written forms. Even the novel reproduces dialogue within a writerly frame. So European 'literature' engages in a massive subversion of the written code, and a masked equivocation with the oral. Far from being a problem or a scandal for the dominant White discursive form, the rootedness of Aboriginal culture in oral forms is part of a familiar paradox which could give the highest of statuses to the despised. We quote Bruce Shaw again: ' The (Aboriginal) narratives, then, contained a mix of history, mythology, legend, customary law and art and were thereby characteristic of oral literature in general (including its written forms in other societies—Homer's *Iliad*, the Bible and the *Ramayana*.)' (1981:9).

Since the category of 'oral' is commonly used so reductively we need to emphasise the full scope and complexity of what is labelled 'oral culture'. An oral culture is a complex semiotic system which is by no means exclusively oral. Various forms of art and performance play crucial roles in the totality of cultural production and reproduction. In such a system the oral mode will consist of a set of genres which will not all correspond exactly to any equivalent in English. Finally and perhaps most in need of emphasis is the continuing viability of all these constitutive semiotic modes. Speech as such has not in any sense been made obsolete by developments in other media. There has been something particularly misleading about simple evolutionary schemes which trace the development of culture from 'simple' oral forms to advanced cultural forms, especially the forms of literate societies. As McLuhan, among others, has pointed out, the culture of the electronic 'global village' threatens the privileges of literacy with obsolescence, in its return to a transformation of oral modes.

Evolutionary premises have underpinned two more sets of false dichotomies at the core of 'Aboriginalist' reading regimes. The first concerns realism, a quality that is normally seen as thoroughly unAboriginal. It is undoubtedly the case that Aboriginal art is typically highly patterned and formalistic, apparently neither realistic nor representational. Aboriginal myths appear to be similarly abstract and remote from any attempt to represent the real. This quality of the two kinds of text makes realism itself seem to be an unAboriginal quality. Yet it was equally striking a quality of traditional Aborigines to possess an extraordinarily precise knowledge of their territory and an ability to read signs in the landscape that were invisible to Whites.

Just as the multiplicity of specific images of a film can be understood by reference to a single grand schema (a 'grande syntagmatique' to use Metz's term), so the abstract forms of Aboriginal art and myth were decoded by Aborigines by reference to highly detailed realist texts, which were mediated through both speech (kinds of commentary) and action (rituals and acts of demonstration). So the realism of White forms that are presumed by many people to be unAboriginal (e.g. realist painting, film and television, novel, biography and history) is by no means absent from traditional culture, although it has a different place in the economy of forms. But as we shall see, not all forms of realism are equally available to Aboriginal artists, as Aborigines. In one way or another, Aboriginal realist texts are always structured by an underlying abstract text which is a primary means of encoding Aboriginal meanings and the metameaning of Aboriginality itself, just as Aboriginal formalist texts always encode concrete realities of Aboriginal social life.

Notions of realism have been used as a barrier to keep Aboriginal culture out of the present. So the easy connections that are often made with archaic forms—even with the great epics at the foundation of the Western tradition—prove to be a double-edged weapon, ensuring the irrelevance of Aboriginal meanings at the moment they seem to celebrate their status. That is why the category of anti-realism has been used so often to liberate Aboriginal forms of art from Aboriginalism. As with every move in relation to Aboriginal culture, this one has its dangers, in the hands of those who wish to exploit Aboriginal artists. Forms of modernist aesthetics deployed on traditional or transitional art can have an effect that is analogous to Aboriginalism. But here as elsewhere, the crucial issue is a matter of control, and it is by no means clear that Aborigines are more open to exploitation or misunderstanding at the hands of agents of the international art market than they were under the benign protection of the previous generation of Aboriginalist cultural guardians.

THE POLITICS OF MEDIATION

Aborigines are unequivocal about the importance of their culture to them. 'Mythology, sacred or secular or in between, is the basis on which Aboriginal life is constructed' write the Berndts in their influential introduction to Aboriginal life (1964:94). Here it seems that Aborigines and anthropologists agree. This easy consensus, however, is startlingly at odds with the typical way in which these texts have been packaged for consumption by the English-speaking majority. The genre of 'Aboriginal myths in English' typically consists of short and pointless narratives, full of acts of unmotivated sex and violence, with punch-lines consisting of implausible 'just-so' scraps of natural history. The language used is a curious form of standard English, which manages to be both childlike and dull, pedantic and imprecise. The puzzle is, then, just how anyone could accept that such paltry stuff could be the basis of anyone's way of life, and what is going on with the English-speaking majority in consuming it so eagerly and accepting such discrepant claims about it.

What we have here, that is to say, is not just massive distortion and suppression of Aboriginal forms and voices, but a kind of doublethink, which attempts to restore in one discursive mode what it has first taken in another. We will illustrate the process by reference to one text, typical enough of its period: *The Dreamtime: Australian Aboriginal Myths in Painting*, first published in 1965 with text by Charles Mountford and illustrations by Ainslie Roberts. This book deliberately set out to popularise Aboriginal myths, and it succeeded in its own terms. Between 1965 and 1979 it went through 15 printings, averaging one per year. It was elegantly produced, with each story as told by Mountford occupying one page, accompanied by a painting by Roberts reproduced on the opposite page, richly coloured modernist works in which the influence of Nolan is most prominent. This coffee-table format assured its presence in many middle-class homes in White Australia, where the authors could justly feel that it brought a positive image of Aboriginal Australia into contemporary suburbia.

It is interesting to see the terms that Mountford uses in describing his material:

> One has only to consider the incalculable influence of the myths of ancient Greece on the literature, drama and art of the civilised world for over 2000 years, and that of the Nordic myths on the music, drama and literature of Northern Europe, to realise how the living myths of the aborigines, which belong so fully to Australia, could contribute to the cultural life of this country.
>
> But as yet our writers, musicians, dramatists, and artists, dominated by the influence of overseas culture, have been but little inspired by the beauty of the mythical beliefs of our native people. (1965:14–15)

The position is so exemplary that it is worth noting the contradictions and sites of slippage that constitute it. The positive premise is a combination of nationalism and a form of Aboriginalism, in which grandiloquent claims are made for the world-historical stature of Aboriginal myths, riding on the coat-tails of the Greeks and prestigious others. These myths are then declared a resource just waiting to be exploited by 'our writers'. Taken for granted here is the assumption that none of 'our writers' could be Aborigines, and their myths 'belong . . . to Australia', in a relationship of confident possession by the White majority.

But there is a curious precision in this seemingly loose rhetoric. We note that it is only 'the beauty of the mythical beliefs' that has an inspirational quality according to Mountford. Is there beauty, artistic skill or complex social meaning in the texts themselves? We would not know, from the 30 stories that follow. The myths are attributed to no author, no tribe or community, no language, no context. In practice Mountford wasn't totally indifferent to issues of authorship and possession, however: Roberts' authorship of his paintings is always acknowledged, and their current owners are also individually named. In the verbal text, all traces of oral form have been effaced, including narrative strategies, purposes and situations—everything that could justify claims about artistic value or social meaning. What is left is content without form—or more precisely (since that is impossible) a 'content' ruthlessly extracted from its original conditions of existence, deprived of life, energy and the possibility of beauty. Homer treated in this way would not have inspired the civilisation of Europe for a minute.

There is a total contradiction between Mountford's claims and his editing practices. But this contradiction is not a personal failure of Mountford's. On the contrary it is underwritten by the genre itself, not normally remarked on or noticed by readers or reviewers and not in need of defence by Mountford. In the 1990s the overwhelming impression may be the vacuity of content of such texts, but it is important to recognise that Mountford's appeal to his readers was not simply the worthiness of his aim but also the risk of the enterprise itself: the spectacle of a heroic individual who has crossed over to make contact with the Other, and is discreetly protecting his suburban readers from the full force of unmediated contact. The strategy is a potent mix of celebration and contempt, which works by positing, as an act of faith, that there must be some people, accredited anthropologists, who can see the meaning and worth of these materials on behalf of other Australians, who buy this belief as the commodity that they purchase for the price of the book. The faith may not always be justified, and the editing practices of these 'popularisers' are not always such as to inspire confidence in readers. Peter Sutton, a modern anthropologist and linguist, commented on Mountford's expertise in the following terms: 'the languages he worked in were basically unknown to him; his linguistic training was minimal; (and) he suffered from partial deafness during the period of collecting represented here' (1988:245).

But such deficiencies as Mountford personally may have had are not the only problem facing prospective mediators of traditional Aboriginal culture as it has been produced in the traditional languages. Even today there are as many as 260 Aboriginal languages in use, some with only a few surviving speakers, but no single one is acknowledged by Aborigines as the dominant or common form. No-one, Aboriginal or nonAboriginal, can hope to understand more than a small proportion of 'Aboriginal literature' in its original linguistic form. Yet in every culture the resources of the specific language as deployed by the artist are a crucial dimension of verbal art. Aborigines attach a very high value to the maintenance of their languages as a vital dimension of cultural maintenance. So translation it seems is both essential yet insufficient, if Aboriginal literatures are to be able to go beyond a very small circulation.

This dilemma is real and inescapable, but it doesn't rule out imperfect solutions, and imperfect solutions are better than none. In this instance there are two broad strategies that have been drawn on, which mirror the two kinds of response of other colonised peoples to the opposition between indigenous and dominant language forms. One is to give due respect to the forms of the indigenous language. Among other things, in the case of Aboriginal languages this means the promotion of more scrupulous and imaginative standards of scholarship in the transcription, translation and presentation of texts in Aboriginal languages, supplementing a transcription with a variety of texts and commentaries that together can communicate specificities of language and meaning that escape the translation process. The other is to accept the role of Aboriginal English as a valid language in its own right, not a defective form of English as many people judge it but already a sensitive medium of artistic expression, which Aborigines have developed into a rich continuum of forms that they already use with great facility and precision in the task of mediation. The two strategies are not mutually exclusive. On the contrary, each can support the other, in the impossible but necessary task of giving Aboriginal literature a much larger number of understanding readers.

Two pioneers of the first strategy have been Strehlow, in *Songs of Central Australia* (1971) and Ronald Berndt *Love Songs of Arnhem Land* (1976), both of which were books aimed at a nonspecialist reader and included Aboriginal text plus extensive commentary designed to guide the English-speaking reader. But most of the texts of this kind that have been published so far have been produced by linguists studying a particular language, who have followed the formula of providing a transcription of the original text with word-by-word interlinear translation, followed by a 'free' translation, sometimes adding a 'verbatim report' by the informant. These books are normally cheaply produced for what is seen as an extremely limited professional market. They are usually subsidised by some body such as the Australian Institute of Aboriginal Studies, regarded as a record for scholars and not for use by the Aboriginal community or the White Australian public. There is unsurprisingly a lot wrong with their forms and conventions for this wider purpose and use, but even so they already constitute an impressive body of texts in Aboriginal literature, promising tips of a formidable iceberg. It is paradoxical that their sheer difficulty, which is so off-putting to most White readers and which is the most striking difference from the genre of popularisations, is closer to the typical condition of Aboriginal texts, constructing an inner circle of privileged (but nonAboriginal) readers, bonded by their access to a secret meaning.

To show some of the possibilities of these texts, and more importantly the artistic resources of the Aboriginal languages of their originals, we will look at just one, a story about Nativecat and Blackheaded Python. This was recorded by Peter Lucich, using a Worora woman as his informant, and published in 1969 as *Children's Stories from the Worora*. We will present Lucich's text in italics, with interlinear glosses in roman type, modifying his presentation only by organising it in lines (his text is continuous).

Widjingara   a Maungunje   Lalai
Native Cat and Blackheaded Python long time past

ge   ganandiri Maungunje   a Widjingara
and they lived, Blackheaded Python and Nativecat,

njina aua   mangganeganje
she he wife

Djaraganbarwuna   baradum
They came in on them in the war

arga wali wulan gadjingiri andje Widjingarangari
they while sleeping were, these Widjingara people

bradenjege   djaraganbarwuna   manemanengari
just before daylight they came in on them quickly

'Wangalalunguje ge gararanunguri ge argumbarbelidjier,
'Children and their mothers and the old folks,

wardeward wuramera' gubadjunganunguri
hide yourselves' they told them.

Arga ibandje   garganemalina
They the men only they fought,

ge Widjingara gauwanananga umbaran
and Nativecat was speared his side/leg

dai   gunjenggananangu
through it went through

manugauaramanga   djerdbunguru
They carried him to the shade

wer gaualira
lay they laid him down.

Lucich's method of transcribing involved the use of a note book: a cassette recorder would now be standard equipment, and would not remove many oral features that are missing from Lucich's text. He attributed the interlinear translation to his informant, who also provided her own English text. What we have, in the 'English' version, is neither correct English nor an Aboriginal text. This makes it all the more surprising that it still reflects Aboriginal aesthetic qualities so much better than the efforts of a Mountford, or Lucich himself when he tries to give a straightforward neutral translation.

We will point to a few of the most important of these aesthetic qualities. First there are the significant patterns made possible by repetition. The text begins with the two main characters, Widjingara and Maungunje, in that order, and then repeats them in reverse order, a version of the rhetorical figure *chiasmus* we could say, if we wished to give high status to the device. The patterning is significant in narrative terms, since it mirrors the transformation which is to come in the narrative focus, from the man to the woman. The word order, although it is slightly different from standard English, is close enough to follow, and it has the expressive potential of montage. The startling *djaraganbarwuna*, 'they came in on them' is as sudden as an ambush the first time it occurs, and then is repeated, stabilised now by adverbs on both sides. This contributes to the pace of the narrative, starting *in medias res* as Latinists would put it, with a sudden irruption of unnamed enemies in an unexplained fight. This mysteriousness is typical of Aboriginal narratives, which are often allusive, taking for granted an open set of prior texts not all of which will be known to most of the hearers, whereas Aboriginal myths as retold in the Mountford style are closed, selfcontained texts that shadow no secrets. Finally there is the dramatic use of snatches of dialogue, another typical quality of Aboriginal oral texts that is normally absent from the standard summaries. Translation is an art, and much could be done with this text by a good translator, but it is important to note how expressive the interlinear translation already is without even trying: an expressiveness that can only be recognised, however, if we employ a reading regime made possible by modernism with its assault on the role of Standard English in literary discourse.

The narrative goes on to describe Nativecat's death, and the rituals that Python performs. Intertextual relations between myth and ritual texts are very common indeed in traditional Aboriginal culture, positioned in different ways to everyday life. This is a story told by a woman, designed for children, making psychological connections between death and the rituals that accommodate it. At its core is a powerful narrative moment, a resurrection which is not welcomed by Python:

> *While she was making a fire*
> *when he had slept for three days*
> *Nativecat he got up from the grave*
> *and there he stood,*
> *right there.*
>
> *She got a surprise*
> *'Why have you come?*
> *Go back to the grave,*
> *go back!*
>
> *My hair has been cut*
> *I've rubbed myself with charcoal!'*

> He was there and turned away
> he went back to his grave
> he lay down.

The motif of the ghost of a dead warrior returning to horrify his living wife has classical precedents, if we want to look for them—in Homer, for instance with the ghost of Protesilaus, or in Propertius's powerful *Elegy 19*—and it may be that those texts had an origin in a ritual-related text like this one. Here the *frisson* is functional, the desire to see the beloved again turning out to be a horrific experience from which the rituals of mourning provide protection. The power of grief is recognised and mobilised yet also averted and neutralised by the combination of ritual and narrative. The fundamental theme of the narrative, as of most Aboriginal texts, is control not expression of strong and disturbing feelings and expressions, and in order to understand how it works as a text we need to recognise the scale and potency of the feelings that it exists to manage.

For all the glimpses of literary power of texts in this form, nonWorora readers are left feeling that they are scanning the traces of a literature that has been filtered too many times. Too much is left to the nonAboriginal Lucich, whose control of the text is all-pervasive in spite of his intention to provide a simple objective record. The publication in 1983 of *Gularabulu: Stories of the West Kimberley* by Paddy Roe, edited by Stephen Muecke, marked what will come to be recognised as a watershed in the production of Aboriginal literature.

Part of the merit of this book comes from the innovative strategies of Muecke as editor, his self-negation as editor allowing a space for the oral texts of Paddy Roe to exist in print. Paddy Roe's mastery of the resources of Aboriginal English establishes at a stroke the viability of that despised form as a literary language. Muecke incorporated into the printed text some of the expressive devices of Paddy Roe's oral art, the use of his voice, the repetitions and seeming untidinesses that all other editors had conscientiously erased from the record. But the conventions that Muecke established were not backward-looking, insistently recalling some preHomeric age. He set the words on the page in lines of uneven length, each marking the natural rhythm of the spoken phrase, looking like modern poetry rather than primitive verse.

As an accessible instance of the polyphonic strategies of traditional oral narrative we will take the opening of Paddy Roe's story 'Mirdinan', as meticulously transcribed by Stephen Muecke:

> *Yeah—*
> *well these people bin camping in Fisherman Bend him an his*
>   *missus you know—*
> *Fisherman Bend in Broome,* karnun—

> *we call-im* karnun—
> soo, the man used to go fishing all time—
> get food for them, you know, food, lookin' for tucker—
> an' his, his missus know some Malay bloke was in the creek,
>   Broome Creek—
> boat used to lay up there—
> so this, his missus used to go there with this Malay bloke—
> one Malay bloke, oh he's bin doin' this for—
> over month—

This text everywhere carries traces of the dialogic situation in which this version of the narrative was inserted. A core meaning here is the nature of the interaction itself, between Paddy Roe and Stephen Muecke, Aborigine and White, with Paddy tactfully in control of the discursive process and consciously mediating Aboriginal language and culture through Stephen to a wider largely White audience, trusting Stephen to complete his act of mediation responsibly.

An obvious instance of this concern with mediation is the translation of key Aboriginal words in this multilingual text. Less obvious is the way he constructs the dimensions of the world of the narrative in Aboriginal terms, giving the characteristically precise spatial location of these events, even though it is not relevant in terms of plot. A more subtle trace from the oral text can be seen surrounding the use of the word 'missus'. This is a word in Aboriginal English which sounds like a conventional English word, but as Paddy knows it does not correspond exactly to dominant English meanings or social patterns, particularly the idea of a lawful wedded wife bound to her husband by church and state till death do them part. But each time he uses the word there is a slight hesitation ('his, his missus', 'this, his missus') marking a site of disturbance which Muecke's methods of transcription are sensitive enough to pick up, but which would be edited out with most other protocols: showing how nontrivial is the loss due to those other methods, how essential is the Muecke method if the meaning potential of oral texts is to be preserved beyond the initial occasion.

The narrative begins in a realist mode. Mirdinan follows his 'missus' and sees her making love with the Malay bloke. When she returns he accuses her but in a seemingly tolerant tone. She denies the accusation, and he seems untroubled:

> '*I know what's goin' on*—
> *so never mind*' he said '*Tha's all right*—
> *never worry*'—
> say '*Come on yunmi better go*—
> *see if we can get some*—
> *we go this way bush*—'

Paddy Roe constructs action and motive almost entirely through speech, through Mirdinan's deceptive platitudes that mask a murderous rage. Once he has lured the woman into the bush he kills her. The reassurance comes through English cliches ('never worry') and through the specific forms of Aboriginal English ('yunmi' from 'you and me' is the 'exclusive dual' form of 'we', a frequent form in varieties of Aboriginal, carrying a sense of intimate togetherness that the Standard English 'we' does not have). Mirdinan is a hypocrite, totally manipulative in his use of language, a manipulation that is repeated and seemingly endorsed by Paddy Roe as narrator. This may hardly seem worth remarking, except that characters in 'Dreamtime' narratives are normally represented as too simple to be capable of duplicitous discourse or fissured consciousness.

Neither here nor elsewhere does Paddy Roe describe Mirdinan's feelings or motives, the complex set of reasons that would shadow the narrative in the classic literary narrative. The fractured objectivity, the discrepancies between speech and event and the absence of any controlling authorial point of view, gesture at a plenitude of competing explanations, social, psychological, and magical. After the murder Mirdinan is tracked by both Aborigines (the murdered woman's relatives) and the police, but he is a *maban*, a man with magical powers who is able to escape at will by changing himself into an animal. He is finally caught and taken to Fremantle to be hung, but at the last moment he is transformed into an eaglehawk and escapes the noose. He is captured again, and this time the police are cunning enough to get him drunk. In this state his magical powers are neutralised, and he is shut in a box and thrown into the sea, where he drowns.

So Mirdinan is an angry and jealous husband who has offended against Aboriginal as well as European law, and an Aboriginal hero with magical powers, in a text that invites then renounces a precisely realist reading. The commentary that it witholds is an unmediated contradiction, in which Mirdinan is morally ambiguous, and the resources of Aboriginal magic are made available to support the stratagems of a recognisably flawed trickster figure. So his exploits seem to be celebrated by Aborigines, yet apart from discomforting the police he seems to have done nothing for anyone else, by Aboriginal or European standards. In this respect he is not dissimilar from most characters in traditional narratives, who are typically transformed into objects of veneration after equally dubious life histories. But at the same time Mirdinan has the ambiguity of the kind of character who is often thought of as a unique invention of the 20th century: the anti-hero.

Muecke's text does not insist on any of these modernist/ postmodernist characteristics. The 'modern' feel comes from his strategy of refusing narrative closure, allowing the shifts and instabilities and irrationalities of the original to be transmitted with a minimum of editorial intervention. The move is legitimated by a modernist aesthetic, which is sustained by seeming to see itself in the primitive Other. The tactic in literature parallels the similar move in the field of art, where the conventions of modernism have provided a far more appropriate frame for reading and valuing traditional art than either the reading regimes of anthropology or the aesthetic regimes of realist art. The acrylics of the Western Desert school are reassuringly reminiscent of abstract art, while encoding important traditional knowledge. Papunya art like Aboriginal oral narratives is seriously misunderstood if we do not recognise the strength of its roots in traditional meanings and modes of production. But it has also been true that the recognition of the affinity with some aspects of modernism has been a liberating tactic in the reading of Aboriginal culture. It has deconstructed some of the most powerful premises of the reading regime that previously dominated and limited the interpretation of Aboriginal textual production. It provides a salutary corrective to the one-sided (and unexamined) connections that had been made with the oral culture that predated the classics of Greece and Rome. Both connections have a partial truth, and together they create a space in which the many kinds of contemporary Aboriginal artistic form can be situated.

THE FUNCTIONS OF MYTH

Qualities of form and language are crucial dimensions of Aboriginal texts, and strategies of mediation that ignore them are obviously defective. But there is a danger in over-emphasising such qualities at the expense of a concern with the social functions and meanings of such texts within Aboriginal society. Aborigines make strong claims about the importance of these forms as encoding the basis of social life. To begin to see how these claims might be true we need to look at texts from a different point of view, attending to different aspects of these texts, and different kinds of connection that link text to text and culture to social life in a close and dynamic complex.

There has been a small amount of work that has tried to give this kind of perspective on Aboriginal texts as they function in Aboriginal culture. Pioneering work was done by the Berndts, in a series of works that reproduced Aboriginal art and artefacts, primarily from traditional societies. More recent work has tried to combine scrupulous, exacting and comprehensive standards of scholarship with efforts to reach the kind of wider nonAboriginal audience that sustained Mountford. The work that incorporates this new approach most impressively is *Dreamings: the Art of Aboriginal Australia* of 1988, edited and substantially written by Peter Sutton. This is a coffee-table book, retailing at a recommended price of $60, containing many sensuous reproductions of

Aboriginal works of art. At the same time it makes a concerted effort to show how Aboriginal people would produce and understand such works, taking the risk that nonAborigines will be prepared to work hard to learn what they need to know for the meanings to be mediated.

As we have said above, until very recently there were two forms in which Aboriginal texts were fixed for use by White culture, which we classify in terms of the politics of literature as separationist or assimilationist. The separationist genres consist of transcriptions and summaries by anthropologists and linguists, usually according to recondite and inconsistent protocols, circulated amongst a small circle of 'experts', who normally do *not* include the Aboriginal communities from which the text was 'collected'. Assimilationists like Mountford are prepared to sacrifice almost any Aboriginal quality of the text in the quest for a nonAboriginal audience which is assumed to be as lazy and uninterested as the Aboriginal text is meaningless and uninteresting.

The virtue of Sutton's work is that it employs sound scholarship as aspired to by the separationists, and addresses the task of mediation with greater respect for both Aborigines and nonAborigines: the only basis on which an attempted mediation could hope to succeed. An exemplary instance of his approach is his treatment of the statues of 'Two Women' from the Cape Keerweer region. These two figures make up a text, which could be sited in a museum, behind a glass wall, or as here reproduced in colour in a book. In either form they would be virtually meaningless to the uninformed observer. This is true of almost all Aboriginal art and artefacts that are bought or displayed, all traditional Aboriginal verbal and musical texts. The task of a mediator, then, must start by acknowledging this central fact: Aboriginal texts are secretive, opaque texts, concealing the most important levels of meaning as a matter of policy. They are difficult texts, with precise entry conditions and circuitous semiotic routes through their patterns and levels of meaning. The difficulty is not extrinsic, a result of unfamiliarity by White readers with the language and conventions at issue, though this adds to the problems of decoding: it is more akin to the quality of difficulty that T.S. Eliot once declared was essential to modernist writing.

Sutton adds a commentary to his reproduced text. But he also adds a series of other texts which together constitute the minimal object of interpretation. First he gives the authorship and the occasion. These figures were carved by three men from the Aurukun community to play a role in a ceremony performed over the death of a young Aboriginal man who died after an attempted suicide in Aurukun Jail. The information allows us to see the terms of a link between Aboriginal art and the issue of Black deaths in custody, two domains of textuality that are normally kept entirely distinct but which must be significantly connected if the mythic texts are as basic to Aboriginal life as is claimed.

Sutton adds two other kinds of text. One is the myth of the Two

Women, the story behind the statues which presumably was incorporated into the ceremony as well. The other is a map (with photographs) of the area where the events of the narrative occurred. The story itself is reported in the same kind of form as Mountford employed, with no attempt to incorporate features of its original spoken form. In summary, it describes how a baby fell sick and died, and was mourned by the two women, sisters who lived on opposite sides of the Kirke River estuary. But the relatives of the baby did not mourn sufficiently, so the two women crossed to the centre of the estuary, where they sank beneath the water into a cave, where they turned into sharks. The others who had not mourned turned into birds. Later on, when a mother shark comes to shore and is speared two young sharks are taken from her belly. The people then sing, three times, and the third time she swims away. The narrative concludes with the explanation that the spots on the women represent clear water, and hence the Freshwater shark.

Mountford's book organised its texts into a series of two-part forms, a verbal narrative facing its distorting mirror in the corresponding painting, neither connected to anything else. Sutton's account makes us recognise that there is a much more complex and dynamic process involved, one which draws on a range of texts and fields of experience. In this process, the 'myth' as summarised by Sutton is normally an abstract structure, a meaning-potential rather than a set narrative which exists as he has described it. It is reproduced in a series of tellings, which will be different depending on occasion and purpose, narrator and audience.

Among these differences, a decisive role is played by two other kinds of text. One we will call a 'life stage' text: the series of ritualised events, including death and mourning, that organise Aboriginal life. The other is the series of particular events that occur to particular individuals, as represented in a 'realist text' which deal with the disturbing issues and emotions posed by deaths in custody and their impact on the whole community, particularly this instance. These issues are not foregrounded in the myth, but that is not an indication that they are unimportant, or that Aborigines forget the 'realist text' in the performance of the oral and ritual texts. On the contrary, the series of enactments (including ceremonies, statues, dances and stories) all serve to recall as well as to exorcise the power of the painful emotions.

The narrative of the Two Women is the point of intersection of the two important cultural texts (the abstract myth and the 'lifestage text') that together help to organise the meaning of the suicide (the realist text). The narrative encodes a double response to the fact of death and the experience of mourning: the deficient grief of the other relatives, and the excessive grief of the Two Sisters. The first turn into birds, the second into sharks. We could take these transformations as moral judgments, as punishments for the different responses, but they are not only too harsh as punishments, they seem to be inappropriate, since the grief of the Two Sisters is hardly a capital offence. And in the last section of the myth the logic of punishment is even more difficult to apply. The two sharks seem to turn into one, who gives birth to two children instead of one, the killer is killed and those who killed her give her life through their song. So there is a death and a resurrection/rebirth for both mother/mourner and child/mourned, and those who did not mourn are both punished and punishers, and finally restorers of life. The emotional trajectory of the narrative is clearly well suited for it to perform its therapeutic function, but it also expresses a profound emotional truth about the processes of grief, an intensity turning into an uncontrolled destructiveness, and the inability to grieve itself being a kind of punishment.

The text works with powerful general categories of meaning, up and down, death and life, sky and water (birds and fish). But it is also located specifically in a known landscape. The narrative specifies exactly where the two women start from: one on the north-west bank of the Kirke River estuary, the other on the south-east bank, one speaking one local language, the other speaking another. Sutton provides the further political and geographic background that fills out the specific meanings of this spatial arrangement, but its overall intent is clear from the structure itself. The Two Women represent two distinct clan groupings, who meet together on the imaginary boundary in the water between the two areas, united by their grief, a grief which bonds the two groups. Sutton also mentions another myth describing the formation of the landscape, in which the north-western hill was created from shellgrit deposited by Shark's tail, while the south-eastern hill is what is left of a mountain which Quail moved to Coen, about 240 kilometres to the east, near the east coast of Cape York Peninsula (Cape Keerweer and Aurukun are on the west coast).

This other myth has been inserted into this version of the Two Women story, with one of the women now a quail, a dappled bird, and the other a shark; that is, the Two Women in this narrative divide into fish and bird, where in the other narrative they are both shark, opposed to others who are bird. The second myth establishes a larger space as the context for the action. Aurukun, which is not mentioned in the Two Women text but is central to the realist text (where the suicide occurred and where the Aurukun people live) is about 50 kilometres north of Cape Keerweer, and Coen is 240 kilometres to the east, thus giving a broader scope to the alliances that are necessary for the people faced with this threat to their cohesion. The 'Yu'angka mob' describes a loose political federation of clans from the Cape Keerweer area, one whose links needed constant maintenance (Sutton 1986). The two hills from which the Two Women mourn express mediations of these two kinds of place: north-west and south-east, fusing the two kinds of otherness that the people must recognise (White civilisation and other Aboriginal people).

So the texts together fuse a personal message, about the necessity and dangers of excessive grief, with a political message, about the need to sustain relations of solidarity across the Aboriginal communities, drawing on the energies released by grief to do so. These meanings, and the strong emotions that they express and organise, are not clearly present in any single text. Most of the texts in fact seem bare and abstract, lacking both depth of feeling and engagement with the everyday, but those absences are precisely what the formalised texts are working with and against.

Sutton for his purposes was more interested in the statues, which from his account we can see as the point of intersection of a number of powerful and significant structures of meaning, which the statues in turn come to carry. Those meanings are mostly different from the associations that an uninformed nonAboriginal would come up with. The statues are the almost arbitrary encapsulation of a narrative or set of narratives, at the same time as they also recall the specific ceremony and its occasion. This way of encoding meaning is different from the way that sculpture functions in contemporary European society. So also is the importance of the meanings at issue, and the directness with which they serve social and political purposes. The verbal narratives have similar qualities, linking current experience to traditional structures that generalise and control what is problematic in life. Because the issue of deaths in custody is so vivid and pressing for the White community as well as Aborigines, this text is a good one to illustrate something of the economy of Aboriginal textual production. The story doesn't rewrite the painful history or help the dead youth to resolve his anguish, but it mediates the effect of his death so that the community will be strengthened and made more cohesive by the tragedy. Literature that can do that doesn't need to be justified by reference to the distant myths of ancient Greece.

5 Aboriginal voices

The assault on traditional Aboriginal culture has been so unremitting for so many years that to many observers its fragile and wounded forms have seemed in need of preservation at whatever cost, as the single most important way of enabling Aboriginal society to resist the assaults and to re-form its own identity. But to reduce the traditional culture to a set of fixed invariant forms is itself an assault on its capacity to fulfil its primary social functions. That culture always minimally consisted of a set of forms and a set of transformations, constantly renewing the repertoire, continuing to provide meaning and stability. So Aboriginal cultural production is always situated on a transformational continuum, between what seem more and less traditional positions, and each text is always positioned along a stretch of this continuum, never at a single point. Texts that seem more 'modern' encode a transformational relationship to the tradition, while more traditional seeming texts produced today still attempt to incorporate meanings and problems from the present.

This essential transformational capacity of Aboriginal culture is like a mirror image of Australia's colonial culture, as described by the Hartz thesis. According to Hartz, the colonial fragment froze when detached from its metropolitan complex of contradictions, lacking a dynamic principle of growth. Aboriginal culture at the time of the invasion was on the contrary itself a highly complex and differentiated culture, whose complexity was held in place by homeostatic mechanisms of formidable force, so powerful that Aboriginal society had seemed able to resist change for millennia. The effect of the invasion was to turn a whole into a part, a complex set of cultural forms into components of a single fragment. It also reversed the cultural imperative. Instead of the appearance of stasis being the primary goal, survival required a capacity to adapt and transform. Yet these transformations could not be allowed to become negations of the original base, since such a negation would be the abandonment of all claims.

This set of contradictory requirements has given a distinctive quality to Aboriginal cultural production, a quality that has made its fundamental coherence and unity difficult to recognise. This quality is a particular way of combining extraordinary innovation with a kind of serene stability, an explosive cultural voraciousness with a capacity to negotiate a series of strategic returns in a distinctively Aboriginal equivocation with Aboriginality. How long this will last is not clear. But one thing that is certain is that these qualities underpin an Aboriginal cultural renaissance, a flowering of Aboriginal artistic achievement that has already made its mark in Australian cultural life.

LAND AS THEME

For Aborigines today the issue of issues is land rights. So it is surprising at first glance that Aboriginal art and literature is not rich in references to land and evocations of landscapes. Aborigines' love of their own land and their precise knowledge of its topography are not in question, yet it was traditionally not an explicit theme in visual or verbal art. The situation of contemporary Aborigines is now very different. Instead of the confident assumption of identity tied to and established through links to a country, dispossession to some degree is their universal experience. But there is still a continuity between traditional and contemporary forms of cultural expression of this theme amongst Aborigines. Traditional culture provided a highly flexible set of ways of encoding a nexus of rights and obligations towards the land. It gave rise to aesthetic statements which were essentially political and juridical rather than personal and expressive. This quality made it equally well adapted to the needs of Aborigines today, all of whom are in some respects fringe-dwellers in their own land, needing a means of relocating themselves in White Australia, reconstructing an identity which is fully Aboriginal yet adequate to the new situation.

In looking at these kinds of adaptation we need to recognise the validity of the two broad strategies adopted by Aboriginal people as these are reflected in cultural forms. Many Aboriginal groups in northern and central Australia are trying to reestablish traditional ways of life, as close to their traditional territories as is now possible. The acrylic art of the Western Desert peoples and the maintenance of traditional languages are important to this strategy. But for many Aborigines in the south the route back has been disrupted, so that the direct link with a specific piece of country is no longer viable. For these Aborigines, urban dwellers or fringe-dwellers in country towns, the achievements of Western Desert artists are inspiring but unavailable. The writers who speak for them include all the Aboriginal writers who are well known in the White community: Jack Davis, Kath Walker (Oodgeroo Noonuccal), Colin Johnson (Mudrooroo Narogin), Kevin Gilbert, Robert Bropho and Sally Morgan. Yet each of these distinct strands of Aboriginal art is equally Aboriginal, equally crucial to all Aborigines, since one establishes the Aboriginal base, while the other opens up the transformational freedom that is equally important to all Aborigines, wherever they are placed.

As an instance of traditional adaptations, we will take two texts by Peter Skipper, a painting and a story. Peter Skipper's Walmatjari-speaking group was part of the exodus of Western Desert people who moved east, out of the desert area, in closer proximity to areas of White settlement in the north-west of Western Australia. His community is established near Fitzroy Crossing, where Peter Skipper is an important elder who is concerned to retain traditional forms of life in this new situation.

The story we will look at was reported to a linguist, Joyce Hudson, and transcribed by her as an example of the Walmatjari language. In that form (part of a grammar of Walmatjari for use by linguists and educators) it has the low aesthetic status and small circulation typical of this genre. It seems a casual and uninformative anecdote, yet like so many such texts it has a complexity of structure and depth of meaning that repay much closer scrutiny. Our reading, we should point out at the outset, will barely scratch the surface of the meanings of this text which are 'owned' by Peter Skipper, to which we have no way or right to access. We will begin by giving a translation of the complete text, drawing on Joyce Hudson's translation and commentary:

> *In the wet season they eat plant food, Janiya*
> *and meat, lizard—*
> *meat, lizard and wild onion plants, wild onion.*
>
> *In the wet season they eat them,*
> *bush-walnuts as plant food, bush-walnuts they eat.*
>
> *In the sandhills they lived like this*
> *the people lived in that former time in the sandhills.*
>
> *They were eating meat and plant food.*
> *Plants that they ate were various, various.*
> *They were eating all kinds of plant food,*
> *all kinds of plant foods they ate,*
> *until what they ate was finished,*
> *a finish to eating plant food and meat.*

> *Well, they ate meat only,*
> *then that finished.*
> *And the people they went this way*
> *to other kinds of plant food, Whiteman's tucker.*
>
> *Well, those people too, they went north to the stations.*
> *Then they gave them plant food,*
> *the people from the sandhills.*
>
> *Those people went for good,*
> *never to return.*
> *Well, they went on a journey for plant food,*
> *Whiteman's tucker.*
>
> *Then they stayed there, those people.*
> *So they ate the plant food of the Whiteman,*
> *and so they stayed there, the people,*
> *never to return.*
> (1978)

In terms of comparable White genres, this is closest to a lyric of loss and dispossession, stately and formulaic, almost literally a structure of feeling organising a temporal and spatial map. There is no comment, no explanation, no justification of either present or past, only a recurring set of organising categories that can be applied to both. Why did the food supply disappear? Was it a natural disaster, an extended drought, or was it the incursions of Whites with their stock and excessive demands on the fragile ecology? Peter Skipper gives no answer, or not explicitly. The text does evoke the plenitude of the desert land for its people, emphasising the abundant supply of food rather than its beauty. But 'The wet season', repeated twice, sets the framework for the movement from plenty to scarcity, for the Wet was always followed by the Dry in the desert, which in turn was followed by another season of plenty. The text gives the narrative of a pessimistic linear history, but sets it in another time-frame, the circular time of the passage of the seasons, but this more optimistic perspective, like the criticism of the Whiteman, remains understated.

Another principle of the structure, which our translation can only indicate with some clumsiness, is the repetition of the two categories of food, *kuyi* (meat) and *miyi* (plant). These two words insistently classify the natural environment as kinds of food to be hunted or gathered in the gendered division of labour of traditional society. The progression that Skipper describes has three stages. In the first, normative stage, there is both *miyi* and *kuyi*, gathering and hunting. In the second phase, there is only *kuyi*, hunting. The tucker supplied by the Whites is referred to every time as *miyi*, plant foods. Flour and sugar may have been the main staples provided by stations, but there was meat too, from occasional killings. Skipper classifies this food in social not in biological terms as *miyi*, implying a comment on its effect on the traditional roles of Aboriginal society. He does not cast back to a time when men as hunters were exclusive or dominant providers—that phase in his scheme was a result of a breakdown in the natural order. Instead in the landscape of plenitude, in the Wet season in the past, men and women were coequals. That is the situation that can and must return, when another Wet succeeds the present Dry.

There is no statement of regret, though the repeated 'never to return' unmistakeably suggests a sense of loss. What the text does is to carry the values of the desert and the past into the new situation, not as a legitimation of the present (a form of existence which is still radically incomplete) but as a kind of charter for change. The text is neither militant nor resigned, but its criticism and its optimism are so understated as to be almost invisible. Its dominant qualities of balance and poise are aesthetic and political, and even its self-effacement is part of a strategy of survival. And although this past is a remembered historical past it also has something of the structural form of what is called 'the Dreamtime' by Aboriginalists: that is, a time in the past whose values are still active in the present.

Peter Skipper painted *Jila Japingka* in 1987, a text which is reproduced in Sutton (1988). The style of the painting is typical of the acrylics of the Western Desert artists, though it has its own distinctive qualities. As is normal for such texts, the first impression is the sense of formal patterns, produced by repetition of a small number of elements, as happens with his verbal text also. The meaning of the text is otherwise almost inaccessible, without further explanation. Sutton provides a gloss, the first aspect of which is its positioning in space and time. The cross-shape (painted deep blue) is formed by rain from the four compass-points, with the top rain from the east, the bottom rain from the west, with rain from the north on the left, and rain from the south on the right.

This, then, is a map of the same landscape as in the story, the all-important landscape in which Peter Skipper and his people have acted out their life. The east, where his people came from, is positioned at the top of the picture, and the west (Fitzroy Crossing, Broome) is at the bottom. As is typical of traditional Aboriginal art, this text makes no attempt to represent the landscape accurately. The symmetry of the four rains implies that rain comes equally from all four directions, which is very far from true in that part of the Kimberleys. But the symmetry is broken by the profusion of water-sources in the dry east, (the arc above the cross and the four water-holes above all painted blue) as against the absence of water in the west. The painting encodes the meaning of plenitude as an attribute of the east (and the past) compared to the west and the present, just as the story did.

The semi-circles and concentric circles are traditional motifs, which carry a complex of meanings, referring to home-centres (campsites,

Peter Skipper: *Jila Japingka*. (*Picture courtesy of Duncan Kentish and Peter Skipper*)

waterholes, fires) or people resting. But the grid of rectangular shapes is not typical. In this text these shapes dominate the west and the north, characterising the spaces of civilisation and Whitemen's ways, seeming not unlike the bars of a cage, symbols of regimented existence. But Sutton's annotation indicates that these rectangular shapes are sandhills, so that western civilisation is reclassified as a kind of desert. 'Desert' in this scheme is partly negative. However, in Skipper's system the actual desert region is constructed as a place of abundance, not as a barren place. This contradictory classification then has a positive implication, making the barren terrain of civilisation a place in which Aborigines can survive as they did in the Western Desert.

Skipper achieves this meaning-effect by drawing on the resources of traditional art, specifically its capacity to use a minimalist system of classification to establish a complex network of connections that in Western traditions is associated with metaphor. We see a more typical instance of this in the use of semi-circular shapes. Sutton's annotation indicates that the two large arcs in the top right of the painting are long sandhills, while the others represent clouds. The semicircular shape acts as a classifier which establishes a metaphoric link between the two: these sandhills are like clouds insofar as both are like people camped around a site. Clouds are the source of water and sandhills are dry, so the link serves to resolve these primary oppositions. But sandhills themselves are encoded as both semicircular and rectangular, rounded open shapes ('home', Aboriginality) and rectilinear closed shapes (White domains, exile). In this and many other ways the painting responds to two opposing impulses, establishment of difference (between desert and water, home and exile, Aboriginal and White) and the resolution of difference.

The verbal text is constructed out of the same fundamental principles, and is concerned with the same crucial issue—coming to terms with the position of Aborigines in White Australia, using traditional resources to express a twin sense of alienation and belonging. If we gave the texts a more formal analysis we would come up with the seemingly implausible elaborations of the kind of structuralism for which Claude Lévi-Strauss is famous. Neither text is a normal object for these forms of exegesis, and the verbal text especially seems far too humble a form to justify any attention to its formal qualities and implicit levels of meaning. We have discussed them in such detail as the only way to make the general point convincing. Very many Aboriginal texts, written and unwritten, recorded or not, deal directly with the fundamental issues facing Aboriginal people, torn as they are between alienation and a sense of belonging. The strategy they use is an adaptation of traditional Aboriginal ways, constructing maps that are designed to represent broad stretches of space and time, to give meaning and perspective, direction and hope on the bewildering journey of the life of themselves and their people.

TRANSFORMATIONS

The words of a traditional Aborigine like Peter Skipper are not attended to by White Australians because of the inaccessibility of their texts. Aboriginal authors like Sally Morgan and Mudrooroo Narogin have a different problem. Because they have the benefits of White education and White modes of literary production the old Aboriginalist premise is invoked, that they couldn't be 'really Aboriginal'. Thus their right to draw on Aboriginal meanings and artistic forms is questioned. Colin Johnson/Mudrooroo Narogin's *Dalwurra* is modelled on the traditional Aboriginal song-cycle from Northern Australia, centring on a totemic animal, the Bittern, which is not found in his area, Narrogin in Western Australia. The songs refer to his own wanderings, beginning and ending in Perth, passing through such nonAboriginal sites as New Delhi, Bangkok, Edinburgh and London, and the journey is encapsulated in a single map, drawn to look like a 'Dreaming' route. Is this a 'legitimate' transformation of Aboriginal forms, or (as Aboriginalists might claim) a parody that subverts them?

Sally Morgan's *My Place* is less insistently Aboriginal, but its title announces its central concern with her 'place' in the double sense, her search for roots and identity that span Aboriginal and White communities, and the places that focus the two—in her case Perth and the Pilbara region in the north-west of Western Australia. Crucial here is her confidence that she does have access to her Aboriginality, even though she claims that she was brought up entirely as White, and was not even aware that she was of Aboriginal stock until she was an adolescent. Again the Aboriginalist doubt is raised, whether her understanding of Aboriginality could be 'authentic', or whether it should be judged to be superficial and exploitative.

The issue can be examined in its most extreme form by looking at the cover of the first edition of the book, a painting by Sally Morgan herself. The map summarises the book's content, in particular its account of the three generations of Aboriginal women who link her own life in Perth with a station in the Pilbara in the north-west of Australia. The overall strategy and appearance of this picture are Aboriginal: this is a map-plus-journey which encapsulates the life of an individual and a family group, though it is the frame with its snakes and dots and semicircles that is more strongly Aboriginal. The figures themselves are more reminiscent of child-art. The visual text does have writing to explain it ('Corunna Downs', the Pilbara station where the narrative starts, 'Ivanhoe' the elegant Perth house where Sally Morgan's half-Aboriginal grandmother went as housemaid to the pastoralist Drake-Brockman, and where she had a daughter by an unnamed White father whose identity remains unstated to the end of the book).

But in spite of this labelling, the visual text remains as highly encoded as Peter Skipper's, its simple surfaces concealing dense layers of meaning that are only slowly revealed, to those who have access to the accompanying set of verbal texts (Sally Morgan's narrative, plus the life-stories of her uncle, her mother and her grandmother which are inserted in the main text). Like Skipper's text it is organised in terms of a double movement, a linear movement (underlined by Morgan with arrows along a white pathway) and a circular movement in which the return to origins is inevitable, with other routes also encoded (here by snakes horizontally and other tracks vertically) that offer alternatives to the linear mode. It is important to recognise that this is not an opposition between linear White thinking and circular Aboriginal thought, since as Skipper's text shows, it is the complex overlapping of these forms which is Aboriginal, not circularity on its own.

The book itself is organised by the classic theme of the Quest, a journey that is both physical and metaphorical, in search of a Secret

ABORIGINAL VOICES

My Place

SALLY MORGAN

Sally Morgan: Cover of *My Place*. (*Picture courtesy of Sally Morgan and Fremantle Arts Centre Press*)

which is nothing less than the key to personal identity and establishment of genealogy and inheritance. This structure underlies the genre of detective fiction, so Sally Morgan's story makes sense to nonAborigines as a satisfying version of that familiar form, but that does not make it less true to Aboriginal archetypes as well. The book is organised around three secrets, each progressively more carefully shrouded, each with more strict entry conditions, an Aboriginal characteristic. The first secret was Sally Morgan's own Aboriginal identity, which she claims she only became aware of under pressure from her White peers as an adolescent. The second secret was complementary, the identity of her white great-grandfather. This was Howden Drake-Brockman, owner of Corunna Downs station, according to her family, though in the book the Drake-Brockman family never admit it. The third secret, which dominates the second half of the book, is the identity of Sally Morgan's own grandfather. Nan, the grandmother, dies without ever giving the name, but the clues mount and the book leads us tantalisingly close to an unspoken and unspeakable final secret. Aboriginal rules of secrecy coincide with White laws of libel to ensure that this meaning (if it exists) does not enter into text.

The book is offered as a realist text, an autobiography/family history. As with all Aboriginal texts the realist text is decisive for interpretation, not simply for the content that is coded into the compressed and displaced formalist text but also for the systems that connect the discursive processes themselves to social life. The book poses the three secrets, and gives enough information to allow them to be unravelled, but it also represents Nan and her family whose secrets they are, and the role that secrets play in family dynamics and construction of personal identity. The secrets matter a very great deal to everyone, especially to Nan. They are the focus of a profound shame, shame at being Aboriginal (she spent many years claiming to be White) and shame at being White, under these conditions. But they are also a source of power, her power within her family group. She is respected as the 'owner' of this knowledge in the Aboriginal way, and her right to this knowledge is respected by her grand-daughter, who we can assume is now its possessor, but who does not reveal it to readers of her book, although perhaps she allows them to guess.

It is paradoxical that Sally Morgan's search for her Aboriginal identity is accomplished primarily by disclosing her White ancestors, paradoxical since it is this search that allows her to come to terms with her Aboriginality in a way that Nan herself found too hard. In the process she discloses to nonAborigines a pattern of White complicity in the destruction of Aboriginal society that is their own buried secret: sexual exploitation of Aboriginal women by Whites which is not resented in itself (Nan and Arthur Corunna, Howden's two children, always speak of him with affection and respect) but which triggers a pattern of guilt

ABORIGINAL VOICES

and suppression which is carried by Whites and Aborigines alike. Aborigines' dispossession of their past and their family roots is widespread, whether because of discreet censorship by important White families, or more commonly because part-White children were taken from their Aboriginal mothers and raised in institutions or by White foster parents, with knowledge of their background withheld from them as a matter of government policy.

Sally Morgan's story is a particular version of this frequent Aboriginal experience. Colin Johnson/Mudrooroo Narogin's history is more typical. He was sent as a boy to Clontarf Boys Home, which formed a barrier that blocked the continuity of his family life and life as an Aboriginal. So neither absorbed Aboriginal traditions in the traditional way, through continuous exposure and running commentary, focused at key stages by ritual and ceremony, though each did have important Aboriginal figures in their early background. Both had to work hard to acquire the knowledge and understanding that they now possess, which in different ways forms a bedrock for their literary and artistic production. Undoubtedly what they write is not fully traditional, but that does not make it any less Aboriginal. The routes that they establish back to traditional forms are passable for other Aborigines as well as for nonAborigines.

People like Peter Skipper are moving in different directions from different starting points but along the same map, whose function is nothing less than to guide the survival of Aboriginal culture and society. This map no longer claims exclusive rights for Aborigines over Australia, in spite of the paranoiac claims of anti-lands rights propagandists. On the contrary it uses maps of physical space as the controlling metaphor in a semiotic system whose aim is to find and assure a place in Australia for Aboriginal people: a place that recognises older rights to specific parts of the country, and newer rights to live and work and find a meaningful identity in contemporary Australian society.

VERSIONS OF HISTORY

One of the most potent legacies of Aboriginalism has been the claim that history is a specifically European construct which is alien to Aborigines, so that Aborigines as Aborigines are incapable of understanding or producing history as it is managed within 20th century European discursive regimes. The claim is encoded as a basic premise in the Aboriginalist doctrine of the 'Dreamtime'. In terms of this doctrine Aborigines divide time into two layers, secular time (in which present and past merge into one) and 'dreamtime' (a period outside time, before time, describing events which have as much, and as little, reality in the present as ever in the past). If this doctrine did in fact describe the

101

temporal dimension of Aboriginal thought, they would be unable to conceive of linear causality of the simplest kind, and any form of historical consciousness would be beyond them.

In spite of the claimed unAboriginalness of an interest in history, especially White history, most Aborigines are fascinated with it. It is the most important subject on the contemporary curriculum for those Aborigines who are concerned with rethinking the school syllabus. The reasons for this are not hard to see, and they are considerably more compelling than the doctrines of Aboriginalism. As C. D. Rowley observed: '(The Aboriginal minority) has hundreds of local histories handed down through the families, and now being recorded; monotonously the same, and cumulatively damning of the inhumanity and injustice of Australian "development" '. (1986:7) Aboriginal society has its own versions of history which do not exist in a different plane but are able to contest the versions of history transmitted through the education system. Aborigines know that White history until a short time ago has failed to observe its self-professed standards of objectivity and truth, on the topic of the role of Aborigines in that history. School textbooks of the past have repeated and expanded the errors of academic historians.

Historians like Rowley and Reynolds have begun to correct the record, and school textbooks today no longer contain the crude prejudices of earlier ones. Modern historiography recognises that claims of objectivity and comprehensiveness can never be absolute. Historians normally work over their 'evidence', sets of documents or texts, interpreting them according to specific protocols. But equally important in shaping historical narratives is the way that they are calibrated against a repertoire of 'grand narratives', maps of 'truth' whose criteria of relevance and plausibility act coercively to produce truth-effects. So Aboriginal histories can contest the dominant version of history on three different kinds of ground: different classes of document, different modes of interpretation, and different grand narratives.

Aboriginal literature among other things includes a set of historical documents, representing an oral tradition which consists of a large set of individual narratives. These documents for a variety of reasons have usually not been allowed into the record, excessively ignored or distrusted. Undoubtedly oral texts and oral traditions do have a number of weaknesses compared to histories that are inscribed in written documents and transmitted in a literary tradition. Yet as Rowley observes, their cumulative weight has carried a particular grand narrative into general circulation, as a theme that the dominant history for many years ignored but now acknowledges as valid.

Just as nonAboriginal historians can and should pay attention to Aboriginal oral versions of Australian history, so Aboriginal writers (in spite of the edicts of Aboriginalism) have shown themselves well able to interrogate White histories and the documents on which they are based.

In fact Aboriginal writers have displayed a more intense interest in history, in 'what really happened' (Hercus and Sutton 1986), than is the case with the mainstream White tradition: whether fidelity to a specific slice of time or addressing the full scope of contact history. Here the significant works are the television series *Women of the Sun*, and most important of all Jack Davis's series of plays, *Kullark, No Sugar, The Dreamers* and *Barungin*.

The phenomenon of Aboriginal fascination with history can be usefully understood by setting it in the context of Georg Lukács's (1971) theorisation of historical consciousness in the 19th century, and its effects on forms of the historical novel. According to Lukács, a grasp of the social totality is a defining feature of great art. In his account the 18th century had as its supreme literary form the classic novel, which had society itself as its object, but society constructed as static object, as a given, not as a process which can be understood and changed. The revolutionary upheavals at the end of the century briefly offered new possibilities of understanding, a new form of historical consciousness. Individuals could experience at first hand the clash of different forms of society and the processes whereby one order is destroyed and a new one arises to take its place. The result was the possibility of a new theoretical grasp of history, and new literary forms. Hegel's philosophy of history represented this new historical consciousness, which was also exemplified in the historical novels of Scott. But the gain, according to Lukács, was not to be permanent. In the post-revolutionary period, the historical sense again shrank to become nostalgia, and history once again became merely a colourful backdrop in literary forms.

Davis's historical project began with *Kullark*, a play that was designed specifically as an intervention, produced for the Western Australian sesquicentennial celebrations in 1978. It directly incorporated archival material—from White archives, of course—organised as a chronicle that spans over a hundred years, from 1830 to the 1940s. This is the linear view of history that is seen as quintessentially European and nonAboriginal, although in fact it is regarded as simplistic history by modern academic practitioners. But the text is also organised by another principle. In each slice of time that it takes, there is an Aboriginal couple with a son. The modern couple are the Yorlahs, Alec and Rosie and their son Jamie. In the 1930s we have the Yorlah family again, with Alec as the young son and his parents Thomas and Mary. In the 1830s we have the historical Yagan and his parents. In the original Perth production the parallelism was reinforced by having the same actors play the corresponding members of the family group.

By using this dual principle of organisation, Davis was able to fuse what have been seen as the two opposing kinds of history—linear European and circular Aboriginal—to represent both the continuities across time and the different possibilities offered by different circumstances.

The grand narrative that recurs deals with the twin themes of Aboriginal victimisation and Aboriginal resistance, a narrative that in 1978 had still hardly entered the official history. The young Alec of the 1930s struggles to affirm his dignity but is forced into passivity and compromise, but his son, Jamie, is training to be a school teacher, taking a different route from Yagan, the first son, who initially welcomed the Whites but was provoked into resistance and finally destroyed.

This use of a repeated structural form to apply to different specific referents, constructing an economical and subtly changing pattern of meanings, is a characteristic feature of Aboriginal culture, as we have seen. Here we can see how Davis uses it to juxtapose two kinds of response to the past, one angry and linear, the other more detached and compassionate, flexible and resilient as it contemplates the possibilities for Aboriginal people. So Yagan's doomed heroism is not opposed to Jamie's different kind of resistance, though the differences do not disappear. The result is a mode of understanding the past that always makes it available for action in the present. In this respect it functions as 'the Dreamtime' is said to, but as a form of practical consciousness of the past, not as an otherworldly mode of knowing that cannot accommodate the harsh exigencies of everyday life.

Jack Davis adopted a chronology that was calibrated against White history, but he also drew on the kinds of documents that make up the evidence for 'people's history', texts that encode the different refractions and interpretations of events and their possibilities of those who made that history, Aborigines as well as Whites. To illustrate the kind of truth that these texts have, and the mode of reading that these texts require, we will look at a single instance, the story of Jandamarra, also known as Pigeon, as told by Banjo Wirrunmarra on two occasions, once to Stephen Muecke in 1977 and once to Alan Rumsey in 1984. The two versions were published together in 1985 (Muecke, Rumsey and Wirrunmarra 1985) with a commentary that was itself a significant contribution to the understanding of Aboriginal oral narrative and its role in the constructions of history.

Jandamarra was an Aborigine from the Kimberley district of Western Australia who for a few years in the 1890s managed to conduct a successful guerrilla campaign against the police and the White settlers in the district, before being shot in 1897. The events of this brief episode were recorded in various written documents of the time, primarily police records and newspaper accounts. From these sources, a consensus narrative has been constructed which satisfies the requirements of White historians, especially given the relative insignificance of the episode in its grand narrative. But the police were biased reporters, ignorant of many incidents and motives, and the news media of the day refracted their unreliable sources in terms of their own preconceptions. A conventional historian genuinely interested in 'what really happened' would not want to ignore Aboriginal oral accounts.

But the oral versions have another more important function. Jandamarra was important not only for what he achieved (which was not very great, in practical terms) but for what he meant, to Aborigines of the day up till the present. He is a comparable figure to Yagan, who was recognised as a significant Australian by the Bicentennial committee who sat in judgment on such things, and he acted out Aboriginal resistance at much the same time as Jimmy Governor, the origin of Keneally's Jimmie Blacksmith. His story was retold by Ion Idriess in 1952 as *Outlaws of the Leopolds* and it played a significant role in Colin Johnson/Mudrooroo Narogin's *Long Live Sandawara* of 1979. Johnson's interest was not in Jandamarra (Sandawara)'s story as a fixed text, but in the significance it had for a group of young urban Aborigines in Perth in the 1970s. His novel describes their ill-conceived and ill-planned attempt to rob a bank, inspired by vague dreams of heroic resistance nourished by the story of Sandawara as they understood it. And it is an object of this kind, a specific refraction of an event rather than its 'objective truth', that an oral version allows us to reconstruct.

The form of the oral texts as they were published by Muecke and Rumsey is exemplary. They are meticulously transcribed according to the conventions established by Muecke in *Gularabulu* of 1983, and Aboriginal regimes of truth are explicitly deferred to, in terms of which Banjo Wirrunmarra is acknowledged as legitimate 'owner' of the story. Two texts are printed, collected seven years apart. Together they relativise the notion of a single authoritative text, a 'correct version', while maintaining an effective unity. Muecke and Rumsey point out the basic stability of the text, structured around the geography of the terrain and the details of a journey, a principle which we have seen is pervasive in Aboriginal art. They do not point out another quality which is also common in Aboriginal texts: the way in which each telling is incomplete in itself, referring outwards to an unstated totalising version. Most of the differences between the two tellings are of this kind: a different selection from a common matrix, rather than unequivocally a different story. To Muecke, speaking entirely in English, Banjo gave a more complete and sequential narrative, but without a number of important aspects that appear in the Rumsey version. For Rumsey who understood Bunaba he began, in Bunaba, with the moment when Jandamarra first became an outlaw, the symbolic moment when as Black tracker bringing his people into punishment he suddenly switched sides, and shot the policeman instead, and he included a significant commentary on the action, again in Bunaba, which is not present in the Muecke text.

There are three important ways in which the official Aboriginal story (as projected by these two texts) differs from the official White version. One is the crucial role played by 'Mincko Mick', an Aboriginal tracker and 'Wit Doctor', in the capture of Jandamarra. In fact Mincko Mick emerges as almost the hero of Banjo's narrative, in a battle of Aboriginal ingenuity and magic in which the Whites are largely irrelevant. As a matter of historical fact, this emphasis is probably closer to 'what really happened' than the official White version, which follows police records in virtually eliminating the crucial work of the Black trackers. Banjo's version restores Aboriginal presence and Aboriginal agency to the narrative, while also foregrounding the problem of the narrative for Aborigines. After the story he reflects on this dilemma:

> BW: but I—where—I don't understand why this—wit doctor—went up there this is the thing that I don't understand
> AR: yeah
> BW: and he bin take a life of a BLACK man and BLACK man been get shot by WHITE people WHY couldn't he leave ALONE?
> AR: yeah
> BW: that was the story that I understand, you know

The comment shows that the function of this story for Banjo is to encode not simply Aboriginal heroism but also Aboriginal complicity, or more precisely, the fatal failure of Aboriginal solidarity as itself a kind of Aboriginal affirmation. The narrative pivots around this dilemma in Rumsey's version. It begins with Jandamarra renouncing his role as police aide, siding with the Aborigines that he has helped to capture, and it ends with Mincko Mick using a high level of Aboriginal knowledge on behalf of the police. Jandamarra's heroism is thus bracketed, as a contained moment not a continuing possibility. The heroism is not discounted but is not to be supposed to be acted on. Colin Johnson/Mudrooroo Narogin's *Long Live Sandawara* used a different formal strategy to carry the same complex message. His young urban terrorists are inspired by the Sandawara story to a bungled and doomed revolt, but the Sandawara story functions in the novel as a parallel structure of meanings not as a lesson to follow.

There is one element in the Wirrunmarra narrative that would seem to destroy its credibility as reliable history. This is the role played by Jandamarra's thumb. According to Banjo, Jandamarra was invulnerable to wounds everywhere except for this thumb. It is Mincko Mick's knowledge of this weakness that proves decisive: Jandamarra is shot in the thumb and dies instantly. Clearly this has nothing to do with 'what really happened'. Its real affinities are with famous heroes and antiheroes of other mythologies: Achilles' and Adam's heel, Duryodhana's loins, Siegfried's shoulder, Ravana's navel. The anatomical site is not crucial: in other versions of the story it is sometimes Jandamarra's foot or his hand which is the affected part. The physiological implausibility of the episode allows us to recognise this element for what it is: *not* a 'historically correct' fact but a marker of intertextuality, the site of intersection of an important set of texts of very great antiquity.

The effect is to connect Jandamarra with totemic ancestor-figures, figures whose potency was inseparable from their transgressive acts. Banjo Wirrunmarra spells this aspect out to Rumsey, but switches to the cover of the Bunaba language to do so. When Rumsey asks how Jandamarra acquired magical powers, Banjo responds: 'Well only you and I say this—*murlal jirri* (he was incestuous)'. Jandamarra's reported 'incest' involved relations with his father's sister, his sister, and his wife's mother, all taboo relationships within traditional society, with the wife's mother the most powerful of the taboos. This information may have been true, or said to have been true, of the historical Jandamarra, which would explain some of the distrust that contemporary Aborigines felt towards his revolt, but Banjo does not mention it in this context. Rather, it is the explanation of his magical potency and mythic status.

The phenomenon is not without its parallels in other mythic heroes. A recent example is President Kennedy's damaged back and prolific womanising, which have proved no impediment to his cult status. This status is a social fact, in the case of Kennedy and Jandamarra alike, which carries meanings and effects into the present and beyond. It is this process which is illuminated by those texts in the oral tradition which construct and transmit those meanings and those effects. From a literary point of view it gives the stories the kind of resonance and density of meaning that the epics of Homer or *The Mahabharata* have acquired. From the point of view of historians it guarantees that these will always be fissured texts, never reliably about 'the facts', never of one piece or one time, but never without reasons and meanings that are as important as their Aboriginal guardians claim.

ABORIGINAL POLYPHONY

The Aboriginalist conventions for transmitting Aboriginal narratives were designed to eliminate Aboriginal authorship, Aboriginal control, the Aboriginal voice. But paradoxically one of the unfortunate effects of Aboriginalism even for many who resisted it was to create the illusion that there is an 'Aboriginal voice', spoken by a unitary Aboriginal subject, that preexisted in the first place. Aborigines on the contrary normally insist that they are a plurality of Aboriginal nations. Their literature is composite and federalist, with specific components 'owned' by different groups, speaking different languages and living in different places. Cutting across this emphasis on diversity is a characteristic set of strategies for dealing with difference. Traditional Aborigines were multilingual, and contemporary Aborigines have their own urgent reasons for a fascination for and facility with linguistic pluralism. Aboriginal literature both traditional and modern is characterised by its dialogic qualities, multilingual and multimedia forms that manage diversity by giving it full play in polyphonic genres of text.

The writings of Kevin Gilbert have been central in the construction of Aboriginality, articulating a voice and a speaking-position for Aborigines in White Australia. His polemical work *Living Black* succeeded powerfully in this aim, winning Gilbert an Australia Council Award and reaching many White Australians. This text illustrates nicely the problems of the Gilbert project, of making space for an Aboriginal voice in an adversarial political climate. Gilbert collected and edited taperecorded interviews with various articulate Aborigines. These people make many intelligent points about 'living Black' in Australia today, but the book overall is surprisingly monologic in its effect, with none of the 'grain of the voice' or play of roles of *Gularabulu*. This is partly due to Gilbert's editing conventions, but the editing preceded his own intervention, as speaker after speaker made sure that nothing derogatory was said about Aborigines. He noted this sanitising impulse in his preface, but as a writer he did more than complain. His book of poems, *People are Legends* of 1978, assembles a cast of characters and a play of voices from across the spectrum of Aboriginal life, from drunks in the gutters to proud, indignant Aboriginal people.

This is also the key to Jack Davis's achievement as a dramatist, and it is no accident that it is the theatre which provides the most congenial context for this achievement. Davis's poetry tends to be conventional in form and subject matter, and has not reached a wide audience. His plays, extensively workshopped with their predominantly Aboriginal casts, have incorporated the range of voices of urban Aborigines, drunk, vulgar, full of energy and humour, anger and warmth, with as much fidelity as a Muecke transcription, but shaped and refined to a condition of typicality.

Like Gilbert, Davis runs the risk of seeming to offer Aborigines up for ridicule, confirming the worst White prejudices, but this is not the effect of Davis's plays, for Aborigines or Whites. Aboriginal audiences typically respond to the bawdy realism and earthy dialogue of the plays with the joy of recognition, along with a sense of release from the disabling and oppressive stereotype of the heroic unitary consciousness of the oppositional Black. Whites on the other hand are given the privilege of entry into intimate areas of Aboriginal life, but at the same time this life is shot through with voices and meanings that are left unexplained and mysterious to monolingual Whites. Aboriginal words weave into the dialogue, and characters repeat fragments of old stories or songs that carry old patterns of belief into contemporary life to a remarkable degree, giving meaning and dignity. What Davis is dramatising is the resilience of Aboriginal customs and beliefs, and their depths of resource in coping with conditions that would destroy the dignity and will to live of most nonAborigines. His theatrical strategy conveys this to Whites by intermittently disabling them, juxtaposing the limits of their monologic state to the dialogic mode of Aboriginal culture.

The problems of negotiating Aboriginal voices and Aboriginal forms are at their most acute with the novel, that quintessentially Western invention as it has been called. Derrida has suggested that colonised poets will be 'attempting to speak the other's language without renouncing their own' (1985:294) but Derrida's lapse into the singular here underestimates the plurality of both sides of the language equation. Colin Johnson/Mudrooroo Narogin has pushed the Aboriginal novel into new territories, while constantly reflecting on the preconditions of his hybrid form. We will illustrate something of his strategy by reference to his first novel, *Wild Cat Falling* of 1965, and the screenplay he wrote 20 years later for a film of the novel—a film which for interesting reasons does not yet exist.

The novel adopted a first-person persona, that of an aimless Aboriginal youth who at the start of the novel is leaving prison, and at the end is arrested, about to return there, certain to be found guilty of the attempted murder of a white man. It seems the account of a pointless but typical experience of an Aboriginal youth of the time, a work in the realist mode. It is organised in three parts, 'Release', 'Freedom' and 'Return', English words which however have a complex meaning in this text, positioned as they are between two kinds of experience, two principles of meaning. The 'release' refers to his release from jail, but also the lack of release of the nameless hero's feelings of alienation and anger. 'Freedom' has a similar irony for the Aboriginal youth. 'Return' however has a non-ironic double meaning. He returns to jail, confirming both White expectations and Aboriginal circular patternings of experience, but he has also returned to his own country and established some contact with his roots among his people, and his dream and identity as Wildcat is located in relation to an Aboriginal myth.

This pervasive, often nearly invisible reference to and use of the resources of Aboriginal tradition is almost universal in Aboriginal texts. It's still worth pointing this out, with texts that disguise or displace this dimension, and at the same time take huge risks with the other voices and traditions that they take on and incorporate. Print tends to drain the 'grain of voice' from Aboriginal speakers, even with the Muecke conventions. The opening of *Wild Cat Falling*, which establishes the narrator, does not strike most readers as especially Aboriginal:

> Today the end and the gates will swing to eject me, alone and so-called free. Another debt paid to society and I never owed it a thing. Going outside into the fake heaven I have dreamed of these last eighteen months. Lifetime lousy months. Lifetime boredom of sameness. Same people, same talk, sick

sameness of dirty jokes. Same sick sagas of old jobs pulled and new jobs planned. Heroic memories. Swell hopes.

There are no signifiers of accent or indications of the spoken here. But there are deviations from the standard forms of spoken English, including the 'incomplete sentences' which are frowned on in the written code but common in speech, both Aboriginal and White. There is a curious absence of genitives ('Lifetime lousy months') which however is not an uncommon characteristic of Aboriginal English. Finally, the basic narrative is in a form of the present tense, which departs from the expected past-form of classic narrative by not situating the narrative comfortably in a fictional past. This is odd in English, except in modernist texts, but is again a normal feature of Aboriginal languages, which typically use a form of the present as the usual narrative mode. Into this linguistic matrix, however, are inserted fragments of official discourse ('Another debt paid to society') and contemporary slang ('Swell hopes'). The result is a fissured consciousness, in which the boundaries between Aboriginal and White are constantly shifting, speaking a language which is both crushingly banal and ordinary yet also aberrant, marked, experimental, a form of modernist writing.

In 1965, this style, liberating Johnson/Narogin's complex sense of decentred Aboriginality, was only possible because of the terrain opened up by modernist works. Samuel Beckett's *Waiting for Godot* plays a crucial role here, in both the book and the screenplay written 20 years later, as an alien voice which Johnson/Narogin found an essential mediation of his own. There are extensive quotes from *Waiting for Godot* in the book, with wry but affirming comments from the character, but in the screenplay their role is even more structural, presented as 'surrealist' projections of Wildcat's own state of mind. *Wild Cat Falling* was published in 1965, the same year as the second edition of *Waiting for Godot* appeared in paperback. It is clear that Johnson/Narogin, like many other readers of the 1960s, shared the excitement of a work which suddenly broke new ground and gave him a new mode of representation, one which he found more compatible with the expression of Aboriginality and its themes and voices than the dominant forms of realism. This was a route followed independently later on by the acrylic artists of the Western Desert. This invocation of modernism is the second essential enabling move in contemporary Aboriginal literature, counter-balancing the oppressive weight of its vaunted 'primitivism' and antiquity to give at last an adequate space in which it can speak.

The sections from Beckett's play which Mudrooroo Narogin incorporates into the screenplay are those which gesture towards the possibility of an ambiguous redemption ('One is supposed to have been saved and the other ... [damned]') or endlessly trap us in an unbounded time and space which is created by discourse. So Wildcat's memories of the

Boys' Home in which he spent his adolescence lead to a lengthy 'cut to surreal setting' in which Wildcat is the Boy,' the principal of the school is Vladimir and an old Aboriginal man in ragged clothes is Estragon. Here the discussion is about a message from 'Mr Godot' which remains unsaid. For Narogin, however, Vladimir/the principal's question is crucial:

Vladimir:	Are you a native of these parts? (silence) Do you belong to these parts?
Wildcat as a child:	Yes, sir.
Estragon:	That's all a pack of lies. (shaking Wildcat by the arm) Tell us the truth.
Wildcat as a child:	But it is the truth, sir!

At this point in the screenplay the voice of June, a psychology student Wildcat met at the beach on the day of his release from prison, is heard:

(voice off):	So here you are, lost to the world in a book. I hoped that you would turn up.

The voice from the realist text labels the experience of the book as a 'loss' of the world, but that parallel world is frighteningly apposite, asking of the Aborigine 'Do you belong in these parts?' and refusing to believe the answer.

The transition from book to film had to reflect the intervening 20 years of experience, Narogin's/Johnson's and his audience's. It also had to confront textual politics in other ways, specifically the kinds of control that are built in to the systems of film production. The director-designate of the proposed film version asked the author to change the ending of the screenplay to give a more 'dramatic' end to the story. The original screenplay followed the novel, in which the hero was arrested by the police. As we have seen, this would have been both repetition and difference, representing a cyclical wisdom about the fate of Aborigines in White juridical (prison-oriented) culture, in the form of a possibly new version of that old pattern. In the new ending the screenplay ends with a 'freeze' after Wildcat is shot by the police. This ending endorses the concept of 'tragedy' and 'peripeteia', the essentials of closure in this cinematic genre. The difference concerns the relations between life and text. Johnson's/Narogin's Wildcat is in prison again, but able to learn and understand his situation: in the revised screenplay his heroic status would have been imaged as immobility, an incapacity to act, the character a safe spectacle for the cinematic gaze, encapsulated in the White version of a 'Dream time'.

111

Narogin's/Johnson's novel is still not a film. What does exist in public form is another text, *Doin Wildcat* (1988) which Mudrooroo Narogin subtitled 'A Novel Koori Script'. This traces Wildcat's return to the sets of a film based on his screenplay which is being produced by Al Wrothberg. In the filmic reconstruction of Wildcat's life (*Wild Cat Falling*) the Aboriginal protagonist of the original novel views the filmic reconstruction of his (fictional) life as a kind of a representation of the repressed.

The sanitised reconstruction fakes reality as its homogeneous White discourse is at odds with the vibrant Aboriginal discourse in which Wildcat's commentary is written. In the process the writing of Aboriginal history is situated as two kinds of impossibility: a White filmic mode which is concerned with local effects for its American viewers and a Black consciousness which can be articulated only after massive historical compromises. The Noongar/Koori discourse of Wildcat is thus both an authentic and an alienating discourse since what it represents is beyond representation. Instead Narogin opts for a writing which may be called anecdotal writing. This allows a large number of Aboriginal stories to intervene in the realist narrative of the film and disrupt its linearity.

The return of Wildcat to his origins, to the place to which, as an Aborigine, he can no longer belong, thus becomes a critique of White-Aboriginal relationships generally ('I'm what's called institutionalised, bin in one place or another most of me life' (p. 85)). Fremantle prison (where a large part of the screenplay is filmed) signifies a 'space' all too familiar to Aborigines. The prison also demands that Aborigines accept the White legal system. When Ernie, the actor who plays the role of Wildcat, asks the author why he didn't give the screenplay a more radical ending, ('Well, yuh ended it wrong, yuh did. All yuh got is another blackfella endin up in jail' (p. 112)), Wildcat replies that for Aborigines even writing functions within a White socio-cultural imperative. The penitentiary demands penance, and truth must therefore be compromised so as to find release. In this respect, says Wildcat, his fiction cannot utter what White society does not want to hear.

Real history must be hidden, its messages distorted, like the mysteries of Aboriginal ritual or painting. And so the polemic is muted, the anger subdued, the penance foregrounded. But for the Aboriginal there is still his own antilanguage, a usurpation and transformation of the language of the coloniser, through which his history can be told. In this perspective, *Doin Wildcat* is a significant 'moment' in Aboriginal literature since here Wildcat (Narogin) returns to his original text (*Wild Cat Falling*, 1965) and effectively rewrites it in a different discourse, through his commentary on the screenplay as this is transformed by White discursive processes.

Aboriginal literary production will never be sufficient on its own to challenge the dominant construction of Aboriginality. Literary criticism will become the site of a new form of Aboriginalism unless Aboriginal voices are given their due place within the discourses that constitute it. That is why Mudrooroo Narogin's *Writing from the Fringe* (1990) is so important a contribution to Australian literary criticism: as significant a landmark as Frederick Sinnett's 'The Fiction Fields of Australia' of 1856, by a critic who is a major writer in his own right, as Sinnett was not.

Narogin's text still has a difficult job to do, as can be seen from a hostile review which greeted its publication, Simon During's 'How Aboriginal is it?' (1990). During's brief polemic shows how easily an up-to-the-minute version of postmodernism can provide a cover for the time-worn premises of Aboriginalism. During asks of Narogin's work, 'How Aboriginal is it?' and confidently finds it deficient, falling foul of the purity premise: 'Any primordial Aboriginality would itself be hybridised, textualised as soon as it is expressed in writing' (1990:21). But Narogin's tactic is clearly a long way from any naive commitment to primordialism or purity, so During takes him to task for venturing into White territory, High (French) Theory: 'Roland Barthes puts it like this in a phrase which Narogin repeatedly cites: "The text is a tissue of quotations drawn from the innumerable centres of cultures". Apparently Narogin does not realise how Barthes' proposition resists incorporation into his larger argument' (1990:23). During, it seems, effortlessly understands both Barthes' and Narogin's 'larger argument': and also understands that Narogin doesn't understand that he doesn't understand.

Certainly Narogin claims the right to read and use European works in his theory as he does in his novels. He quotes or paraphrases the offending phrase from Barthes at least three times as he develops his own complex social semiotic approach. He advances an Aboriginal critical practice which, in its postmodernity, is a politics as much as it is criticism. Aboriginality as he proposes it is an 'advanced coherence' in literature, a concept based upon a strategic (and extremely functional) reading of Michael Riffaterre's use of the matrix and the hidden intertext (1980). Narogin is concerned with the hidden metatext, the core which signifies Aboriginality and is the defining feature of an Aboriginal text. In terms of this theory, an initial minimal reading of a text along purely representational (mimetic) lines must give way to a retroactive reading which uncovers the work's 'significance'. This 'significance' is directly related to a text's Aboriginality, which literature, like the processes of Buddhist nirvana, unfolds as it disentangles or lays bare the world of illusion. In this way Narogin uncovers the multiplicity of 'tissues' that constitute the Aboriginal text.

Narogin sets his enterprise in a historical frame, scrutinising White versions and proposing an alternative periodisation along Aboriginal lines, with only the year 1788 being common to both White and Black Australian histories. He also offers an archaeology of crucial Aboriginal 'moments', such as the history of the publication of the journal *Identity* (1972–1982), the White writing of 'trustories', the 'consumption' by the White community of the 'battler genre' of Sally Morgan and Glenyse Ward, the place of popular music, especially reggae rock in Aboriginal society, and so on. The endlessly reiterated lesson of this history is the unresolved contradiction that Narogin like all Aboriginal writers must wrestle with: Aboriginal texts are written in an alien language (English) for an audience which is predominantly White, in what he calls a peculiar schizophrenia (p. 125).

In exploring this contradiction, or schizophrenia, Narogin points out how Aboriginal literary production is trapped in an entire history of Australian assimilationist policy. This policy of assimilation valorised conformity at the expense of difference and led to a form of literary imprisonment. A particular discourse (standard English), a particular ethic (Christianity) and a particular genre (the ballad or hymnody) denied Aborigines access to the great and complex texts (and experiences) of the metropolitan centre as well as of Aboriginal tradition itself. Black Australian writing was trapped in this generic and linguistic continuum since the Black writers were told no other, with their own way forcibly suppressed (as primitive, pagan, or whatever). Oodgeroo Noonuccal, Kevin Gilbert, Jack Davis and Narogin himself are all part of a generation 'scarred by assimilation' (p. 49), part of a racial 'splinter' who had no 'natural' family (p. 79) and who show how 'assimilation has hindered Aboriginal creativity rather than helped it' (p. 86).

Yet Narogin is no simple romantic. He recognises that cultures must never fossilise (as indentured Indian culture with its mimicry of the coloniser's values has done) since this would only confirm their 'museum' status as a 'calcified colonised society' (p. 144). Their vibrancy must never be sacrificed and for this they must be self-reflective as well. The theoretical cosmopolitanism of Narogin's criticism with its strong basis in French post-structuralist theory is part of this self-reflexivity and 'de-calcification'. What is needed is a generic freedom as well as a refined sense of the Aboriginal struggle. The defining feature of the Aboriginal text to which Narogin returns over and over again is its Aboriginality. This remains a structural and a thematic dominant because of a fundamental, inalienable fact of history: 'being born in a white world is no joke for a black man or woman' (p. 136).

Given this fact, compromise, manipulation, abuse and misuse are all part of the processes through which the colonised negotiates with the coloniser, with the ever present threat of collusion and complicity. The Black writer exists at the very interface of this ambiguity, and feels like a 'shuffling Beckett character uttering parables into the recording apparatus of white dominance' (p. 151). Narogin is acutely aware of the paradox: 'It is a curious fate to write for a people not one's own, and stranger still to write for the conqueror of one's people' (p. 148).

Thus Aboriginal writers must use (White) literary genres as a political weapon with which to challenge White hegemony. They must redefine genres, explode discourses, delegitimate standard English, subvert expectations, challenge assumptions while maintaining their rage and their centrality in an Australia which, after all, ultimately and preeminently, belongs to them. This literature participates in forms of magic realism as it mixes fantasy and reality, dreamtime and chronology, fact and myth. But reading—our own reading—also requires an Aboriginal reading practice, an Aboriginal strategy of unearthing mythic, totemic meanings which Narogin demonstrates as an exercise in radical practical criticism in the final chapter of this challenging, and disturbing, work. Like a taboo, a sacred ritual, Aboriginal literature does not open its secrets readily to the uninitiated.

For Narogin as for other Aborigines, writing is a matter of political struggle through which the very strangeness of alien discourses may mark them as legitimate modes, as 'belonging' to Aborigines. Colin Johnson/Mudrooroo Narogin with his self-reflexivity and fractured discourse is not an aberration in the emergence of Aboriginal literature. The issue at stake is not the definition of authenticity or Aboriginality, but on the contrary, how to explode the processes, energies and investments that have gone into the construction of such spurious unities. In this chapter we have not tried to fix or define any unitary essence of Aboriginal literature. On the contrary, we have tried to offer a more Aboriginal kind of object, a map which is a journey and a set of possible journeys, which has places for Colin Johnson / Mudrooroo Narogin and Peter Skipper, Sally Morgan and the people of Aurukun, recognising continuities and differences but deferring for ever an imperialist move to unity, whether the unity of Aboriginality or the unity of Australia which might subsume both Black and White.

6 Crimes and punishments

Australia was founded on a double guilt: the dispossession of the Aboriginal people and the excessive punishment of large numbers of British and Irish people, mainly from the poorer classes, for crimes against the property of the ruling class. The last convicts were brought to Australia over 120 years ago, but Australia still has a legal system that constructs criminality and incarcerates deviants. It has now granted citzenship to Aborigines, but they take up a disproportionate share of space in Australian prisons. This juxtaposition of the two ends of White Australian history is of course simplistic, but it raises an important problem in a usefully stark form. How are we to link the historical reality of the convict era to the set of representations over time reaching up to the present? How should we read the patterns of similarity and difference in these representations against the background of developments in the construction and control of criminality and deviance? What is the social meaning and function of the theme of criminality in Australian mythology, in its double form, the virtuous convict and the heroic bushranger?

The Hartz thesis is again a useful starting point for grasping the dynamics of the foundation event. As purely as any instance of European colonisation, the colony at Botany Bay was constructed as a fragment, an intractable component of a much more complex metropolitan structure. With the loss of the American colonies the British penal system was in a state of crisis, unable to accommodate the prisoners who swelled the notorious hulks, who previously would have been sent to America. Transportation was only one option in a penal system that was only one part of an overall system of control. Over the period of the foundation event, that system itself was subjected to massive pressures for change. So the society that Governor Phillip presided over was a gross and unstable parody of the metropolitan situation. The legal system in Britain at the time was an instrument in a class war, but the alignments in that war were complex and shifting. The colony of Botany Bay, however, had an elemental simplicity. It was virtually a society of prisoners and warders, with a palpable opposition of interests between the two. It also had a contradictory double brief, as a penal colony and as a self-sufficient or even profitable component of Britain's maritime empire.

So from the outset the colony was not just a fragment seeking the completion of the metropolitan whole. It incorporated contradictions from the centre in a dynamic and unstable form. It is this fact which helps to explain the tenacity with which this early pattern has survived into the present. Ideological forms and patterns of behaviour that were laid down at this time were designed precisely to cope with the continuation of the penal system in another guise, so that the passing of convictism was in some respects just the operation of one tendency of the system, following transformational lines that were always implicit in it. The set of representations which is our particular concern in this chapter was therefore able to make the transition beyond the end of the convict period. However, the meaning and function of these forms, even when they apparently remained the same, was often transformed by the new place they occupied, in the new situation.

To understand how this worked we need to say a few words about the general relationship between the set of representations and the social conditions out of which they arose and which they ostensibly are about. We draw here on Althusser's (1971) distinction between what he calls ideological state apparatuses (ISAs) and repressive state apparatuses (RSAs). RSAs include the police and military and the penal system, physically coercing those who resist or defy the state. ISAs include religion, education and the media, systems that according to Althusser not only control systems of representation but also the construction of the subject. We will extend Althusser's scheme to theorise various important aspects of the history of representations of criminality in Australia. From the point of view of a ruling class, one of the functions of an ISA is to complement the operation of RSAs, legitimating the use of power and making it redundant. The direct exercise of power is expensive and divisive. The exercise of power through ISAs is naturalised and accepted, but needs the reality of state power as its sanction and support.

ISAs in this view are not simply sets of representations. They also incorporate rule systems of their own, which are part of their meaning. These rules, however, express not only the will of the rulers but also their recognition of the effective resistance of the ruled. The set of representations, in turn, incorporate a number of contradictions. Firstly we must note that they work with different media to construct radically different kinds of text. They construct various symbolic forms, images in words or pictures. They also inscribe meanings on bodies, coercing various individuals or groups to act out specific legitimating meanings. These are various categories of 'deviant', whose existence, far from being an embarrassment to the system, is essential to its smooth operation. The deviants justify the repressive apparatus, aligning the 'normal' majority with the rectitude of the state. The construction of deviance is carried out by a collaboration between RSAs and ISAs, and then confirmed by systems for the circulation of images.

But so far this account has given too much weight to the capacity of ruling classes to control all forms of representation. The degree of dominance of the dominant is variable, as is the cohesion of challenging groups and their capacity to achieve recognition of their competing interests and ideological forms. In the case of convictism in early Australia, the material and ideological control of the ruling group was never absolute, and there were profound divisions within the society that left its mark on the major ideological forms that it transmitted to succeeding ages. In this chapter we will outline some of the major fissures in the original construct, focused through the double figure of the convict and the bushranger, and trace the way in which later groups at later stages were able to make use of these forms for their own distinct but analogous purposes.

THE CONVICT SYSTEM

The system of transportation to Australia was not a unique phenomenon. It had well-recognised roots in developments in England and Europe at the time. We will use the important thesis of Foucault (1979) on the development of modern European carceral systems as a source of ideas to organise our sketch of the background and issues involved. Foucault argued that between 1760 and 1840 there was a profound change in the European system of punishment. In his view the previous regime worked through spectacles of punishment, dramatic displays of state power as in the grisly ritual of public executions. The later system emphasised surveillance, correction and reform. The spectacle of punishment was the inverse image of monarchical strategies for exercising control, which operated through spectacles of royal power as exercised through ceremony. The system of discipline, associated with bourgeois rationality, has now become the dominant force in modern society according to Foucault. We could expect, then, that insofar as the founding premises for Botany Bay were formed by the regime of the spectacle, then its ideological value today would be complex. A fierce attack on its brutal inefficiencies might even function as a kind of affirmation of the modern attitude to the carceral society.

We shall see that something like this was sometimes the case. But it is also important to recognise the contradictory and transitional nature of the system of transportation itself. Transportation was used as the opposite of a spectacle of punishment. The English legal system had proliferated so many capital offences over the 18th century that the spectacle of punishment could have solved the problem of carcerality at a stroke: but this was not a realistic possibility. Transportation was the transformation of the death sentence into another spectacle of punishment which was also useful behaviour (working in a distant part of the world). The sentence was intended to signify the meaning of royal mercy as well as royal power, a contradiction that was inherently unstable. No less than Jeremy Bentham attacked the whole Botany Bay scheme, and since Bentham's proposal for a 'Panopticon' was taken by Foucault to be the exemplary instance of the new attitude we might suppose that transportation was linked to the old penal regime. The old system in practice had always needed some system of surveillance: its extravagant shows were only necessary because its means of surveillance were so ineffective. And the new system needed its own kinds of show, and its own forms of coercion of bodies and control through pain.

We can see both elements in the Australian penal colony as it evolved. Governor Phillip was a representative of the new attitudes to punishment, but others maintained the punitive practices that were also intrinsic to the system. The split that gave birth to the colony spawned analogous divisions within it, displacing fragments of penality from Botany Bay into such notorious settlements as Norfolk Island, Port Arthur and Moreton Bay. These acted as 'spectacles of punishment' for the colony, as the hulks and Botany Bay did for England and Ireland. Tales of atrocities circulated about these which fed into the myth of convictism. They came from both above—from reformers of the kind whose enlightened views were to prevail—and below, from convict victims expressing their anger and opposition. They functioned as spectacles, to reinforce the image of the might of the state if not its justice. They also incorporated into the myth the radical premise that state justice can be not only excessive but even unjust, that criminality can be a social construction on behalf of a venal ruling class. But once they were located safely in the past, they served to confirm the legitimacy of a new ruling class by its contrast with the practices of the old.

Out of this contradictory situation came two characteristic forms of consciousness which are the legacies of this period, though as we have said they have been continually renewed by an endless supply of analogous contradictions. One is the construction of doublets, that is, images and values which appear simultaneously in two opposed and incompatible forms. The image of convicts and bushrangers alike as both heroes and scum is a case in point. The split image of women as 'Damned whores and God's police', in Anne Summer's graphic phrase (1975), is another instance. But doublets are best seen as one way of resolving a more endemic quality of consciousness: double-think. The ambiguous coexistence of two systems of values leads to paranoia from above and from below, as each scans the texts of the other for their hidden content of hostility and opposition.

With these concepts in mind we are able to trace the shifts and contradictions in representations of crime and punishment from the foundation of the colony to the present, as they affect the reading of literary texts and cultural forms. In the 19th century convict and bushranger were sometimes constructed from above as romantic figures who were celebrated for their noble and convenient suffering and demise. Plot, character and setting were influenced by the conventions of Gothic, a genre that was far more prominent in Australian literature than in contemporary English fiction, one that was especially appropriate because of its obsession with guilt and its paranoid textual strategies. But at the same time from below came protest texts about injustice and cruelty against convicts, and popular celebrations of acts of resistance, especially the exploits of bushrangers. The two kinds of text circulated alongside each other, both of them available for various writers and artists to draw on in a complex and unstable tradition.

In the last quarter of the 20th century the theme is positioned against a different situation. The words 'convict' and 'bushranger' are archaic and no longer refer to contemporary prisoners, inmates or criminals, thus establishing a barrier against connections between past and present. But links can still be seen. It might seem fanciful to suggest that contemporary Australia is in some respects only a more complex and extensive disciplinary machine than Botany Bay was in 1800. But mechanisms for constructing deviance and maintaining surveillance still exist, in direct line of descent but more efficient and better resourced, with new objects of the disciplinary gaze to join the old. The connections between various sites and objects of discipline in the present and the past are not merely fanciful metaphors, in terms of a Foucauldian framework. On the contrary, they help us to understand how these texts and genres were interpreted in the past and how they can be read now, and with what functions and effects.

THE SPECTACLE OF PUNISHMENT

The history of convictism in Australia is complex and subject to theories and revisions by different historians. The process of interrogating the surviving texts, however, is continually crossed by another history, the history of the construction of the convict myth, which provides the momentum and agenda for the other histories. To give the terms of this second process in schematic terms, we can see its characteristic ambiguities and complexities as deriving from its double source from above and below, representing different experiences of different groups with different interests. For a variety of reasons, constructions from above have dominated in later versions of this piece of history. Amongst these, a decisive role has been played by Marcus Clarke's *His Natural Life* (1870–72) and its abridged 'novel' version, *For The Term of His Natural Life* (1874) which we shall read as a single composite text. But in spite of its spectacular success as the definitive convict novel, this work and its meaning were dependent on other sources and traditions which it worked over and incorporated and helped to bury from view. These came from below, from popular traditions, often in oral form, which have now become barely accessible. To reconstruct something of the dialectic between the two sources of the convict myth, we need first to be able to go some way towards recovering the buried form.

The essential feature to recognise about the popular tradition was its closeness to traditional forms of oral culture. In early periods of the settlement it performed a community-sustaining role, contributing to the identity, cohesion and morale of a whole group. But the scope and richness and diversity of this cultural form has until recently been almost entirely neglected by historians and literary critics alike. The relevant texts have not survived in the prolific manner of written texts, and where they have, the reading practices of both disciplines have not been adequate to such texts and such cultural forms. Because they are now so scarce, given that they were once so widespread, a method more akin to archeology is needed, one which systematically over-reads the few surviving texts, to compensate for the asymmetrical action of time on their distribution. In the same way, archeologists reconstruct vases from fragments, and human beings and societies from bits of bone and pottery.

Texts from the early period survive in collections of ballads and unreliable scraps of prose and song, whose provenance is often worryingly uncertain. One way of dealing with this uncertainty comes from an understanding of the dynamics of oral cultures. In oral cultures, individual texts are not tied so closely to a single author, nor to a single version. As versions circulate, they accumulate differences that are themselves significant, establishing a meaning which is irreducibly social. But the opposition between oral and literary cultural practices should not be pushed to an extreme. In ancient Greece, Homer worked with a rich set of oral sources in ways that were characteristic for oral cultures, but at the same time he produced a definitive text, as an individual, highly valued performer. In the same way, the anonymous oral convict tradition produced a single major figure, who became known as 'Frank the Poet'. Only a few poems can be attributed to Frank the Poet, none of them in a text that can be relied on. None is on the scale of a Homer. These are not unrecognised 'masterpieces' of western culture. But Frank the Poet's importance is part of his meaning within his own culture. The connections between different versions of the works that can be included in his oeuvre give a social resonance that goes beyond the meaning of individual texts, in a way that is impossible to reconstruct from any other kind of source.

Frank the Poet has only recently begun to exist as a possible object of knowledge as the result of the effort of two historians, John Meredith and Rex Whalan (1979), who have painstakingly established a corpus of poems (sixteen only, some in several versions) and a historical identity. Their book is cheaply produced and leaves many questions unanswered, but it provides an indispensable starting point for future scholars to build on. They identify Frank the Poet as Francis MacNamara, born 1811, transported for seven years in 1832 for larceny (stealing a plaid). His biography illustrates one of the archetypal patterns of convict life. First there is his Irish nationality, which established him as part of that potent subclass of convicts. His crime is typically trivial compared to his sentence, and Meredith and Whalan cite evidence to suggest that there were political overtones to his case. On reaching the colony his fate showed one of the two outcomes of convictism: not reform and incorporation into useful membership of the new community but stubborn opposition and consistent punishment. His original seven year sentence grew to seventeen years. He was flogged on fourteen occasions, receiving a total of 650 strokes of the lash. He did three and a half years hard labour in irons, and three months on the treadmill. Meredith and Whalan comment on this history: 'He became hardened and more abandoned after each punishment' (1979:4). The main 'crimes' that led to this savage increase in his sentence were running away and 'insubordinate conduct' or 'refusing to work'. To a rational observer from another time it is a minor mystery why he was so foolish as to accumulate such severe penalties for so little cause. Clearly his body was used as a spectacle of punishment, and his mind remained uncorrected and unreformed.

The other aspect of his history was less typical. This is the importance of his role as 'the Poet', a function that was evidently of the utmost importance to him and to his community. It had roots in Celtic tradition, in the role of the Bard in social life. Frank fulfilled this function in the new situation in Australia, where the Irish population needed cohesion and identity. Frank's poems include commemoration of heroes and great victories: his version (or versions) of the lives of the bushrangers Jack Donohoe and Martin Cash contributed to the construction of the bushranger myth. His celebration of the mutiny that led to the capture of the *Cyprus* helped to establish this as a symbolic triumph, an Antipodean *Battleship Potemkin*. The Reverend West writing in Tasmania in 1850 is quoted as acknowledging the effectiveness of this form of protest: 'The prisoners who waged war with society regarded the event with exultation; and long after, a song, composed by a sympathizing poet, was propagated by oral tradition, and sung in chorus around the fires in the interior' (Meredith and Whalan 1979:56).

Marcus Clarke adapted the *Cyprus* incident (and neutralised it, as we will see) in his novel. Ned Kelly incorporated an adaptation of some of Frank's most famous lines in the successful propaganda of his 'Jerilderie letter' of 1879, and Dan Kelly sang a song by Frank the Poet to inspire the beleaguered gang during the siege at Glenrowan. Frank was not a participant in most of the events that he chose to celebrate. His role was more public and almost official: to draw together and shape an alternative mythology, an alternative version of history which was not, however, his own individual creation and which was transmitted and recreated much more actively by his community than would have been the case with written texts in the dominant culture. The scale of their influence is now impossible to determine with any precision, but it clearly had an important role in constructing the images of the convict and the bushranger as potent organising principles for the Irish community, carrying this alternative version of events into the wider community. This oral tradition undoubtedly played its part in preparing the roles of both Ned Kelly and the community which sustained his act of rebellion. More importantly, its reading of those events had a powerful impact on the aftermath of the Kelly trial, and the construction of the Kelly legend itself.

Given the unreliability of the texts that have survived and the impossibility of assigning every word to the conscious hand of the individual poet, traditional literary criticism would find it hard to pronounce on the literary qualities of Frank the Poet. Nonetheless there are many qualities shared by the texts in the corpus, even between different versions of the same text, which give unity to the construction of 'Frank the Poet' as a social fact, irrespective of the mechanics of authorship of individual texts. We will take as an instance one of his most famous poems, called variously 'The Convict's Arrival/Lament' or 'Moreton Bay'.

Moreton Bay was one of the notorious penal settlements, part of the spectacle of punishment that was invoked to control the convict population. The poem includes mention of savage and unjust punishment:

> *For three long years I've been beastly treated,*
> *Heavy irons each day I wore,*
> *My poor back from flogging has been lacerated,*
> *And oft times painted with crimson gore.*

This is a description of a spectacle of punishment which had no intent to reform. But the terms of it seem slightly disappointing, if this was to be a denunciation of the brutality of a convict's life. Frank the

Poet was not sent to Moreton Bay, but he did endure three and a half years (not three) on a chain gang, and his back was indeed 'oft times painted with crimson gore'. But there are far more vivid descriptions of floggings elsewhere: 'I was to leeward of the floggers ... I was two perches from them. The flesh and skin blew in my face as it shook off the cats' wrote Joseph Holt in his journal in 1800, of a savage flogging administered to two Irish convicts suspected of treason, quoted by Hughes (1987:189).

Frank the Poet is deliberately understating the reality of brutality, and from the point of view of a convict bard it is easy to see why. A melodramatic description of flogging would do the work of the enemy, constructing and endorsing the spectacle of punishment. The quaintly colloquial 'beastly treated' (complete with Irish accent) undercuts the force of the image in one way, while the poetic diction of 'oft times painted' neutralises it in another. Physical suffering is thus acknowledged but not made central. The poem goes on to emphasise the 'excessive tyranny' of everyday life, and the demands of 'daily labour' made by these tyrants. Forced labour is presented as a major injustice, and refusal to work (under these conditions) as one of the most significant acts of resistance. And in practice, this was the cause of most of Frank's own floggings. So the poem carries the anti-ideology of convicts, in a situation that explains and legitimates it.

The poem not only records daily life in Moreton Bay, it also recounts the death of a notorious 'tyrant', Captain Logan, who was killed in an ambush by 'a native black'. This act of liberation is attributed to 'kind Providence' not to any convict initiative, and the unproven contemporary assumption that the killer was an Aborigine is kept intact. Again we see that the poet avoids specious consolations, establishing instead a nexus of connections (between convicts, Aborigines and Providence) that is comprehensive and positive but still sufficiently loose so as not to contradict the reality of convict life.

This structure of positive and negative aspects of convict life is set in a complex frame. It begins with the singer:

> *I am a native of the land of Erin,*
> *And lately banished from that lovely shore,*

and traces his journey from Ireland to Sydney Harbour, 'in transient storms'. But on his arrival he receives a further sentence, to Moreton Bay. The singer there meets another prisoner:

> *Early one morning as I carelessly wandered,*
> *By the Brisbane waters I chanced to stray,*
> *I saw a prisoner sadly bewailing,*
> *Whilst on the sunlit banks he lay.*

After this moment of lyricism, with its echo of the Babylonian exile, the rest of the poem contains the inserted narrative of this other prisoner, who as it emerges has done his time and is about to leave Moreton Bay. The two narratives intersect, the arrival and the departure, the prospect of suffering and the fact of survival. The poem concludes on an optimistic note:

> Fellow prisoners be exhilarated,
> Your former sufferings you will not mind,
> For it's when from bondage you are extricated,
> You'll leave those tyrants far behind.

Another version has the more interesting 'We'll leave' in the last line, a complex relationship of identity and difference between new and old prisoners, but both versions construct solidarity and affirmation ('exhilarated') out of the normal conditions of convict existence. The simple diction masks a complex rhetorical strategy, whose reassurance stays close to the problematic reality that it has to work over. We can see why the ballad proved so durable and inspiring.

Marcus Clarke's treatment of convict life has a very different quality to Frank's restraint. His passionate indictment of the system reads like a clarion call on behalf of the convict oppressed, but it was produced after the end of transportation, from a different point of view. Clarke did work with popular traditions, perhaps including texts produced by or derived from Frank the Poet. Meredith and Whalan speculate that he and Frank once met, as recorded in a description by Clarke of a trip through back-alleys of Melbourne in 1868: 'One of the men around the table, a little Irishman, with a face that would make his fortune on the stage, is a well-known character in the low public houses. He is termed the 'Poet', and gains his living by singing his own compositions' (Meredith and Whalan 1979:24). Clarke seems to have been quite impressed by the 'Poet's' skill at improvising ditties (he calls him 'really clever') but he dismisses him as 'an unconscionable drunkard', and Clarke's party, 'having made him temporarily grateful by the bestowal of largesse', continue their tour of this delectable low life. Whether or not this 'poet' was Frank, the passage shows Clarke's ambiguous relationship to the popular tradition, his Bohemian fascination with 'low life' along with his patronising sense of superiority.

The ambiguity of Clarke's position is crucial to his role as the gateway for the convict experience, the mediator of this part of the past into the official Australian consciousness. Clarke's origins were in the legal system not the criminal underworld. His father was a barrister, and the uncle who was in Australia when he emigrated there was a County Court judge. When Clarke arrived in Australia in 1863, transportation had ceased in the eastern colonies of Australia for over a decade, and the abolitionists were mounting their successful assault on the last bastion of the system, Western Australia, which was to end transportation in

1868. So Clarke's work has the passion of a reformer, after the evil had ceased to exist. It celebrates the triumph of the reformers, writing the history that legitimates their victory. At the core of its rewriting is the representation of the essence of transportation as a spectacle of punishment that was lurid, seductive and inadequate. Its subtext, then, is the superiority of bourgeois discipline and bourgeois rationality over the irrationalities of the previous system. This ignores the extent to which transportation itself was a hybrid form that incorporated many of the tendencies of the newer ideology of penal reform.

The novel on which Clarke's fame rests was in fact the end product of a process which itself was significant and revealing. Clarke worked at first with records and first hand reporting, producing journalistic accounts of convictism and its remains. He then drew on this body of materials to write a lengthy serial, which was published without great acclaim between 1870 and 1872. Finally in 1874 he compressed the serial down into the novel itself for which he is now best known. This transformational chain is not simply the record of a creative process. Since the novel was valued so much more highly than the other two texts, we can use the sequence diagnostically, to pinpoint the social functions the novel served, and the forces that it expressed.

As a sample of Clarke's journalism, here is a piece from one of a series on Port Arthur in Tasmania, published in the Melbourne *Argus* of July 1873, describing his visit to the prison there, now converted to an asylum. They are conducted around by a guide, 'Mr Dale', and see the human degradation of the inmates, many of them convicts. Mr Dale gives them a list:

> ... and with a bow (and a touch of rum) he departed.
>
> The list was as follows:—
> | | | |
> |---|---|---|
> | Convicts | 301 | |
> | Do., invalids | 13 | |
> | Do., insane | 8 | |
> | | | 322 |
> | Paupers not under sentence | 166 | |
> | Lunatics do. | 86 | |
> | | | 252 |
> | 26th Jan., 1870. | | 574. |
>
> How shorn of its glories was Babylon! How ill had the world wagged with it since the days of the settlement of Port Phillip in 1835, when the prison owned 911 men and 270 boys, their labour for the year being valued at £16000! (Clarke 1976: 525)

Clarke's target here is the convict system at a moment of transition into the system that succeeded it. The collection of inmates, convicts, lunatics and paupers neatly encapsulates the major categories of deviant that the new system would control (only Aborigines are not represented here). In repeating the list, with a gesture of contempt at the official who is so totally satisfied with this as a strategy of control, Clarke satirises the new mentality, whose bureaucratic indifference to common humanity is as reprehensible as the overt brutality and injustice of the old.

If we turn from this piece of journalism to the narrative of the serial and the novel, we can see a progressive elimination of history and its connections with practices and problems of the present. The serial begins with the evening of 3 May, 1827, but flashbacks in the first book take the story back to the earlier story of the main protagonist, Richard Devine. The serial takes events up to the 1850s, the period of the goldrush and the end of transportation in the eastern colonies. The novel slices off the beginning and end, compressing the earlier narrative into a brief prologue, and eliminating the last section, so that nothing can distract from the pathos of its hero's unjust death, clinging in death as he could not in life to the beautiful woman who in all innocence was responsible for much of his suffering. The openness of the journalism is transformed into the elegant closure of the novel, which intensifies the past in order to colonise it.

The central character of the serial and the novel does not come from any records or observations of Clarke's. Richard Devine is a figure from Gothic literature superimposed upon William Godwin's Caleb Williams. Of wealthy or aristocratic birth, he is sentenced for a crime that he did not commit, and is transported under the name of Rufus Dawes. By putting him at the centre of the novel, Clarke effectively displaced the problematic reality of the experience and ideology of convictism as represented by Frank the Poet. Instead of a vindictive system of justice that discriminates against the poor and the Irish, conflating political and social crimes, Devine/Dawes is the innocent victim of a series of malign coincidences, so extraordinary that no system of justice could be expected to circumvent them, culminating in the heroine, Sylvia, being overcome with amnesia when her story could have saved Rufus before the novel was half-way through. The problem, clearly, is not with the system of justice but the conventions of a genre that legitimates such implausible plots.

The obsessive theme of the genre that attracted Clarke and his audience was legitimacy. He shared the concern of romance with genealogies, and genealogies drive the action of both serial and novel, though he made some significant changes between the two. In the serial, Richard Devine is the reprobate son but rightful heir of Sir Richard Devine, a wealthy merchant. The son is about to be disinherited on behalf of his cousin, Maurice Frere (cf. the French *frere*, brother), when he is accused of a murder that he did not commit. He assumes the name of Rufus Dawes in order to serve his time in Australia without disgracing the family name. Frere also goes out to Australia, as lieutenant, warder, and implacable foe of Dawes/Devine. In this scheme, Devine and Dawes are a doublet, reprobate heir and innocent criminal. This double character also forms a doublet with Frere, as usurping and usurped brother and warder and prisoner. The serial first establishes Australia as the site where values are inverted (so that the criminal is innocent and the warder is illegitimate) but Dawes finally triumphs over adversity, proving his innate worth which shines through even in such adverse conditions. His career thus parallels that of his father, Sir Richard, who likewise rose by sheer ability to a position of great wealth. In this sense the serial can be seen as a romance of high capitalism, and a vindication of the innate abilities of the ascendant bourgeoisie.

The novel shifts these alignments in some important ways. Devine finds out that he is the illegitimate son of an aristocrat, Lord Bellasis, and it is Lord Bellasis that he is now falsely accused of murdering. Frere, still the nephew of Sir Richard, is now a more legitimate heir to Sir Richard's wealth, and his role as nemesis of Dawes is not complicated by the earlier pattern of similarities. The contradictions are now concentrated in Dawes/Devine, who contains in his two personas the extremes of nobility (compromised by illegitimacy) and criminality (and innocence). The action of the novel then eliminates this contradictory structure, since Dawes dies heroically but without inheritance or issue. His vindication is purely symbolic, his life a proof that blood and breeding do matter after all, in even the hell-hole of a penal settlement.

The novel has other doublets. One is the opposition between Rufus Dawes and John Rex, the imitation and the real convict. Rex (some of whose exploits are based on historical incidents, including the *Cyprus* affair) is an unscrupulous survivor. Clarke's narrative gives a realistic portrait of Rex's role, but shifts the centre of attention from the mutiny organised by Rex (the core of Frank the Poet's narrative) to Dawes' selfless act of rescue of Frere and the beautiful Sylvia. In the historical incident on which this was based, the convict Popjoy received a free pardon. Clarke's Frere pleaded successfully on behalf of Rex, and denigrated Dawes. So in this indirect way, Clarke affirms the 'real' convict against Dawes, though Dawes' superior virtue is not in doubt. The alliance/opposition between Frere, Dawes and Rex is also played out in the double construction of woman. The heroine, Sylvia, is loved by both Frere and Dawes, but marries Frere. Golden-haired, virtuous, infantilised, she is opposed to Sarah Purfroy, who is introduced as her mother's maid, with 'black hair, coiled around a narrow and flat head' (a criminal skull) and 'scarlet lips'. The pair represent a form of the Madonna–Whore double, with class affiliations. On the voyage out, Sarah seduces both Rex and Frere (and others), but her primary alliance is with Rex. Clarke's characterisation of both women is two-dimensional but they are structural in his scheme, making a direct connection between the social structures of the class system under conditions of a penal settlement, and this recurring construction of women and sexuality.

In his fiction, Clarke yoked together a European literary tradition—more specifically Victor Hugo's *Les Misérables* (1862)—with a serious historical concern to produce a powerful but contradictory hybrid. It was primarily with the historical background that Clarke made use of his research into convict conditions, and this gave considerable authority to what otherwise would have seemed an attractive but familiar and implausible generic text. The generic elements clearly made the convict experience more palatable, leaving it comfortably on the margins of a pleasurable reading experience. But there was also a significant interaction between historical case and novelistic conventions that further subverted the effects of the historical case.

To show how this worked in practice we will consider the following passage, a reflection on Rufus Dawes' despair after six years in the colony:

> Is it possible to imagine, even for a moment, what an innocent man, gifted with ambition, endowed with power to love and to respect, must have suffered during one week of such punishment? ... We know that were we chained and degraded, fed like dogs, employed as beasts of burden, driven to our daily toil with threats and blows, and herded with wretches among whom all that savours of decency and manliness is held in an open scorn, we should die, perhaps, or go mad ... No human creature could describe to what depth of personal abasement and self-loathing one week of such a life would plunge him ... Imagine such torment endured for six years! (Clarke 1969:116)

We have compressed the exposition somewhat, because the passion of Clarke's denunciation is not in question. His plea for compassion for such as Rufus Dawes includes some of the grievances mentioned by Frank the Poet. But there are other grievances, the climax of his litany, that had no place in Frank's poem. The contempt for the 'wretches' with whom one must be herded would include Frank and all his companions, who did not see that as part of their degradation at all. This victim is totally helpless, entirely passive, without dignity but at last without guilt because of the sheer scale of his sufferings. Frank and his convict fellows retained lyricism and wit and self-respect, the capacity to endure and even to resist. If Dawes were typical, then Clarke's compassion would be safe, because such a convict could represent no threat. But of course, he is not typical. He is innocent (the term accepts that there is a single moral system which normally underpins the legal system, except in aberrant cases like the present). He is also like 'us', the comfortable, secure middle-class readers who are only tentatively asked to 'imagine' this situation, not to see it or enter into it. Clarke carefully constructs the reading position from which the whole novel is viewed, entirely on one side of the class divide. The focus on the middle-class Devine/Dawes, then, gives the *frisson* of engaging in an imaginary experience which gains its power precisely from the strength of its repudiation of real convicts, provoking a reaffirmation of the solid certainties of bourgeois existence.

As is to be expected with so successful a work, Clarke's novel performed a number of distinct functions with elegant simultaneity. At a single stroke it put Australia's convict origins on the agenda while constructing a melodramatic substitute for historical understanding. Readers relied on Clarke's genuine if partial research into the history of convictism to trust his novelistic account and inquire no further. The reassuring lesson from the ghastly past was that the present was now much better. The complex meaning of transportation as a penal strategy was simplified and encoded as a pure symbol of the past, obscuring its real connections with carceral regimes in Clarke's present, precisely at the time when those regimes were beginning to enlarge their scope.

But this strategy of displacement is also Clarke's strength since melodrama and sentimentalism rendered through essentially Gothic categories of genre becomes, for the Australian, a means of by-passing the tyranny of history. In reconstructing history through melodrama the legend of brutalisation, hitherto rendered in realist texts through an excessive deferral towards historical truth is transformed into the text of the colonised. If history can be legitimated only by the guardians of its 'truth-conditions', the English aristocracy, then it is only through explicitly anti-historical forms that the merit of the colonised could be given expression.

In addition to this complex ideological work, Clarke was able to restate the long-standing Australian concern with legitimacy. Dawes represented in a dramatic form the experience of the early settlers, their sense of dispossession from the old land and alienation in the new. His real innocence was as important in constructing this effect as his savage punishment. His acceptance of a guilt that was not his meant that he could expiate the guilt of others who could feel equally innocent yet still be in need of expiation. The serial allowed him to live and prosper after his expiation was complete, merging in with those he had justified. But that personal benefit detracted from his capacity to act as a scapegoat for the whole society. As Clarke came to realise when he revised his text, middle-class Australia had more need of a purified Dawes locked safely in the past than a reformed Dawes living on into the present. And if injustice has to be acknowledged in the foundation event of Australia's history, better that it be done by a Marcus Clarke than by such as Frank the Poet.

THE BUSHRANGER MYTH

As a social phenomenon the Australian bushranger was an instance of what Hobsbawn (1969) called the 'social bandit', a figure who rose from an oppressed and subordinated group and whose 'criminal' career had political overtones and a large measure of popular support. Ned Kelly has entered into Australian mythology as the archetypal bushranger, but it is a fact with its own significance that Kelly was the last of the bushrangers, the end as well as the symbol of the tradition.

In doing justice to the meaning of the bushranger it is especially important to both recognise and go beyond any simplistic dichotomy between 'fact' and 'myth'. Throughout the eight decades when bushrangers flourished it is always possible to question the purity of their 'real' motives, and discover desperate or brutal acts that would tarnish the romantic image that has been constructed on their behalf. It is also the case that never in this period were bushrangers a numerically large group, able on their own to constitute a serious threat to existing authorities, though some of the outbreaks, that of the Kellys included, did give rise to considerable anxieties. They were neither entirely noble, nor really effective in immediate terms.

But an analysis in these terms misrepresents the nature of the phenomenon itself, and uses inappropriate means to analyse it. At its core the bushranger phenomenon was always important primarily as a symbolic mode of action, a set of texts enacted with actual bodies and actual bullets, a hyper-real form of political theatre. The key events themselves were performance texts, the site where prior texts intersected and around which subsequent texts wove their further acts of meaning-construction. Things would not have happened as they did (whatever that was) but for these prior texts, and the performance-text was neither stable nor powerful enough to control the meanings that came to be assigned to it. What we have, then, is not a gap between truth and fiction, but complex processes in the social construction of meaning, processes which had material agents and conditions and effects at every point, and a history that is not without significance.

The bushranger was a spectacle of resistance constructed from below, and it is with this point of origination that we must begin. As an example of the phenomenon we will take the short career of 'Bold Jack Donohoe', an Irishman who was transported at the age of 18, convicted of 'intending a felony' according to Meredith, who suspects that it was of a political nature (Meredith 1960:1). In 1828, aged 21, he was indicted on a charge of highway robbery but managed to escape. He remained free for the next two years, but was shot dead on September 1, 1830. During this period he achieved no spectacular successes as a robber to match the Kelly gang's exploits, but the powerlessness of the authorities to capture him was reported enthusiastically, as evidence of their incompetence and the depth of popular support. With his death the interest in him did not die. On the contrary, he became the central figure in a series of popular ballads that became associated with the name of Frank the Poet, part of a broader complex that included perhaps the most famous of all Australian ballads, 'The Wild Colonial Boy' in its many versions. At precisely the same time, his fate was the subject of the first important dramatic work written by an Australian, Charles Harpur's *The Tragedy of Donohoe* of 1835, later revised over a 30-year period to become *Stalwart the Bushranger* of 1867. This set of texts (including the life of Donohoe as itself a text) makes up an exemplary as well as a historically important instance, and we will look at the interrelations from both points of view.

With the ballad tradition we face again the seeming problem of deciding which text we look at, and perhaps which text did Frank the Poet really write. But the need to suppose that Frank was responsible for only one of them (as assumed by Meredith and Whalan in their otherwise excellent edition) is as unjustified as the supposition that Clarke or Harpur could have written only one of the versions of their text that survive. There are many differences in the surviving ballads of Donohoe, but there are two levels where we find recurring patterns. One is the overall structure. Some versions include some of Donohoe's early triumphs, but all focus primarily on his death and his defiant last words. And weaving through the Donohoe and Wild Colonial Boy texts there are recurring phrases, nomadic formulae wandering from poem to poem almost disregarding their context, with every fresh recurrence signifying their truth and their immortality.

As an example of such formulaic phrases, here is one line in the version that Meredith and Whalan attribute to Frank the Poet:

He'd scorn to live in slavery or be humbled to the crown.

This phrase recurs in versions of 'The Wild Colonial Boy', like a defining property rather than an incidental description. This gives it a much greater salience in the construction of the narrative and its social meaning, along with another such phrase, 'We'll fight but not surrender, our freedom to maintain'. The narrative becomes a fluid setting for the repetition of these phrases, rather than the phrases relying on the narrative to prove them true.

This quality, a typical resource of oral narrative, accounts for the paradoxical effect of these texts, which seem to dwell on the moment of failure of the act of rebellion but communicate instead the opposite feeling, a sense of optimistic celebration. It's no coincidence that the death or capture of notorious bushrangers, whether Donohoe or Kelly, by no means cast their admirers into a state of passivity or despair. This kind of text, in its verbal and enacted forms, could incorporate defeat and death effortlessly and endlessly, because the repetitive form of the celebration guaranteed that the defiance likewise would always recur. By foregrounding the moment of apparent defeat it was able to negate it, using it to carry on the message of freedom. In this way it constructed a spectacle that was designed in advance to negate the official spectacle of punishment, by refusing the official spectacle the right to end the show.

Harpur's version of the myth came from a complex point in the social structure. Harpur was a literate and educated free citizen of radical views, but he was also the illegitimate son of a former Irish convict, an emancipist who for a while made good in the new colony, proof of the ability of the system to deliver reformation. We would expect a profound ambivalence in his treatment of the Donohoe story, and this is indeed what we find, within each text and between them over time. The first text is called *The Tragedy of Donohoe*, the last one *Stalwart the Bushranger*. We see even in the title the transformation of the historical Donohoe to the abstract type 'Stalwart', an ever greater distance from the originating Irish performance text. But even in the first version the term 'Tragedy' distances the form from the popular ballad tradition of a Frank the Poet. This text included a mixture of blank verse and prose. Harpur was advised to increase the amount of prose, but instead he turned it all into blank verse. English classic literary texts overwhelmed traces of the Irish popular tradition in Stalwart, in particular Marlowe's *Dr Faustus* and Milton's *Paradise Lost*, which between them provided the inspiration for the central character as well as much of the diction.

In this and many other ways, Harpur constructed a fissured text. Where the achievement of the traditional ballad was to link activity and passivity, success and failure into a single persuasive unity, Harpur wrote along the lines of cleavage in the myth. His working-class Irish hero has the mental baggage of a member of the English middle-class, and the cast-list is full of split or doubled forms. In the earlier version Donohoe is opposed to the virtuous William, a respectable settler and the lover of Mary. Donohoe falls in love with this Mary, and out of envy at William's good fortune he kills him. But Donohoe is himself loved by another Mary, the daughter of Mrs O'Brien, a small-time criminal. The opposition between the two men corresponds to the two responses to convictism (though William is not specified as an emancipist). The sense that these two are alternatives is reinforced by Harpur's renaming of William as Abel, in the later version, thus constructing Donohoe/Stalwart as Cain. The two women are both identical (both named Mary) yet opposed, as a mirror image of the opposition between the men. But although in these terms this seems a repetition of the classic opposition between citizen and criminal, damned whore and virtuous woman, Donohoe/Stalwart is not debased or evil, only desperate, and Mary O'Brien (later Fence) is by no means a whore. On the contrary, Donohoe feels that she also is too good for him in his present state.

Harpur's radicalism emerges in the critical stance that he takes towards the forces of the law. In the *Tragedy*, these are represented by the venal constable Bomebard, the hypocritical Canterbury and the implacable chief officer Dreadnought. In the later *Stalwart*, Canterbury becomes 'Cant', and the cast also includes Roger Tunbelly, JP and Wealthiman Woolsack Esq, JP, whose qualities are clear enough from their names. *Stalwart* contains vigorous satire at the expense of all these except for Dreadnought, who is competent and effective in spite of the quality of his troops. So the forces of the law are split along the same lines as Donohoe/Stalwart and his women: three sets of parallel contradictions locked into a symmetrical pattern. Instead of the monolithic unity of Donohoe in the ballad tradition, every entity in Harpur's text carries its self-cancelling shadow wherever it goes. In the ballad tradition, defiance and defeat alternate in an eternal dance. In Harpur, the ambiguity of agents is so acute that every action carries contradictory meanings. Donohoe's resistance is both justified and criminal, and his crimes are also punishments. It is a very different kind of moral universe from the world of the ballads. Since it works over the raw materials of the bushranger legend, in some respects it is an attack on it, demolishing it from the inside as well as from the outside. So it is interesting to note that at the time it was written, noone wanted it. It was not performed as a play, and it made no inroads at all on the thriving oral tradition. It was without influence and effect in its time. But it also laid down patterns which can be seen in works in the subsequent tradition.

Here the crucial date is 1880, when Ned Kelly was captured and executed. The remaining years saw the final political accommodation with bushrangerism, with trials of police, promotions and demotions, and new policies towards the disaffected supporters of the Kellys. Ned Kelly's superb performance was the spectacle that ended the possibility of a repeat, just as Marcus Clarke's novel only a few years earlier marked the end of the spectacle of convictism by constructing its definitive form. Boldrewood/Thomas Alexander Browne's extremely successful *Robbery Under Arms* of 1888 played a role in relation to bushrangers similar to the relation between Clarke's novel and the convict system. Because it was so positive about bushrangers (while not allowing them to be seen to escape capture and punishment) it acquired the same authority as Clarke did with his negative image of the penal system. In both cases, this was only possible, and greeted with such relief, because the community believed that the problem was now resolved. Thus their relation to the performance texts to which they referred differed from that of earlier works. The ballads and even Harpur were part of a single textual complex that included performance texts, i.e. 'reality' itself, where literature could affect the meaning of 'reality' and vice versa, in a dialectic process. After 1880 the definitive images of the bushranger and the convict could be endorsed from above, undisturbed by the threat of revolt from below.

Boldrewood worked with the romantic image of the bushranger, appropriating it on behalf of a progressive politics. But the figure itself had other possible structures of meaning, which allowed it to be used as Harpur had done, as a way of exploring major fissures in Australian social life. One example of this strategy is *Outlaw and Lawmaker*, written by Rosa Praed and published in 1893. Praed's novel deals with a character who is totally split: Morres Blake, Baron Coola, member of the Legislative Council and Colonial Secretary, is also Captain Moonlight, a bushranger whose illegal gains go towards the Irish cause to which he is fanatically faithful. But Praed's concern is with women rather than men, and Blake/Moonlight is only one counter that she uses to explore the contradictions of women's position in 19th century Australian society. Her central character is not Blake but Elsie, who is in love with Blake but is pursued by a large collection of other men, virtually every male who meets her, as it seems. The attractions of Blake compete with the attractions of other 'lawmakers', Frank Hallett, virtuous and without a stain on his past, and Trant, who is also Captain Moonlight's less idealistic offsider. Hallett proposes honourable marriage, while Trant abducts her.

Blake is implausibly ideal in both roles, as lover and as romantic outlaw with a dark past, but he plays a part in Praed's exploration of the possibilities facing a young woman of marriageable age. The sexual excitement he represents is cancelled out by the dark secret. Hallett's worthy love is without passion. Blake contrasts the two as a 'shortlived rapture (which) might be worth more than a long married life of decorous commonplace conventional happiness—a Frank Hallett kind of happiness' (Praed, 1988:114). Trant's passion is more urgent than Blake's noble selflessness; aggressive, acquisitive and dangerous. Elsie's life, during the period covered by the novel, is a frenetic whirl of seduction and resistance, as the males circle like sharks in a feeding frenzy. She is not exactly a whore, though she is rather unchaperoned much of the time. But after the death of Blake, her only love, the novel summarises the rest of her life in one page, as a celibate existence lived out in faithful devotion to the dead Blake.

There is some parallel here with Rosa Praed's own life. Praed too had a period of hectic gaiety between 1867 and 1872, as the daughter of a widowed member of parliament with duties to entertain. In 1872, aged 21, she finally acquiesced in her father's pressure on her to marry, and found that marriage to the wealthy Campbell Praed was an oppressive form of existence. There was a stark contrast between the courtship stage, where she was expected to be attractive to all males, and the marriage stage, when she must be faithful and subordinate to one (who felt himself to be under no such obligation). It was this opposition between the roles that women were socialised into that underlay the polarisation into madonna/whore. Praed's novel has the merit that it explores this opposition from the point of view of a woman's experience, instead of seeing it as purely a construct of male attitudes. It is the corresponding split in male identity that is projected in the characterisation in her work. And here the image of the bushranger lay ready to hand, ambivalent and yoked to his double the lawmaker, allowing her to externalise and express her own sense of self-division and ambivalence as woman.

By the 1890s, then, the myth of the bushranger was no longer an active part of the social and political struggle of a distinct group of oppressed people. No longer anchored in that struggle, it was available as a metaphoric resource, to express a contradictory relationship to contradictions of power throughout society. In plays such as Stewart's *Ned Kelly* of 1943, in paintings such as Nolan's famous Kelly series, in films dealing with Ned Kelly or in successful TV series such as *Ben Hall*, the bushranger myth poses general problems of justice and the role of the individual caught up in an unjust society. The specific themes that can be thought through this figure are various: Nolan's concerns are very different from Rosa Praed's. But there is one dimension that is almost always necessarily lacking from later uses of the myth: the political dimension that in many obvious and less obvious forms was always part of the early traditional use. There is only one exception to this, but a significant one. The Aboriginal oral tradition celebrated its trickster figures, its unsuccessful heroes of resistance, in similar ways and with similar strategies to the Irish bards, and that resistance was a fact of experience within recent memory. Colin Johnson/Mudrooroo Narogin's *Long Live Sandawara* of 1978 engaged in a task similar to that faced by Harpur over 100 years before, coming to terms with the oral culture and political struggles of his people using the dominant literary modes of the day.

THE USES OF DEVIANCY

Historians dispute the value of the convict heritage, and the extent to which it has come down to the present. Russel Ward (1958) is at one extreme, with his influential claim that the convict experience contributed its brand of anti-authoritarianism to the Australian ethos, what he called 'The Australian Legend'. Humphrey McQueen (1970) at the other extreme is contemptuous of actual convicts and unimpressed by claims that they have any continuing influence. Robert Hughes, in his massive study of the convict era, is seemingly more confused in his assessment. On the one hand he talks of 'the defensive, static, levelling, two-class hatred that came out of convictry', but he also doubts the influence of the 'convict past' today. 'Thus, it made Australians cynical about Authority; or else it made them conformists.' Then he has further thoughts: 'Perhaps there are roots of social conduct that wind obscurely back to the convict era, and the familiar Australian habit of cursing authority behind the hand while truckling to its face may well be one of them' (Hughes 1987:596). There is only one legacy that he is sure of: that the stain of convictism helped Australians to forget the past and replace it with images of 'grand guignol', epitomised by the work of Marcus Clarke.

Hughes's uncertainty in fact reflects the contradictions in the nature of convictism and its representation over time, better than either of the extreme positions on its own. The continuing relevance of the image of the convict/criminal comes from the issues of carcerality as outlined by Foucault as they play on the present. In Foucault's account, the disciplinary system has not only triumphed in the restricted realm of the penal system, it has now become ubiquitous. 'Is it surprising that prisons resemble factories, schools, barracks, hospitals, which all resemble prisons?' he asks (1979:228). Secondly he suggests that the apparent failure of the prison system to eliminate crime in fact should be seen as a systemic success, producing 'delinquency . . . . a politically or economically less dangerous—and, on occasion, usable—form of illegality . . . . producing the delinquent as a pathologised subject' (1979:277). David Ireland in *The Unknown Industrial Prisoner* of 1971 portrayed Australia in these terms, as a single continuous penal colony, an Australian dystopia in the tradition of Orwell's *1984*.

This is a system which could produce docile delinquency in all Australians, viewed as the inhabitants now of an open prison that covers the whole continent. We can see why Hughes very properly doubts whether the characteristic Australian double-think towards authority should be blamed entirely on the convict past. But the continuity also allows the forms from that past to function powerfully into the present, both as the instruments of control and as the focus of resistance. And part of the tradition is an effective strategy for appropriating history, replacing the surveillance of the past by various spectacles, a kind of screen memory to use the Freudian term. But none of these devices is new, or irresistible. Throughout its history the construction of deviance has always been contested, and this history of effective resistance has also left its traces on the tradition.

The double messages of this open prison produce the classic symptoms of paranoia as described by Gregory Bateson (1973). In a lighter vein, the first chapter in *How to Survive in Australia*, a popular satire of the Australian character by Robert Treborlang, is entitled 'For a Start . . . Don't Ask Questions'. Treborlang illustrates his proposition, that 'asking questions is the one thing a true Australian never does', with the following anecdote:

Let's say you are having lunch with some new friends at the factory cafeteria or at the office where you have found employment. Excited and curious, you decide to get things going by making what you believe to be innocuous conversation.

YOU: What do you folks do on weekends?
THEM: (An embarrassed silence and interchange of looks followed by an outbreak of mysterious unease).

Without knowing it, you have just made the following thoughtless allegations:
1 What gay bars do you frequent?
2 Don't your Alcoholics Anonymous meetings interfere with your weekend social life?
3 Do you happen to own a truck that could help me move my things on Sunday? (Treborlang 1985: 9–10)

Treborlang's satire represents the typical Australian as a rampant paranoiac, misinterpreting the most innocent of questions. What he himself seems not to notice (like other anthropologists collecting data on other exotic tribes) is that his question and manner are not entirely simple. There is some contradiction between being 'excited and curious' and trying to ask an 'innocuous question'. Then there is the curious word 'folks' (in the plural, too) implying that his hearers have the quaintly primitive status of proper objects for the anthropological gaze. The general present of 'do', along with the plural 'weekends', in Treborlang's mind removes the question from the dangers of particularity, but instead they suggest the greater intrusion of a sociological survey. These people are being asked, by an obviously over-educated factory worker, to summarise the pattern of their lives for some act of surveillance that has not been declared. Treborlang is right to notice the paranoiac overinterpretation, but he fails to recognise his own double messages, of power and pseudo-friendliness, that have provoked it.

This text comes from a satire on Australian life in general. The same prohibition on asking questions is emphasised in a text about prison life, Gabrielle Carey's *Just Us* of 1984. Gabrielle Carey fell in love with Terry Haley, a long-term prisoner in Parramatta jail, when she was visiting the prison. *Just Us* was an autobiographical account of the relationship. For a long time Terry totally refused to answer any questions even from his lover. In a text included in the book he describes the double message system in a modern jail that gives rise to such paranoia: 'You'd think if they really believed in all this crime and punishment shit that they would tell you—so you'd know when you'd been bad (by their books) and you wouldn't do it again—so the whole system would be put to work the way they reckon it works. But that's far too rational for them. Far too fucking rational' (Carey 1984:17).

The result of this contradiction in the very aims of the system, as it is perceived by the prisoner in the modern penal system, is what he calls paranoia: 'In gaol you get to develop this sort of sixth sense because everyone's so paranoid, you can't find things out through the normal channels. Noone trusts anyone else enough to talk about stuff truthfully. So you have to feel everything. And you get pretty good' (Carey 1984:18).

Haley here describes the radical distrust that generates paranoia, emanating from above, in the double messages that express the double ideology of the modern penal system, and also affect communication from below. He also illustrates the kind of pared-down language which evolves to meet the need to communicate in these conditions: apparent vagueness, behind which multiple meanings lurk, and a rigid, formulaic repetitiveness, in which whole clauses reappear unchanged in new contexts. Along with this seeming rigidity and simplicity goes an extraordinary sensitivity to under-messages and a dangerous trust in the ability to read them. If Treborlang had read this text, he might have understood the aberrant response of his almost-mates.

Haley as described in this book had been constructed as a classic 'delinquent'. First institutionalised at the age of nine for 'illegal use of a bicycle', he had spent only one year outside surveillance up to the age of 35, when the book was published. The pattern seems hardly changed from the days of Frank the Poet. But if Haley seems to be a typical 'delinquent', Carey his biographer and lover is much less typical. In 1979 she co-authored the very popular novel *Puberty Blues* with Kathy Lette, and she met Terry for the first time in that year. The novel describes the encounter of two girls with the surfing subculture of a Sydney beach. The rules and rituals of this antiworld are implacable and sexist, a persuasive and cohesive alternative to school discipline, a mirror image of the dominant hierarchical structures. The narrative follows the initiation of the two girls into this world, and their progress to an autonomous existence as women, outside the oppressive and ultimately suicidal world of the surfies.

Surfies are one of the modern faces of the Australian legend, carrying on the long tradition of defying authority and the values of the work ethic. But Carey and Lette deconstruct this group's claims to dissidence by adopting a stance as outsiders in this world of outsiders: as females who are oppressed by the traditional sexism of the Australian male. In the book they frame the narrative with another form of discourse: academic social theory. The novel begins with a description of the surfie rule system governing the beaches of Sydney, in the tone of a 'participant observer' as anthropologists would put it. It ends with an appendix listing the fates of the members of the surfie group, mostly a sorry tale of drug abuse and delinquency, like a social worker's case file being brought up to date. The film of the book dropped this alienating conclusion. It showed the two girls walking off together, two free individuals, after they have learned to surf and just demonstrated their skill to the amazed surfies and their chicks. This jaunty feminist conclusion was made for a popular film in the 1980s, but in spite of such differences there is the same fluid pattern of contradictions in the stance of Carey (as author or coauthor of both *Puberty Blues* and *Just Us*) and in *Puberty Blues* (as book and film). The three texts have an intertextual relationship that is analogous to the oral tradition of Frank the Poet. In their different ways they all show the ambivalent fascination felt by 'straight' outsiders for the frighteningly recognisable inverted world of the officially delinquent.

The fascination can be seen in the success of two TV series of the 1970s and 80s, *Prisoner* and *A Country Practice*. *Prisoner* attracted huge ratings and equally intense opposition from anti-television lobbyists for its subversive construction of the antiworld of a woman's prison. The women prisoners were sympathetic characters, totally opposed to the 'screws' though in a more gentle way than in male prison or convict drama since 1788. The locale allowed an audience including many children to make the Foucauldian connection between prison and school, and explore issues of power and authority in a stark and demystified form: precisely the legacy of the convict tradition. And for that reason lobbyists committed to the ideal of benign discipline were hostile to it. *A Country Practice*, however, has had no problems of acceptability. It is set in an idealised country town, where its stable, loveable and caring characters deal with one social problem after another, each carried by a single representative guest 'delinquent'. The challenge to the Wandin Valley community and to the audience is to expand its sympathies to recognise the humanity and the pain of each kind of delinquent, so that they can all be reincorporated into a caring community. Although *Prisoner* was the earlier of the two programs and is no longer a competitor for top ratings against *A Country Practice*, it would be unwise to see a definitive change as having occurred. The two programs represent two alternative attitudes to the image of the 'delinquent' which have coexisted for 200 years already, and are likely to last longer yet.

There is, then, not a single image of the criminal or the delinquent that defines Australian culture. On the contrary what the culture contains is a rich and complex meaning-resource, one that allows a range of different issues of power and authority to be explored or mystified or both. And certain dimensions of the experience of incarceration offer in a usefully heightened or extreme form some of the most problematic elements of the Australian consciousness, elements that are not of course unique to Australians. It is in this respect that the experience of Aboriginal people comes to have an unacknowledged function for other Australians. Rowley (1970) and others have documented the ravages of forced institutionalisation on Aboriginal society, when the term 'Aboriginal Protection' was enshrined into the very Acts of parliament which legitimated a whole range of punitive actions towards Aboriginal people 'for their own good'. Hardly an Aborigine today is not scarred in some way by this still recent history. The carceral mind is one of the central themes of Australian culture today, and Aborigines as a group are Australia's experts on carcerality.

It is undoubtedly an overwhelming theme, directly or indirectly, in contemporary Aboriginal writing. Many works deal with life on Aboriginal reserves. Jack Davis in *No Sugar* reconstructed a traumatic but typical incident on the Moore River reserve in Western Australia in the 1930s. But his more recent *Barungin* of 1989 takes his exploration of the theme one step further. The play was written as a reaction to the death of John Pat, victim of police brutality and one of the triggers to the Commonwealth Government Royal Commission into Black Deaths in Custody. That commission had a brief that was similar to those of many inquiries that have been held since 1788, all investigating spectacular instances when the penal system has lapsed from its professed ideals and standards of custodial concern.

Most of Davis's play, however, seems to ignore the basic issues of law and justice that such a commission must address. He depicts a typical Aboriginal family, with a typical dependence on the welfare system, and a typical number of its members in trouble with the law for minor offences. The play seems a realist text, characterised by humour and insight into aspirations and tensions of such a group. Then towards the end of the play Peter, a young Aborigine, is released from gaol, and he goes off with a group to a party. His younger brother, meanwhile, has engaged in some petty theft, accumulating an excessive stock of electronic equipment. His uncle, meaning to protect him, puts the stolen gear into the boot of a car—the car that Peter takes. The uncle's well-intentioned if slightly criminal act then has catastrophic consequences. The police find the gear and presume Peter's guilt, and in the process of their pursuing their enquiries, Peter is killed. The play changes dramatically from social realism to tragedy. It closes with the mother of Peter intoning the list of black deaths in custody that were matters of public record at the time of writing, but she goes back to Yagan, the Black resistance leader who was executed in Perth in 1831.

The reading of the list is clearly an overt political statement, reinforcing Jack Davis's message about black deaths in custody. But the form of his play at first seems curiously indirect to support this theme and the final speech. What he shows is a connection between crime and punishment as oblique as in Clarke's novel, yet inexorable. There is a crime— Peter's brother's theft, and his uncle's complicity—and there is a punishment, the catastrophically excessive death of Peter, the wrong punishment for the wrong person. But the real 'crime' is different: the whole family are being punished for their Aboriginality, for the whole complex of ways of coping that this group has had to evolve to survive in White society. The play constructs the experience of this mentality, where there is an inexhaustible requirement to expiate a crime which has been in fact committed against, not by, these people, and a threat of

141

punishment hangs over every unassimilated head that is Aboriginal, as the price of its Aboriginality.

The shattering force with which the cataclysm descends on the very ordinary household recreates this experience for the nonAboriginal audience as well. In a White family this would be a paranoid view. In Aboriginal society it is an instance of the contradictory logic of the system under which they have lived for so long. It is also tinged with paranoia, however, just as the world of the Irish convicts and modern prisoners was and is both true to its conditions and yet self-destructive in its excess. That is why the form of Jack Davis's conclusion is so effective. The list is the product of another discourse, the discourse of the dominant legal system announcing its own inadequacies, and it is spoken by an Aboriginal woman with full knowledge and control. Not only does it have polemical force through its acknowledged 'truth': it is also the kind of nonequivocating discourse that is the only safeguard for Aborigines and nonAborigines alike, against the endemic Australian condition of paranoia and double-think.

Davis's play allows us to see the curious irrelevance as well as the importance of history for understanding how images of crime and punishment function in Australian literature and culture. The Australian 'criminal past' for Australians today is an abstract but potent metaphor for a kind of legal double-think, a crime that is not a crime, committed by society on criminals, by warders on prisoners and by the system on warders, threatening the destruction and purification of society itself. The events that happened and the repressive apparatus that was constructed in the early days of the colony had repercussions at the time, as confused and contradictory as the system itself, with structural consequences that have continued till now. But the force of the metaphor in the present comes from the schizogenic processes by which delinquency is still constructed and managed, in terms of which social life is organised by the double message of the disciplinary regime. Australia demands its images of convicts and bushrangers, criminals and victims, if only for the sake of its collective sanity.

7 Reading the country

From the beginning of the colonial period, the landscape of Australia has been a dominant presence in art and literature. For much of this time, Australian social life has been located in its few cities rather than in the countryside. The contradiction involved here is so massive and so obvious that many have noticed it, but usually with a kind of puzzlement. 'I propose instead to advance the view that this preoccupation with landscape has been largely responsible for the creation and maintenance of a false consciousness of what it is to be Australian' remarks Professor Bernard Smith, the doyen of Australian art historians (1976:87), implying that artists have unfortunately mislead the majority of their fellow citizens, while not really meaning to. We need to look deeper than this into the reasons for the contradiction, understanding its sources and different forms in the past and its continuing functions in the present. At issue is perhaps the most important single problem facing the student of Australian culture; how so many people have been able to say such silly things for so long about the nature of Australia itself.

Smith is, of course, absolutely right that this 'false consciousness' is a crucial component of Australian consciousness and Australian identity. That has been its function in the past and that is its function today, mediated through advertising and the mass media and sustaining the burgeoning tourist industry, as well as affecting many other aspects of Australian political and social life. Our concern in this chapter will be with its operations in the fields of literature and art, but it is part of the everyday sense of themselves that most Australians share, in spite of being so manifestly absurd when looked at more closely.

One function of this contradiction is to legitimate the illegitimate. As we have argued, the prior rights of the Aboriginal peoples are the largest barrier to nonAborigines' sense of their right to be here. Because of this, constructions of Australianness have tacitly deferred to and incorporated the basis of this competing right. Aboriginal possession of the land over which they roamed was affirmed through their intimate knowledge of it: 'Reading the Country' as Stephen Muecke has called it, in the title of a recent book (Benterrak, Muecke and Roe 1984). So the new possessors must claim to know and love the land as much as those they dispossessed. In Patrick White's *Voss* Laura Trevelyan defends the German explorer's rights to the land in these terms: 'It is his by right of vision' (White 1957:32). For contemporary Australians, tourism and the practices of leisure provide many opportunities to (re)create a national identity, compressed into week-ends and the four weeks of annual leave. But over and above this there is the further need, met by art and literature and other cultural forms, to *represent* the country, to provide a set of images that can substitute for this country that they have an obligation to read and know and to possess, from the inconvenient but secure base of their suburban homes.

But these images are not constructed purely out of a need for legitimation. In the history of images of the country we can note two main ways they have been used in art and literature. Sometimes images of the country are provided as the context for human actions, and in these cases the context (location, setting, landscape) provides a complex comment on the main action being represented. On other occasions, images of the country function as transformations of people or aspects of people (e.g. women or Aborigines, fear or desire). In these cases the interaction between characters and the transformed landscape as itself a major actor, is often the main action in the narrative. Both these kinds of use of the landscape are very widespread. Both carry important social and ideological meanings. But they do so in very different ways, requiring very different modes of reading. In the rest of this chapter we will try to clarify this set of differences, and show how the two modes of reading work in practice.

NEGATIONS OF THE REAL

From the early days of the colony artists and scientific writers like Cook or Banks or Darwin were capable of accurate and realistic depictions, but it is generally agreed that it was not until the 1850s that artists and writers in the mainstream culture represented 'the country' in convincingly realist terms, though they claimed to be trying hard to do so. The definitive triumph of this realism was deferred until the 1890s, when nationalists used this as proof that the nation was at last ready to exist in its own right. But this summary of the dominant content of the images does not reveal what was the significance of these less than 'real' earlier images, what forces acted through them, and what functions they served. Shadowing this apparent history of the triumph of the real is an exactly contrary history, which helps to account for all the contradictions that have bedevilled attempts to describe Australian attitudes to the physical landscape. This second history is a slow, imperceptible emptying out of the reality of the land, not least at moments when the reality seems to be its most obvious characteristic.

As a first exemplary instance of the dynamics of this process as it acted over time we will look at the following prose text, part of a letter written by Georgiana Molloy, an early settler in Western Australia, to a friend in Scotland, Helen ('Nelly') Story, who had just lost a child:

> I was indeed grieved, my dear Nelly, to hear of the poor infant's demise ... I could truly sympathise with you, for language refuses to utter what I experienced when mine died in my arms in this dreary land, with no one but Molloy near me. O, I have gone through much and more than I would ever suffer anyone to do again. I fear—I need not say fear—I know, I have not made the use of those afflictions that God designed. It was so hard I could not see it was in Love. I thought I might have had one little bright object left me to solace all the hardships and privations I endured and have still to go through. It was wicked and I am not now thoroughly at peace ... Your dear little one, did you call the dear infant after me? Mary told me of your affectionate kindness in thinking of me. The one I called after dear Mary was like 'a little angel'. Its grave, though sodded with British clover, looks so singular and solitary in this wilderness, of which I can scarcely give you an idea. (Hasluck 1955:73)

We have quoted extensively in order to give a context to the sentence that we will discuss, the last one. Georgiana's dead daughter, Mary, had died three years earlier. According to Hasluck this is the first time she had been able to mention it to Nellie, one of her closest friends. The mechanisms of suppression here operate in an obvious way: the not mentioning of the daughter's death is not of course a sign of Georgiana's indifference, but of the opposite. Similarly it is not to be supposed that she did not 'see' the 'dreary land' when she planted the sods of 'British clover' on the grave. On the contrary, the oppressive site of reality was located in that dreary land, and the British clover was invoked purely to negate it. But it could not be successful, as she also indicates clearly: the grave looked 'singular and solitary' in the actual landscape, whose actuality was not in doubt.

The pattern of negations at work in this everyday text can be read against the model of the Hartz thesis. Georgiana Molloy is and perceives herself to be a fragment, part of a social whole now constituted and sustained only by the written discourse of her letter. Her actual everyday material existence and its context is a brutal negation of this social whole, a negation so total that most of it is inexpressible in the shared language which holds it together. But for whatever motives, Georgiana herself is the agent of that negation, or at least she endorses its action. So the British clover (symptomatic of a whole set of markers of Britishness) is not and is not perceived to be a full presence. Rather, it is only a double negative, and it has the modality and truth value that goes with that form: the flimsy denial of a truth that overwhelmingly breaks through its pretexts. It is consistent with this that Georgiana Molloy later became an indefatigable collector of Australian plants and seeds, sending them off, carefully catalogued, to England the home of British clover, where they functioned in their turn as intractable fragments inserted into the British botanical scheme.

For many of the early settlers like Georgiana Molloy the primary reality of the Australian landscape was too obvious to need insisting on, and it determined their interpretation of the fragments—whether material items from the British repertoire or discursive forms from British culture. To establish an explanatory space we will jump forward more than a century to a poem by another woman, Judith Wright, commemorating her own ancestors as pioneers.

Old House

Where now outside the weary house the pepperina,
that great broken tree, gropes with its blind hands
and sings a moment in the magpie's voice, there he stood once,
that redhaired man my great-great-grandfather,
his long face amiable as an animal's,
and thought of vines and horses.
He moved in that mindless country like a red ant,
running tireless in the summer heat among the trees—
the nameless trees, the sleeping soil, the original river—
and said that the eastern slope would do for a vineyard.

Where Georgiana Molloy is trying to forget, Judith Wright is trying to remember, and what she is trying to remember is the reality of pioneer life that was too present for Georgiana. The tangible reality of the old house and the pepperina tree and the vivid image of the red ant function here to guarantee the reality of the great-great-grandfather whom Judith Wright never knew. But conversely his unreality, his ghostly form of existence affects their status as real, while it relies on their ambiguous reality for itself to be believable. For pepperinas have the same kind of partial reality to urban Australians reading Judith Wright as British clover had in early 19th century Augusta. It's possible to believe that they are actually there, if the writer tells us so, but we also know that they are out of place, not guaranteed by the everyday suburban world which is the base-line of the real.

In fact the ambiguous reality of the pepperinas and red ants is crucial to the strategy of the poem, meshing in with the even more ambiguous reality of the dead and absent ancestor, whose ghost could only exist with this potency in this kind of environment. The bush is (from the suburban perspective) not-here, the negation of suburban existence, just as the Australian bush negated Georgiana Molloy's British existence. Because it is not-here it can by extension accommodate the not-now. This transformation is endemic in Australian literature. The bush allows reveries of the past, not as history but as partial survival into the present, as though the bush does not exist at a point in time but slides back over an indeterminate period. In 'Old House' Judith Wright's ancestor exists along with Aboriginal people, both long gone but now joined in harmony in this twilight existence. It is a common theme, in her poetry and in many other forms. The bush, because it is both real and unreal, allows present and past to fuse, and resolves the antagonisms that drove the history of the past as it drives the present.

We are not saying that the bush has a single reality value. On the contrary, it is its shifting reality value, its instability between different writers and readers, even for the same writer, that makes it so potent a factor in the construction of literary works. The way it operates is comparable to the opening pan shot of the classic Hollywood western that establishes the generic form. The single continuous shot, in that case, establishes not only a place (the 'West') but also a time-that-is-not-a-time (even if a written text claims a precise historical incident at its base) and a mythic mode of reality. The important difference between the Hollywood western and the role of the bush in Australian culture is the scope of the Australian theme, the degree to which it is embedded in the national stereotype. The western is a specific genre among many that construct the American myth: categories of the Outback are part of the very conditions of Australian mythology. It is undoubtedly true that as Frederick Turner has argued, the myth of the frontier is an important foundation myth for American culture, and this feeds into the significance of the western for Americans. However, we believe that the myth of the Outback plays an even greater role in Australian life, and is more insistently constructed as a contemporary reality.

The phenomenon of course is not without its contradictory forms, and is itself not outside history. In tracking that history we can say that the structure has been relatively stable since the 1890s, which act as a pivot around which the process of constructing the Australian country swings. The role of the 1890s in the process has been well enough documented for a brief illustration to suffice. 'Banjo' Paterson's 'The Man from Snowy River', title poem from his hugely popular first volume of poetry of 1895, begins with dramatic immediacy:

> *There was movement at the station, for the word had passed around*
> *That the colt from old Regret had got away*

But after the exciting narrative the poem ends:

> And where around The Overflow the reed-beds sweep and sway
> To the breezes, and the rolling plains are wide,
> The Man from Snowy River is a household word today,
> And the stockmen tell the story of his ride.

The last two lines suddenly situate this story in a vague past, its hero part of a legend which only existed (until the poem was published) in the unreal world of The Overflow, with its fictional stockmen authenticating the fictional tale. The film *The Man from Snowy River* (1981) was shot on location in the Blue Mountains, which carry a similarly ambiguous reality value for late 20th century film audiences, reinforced by filtered lenses and soft focuses. The biggest difference, in these terms, between the film and the poem was the film's skilful use of the discursive fact that 'The Man from Snowy River' is indeed a household word today, in the minds and discourse of urban Australians rather than among the fictional stockmen of Paterson's poem. This apart, we can say that the reality value and meaning of Paterson's bush shows a remarkable stability across nearly 100 years.

This stability is one of its most significant properties. But it is equally important to recognise that this value is not natural and inevitable: it has a history, even if it is a hidden history, requiring a careful archeological reconstruction. As an initial sounding we will take two important documents: Sinnett's early claims on behalf of 'Australian' fiction of 1856, nearly 50 years before 'Australia' existed as a nation to have any fiction, and the reception of Charles Harpur in the 1840s, as the first candidate for the status of major Australian poet.

Sinnett begins his article by announcing 'the distinct conviction by which we are possessed, that genuine Australian novels are possible' (Barnes 1969:9). In spite of the ironic tone, Sinnett is a proselytiser, but he is more keenly aware of the problems than of the possibilities. The first problem that he addresses is precisely the function of the setting:

> It must be granted, then, that we are quite debarred from all the interest to be extracted from any kind of archaeological accessories. No storied windows, richly dight, cast a dim, religious light over any Australian premises. There are no ruins for that rare old plant, the ivy green, to creep over and make his dainty meal of.   (Barnes 1969:9)

Again we have the typical pattern of negations, deployed on the repertoire of English literature going back to Milton. But the insertion of the fragment from Milton, like Georgiana Molloy's sods of clover but even more strongly, is seen as ridiculous in its new setting, geographical and linguistic (alongside the prosaic 'Australian premises'). We can see from this that the revaluation of the Australian environment as taken-for-grantedly real is already far advanced, and no longer an issue. What is still an issue is the opposite development: the establishment of its ambiguous unreality for literary and cultural purposes. Sinnett recognises that this is still an unsolved problem, and it is the most important such problem that he poses. And the problem he draws attention to is the absence of a marker of a kind of reality in which differences of time are blurred, and the past can become a tangible presence, as it is in later literature like Judith Wright's.

Sinnett is writing specifically about the possibility of Australian novels, but his example shows his awareness that the genre entrusted with the task of legitimising the new valuation was poetry. Charles Harpur was acclaimed and saw himself as 'the Bard of (his) Country' in a poem published in 1843. 'Australia has now produced a poet all her own' announced no less than Henry Parkes, reviewing Harpur's first volume of poetry in 1845. So it is interesting to juxtapose these claims of authenticity to Harpur's poetic productions. His 'To an Echo on the Banks of the Hunter', for instance, was republished in the *People's Advocate* of 20 January 1849 with the following endorsement: 'We venture to assert that the following is the most beautiful poem belonging to the infant literature of this country'. The poem as it appeared in 1849 begins:

> *I hear thee, Echo, and I start to hear thee,*
>   *With a strange tremour; as among the hills*
> *Thy voice reverbs, and in swift murmurs near me*
>   *Dies down the stream, or with its gurgle low*
> *Blends whisperingly—until my bosom thrills*
> *With gentle tribulations, that endear thee,*
>   *But smack not of the present. 'Twas as though*
> *Some spirit of the past did then insphere Thee*
>   *Even with the taste of life's regretted spring—*
> *Waking wild recollections, to evince*
>   *My being's transfused connexion with each thing*
>   *Loved though long since.*

A modern reader might react to this as a subWordsworthian effusion without a trace of local colour bar the title. From the terms in which it was praised it is clear that this was not how it was read at the time. Crucial here is the acceptance of the reality and Australianness of the scene itself. The Hunter river was within 100 miles of Sydney, reached by easy coast roads. Harpur's poetic achievement which was so valued by his readers was in fact to rework this reality value, to prise it free of its every day quality not only by using Wordsworthian diction but more importantly by investing it with a specific history. The echo is itself a symbol of what he is trying to do: to superimpose tangible images from distinct layers of time so that the 'reality' of each is cast into doubt. On the one hand this half-negates the reality of what is before him, this particular part of the Australian bush. On the other hand he is then able to see or hear the past itself, a 'spirit of the past' that then becomes generalisable into a kind of mystical experience which is nonetheless accepted as distinctively Australian.

There were other subterranean connections between Harpur's poetry and its reception and more directly political attitudes to the land. Henry Parkes, champion of the poetry and later one of the fathers of federation, was not uninfluenced in his opinion of Harpur's poetry by Harpur's role in the Free Selection movement, in which Parkes played a dominant role in NSW of the 1850s. Initially it may not seem easy to make the connection between Harpur's effusions about echoes and his political support of free selection and land reform. But each is in its way a kind of claim to the land, an appropriation of its essence, with the poetry no less insistent in its pretensions to ownership. But where the movement for land reform was practical politics (which as is so often the case with practical politics fell far short of its original aims) the poetic program was the opposite: constructing an alternative reality in which the aims of land reform were magically accomplished.

The complex reality-value of the country was not definitively established at one time or by one writer, and we have given only a rudimentary history of its emergence. Another significant marking point might be Marcus Clarke's famous description of Australian scenery, in his preface to the poems of Adam Lindsay Gordon published in 1876. Gordon himself, whose fame rested on his *Bush Ballads* and whose stature in his time was such that he was commemorated in Poet's Corner in Westminster Abbey, was perhaps a surprising figure to provoke Clarke's commentary on the bush, since Gordon was so short-sighted that he could hardly see past the head of his horse, and his descriptive powers were well matched to his focal length. But a negation of reality, however achieved, was the essence of Clarke's vision of the bush:

> The Australian mountain forests are funereal, secret, stern. Their solitude is desolation. They seem to stifle, in their black gorges, a story of sullen despair. No tender sentiment is nourished in their shade. In other lands the dying year is mourned, the falling leaves drop lightly on his bier. In the Australian forests no leaves fall.   (Clarke 1976:645)

This by now is a thoroughly romantic conception of the bush, constructed by a series of negations both of other lands and even Australian botany (gum trees do shed their leaves, as suburban householders with native gardens know). Clarke works with a very different genre to Paterson (and Gordon) so that his picture of the environment seems quite different, but underpinning and accommodating the difference is the same Australian cultural achievement, its construction of the ambiguous reality of the landscape.

Although the landscape has a generalised value of this kind, the precise reality-value of different aspects alters, sensitively responding to changing cultural maps that specify degrees of unfamiliarity and hence degrees of unreality. The place occupied by 'the bush' in the 19th century is now occupied by the desert. There is scarcely a single 19th century painting of a desert landscape, but these are now the signature of painters like Nolan, Drysdale and Williams. The apocalytic landscape of *Mad Max III* (1985) is signified sufficiently by desert scenes, whose unreality can accommodate a doubled time, a post-holocaust future and a return to a primitive frontier age. But the setting does not have a single, unalterable reality-value. *Picnic at Hanging Rock* (1975) for instance is set in the bush at the turn of the century. The unreality of the bush is part of the enabling conditions for the mystery of the film to work, but the unaided bush is not unreal enough. The film of the 1980s had to reinforce the unreality by sound effects and camera work. Nor is all of the bush equally unreal. The precise mix of reality and unreality required in constructing the mythic status of Crocodile Dundee for Paul Hogan was achieved by using the unfamiliar yet known (through tourist brochures) terrain of the Northern Territory's Kakadu Park. Our point is not that there is a single fixed meaning or invariant reality value for the Australian landscape, or that its use is confined to literary texts. On the contrary, it is as potent as it is precisely because it is so variable a resource and so pervasive a phenomenon.

THE MEANING OF DISTANCE

One of the most evocative titles among books on Australian history has been Geoffrey Blainey's *The Tyranny of Distance* (1966). Blainey's specific concern as an economic historian was to show how one single material factor affected many aspects of Australian history and Australian attitudes. But almost incidentally his narrative raised the question of the meaning of distance itself as a potent and complex signifier. Distance, when we inspect it, turns out to be a curious signifier, because it is in fact a kind of absence, the space between two significant points, the space constructed as empty by the emphasis on the points. So distance also implies the intention to travel, and the obstacles in the way.

Blainey linked the development of the colonies around the sea-board to the distance from England and Europe, and the relative ease of sea travel. So the distances inland were a function of the distances for goods to travel to Europe: each mile an extra cost on the way to their European destination. We can say then that the strength of desire for 'home' created the sense of distance, which came therefore to express the sense of that desire as an image of its deferral. We can go further (further certainly than Blainey would wish) to see the sense of distance as having class affiliations: the subjective expression of Australian capitalism's difficult relationship to the European market. Emphasis on distance, then, will mark the expatriate, a member of the possessing class in exile, inscribing the absence of Europe on the visible landscape. The extreme contrast is with Aboriginal representations of the landscape in their art, where as we have seen they typically represent its plenitude, the fullness of places linked to other places without the remorselessly linear directionality that creates distance. European art of the 19th century typically depicted mountains and forests, barriers (solid impediments to travel which could be overcome by effort—and real estate which could be owned and exploited) rather than distances as such. It is only in the 20th century that distance has really come into its own, so that the dominant iconography has now become the desert, not only as the negation of the real but also as the image of absolute distance: the journey without a destination, the distance to a nonexistent point, motionless and objectless desire.

Paul Carter in *The Road to Botany Bay* (1987) has developed a useful distinction that helps to refine the meanings clustered around distance. At the founding moment of the colony he distinguishes between the habits of mind of the explorer Cook and the scientist Banks. The two men, contemporaries and companions, are usually treated as indistinguishable. Carter makes the point that Cook saw the landscape in terms of his own travels in it, whereas Banks assimilated its features to a pre-existing scheme. So in the terms that we have been developing, Cook can construct distance precisely, by reference to the grid of the world (his ability as a map-maker was enhanced by his use of new methods to estimate longitude accurately as well as latitude, Blainey points out). Banks's concern with classification, on the other hand, relentlessly absorbed the complete physical landscape into his expansive but unitary scheme, and in the process eliminated distance as irrelevant to his taxonomies.

Blainey's work allows us to locate distance as a meaning: Carter's work encourages us to try to specify some of its stylistic correlates. The first broad distinction is between the syntax of journeys and the syntax of classification. A syntax that was organised like Cook's journeys would consist of a series of elements loosely chained together in a linear progression, anchored by a beginning and an end but having its bulk in the gap between the two. But Cook was an explorer. Explorers were a significant type of traveller in the construction of Australia but not the only one. However, if we were to eliminate the anchoring end-point it would then proceed in linear sequence to no destination: what we can term nomadic syntax. Below we will argue that nomadic syntax is a quintessentially Australian form. For the moment we will point out that it also describes a kind of plot that is associated with modernism: the narrative that has no destination outside itself.

The antitype to nomadic syntax we can call expatriate syntax, where the end and the beginning are as far apart as Australia from Britain, and the writer crosses huge mountains and dangerous seas in the strenuous quest to reach the longed-for goal. But expatriate syntax is also characterised by relentless accumulation of detail, organised by classification schemes that assimilate and carry off the land, transporting it back, in discourse at least, to the imperial centre. The archetypal figures in Australian mythology corresponding to these kinds of organisation are the explorer, the swagman and the expatriate. We will look at instances of each, to see the play of language, plot and character that weaves around these central meanings.

Historically these types have a specific order: explorer, imperialist and swagman, but in practice they are all available as part of the cultural repertoire, combined in different ways by succeeding writers and artists. We will begin, then, with the most distinctively 'Australian' of these types, the swagman, as it was given its definitive form by Henry Lawson in the pivotal decade of the 1890s. In a relatively late essay-story entitled 'The Romance of the Swag', Lawson expatiates on the meaning of the swagman:

> The Australian swag was born of Australia and no other land—of the Great Lone Land of magnificent distances and bright heat; the land of Self-reliance, and Never-give-in, and Help-your-mate. The grave of many of the world's tragedies and comedies—royal and otherwise. The land where a man out of employment might shoulder his swag in Adelaide and take the track, and years later walk into a hut on the Gulf, or never be heard of any more, or a body be found in the Bush and buried by the mounted police, or never found and never buried—what does it matter? (Lawson 1972a:500)

This passage encapsulates the dominant features of Lawson's style. The first sentence includes an aggressively truncated version of the ideology of the bush and the myth of mateship: the kind of rhetoric that allowed him to be so easily appropriated by the nationalist ideologues of the 1890s. We note that in this part of the text Lawson is using a version of scientific syntax, classifying Australia many times over, accumulating attributes in the same manner as an expatriate. Humphrey McQueen has criticised Lawson, as a representative of the radical nationalist Australian, of simply incorporating a populist version of the ideology of imperialism (McQueen 1970:104). We can see that on occasions such as this, and they are not untypical, Lawson shows the form as well as the content of imperialist thought. But the tone of strident patriotism, as so often in his work, immediately changes totally, in what is technically a single sentence, with each clause loosely tacked onto its predecessor like a journey without itinerary. The image of Australia, in this writer who

153

was acclaimed as the voice of the bush, is reduced entirely to a Blaineyesque image of 'magnificent distances'.

The final 'sentence' begins with a point of departure, in Adelaide as the representative of civilisation and the world of work (or its absence), and immediately disappears into a series of possible journeys, all without substance or point or destination, in a classification scheme which is now the collapse of all classification schemes, since this is a list of alternatives that all come to the same thing. As the negations build up, the sentence is left with nowhere to go but the nihilistic question: 'What does it matter?' The bush has totally disappeared from the text. So, paradoxically, has Blaineyan distance, since there is no desire linking two distant points, no goal, no quest. Even movement has almost gone: there are few verbs, none of them describing active, purposive movements, so that it is almost a surprise that the nameless swagman materialises at the hut on the Gulf.

The closest literary comparison perhaps is with Samuel Beckett's two tramps in *Waiting for Godot*, which so impressed the Aboriginal novelist Mudrooroo Narogin, as we saw in chapter 5. The resemblance may seem odd to Australian readers who are so often assured that Lawson is a realist writer and typical Australian that they do not notice the almost total absence of the bush landscape from his works. His best work is in the form of anecdotes, not short stories of a classic form. Typically the starting point is a piece of 'home-spun wisdom', a fragment of bush-discourse as we are to suppose, taken out of any specific context, to which is attached a narrative which departs from the piece of wisdom, and never returns. Most of them are short precisely because they have nowhere in particular to go. Cumulatively they define a form of consciousness which is rootless, nomadic, fragmented, expressing an Australian inflection of the modernist malaise.

So the contemporary heirs of Lawson are not social realists who depict the rural life he seemed to treat, but modernist avant-garde writers. In the 1970s, for instance, there was a poetic movement that described itself as the 'New Poetry', self-consciously renouncing the dominant realist tradition that seemed to stretch back to Lawson and his era. But the disordered syntax and fractured forms that were the signature of this writing expressed a sense of alienation and pointlessness akin to Lawson's through similar syntactic forms, and the central consciousness that they constructed, the drug-addict as hero, was a direct successor of the alcoholic Lawson.

One of the most interesting of this group was Michael Dransfield, who died in 1973 aged 25. His poem 'Bums' rush' begins:

> Becoming an eskimo isn't hard once you must.
> You start by going far away, perhaps another landmass,
> into the jungle of cold air and make a room a cave a hole
> in the surface with your axe.

The aim of becoming an eskimo initially seems thoroughly unAustralian, but Dransfield is using an Australian formula and the Australian sense of distance. 'You start by going far away': as with Lawson the whole stupendous journey is invisible, finished in a single clause, and 'you' materialise at the destination-which-is-not-a-destination not knowing quite why you are there. As with the Lawson, there is a classificatory impulse, but it represents the progressive collapse of its own taxonomy: 'a room a cave a hole' refers to the same place classified differently in response to the feelings of the poet, not to the necessities of logic. The immense stretches of cold ice are the opposite of the Australian desert, but only as a mirror image, in which the distances are even greater and the desire to journey in it even less. The traveller is as anonymous as Lawson's swagman: 'And identity you need not concern yourself with names you are the last of your species'. The trip is purely subjective, the product of drugs: 'The worst pain is the morphine blue crevasse'. And the conclusion is not simply death but the willed loss of identity, the same terminus as a Lawsonian swagman's:

> *then walk as a human lemming would*
> *out across the bay to where the ice is thinnest and let yourself*
> *vanish.*

The classic text that represents the imperialist mode is undoubtedly Henry Handel Richardson's monumental trilogy, *The Fortunes of Richard Mahony*. Published between 1917 and 1929, the trilogy traced the fate of a character based closely on that of her own father. At the start of the first novel, Mahony is at Ballarat, lured across the world by the gold rush. He slowly and erratically achieves material success, as a doctor rather than from gold, but cannot overcome his restlessness, and finally, for no good practical reason, returns to England. But the same restlessness and a change in his fortunes drives him back to Australia, and the third novel traces his slow disintegration into madness and death.

The double movement, of course, complicates its status as an expatriate novel. Only Mahony's first movement, from Europe to Australia and back, staying long enough to become rich enough to then return 'home', is the archetypal journey of the expatriate. Richardson's position as writer is similarly anomalous: instead of writing from Australia about the desire for return which constructs the necessary distance, she wrote the trilogy from an English base, as an Australian expatriate lovingly recreating an Australian reality, as British expatriates had tried to recreate images of their British past. The result of the double position, the two starting points, is that the journey in both directions compromises the linearity and momentum to be found in the classic expatriate figure, who struggles singlemindedly to return to the starting point. Mahony's position is closer to that of the nomad: a nomad with baggage. Richard Mahony, from a different class to Lawson and his swagmen, is nonetheless a transitional figure moving towards that type.

A three-volume novel is obviously at the other pole to the short fragments of a Lawson or a Dransfield. It is only possible because of the wealth of detail required by its realist conventions, detail carefully assembled by Richardson from archival materials, meticulously situated by her in its period: 'real history'. Where the absence of detail in the nomadic style signifies the emptiness of distance, the empty space between desire and its nonexistent goal, in Richardson's form of realism detail signifies the innumerable barriers that intervene to block the movements of desire. The result is a style which has been criticised for its cumbrousness. In her preface to the Penguin edition, Professor Leonie Kramer commented acerbically on the problem of style: 'One of the reasons for the length of the trilogy . . . is that Richardson's style lacks penetration. A point which can be made in one sentence is often allowed to occupy several; and what follows the original statement is a series of slight variations, or near synonyms, adding bulk but not meaning' (1971:xxiv).

What Kramer objects to is the lack of goal-directed 'penetration' that would lead smoothly and effortlessly to its destination, and the multiplication of obstructions that contribute to delay. As a sample of this style we will take a short passage from early on in the first novel: 'Under a sky so pure and luminous that it seemed like a thinly drawn veil of blueness, which ought to have been transparent, stretched what, from a short way off, resembled a desert of pale clay' (1971:5).

We can see why Professor Kramer was so irritated. All Richardson is saying is that the sky was blue, and that the Ballarat goldfields were like a desert—clichés at best, and not worth the extra verbiage that Richardson weaves around them. But this entirely typical syntax is a form of significant action, itself an important meaning resource. It has two main characteristics. One is self-embedding: a pause in the flow of the syntax to insert a qualifying element (eg 'which ought to have been transparent'). The other, more endemic, is the interminable gap between the beginning of the sentence and the key elements of the main clause, the subject and the verb. And when they come they are a disappointment, not worth the wait. What prevents the sentence from ever really getting started is the obsessive concern with aspects of the context. The sentence is dominated by the opening adverbial phrase which then expands into clause after clause just as Richardson set herself a formidable task of assimilating the history and geography of the period before she could proceed with her novel, and as she continually deferred the study of the man, her father, by intruding details of the context. It is paradoxical that for Lawson, writing in Australia, the material reality of Australia was so taken-for-granted that it almost disappeared from his text, whereas for the expatriate Richardson its dead materiality was expanded by her sense of distance and desire into an oppressively dominating presence.

Simple binary schemes are of course simplistic, since two terms are never enough to accommodate the complexity of phenomena. But with this reservation the generalisation is true often enough to be illuminating, that the critical establishment that has been the arbiter of literary quality in some form or another since the earliest days of the colony has always been dominated by expatriates, who over-value expatriate syntax (complex, self-deferring syntax, complex but carefully wrought plots, characters whose virtue is their ambiguous positioning within the Australian landscape, orderly and precise systems of classification). In contrast the writers who achieve not simply popularity but also a popular recognition of their representative status commonly employ a form of nomadic construction of language, plot and character. This rather than a form of realism is what links Lawson and Furphy, Prichard and Herbert, Humphries and Hogan, Nolan and Roberts. But that is not to say that expatriate structures are always of less value (however that would be determined) or even less 'Australian'. Both types are part of the Australian repertoire, and the case of Richardson is commonplace amongst the most interesting Australian writers, where it is precisely the dialectic between various forms of the two fundamental types, acting at different levels or between different levels, that gives them their scope and fissured typicality.

EXPLORER AS HERO

The role of the explorer in Australian mythology is an interesting one. During the 19th century they had a popular appeal. Public subscriptions subsidised the various expeditions, and explorers received a hero's welcome on their return to a centre of civilisation. They seemed to be a highly successful legitimation strategy for European conquest, their passage across the landscape naming it as they went, being for the time an entirely sufficient claim to the land. But in retrospect we can see that this success had a surprisingly narrow semiotic impact. True, explorers' feats were celebrated in the newspapers and their journals were published, but without achieving the same hold on the popular mind as swagmen or bushrangers or convicts. The major genre that transmitted their image to later generations was the public monument, the bronze statue on a stone block, placed in a prominent place that was still easy to ignore by crowds that flowed around it on their daily business.

As an instance of this kind of text and the ideological work it was designed to do we will quote the inscription on a memorial to three 'explorers', Panter, Harding and Goldwyer, which was placed in Esplanade Gardens, Fremantle in 1913:

> *This monument was erected by*
> *C.J. BROCKMAN*
> *As a fellow bush wanderer's tribute to the memory of*
> *PANTER, HARDING AND GOLDWYER*
> *Earliest explorers after Grey and Gregory of this*
> *Terra Incognita, attacked at night by treacherous natives*
> *were murdered at Boola Boola near Le Grange Bay*
> *on the 13th November 1864*
> *Also as an appreciative token of remembrance of*
> *MAITLAND BROWN*
> *one of the pioneer pastoralists and premier politicians of this*
> *State, intrepid leader of the government search and punitive*
> *party, his remains together with the sad relics of the ill*
> *fated three recovered at great danger from the lone wilds*
> *repose under public monument in the East Perth Cemetry*
> *"LEST WE FORGET"*

The ideological work done by this text is obvious and overdone. C. J. Brockman, a wealthy pastoralist, constructs himself as a 'bush-wanderer', a category nicely situated between explorer and pleasure-seeking bush-walker, giving two points for the urban reader of the text to identify with. Incidentally he nowhere mentions the date that he erected the monument, conveniently conflating the very different situation that prevailed in the 'heroic' age of exploration compared to the time (and place) when the monument was first in position. The primary object of legitimation is the assault on Aboriginal society, constructing the closed circle of a crime and a punishment that first destroyed Aboriginal legitimacy (they are reduced to the status of 'treacherous natives' guilty of murder of explorers, no less) and then killed large (but unstated) numbers of their people. But the last part of the memorial seeks to do further work, linking the image of the explorer to the heavy weight of a triple pair of p's: pioneer pastoralists, premier politicians and a punitive party. The monument tried to do too much work to have any chance of enduring success.

In 1988 a group of historians working under the direction of Bruce Scates and Raelene Frances researched the actual sordid history of the unequal fight commemorated by the plaque, and used this as the basis for persuading the Fremantle City Council to promise to set up another plaque to correct the historical record. But in some respects this counter attack was overkill, just as the original text was betrayed by its own excess. Surveys of people sitting happily on the grass beside the monument show that virtually none of them has bothered to read its involuted message. The remorseless appropriation of the image of the explorer by ideologues of legitimation has left it without force or appeal.

So it is unsurprising that the explorer is not a significant figure in popular culture or in art or literature. Even Captain Cook, perhaps the least problematic of them, figures mainly in the playground rhyme:

> *Captain Cook*
> *Was a dirty chook*

Flinders was the subject of Ernestine Hill's popular history *My Love Must Wait*. In mainstream literature and art the greatest exceptions to this claim are Sydney Nolan's 'Burke and Wills' series, and Patrick White's *Voss*. This last is so major an exception that we need to look specifically at it.

White's novel has a significant intertextual relation to Leichhardt's journals, and his Voss is a fictionalised version of the famous German explorer of the mid-19th century. But White's way of treating the theme is antagonistic to the explorer thematic in two ways. The frame for the novel is White's concern with the process of turning the contradictory phenomenon of the explorer into a safe but neutralised ideological form. Towards the end of the novel, with Voss dead and the process of sanctification under way, there is this comment: 'Johann Ulrich Voss was by now quite safe, it appeared. He was hung with garlands of rarest newspaper prose. They would write about him in the history books. The wrinkles of his solid, bronze trousers could afford to ignore the passage of time' (White 1957:468).

White here overestimates the durability of bronze trousers and official myths, in spite of his heavily ironic tone: perhaps his own myth-creating enterprise was more complicit with those official myth-making processes than he was aware. But in other ways he constructed the novel so that the quest was guaranteed to go nowhere. Leichhardt made two successful trips before his final failure. White's Voss seems to make only one, and during the course of it he is so estranged from himself that it is clear that he could hardly be trusted to cross the road. White provides minimal markers of where Voss got to, in space or time. He left Sydney by boat for Newcastle, then headed north and west from Darling Downs, but thereafter there are no landmarks, and no interest in them. His party is held up by flooding rivers, so we presume that he is crossing the north of Australia, but these floods come in the winter, not the monsoon time in the north. Although nearly half the expedition mutinies, presumably wondering why they were there, noone sees fit to explain it to them or to those who decide to go on. By these means, White removes the issue of the purpose of the journey from the agenda. The journey is its own reason for existing; and in any case the destination is left indeterminate.

Voss's journey towards his death was not only pointless in practical terms. It was always counterpoised against another narrative, the narrative of Laura Trevelyan, who remained at home but was the obsessive theme of Voss's thoughts. Some kind of mystical communication with him is suggested that intensified till near his death, where White cuts between the thoughts and words of the two so that it is as though they are closer at that point, when their bodies are at their greatest remove, than at any other time of their lives. 'You see that separation has brought us far, far closer' Voss writes, to the woman he has hardly met but has proposed to, in a letter that does not reach its destination (1957:231). They become, then, like the inverse image of a married couple in White's construction of marriage: their bodies hundreds of miles apart yet their souls mystically joined. The novel seems to ask us to believe in this mystical closeness, an illusion of closeness that is seemingly endorsed by White's plot and technique. But the setting for Voss's actions is the bush, a place that never achieves concrete reality, whose conventional status as not fully real allows White's complex narrative moves.

This double movement disrupts the classic Australian notion of distance. Voss is never removed from the continual flow of discourse, so in a sense he does not and cannot ever travel, whatever happens to his body. And White's constructions of the landscape are minimal. His syntactic patterns are as revealing as those of Richardson or Lawson. Here is a sample, two sentences that follow the description of a letter Voss wrote to Laura before the journey proper had begun, when he first proposed marriage to her in his own understated fashion:

> Next morning, while the lamps of friendship hovered touchingly in the dew and darkness, and naked voices offered parting advice, the company began to move northward, with the intention of crossing New England. It was a good season, and the land continued remarkably green, or greyish-green, or blue-grey, the blue of smoke or distance. (White 1957:164)

The first sentence has the deferral of meaning characteristic of the expatriate style, but before the action is described he inserts mention of discursive activity, and what follows the action is a statement about intention, itself a discursive phenomenon. The physical description, when it comes, is as vague and lacking content as nomadic syntax. What is elaborated is not the content of this distance, but its contradictory classifications. The series of adjectives refers to changes not in the land itself, but in the narrator's perspective on it, or distance from it. Perhaps. Or perhaps the effect is only due to smoke. White/the narrator does not ever bother to decide between the two explanations, so indifferent is he (or Voss) to the material dimension of distance and the content of the landscape itself.

So Voss, the most celebrated explorer in Australian literature, explores nothing external to himself. The distances that he supposedly travels are as irrelevant as the distances travelled by a swagman, because the goal is indistinguishable from the point of departure. The distances at issue were there from the start of the journey, in the separation from his own desires that created the gulf between himself and all others, men and women; but especially his loved one, his 'wife'. The landscape that he travels through is a metaphor for his own mind, but it is also a map of his social alienation:

> 'You are so vast and ugly,' Laura Trevelyan was repeating the words; 'I can imagine some desert, with rocks, rocks of prejudice, and yes, even hatred. You are so isolated. That is why you are fascinated by the prospect of desert places, in which you will find your own situation taken for granted, or more than that, exalted' (1957:94).

In some senses White's novel is not after all an exception to the generalisation that Australian literature has no major works based on the explorer figure. But in other respects we can say that his novel demonstrates some typical strategies of Australian literature of the 20th century, showing a phantasmagorical figure seeming to move through an unreal space and time, blurring present and past, city and country, truth and fiction, journey and destination; a character who cannot fail because he could not ever succeed, whose alienated creator heaps up endless metaphors of land and belonging, which only serve to reinforce his isolation. The unresisting land is made over, exploited by artists as by miners and pastoralists, to express the devastating human and social consequences of life in Australia.

8 The Australian legend

Russel Ward's *The Australian Legend*, first published in 1958 in the heyday of the Menzies era, has proved to be the most provocative history of Australia of this century. It did not attempt to be comprehensive, and does not compete with monumental histories such as those of Hancock or Manning Clark or most recently the *Oxford History of Australia*. In a sense it was not even original, since the ideas it was working with have been commonplaces in Australian society for at least 100 years, as Ward himself insisted. Ward's originality and provocation was simply to take this body of ideas very seriously, as a version of history which had its own history. The object of his analysis is an undeniable fact of the present: that there is a concept of the 'typical Australian' which has very widespread currency in contemporary Australia, and this myth projects a shadowy history which itself has an unacknowledged potency.

To indicate the reach of Ward's thesis as well as the flaws in his treatment of it, we will refer to the work of two later historians, both of them highly critical of Ward yet in many respects making fertile use of his work. Humphrey McQueen's *A New Britannia* of 1970 was a new Left polemic for its time, attacking the radical nationalism that McQueen associated especially with Ward. McQueen was not opposed to radicalism, nor even (in some respects) to nationalism or at least a real autonomy. What he objected to was Ward's location of it in the past, as a 'heritage' that was a nostalgic compensation for the absence of radicalism in the present (for McQueen the early 1970s, which seemed more hopeful than Ward's 1950s). And when he turned to the past, to find evidence of the reality of this myth, he found its opposite: a self-seeking, servile and class-ridden society whose radicalism was always compromised and whose nationalism was simply an epiphenomenon of Australia's role in world capitalism. So chapter after chapter of McQueen takes a fragment of Ward's legend and mercilessly confronts it with social reality.

One aspect of Ward's enterprise invited this assault. He did claim that legends like this 'spring largely from a people's past experiences' (1958:1). McQueen shows sufficiently conclusively that there was never a stage of reality that conformed to the myth, but the single-minded energy of his assault suggests that he still thinks that it might have done. Richard White in *Inventing Australia* (1981) adopts the more sophisticated position which is the minimal basis for addressing the second part of Ward's project. He insists that Australia and Australians of the legend have never existed in pure materiality, but have always been constructed by specific ideologues at specific times for specific purposes. That process of 'inventing Australia' has its history which White tries to trace. It is this history that we ourselves try to contribute to, in the present chapter. What we will stress, in contrast to White and McQueen, is the contradictions that were present in this ideological complex from the very outset.

The Australian legend was never the Australian reality, as Ward sometimes supposed, but nor was it simply bad history, as McQueen thought, nor a pernicious ideological trick, as White saw it. In different ways it has been all three, at various times, but it has also been more. It has been the vehicle for the transmission of ideological primes, but it has also been used continuously as an instrument of critique, specifically of what seem to be its own first premises. In order to show how this has happened we need to go back to the same category of texts as Ward drew on more than any other historian, texts from literature and popular culture. But we need to subject such texts to a far more critical reading than Ward employed: one that is alert to the shifts and contradictions that are typical of an ideological complex.

A GENDERED LAND

One of McQueen's targets in his critique of the Australian legend is the extreme sexism that is part of the definition. This criticism was forcefully articulated by Miriam Dixson (1976) and Anne Summers (1975), and developed by many other feminist historians. We can see Ward's complicity with this sexism in his opening description of the type: 'According to the myth the "typical Australian" is a practical man, rough and ready in his manners and quick to decry any appearance of affectation in others. He is a great improviser, ever willing "to have a go" at anything, but willing too to be content with a task done in a way that is "near enough" ', (Ward 1958:1-2).

The use of the gendered pronoun here is no accident. The 'typical

Australian' is a highly sexist construct, which removes all women from the national identity at a stroke. The definitive relationships he engages in are exclusively with males: with bosses whom he treats as equals or enemies, and with his 'mates' whom he sticks to through thick and thin, unless they are 'scabs'. So not only are women not part of Ward's 'typical Australian', they are not even part of his social environment, as persons, partners or problems.

This omission, of course, is so gross that many have noticed it as a weakness in the national stereotype. But the absent woman does appear, in a transmuted form, in this complex of ideas: as the land itself, on which the 'Australian' works his will. Kay Schaffer has made this point forcibly, using a sentence by Sir Keith Hancock as an exemplar: 'Many nations adventured for the discovery of Australia, but the British peoples have alone possessed her' (in Schaffer 1987:17).

The gendered pronoun would have come naturally and inevitably to Hancock, since 'Australia' in English (like 'England', 'America' etc.) has covert gender as also happens in other cultures ('Mother India', 'Mother Russia'). But as Schaffer points out, this fact is far from innocent. The gender that has been mobilised through 'Australia' is crucial in the metaphor that then describes and celebrates the relationship between the British peoples and the country 'herself': 'possessed'. So natural is the idea of gendered domination in Hancock's phrase that the distinction between legal 'possession' (as for a man of his wife) and rape does not arise. This is a phallocentric historian taking for granted a specifically gendered construction of the relationship between Australians (the possessors) and their country. We can begin to see why women do not fit easily into the category of typical Australian, although the typical Australian is not the dominant exploiting class foregrounded by Hancock.

The ambiguity of this assumption on the part of the Australian male explains why the avowal of the land as woman is undercut by its disavowal. Precisely because it is hardly marked or acknowledged it becomes a significant means for transmitting gender ideologies and also a whole complex of attitudes to gender which go beyond those ideologies. As one well-known instance from literature, here are A.D. Hope's lines on Australia:

> They call her a young country, but they lie:
> She is the last of lands, the emptiest,
> A woman beyond her change of life, a breast
> Still tender but within the womb is dry.

Hope as a man constructs Australia as a woman who is not really a woman, who is unable either to seduce or to nurture. In the process he expresses a male rage against women projected on the landscape, whose features give Nature's support to a hatred of women that is the other face of the Australian legend.

It is useful to compare this metaphor with what seems a similar theme, but written by a woman: the bravura conclusion to Richardson's 'Proem' that begins her trilogy:

> A passion for the gold itself awoke in them an almost sensual craving to touch and possess; and the glitter of a few specks at the bottom of pan or cradle came, in time, to mean more to them than 'home', or wife, or child.
>
> Such were the fates of those who succumbed to the 'unholy hunger'. It was like a form of revenge taken on them, for their loveless schemes of robbing and fleeing; a revenge contrived by the ancient, barbaric country they had so lightly invaded. Now, she held them captive—without chains; ensorcelled—without witchcraft; and, lying stretched like some primeval monster in the sun, her breasts freely bared, she watched, with a malignant eye, the efforts made by these puny mortals to tear their lips away. (1971:8)

In both, the country is constructed as an ancient mother, but where for Hope she is simply old and useless, in Richardson she is still potent and seductive but actively malevolent, and for good reason. Richardson prefaces the image with a brief account of its social and psychological origins. Frenetic mining is the archetypal activity, The Digger the exemplary type, with the psychological roots to be found in a loveless eroticism, a massive displacement of the entire libidinal organisation away from all relationships involving women. Hope indulges in his contempt for women as though it is something outside himself, a universal fact that is not in need of explanation. Elsewhere in the same poem he is equally contemptuous of urban Australia: ('And her five cities, like five teeming sores,/ Each drains her'); and he does try to end on a positive note ('Yet there are some like me turn gladly home'). But two such negations do not add up to one insight, and his positive is unbelievable. The only unity that could hold his fragments together is the framework that Richardson provides: a recognition that the anger and negativity proceed from a double act of alienation, of man from man in a male-dominated act of exploitation and invasion, and of man from woman in the dominant organisation of sexuality. The gendered land is a reflex of the inadequacies of the Australian legend.

The overt ugliness of such an image is relatively rare, because it is too revealing and because it does not serve one of the primary functions of myth, to integrate a diverse society through seductive images of unity. An exemplary instance of the positive form is a poem by Dorothea Mackellar entitled 'My Country', which has been learnt by heart by many generations of Australian primary school children. Its first stanza begins with the rival landscape of England: 'The love of field and coppice'. Its second stanza then begins the celebration of Australia:

> *I love a sunburnt country,*
> *A land of sweeping plains,*
> *Of ragged mountain ranges,*

> *Of droughts and flooding rains.*
> *I love her far horizons,*
> *I love her jewel sea,*
> *Her beauty and her terror—*
> *The wide brown land for me!*

This is a gentle but unmistakeable form of the land as witch-mother, powerful, mainly negative but also fascinating. But the image is surrounded by the thrice-repeated claim of love, sustained by the simple regular rhythm as a chant of praise. The form as well as the poet's name confirms that this is a feminine utterance, one which would in fact be unspeakable by any representative of the Australian legend. Her gendered voice carries the reassuring message of the poem: that woman affirms her alienated Other, she is not self-divided, so that all will be well (in spite of droughts, floods, and other disasters). For this poem to have its greatest currency in the primary school classroom is itself significant. Even adolescents, female as well as male, would find it slightly mawkish. But by that stage in an Australian upbringing this poem, reduced to a chorus and other fragments, still survives in the memory as a potent source of reassurance. Surprisingly it can coexist with the sentiments of Hope's 'Australia', since it accepts a similarly ambivalent image of the country-as-woman and affirms it from a woman's point of view. This manages to present a hostility to women as somehow not a rejection of women at all: a contradiction, of course, but ideologically a most convenient one, which is especially suitable for children.

But the metaphor of the land as Mother, embedded in more positive models of gender relations, has motivated many critiques of White Australian's treatment of the environment. Geoffrey Bolton's *Spoils and Spoilers*, for instance, was the first extended history of Australians' interaction with the land. The title sums up the dominant note of the history, a sorry tale of catastrophic misuse and uncontrolled exploitation for most of this time. Bolton's conclusion, written in 1981, gives a sombre forecast that the situation will grow worse. Only in the final paragraph does he allow himself to hope:

> It was even possible that the renewed concern for Aboriginal land rights might lead to a subtler appreciation of Aboriginal principles of conservation and renewal and the Aboriginal concept of a religious respect for the land with which Australians identified themselves. For if Australians were learning to abandon the old idea of the country as a hostile force to be tamed they had yet to attain that state of mind present in the wisdom of so many older cultures: the habit of viewing the Australian earth as their mother. (Bolton 1981:174)

In this final sentence Bolton personifies Australia in gendered terms, invoking a rather unspecific and unexamined notion of mothers as the enabling premise for such limited optimism as he can manage. In the rest of the book he uses the word 'Australia' in the manner that is typical of modern Australian historians, referring only' to the place, usually in adverbial constructions with 'in' or 'to'. The primary agents he refers to, as here, are 'Australians', the people who ravaged the land, who are not Aborigines and less obviously are not women either.

Bolton's peroration in fact links the two classes of 'non-Australian', Aborigines and women. He diagnoses the core problems as the absence of both from the category of Australia(n), and the hostile attitudes that have sustained this exclusion throughout most of Australia's history. The conclusion, coming after the book's understated account of a continuous history of environmental rape, serves as a salutary reminder for students of history and literature alike. These buried metaphors not only express exploitative and alienated forms of social life: they also then have further consequences, providing emotional legitimation for some of the most destructive practices of Australian capitalism. In this way attitudes to race and gender do much more than affect how the country is constructed in discourse: they also have material effects that have cumulatively reshaped the land till it is a suitable environment in which that ideology can grow and thrive.

A CLASSIC TEXT REVISITED

Whatever people may think about the Australian legend, it is agreed on all sides that the definitive form was laid down in the 1890s, with the propagandist role of the *Bulletin* magazine, the 'Bushman's Bible', a significant factor. Historians tend to take the propagandistic claims at their face-value, and try to exemplify them in striking quotes. However the most important texts from this founding moment tended to be far more complex and contradictory structures of meaning, the point of intersection of different meanings for different kinds of readers rather than a single fixed meaning that merely illustrated the program. In insisting on this we are not claiming a privileged plenitude of meanings for literature. On the contrary we are pointing to a specific process that has occurred with a specific body of texts that formed the basis of the Australian legend. At the moment of production they were read as popular texts which also possessed an inexhaustible if subterranean meaning potential, though they were also inscribed in much more limited polemical discourses. But within decades they had become 'classics', texts suitable for study in classrooms. And so a process of closure began, shutting off whole avenues of interpretation that had become inconvenient for their pedagogic function. Read in this reductive way most of these texts came to seem rather uninteresting, their fame inexplicable, since they tended to be so slight and fragmentary and self-effacing. Yet the enigma of the legend still hovered over them, giving them a kind of fascination that provoked later writers to work over them again, recasting their themes, sometimes literally rewriting the texts themselves. In the process the closure of the classic was continually challenged, and though the rewritings were not intended merely to release the plenitude of the original, that was one thing that they inevitably did.

We will illustrate the process by looking at one such classic, Henry Lawson's short story 'The Drover's Wife' and a number of versions which in some way or another took this as a precursor text. Lawson's story was written in 1892. In 1896 Barbara Baynton wrote a story which was published in the *Bulletin* as 'The Tramp', subsequently published in 1900 as 'The Chosen Vessel'. While not referring directly to Lawson's famous story, Baynton's text takes up a number of its themes and concerns from a woman's point of view. We will also look at two later works: Murray Bail's metafiction 'The Drover's Wife', apparently based on Russell Drysdale's painting of that title, and Barbara Jefferis's 'The Drover's Wife', a commentary by the wife herself on the various males who have tried to represent her in their art.

Neither Lawson nor this story is an entirely arbitrary choice. Here is Vance Palmer, an authoritative voice on the 'Legend of the Nineties': 'It is hard to realise now the excitement caused by such ballads as Paterson's "Clancy of the Overflow" or such stories as Lawson's "The Drover's Wife"; but to the people who read them they seemed to open new vistas' (in Ward 1958:223). Palmer here records the inexplicable significance of these texts as seen from a later period, the 1950s, when he was writing: but their exemplary status is not in doubt. So it is interesting to note that the historians who have been most fascinated with the construction of the legend of the 1890s, Ward, McQueen and White, do not discuss 'The Drover's Wife' at all. The absence is perhaps most obvious in McQueen because he devotes thirteen pages exclusively to Lawson, but these pages assemble polemical quotations from his poetry to illustrate McQueen's case about Lawson's reactionary attitudes. The meanings coded in narrative texts are left alone.

The most immediately striking property of Lawson's text in fact is its unsuitability to carry the core message of the Australian legend. The gender of its subject is the first disqualifying attribute—the Drover's wife as its centre, rather than one of the male types who make up the Australian legend. The drover himself is introduced briefly, but only to announce that he is 'away with sheep'. Later we learn that he has been away this time for six months, and his absence contributes to her sense of anxiety. But he is neither incompetent nor feckless. He does provide a cheque reasonably reliably and is not without goodwill, but is hardly an emotional necessity to the woman, nor she to him.

In his absence he does not show any of the virtues of the Australian legend. It is his wife who does that. In the course of the short narrative we learn that she has coped with fire and flood (the dangers of 'the wide brown land' of MacKellar's poem), showing the uncomplaining loyalty, ingenuity and perseverance that are core virtues in the legend. But she is a woman, and women in the legend do not exist, much less show the core virtues. Even worse, the text is full of males, real and transformed, who together add up to something like the repertoire of the legend, and almost all are vicious or contemptible. We have mentioned the drover of the title. There is also brief mention of a 'gallows-faced swagman' with malign intentions, and a 'stray blackfellow' who cheats her. Then there are the transformed males. The story itself concerns an incident with a snake, a black snake that enters the house itself. The threat is finally overcome with the assistance of Alligator, her dog, who protects her from vicious swagmen or snakes but once attacked her by mistake, when she was wearing trousers after fighting a fire. The only positive male is Tommy, her eldest son, who professes loyalty to her but also has a tendency to violence equal to Alligator's.

So it is not the case that she is a woman who happens to have the virtues of a man, because no man has these virtues in the world of the story. Nor is this swingeing critique of the masculine form of the legend unparalleled in Lawson's other stories. On the contrary, time after time his male characters show cruelty and superficiality, only partly held in check by the intermittent operations of the 'ethic of the Bush'. Lawson's style, speaking through the persona of a bushman and withholding comment and evaluation, leaves the brief anecdotes morally ambiguous. But it is normally impossible, as here, to interpret the stories as celebrations of the virtues of the legend. And this, accepted at the time as a classic of the genre, clearly works by decentring the materials of the myth, and specifically the gender-assumptions at its core.

The woman herself is only described briefly at the start, as a 'gaunt, sun-browned bushwoman'. Otherwise she appears through her actions, as the preserver of her family and property in this harsh environment. As a mother she is undemonstrative: 'She loves her children, but has no time to show it. She seems harsh to them. Her surroundings are not favourable to the development of the "womanly" or sentimental side of nature' (1972b:50). This is the harsh mother-figure again, but as a social reality not a metaphor. And her harshness is given an explanation, with the opposing virtues relativised by apostrophes, so that the dominant construction of 'woman' is made to seem fake in this more authentic situation. But the absence of expressions of love is not seen as a new virtue: only something that has its reasons, and is less pernicious than it seems.

Henry Lawson's mother was a strong-willed and articulate woman with feminist views, and she undoubtedly influenced her son. Even so, it was he and not his mother who wrote this story, and though he constructed this his most famous story around a female character and point of view, it remains a male construction. Barbara Baynton's 'The Chosen

Vessel' picks up some of the themes of the Lawson story in a way that seems like a critique of it from a woman's point of view. Baynton also deals with a woman alone in the bush, with an absent husband, a shearer only 15 miles away and gone for only a week, but not able to protect her from male threats. Where Lawson's drover's wife gets rid of the swagman with the aid of her dog, and triumphs over the snake, Baynton's wife confronts the sexuality of the swagman without protection and is brutally murdered. But Baynton's brief text has a complex structure, interweaving the narrative of the murder with another narrative of hypocrisy. The wife clutching her baby runs out when she hears a horseman riding by, hoping that he will save her. But the horseman is brooding on images of the Virgin, and thinks that she is just a vision. He rides on, elated by his reverent vision of woman as sacred, while the real woman is left to the swagman's murderous attentions.

Lawson's story casts the woman in a more positive and effective role, but her effectiveness is ultimately there to save the masculine ideal of the legend, rather than to explore the situation of women in Australia. Baynton is concerned more with the actual experience of women than with legends. Her final title, 'The Chosen Vessel', underlies the irony created by the two narratives, where one male's overvaluation of woman leaves the actual woman even more exposed to male hostility and rage. The same split is shown in a less dramatic way, when her husband taunts her at her fears for her safety: 'Needn't flatter yerself', he had told her, 'nobody'ud want ter run away with yew' (Baynton, p.82). (Anne Summers' important study of Australian attitudes to women, *Damned Whores and God's Police*, pointed to a related dichotomy in the dominant construction of women.)

Baynton shows the paralysing effect on the young woman of being an object of violent male desire whose desirability is strenuously denied, with a contemptuous but absent keeper (the husband) and an all-too present murderer/rapist. The idealist rider is the third refraction of the masculine, as anti-rapist (he worships but does not desire) and anti-husband (he is present but does not aid). Baynton's technique is compressed and non-realistic, but her comment is complex and remarkably modern. And we must remember that this structuralist critique of gender relations in the Australian legend was first published in the *Bulletin*, the primary vehicle for carrying that legend.

Murray Bail's version of the story was published in the 1970s. The classic story is not addressed directly: the starting point for Bail's narrative is Russell Drysdale's painting of that title. Drysdale's painting represents a huge woman arising from the earth, earth coloured, a spirit of the land: not doing, like Lawson's woman, but simply and massively being. The landscape is bare, a desert with a few dead trees, but the opulent and fleshy presiding goddess and the warm tones of the landscape negate any sense of barrenness and sterility. Drysdale like

MacKellar has taken the image of the desert as a symbol of woman and used it as an affirmation of woman and country alike. But to do so he has had to transmute the social materials into the status of myth.

It is the mythic claims of the painting that Bail most openly attacks, returning the text to a kind of realism, though not to the kind of realism of the Lawson original. Lawson's story asked to be read against both the claims of the legend and the reality of social life. Bail's metafiction delights in fictionality, happy to take Drysdale's painting as a substitute reality and play games with it. So his garrulous persona claims to recognise the subject of the painting as his wife, Hazel, who had left him and his two children, Trev and Kay, 30 years earlier. The effect of the names and of his own profession—he is a dentist—is to make the pretentious subject familiar and absurd: strictly limited to the world that can be constructed from a suburban lounge (in which a print of the famous Drysdale might hang on the wall). The event exists only in discourse, as a fiction. Since the major event is now a discursive act, however, the result of this move is to restore the chattering husband to the centre of attention. He is represented as a profoundly inadequate middle-class male, without a wife and hardly able to relate to his daughter either, and the drover is now assumed to have acquired the sensitivity with women that was so lacking from the Australian legend.

Bail's target is the suburban Australian lifestyle, not the legend. And though his critique is directed at the Australian male, his strategy takes for granted again the supreme interest of the masculine. But his story ends with the preeminence of the woman, as its final image: 'I recall the drover as a thin head in a khaki hat, not talkative, with dusty boots. He is indistinct. Is it him? I don't know. Hazel—it is Hazel and the rotten landscape that dominate everything' (Kiernan, 1977:10). Here the drover has almost disappeared, and the conclusion repeats the obsession with woman-and-land, woman-as-land that marks Drysdale's painting and the long tradition that goes back to Richardson and earlier. Only the narrator is left, repeating that relationship with the object of his gaze.

Finally we will look at a brief piece published in the *Bulletin* by Barbara Jefferis in 1980. She adopts a similar strategy to Bail's, adopting the persona of one of the actors in the narrative: in her case the drover's wife. She concludes, rather out of character, with some impeccable feminist sentiments: 'What I meant was to tell not so much about me and the drover and the dentist and the rest of them but about how women have a history too, and about how the Bushman's Bible and the other papers only tell how half the world lives' (Jefferis:160).

In Barbara Jefferis' version of the narrative a robust version of the drover's wife meets head-on a succession of males. Since birth, for a woman, has such immense importance, it is this 'moment', made more acute through a difficult birth, which is the occasion for a form of creative gynocriticism. Men—notably Lawson—are thus taken to task for their own bias: 'Funny the way he was more taken by a snake story, the sort that happens to everyone two or three times in a year. But that was the thing about him. Nervous. A nervous man who could never write about things as they really were but only about how they would have seemed to be if he'd been what he would have liked to be' (p. 157).

Jefferis' the Drover's wife adopts with Lawson the confident and kindly authority of a mother with an anxious son. In one sense she is simply recovering a text which was latent in Lawson's original, which constructed the mother as powerful and reassuring: the angular but reliable support for a typical Australian male. Her right to offer a female critique had already been asserted by Barbara Baynton 80 years before. It is important to recognise the many ways in which the Australian legend was introduced accompanied by its critique. But the significant gain of the metafictional mode is that the mode of reading itself, the instrument by which the closure of the classic texts was achieved, is at last foregrounded and thematised in its own right. The opacity of the classic texts was a function of the power of the discourses that controlled their circulation and reception. It is that power that the metafictional mode has attempted to challenge.

THE UGLY AUSTRALIAN

The Australian legend is by no means confined to the museum of culture, of interest only to historians. Various aspects of it pervade contemporary popular culture. To cite only the most spectacular recent instance, Paul Hogan was nominated as 'Australian of the Year' in 1988, and his two *Crocodile Dundee* films have set new records at the box office by recycling his version of the legend. The trade in Australiana in bookshops flourishes, showing the unabated appetite for the legend among contemporary Australians. So the sense that the legend is a highly relevant phenomenon is not in doubt. What is in need of explanation is exactly why this is so. Or to put it more precisely, how so obsolete, irrelevant and ridiculous a construct can serve as the agreed image of national identity to unite Australia.

For there is no doubt that the Australian stereotype is nothing like the majority of Australians, today or even in the past. The normal interpretation of the stereotype of course must acknowledge that, but it does so with a sense of puzzlement, as though this discrepancy has arisen late and has not quite been noticed yet. But the discrepancy has not arisen late, nor has it not been noticed. At least since the 1890s the discrepancy was central to its meaning, whether the uniqueness of a noble bushman like 'Clancy of the Overflow' in 1894 or the ridiculousness of Steele Rudd's 'Dad and Dave' of 1899. At exactly this period, according to a study of the history of incarceration in Australia by Stephen Garton

(1988), the population of lunatic asylums was dominated by male rural labourers and itinerant workers: arrested by the police for being classic examples of the Australian legend.

The obsession with defining this curious object and accounting for its appeal has deflected attention from the discursive and ideological processes that are the key to its meaning. Those who produce and consume the Australian legend are normally middle-class urban dwellers. Their identity as Australians is not constructed by identification with the legend but on the contrary by a common pattern of repudiation of it. The legend is offered as an object for the gaze, not as an ideal to be imitated. Its primary ideological effect proceeds from the reading position that it constructs and the discursive moves that it sustains. The 'real Australian' is not the person who is like the legend, but the person who has the right attitude to the legend.

Neither the legend nor the attitude to him is self-consistent. On the contrary, both are constituted by a set of contradictions, in categories that form the basis of Australian social existence. The legend is masculine, rural, a worker, Anglo-Celtic and of course Australian. Each of these terms forms a bipolar continuum with its opposite, and together they point to the major fissures and sites of conflict in Australian life, across divisions of gender, region, class, race and nationality. In its simplest form the legend overcomes these divisions by removing one half of each polarity. But the legend does not usually exist in this simplest form, because the price of unity is too great: the legend must both resolve oppositions and also seem to incorporate what it has removed. So the ritual practices which complete the ideological work of the legend must combine contempt and repudiation with a kind of complicity, affirming at one level what it has denied or negated at another. This is a complex balancing act which has constantly to be renewed, not the formula for a single unchanging essence. In what follows we will not try to pin down this essence, then, but rather give a schematic account of the range of positions that are available within this formation.

As an instance of one position within popular culture we will take the following advertisement for a piece of Australiana:

A Bonzer Gift Idea
The Great DINGO fence and other AUSTRALIAN ODDITIES
$16.50

> Take a journey back into time, to an amazing fence four times the length of the Great Wall of China. Here, in a unique full colour book, are the strange Outback myths and dry wit of a Dinki-Di Australia. A Fair Dinkum, True Blue look at the cherished oddities of the national language, Strine, and our nation's bizarre rituals, habits and landmarks.

The book itself is part of the cult of Australiana. What is notable about the advertisement is the contradiction between the Australianness

173

that is insisted on in its readers and in the subject matter, along with the strangeness that these readers are encouraged to expect. The commodity that the book is selling, to Australians, is a course in how to be Australians. Or more precisely, how to insert small fragments of this kind of Australianness into the appropriate social contexts. The book and the advertisement foreground Australianness, but against a background of a taken-for-granted urban life-style within Australia. The book, then, is a kind of metatext, reflecting on the social and discursive processes that make for competence within Australian society. Its main ideological message is the unsaid text of normality that must be activated if the 'Australian' text is to be understood or used.

In this instance, Australianness is quaint but charming, and the complicity is more prominent than the critique. In the following joke, the balance is different:

Q. What's the Australian definition of foreplay?
A. 'You awake?'

This joke was written on the wall of a woman's toilet at an Australian university, set among a series of lesbian jokes. The context underlies the meaning of the joke. Its point is the totally rudimentary understanding of women and sexuality of the typical Australian male, who is of course the legend once again. The two word utterance is understood as gendered: of course it must be a 'he' to be so crass and inarticulate. The writer of this joke is accepting the legend's definition of 'Australian' as itself gendered, so that women are not Australian and therefore not included in this critique. Yet the result of this, in this context, is clearly not a loss of identity but the affirmation of identity: a gendered identity which is not only female but articulate, ('definition' is not the kind of word that fits into the legend's vocabulary) and also sexually knowledgeable, and adventurous. So at the same time as it savagely critiques this 'typical Australian' it also projects a very different pattern of sexuality as an ideal. The sexism of the stereotype is put to good use, and its stereotypic status allows the message to be immediately generalised. The legend thus enables a strategy of resistance and critique, precisely because it is so profoundly inadequate and is labelled as such. McQueen is more right than Ward, that the values coded into the legend are not radical or admirable, but that only makes the legend more readily available for radicals to use as a target.

Versions of the legend that abound in 'high' culture, in art and literature, range between the two poles of complicity and contempt, but since the 1940s contempt is the dominant note. The Heidelberg School in the 1890s not only constructed positive images of the country, they constructed a positive vantage point from which to view them, an 'Australian' viewing position which was persuasive precisely because it was itself invisible, outside the picture. The sunlit landscapes of Hans

Heysen continued the position, and Heysen prints still sell well today. But Heysen has no followers among modern artists. Sydney Nolan's Ned Kelly, a human being reduced to a metallic frame, is a descendant of the legend. The most powerful images of the legend as a failure in human terms come in the work of Albert Tucker, whose archetypal Australian is shrivelled to a two-dimensional shape, devoid of feeling or the capacity for feeling, isolated in a devastated landscape that is barely distinguishable from the man.

The status of the legend allows writers and artists to take it for granted that he is radically inadequate, but also that the attack on his inadequacy will carry momentous meanings for their society—even if that attack has been repeated many times before, and in a sense is built into the legend itself. Ray Lawler's *Summer of the Seventeenth Doll*, for instance, was regarded as a major event in Australian drama when it was first produced in 1955. It dramatised the crisis in the life of Roo, a cane-cutter and representative of the legend, and his relationship with Olive. For seventeen years Roo had been cutting cane in Queensland, as the top man in his team, returning to Olive's house in Melbourne for the five month lay-off, bringing back enough money to last till the next season. Each year he gives her a cheap doll to mark the occasion: hence the title. The crisis this year occurs because Roo has lost his position as top man to a younger rival and cannot cope. He tries to adapt to a new style of life, seeking regular employment and normal domestic life with Olive, but by the end of the play it is clear that neither she nor he can adapt in this way.

Overtly the tragedy of the play comes from the death of the legend: Roo's way of life is now obsolete. But the legend was already dead when it was first born, half a century before, and obsolescence is built into it. There had to be more to the play than this belated obituary, for it to have had the effect it had on contemporary audiences. In fact it addressed a similar problematic to White's *Voss*, which was written in the same decade. Like *Voss* Lawler's play was concerned with the crisis in the Australian family, complicated by problems between the public and the private as they impinged on alienated sex roles. Like the drover/shearer husband in Lawson and Baynton, Roo is totally split into a public and a private self. The seven month absence each year is like a hyperbolic metaphor for the split: just as Voss's long absence and huge distance is a metaphor for his relationship to his 'wife'. Within the play, Roo is not constructed as an instance of the legend. He is not insensitive or irresponsible. On the contrary, he has total loyalty to Olive and shows himself to be loving and sensitive, a good companion. Even the inarticulacy which Lawler's stage directions insist on is no greater than that of any middle class male in the audience if his career had reached the same mid-life crisis. The double construction of Roo's character is signalled by his name. It is assumed by everyone (the audience included) that it is a shortened form of 'kangaroo', Australia's national animal, but Olive explains that it comes from 'Reuben', the eldest son of Jacob in the Bible, an archetypal patriarch of impeccable credentials.

The play seems to deliver a heavy-handed judgment on the life of the legend. The symbolism of the doll-ritual is unmistakeable, and various characters underline it in case the audience is too obtuse. These cheap dolls are a tatty modern substitute for the corn-dolls of authentic harvest rituals. They mark time in so repetitive a way that they are in fact an attempt to hold back time. And most damning, their plastic brightness signifies the infantilisation of the women as a prerequisite for the fantasies of the men. At the climax of the play, Roo smashes the seventeenth doll, seeming to signify the end of his dream and his still inarticulate recognition of the higher reality of maturity.

But the power of the play does not come from its affirmation of this highly conventional morality. It is set throughout in a single room of a rather tatty Melbourne suburban home in 1953: 'reality' for its first Australian audiences. The locale of the legend, the cane-fields of Queensland, exists only by report and that is not what is problematic in the play. The audience see instead a house which is strongly marked as a woman's space (owned by Olive's mother, controlled by Olive) in which the men are like boarders. And Olive's intense rejection of marriage expresses a repudiation of everyday bourgeois respectability. Their relationship, as an exclusive couple who are not formally married and have no children, has become a significant trend in Australia in the 1980s. In the 1950s, the pattern was hardly visible, though government bodies were already expressing anxieties about the anti-social tendencies of women to have small families and make use of contraception. Under cover of a play that seems to look backwards, Lawler was dramatising an emerging phenomenon that was to revolutionise the Australian family.

There is another character, Pearl, a middle-aged widow, currently a barmaid, who is invited to fill an empty slot in the world of the lay-off. She mounts a continuous commentary on the 'nastiness' of Olive and Roo's arrangement, but she is ridiculous in her hypocritical respectability. Olive and Roo's crime is to have attempted to be lovers for seventeen years; not at all the kind of crime a representative of the legend would ever have been guilty of. So their achievement is still heroic, in spite of its failure. The failure is compounded by the ethic of masculinity into which Roo has been socialised, which forces him into an absurd competitiveness with his younger male rival. Both Roo and Olive have many unexamined reflexes from their sexist upbringing. Their attempt is also constrained by the alienating conditions of work in contemporary society, where seasonal rural work, the central activity of the legend, still provides a source of metaphors for the gendered division of labour in Australian society. The legend is not here the shadow of an ideal world in the past. It is a magnified image of patterns of gender and work relationships from the present reaching out into the future, which have catastrophic consequences for the ordinary lives of ordinary people.

Lawler's ambiguous use of the legend diffuses the critique, generating a sense of loss that ultimately, for most audiences, leaves the ideology of the legend alive and well and able to damage many more lives in the present. Other uses of the legend are less elegiac, more savage, like nightmares rather than a fading dream. Stan in White's *The Tree of Man* is a monument to the legend, heroically inadequate, as is Voss in a different way. But in other works White gives merciless portrayals of figures from the legend: Norbert Hare in *Riders in the Chariot* (1961), Don Prowse in *The Twyborn Affair* (1979), among others.

In the film *Wake in Fright* the legend definitively enters the condition of nightmare. The central character, a school teacher in a country town, goes off for the vacation, meaning to go to Sydney where his girlfriend is waiting for him. Instead he gets drawn into the world of the legend, preserved in a country town on the way to the metropolis. He gambles his money away, and has to submit to a parody version of the ethic of mateship in order to survive. There is a horrific scene at the centre of the film, a kangaroo shoot which heaps carnage upon carnage, the kangaroos as victims of the violence that lies close to the surface in this incarnation of the legend, as it did in Baynton's earlier version. The all-male bond is translated into a homosexual rape that leaves the teacher disgusted to the point of suicide. At the end of the film he returns to the school to begin another year, but now the shadow of the legend hangs over the bleak normality of the lonely town. Where Lawler and White in different ways use the legend to focus on and magnify specific problems of their society, *Wake in Fright* takes the legend to the limit, establishing it as a more intense and persuasive reality that is so painful that a bourgeois sleep in the safe and humdrum world of the suburbs has to be better.

The legend, then, is not a single set of meanings that always function in a similar way. It is a complex cultural resource which has been inflected in different ways by different people. It is typically hard to decode because it is constituted by contradictions, and many of the meanings that complete the interpretation of the text are left unstated. This difficulty of interpretation complements the bare simplicity of the meanings that the text seems to contain, masking yet making possible the endless shifts and ambiguities that characterise the legend in social use. The last 80 years have more than shown how viable the legend has been for so many people. So protean and inexhaustible a form is likely to have many more years of excessive use.

9 Multiculturalism and the fragment society

'Multiculturalism' became a fashionable slogan in the 1980s, more or less espoused by both major political parties. But this unenthusiastic consensus also provoked a predictable backlash, sparking off a debate that brought xenophobic nationalism into the public arena. For instance, in early 1990 the Australian Law Reform Commission announced that it planned a study of multiculturalism and the law. This was immediately attacked by Bruce Ruxton as a leading spokesman for xenophobic nationalism, who was duly reported in the media:

> CANBERRA: Australia should not consider whether the legal system protected the rights of non-Anglo Saxon Australians, Victorian RSL president Bruce Ruxton said yesterday ...
>
> In a statement, Mr Ruxton said the British legal system had served the majority of English-speaking people for centuries.
>
> 'Any attempt to change it in this country is just not on', he said.
>
> 'The minorities and their cultural values are of no concern to the Australian people.
>
> If these newcomers are not satisfied with the legal system in this country they know what they can do'.
> (*The West Australian* 1 March 1990)

Ruxton's militant nationalism does not stop him claiming an unbroken connection back to the imperial centre, celebrating a legal system that now guarantees the privileged position of British migrants against all others. Although he refers to the 'British', it is the AngloSaxon majority within the British that he identifies with exclusively. Other

THE FRAGMENT SOCIETY

groups of 'newcomers' have posited a monolithic 'Anglo-Celtic' majority as the dominant group in Australia, but Ruxton speaking from the heartland of this nationalistic position does not recognise the existence or participation of Celts. His unitary 'Australian people' clearly do not include any of these minorities, and he claims on their behalf a contemptuous indifference to all other cultural values.

Ruxton received publicity because he is representative, but what he represents is now a minority view. In the last 50 years there has been a major shift in attitudes within the Australian community, which has destabilised earlier definitions of 'Australianness' itself. The end of the second world war marked a turning point, with the development of an expansionist immigration policy which drastically altered the balance of immigrants. Before this time, migrants from Britain were the majority. Since the war, migrants from Britain have made up only 40 per cent of the intake, in an influx that accounts for nearly 60 per cent of Australia's post-war population growth in the 1980s (Storer 1985). 'Multiculturalism' reflects a significant demographic shift.

However, the fashionableness of the term may make it seem a dubious category to use to organise an account of Australian literature and culture over the past 200 years. It has the effect of constructing the recent present as the exclusive site of multiculturalism, leaving the rest of the past as Ruxton territory, an uncontested domain of xenophobia and prejudice. In the present it opens up the dangers of overstatement, since even in the 1980s the population was still over 75 per cent Anglo-Celtic, and with the same demographic patterns it will still be 70 per cent 'British' in 30 years time (Price 1985). What is the explanatory power of a category which is marginalised in the present and excluded from the past?

Against such doubts we will argue in this chapter that in a modified form Australia has been beset with the problems and conflicts of a multicultural society throughout its history. The theme of multiculturalism is a belated recognition of the kind of struggle that is a constant in colonial situations, but its very ubiquitousness necessitates its constant redefinition as it can so easily be appropriated by any ideological position whatsoever. From this perspective the experience of recent migrant groups, as articulated through a still small number of writers, is by no means marginal to an understanding of the construction of Australian identity. On the contrary, since these issues have been so effectively suppressed or displaced from mainstream literature and history, a version of the multicultural perspective has a crucial role to play in current criticism providing as it does, in formal terms, an almost exact mirror image of tendencies outlined in our earlier chapters.

We therefore return to the Hartz thesis to begin to describe the overall process. Hartz focused on the foundation moment, when the initial fragment separated from the metropolitan centre. He proposed

179

that such fragments lack the cultural diversity of the centre. However, the Hartzian unity is simply an artefact of the colonial eye, which fails to recognise the self-division of fragments or the existence of indigenous cultures. In Australia's case the founding fragment consisted of a microcosm of British imperialism. The colonial power arrived accompanied by people from England's first colony, the Irish, who formed a decisive element among the first convicts. The colonial relation back in Britain affected the supposed unity of the 'Anglo-Celt' majority throughout the 19th century, which saw fresh waves of immigrants coming for a variety of reasons, with the Irish making up the second largest group within the colony. This is not a static picture, with a single fragment working out its destiny undisturbed by any further external incursions. Each wave of immigrants can be seen as the insertion of a new set of fragments into a structure that was not a monolith but itself an ordered series of fragments, whose history laid down patterns that functioned to organise and make sense of each new wave.

The xenophobic nationalism espoused by Ruxton is frankly racist, and this racism runs deep in the construction of Australian identity. Australian racism has an impeccable genealogy stretching back to the initial confrontation with Aboriginal people. In this way the conditions of the founding moment laid down tracks that have continued to influence later structures. McQueen has argued trenchantly that 'racism is the most important single component of Australian nationalism' (1970:42). He and others have documented the role of virulent racist attitudes in the construction of the Commonwealth, as exemplified by the central place of the Immigration Restriction Act of 1901, the cornerstone of the infamous White Australia policy.

Racism is a stark and exemplary form of ethnocentrism. Both racism and ethnocentrism have a common set of properties which come together in a syndrome that Adorno (1950) labelled the 'authoritarian personality', a set of traits that he associated with fascist sympathies and racist prejudice. The 'authoritarian personality' shows two characteristics that are logically and psychologically indispensable to ethnic prejudice: an obsession with notions of purity and unity within the group, and a need for strong category boundaries around it.

Racism and ethnocentrism of the kind that Adorno studied are found amongst non-dominant as well as dominant groups. Every group which believes that its existence is threatened by hostile outsiders develops strategies to exclude others and maintain its own homogeneity. These strategies take two forms, in Australia as elsewhere. One is through patterns of marriage, with marriage within the group (endogamy) both signifying and maintaining strong boundaries around the group. The other is through forms of language and culture which have the same function, to sustain group identity and exclude outsiders: forms of antilanguage and anticulture designed to protect what perceives itself as an antigroup.

Different immigrant fragments have different marriage patterns, and these patterns change significantly over time, reflecting the relation of the group to the dominant society, in particular its sense of vulnerability and opposition. Greek immigrants to Australia, for instance, have been relatively endogamous, and marrying outside the community is rarer than for Dutch immigrants (Price 1985). But the pattern for each such group changes with the length of time it has been in Australia. Southern European migrants are now in a second-phase relationship to the dominant society, with Asian migrants the largest group in the first phase.

In general the more secure a fragment is in its place in the overall structure, the less it needs and values high boundaries and strict boundary-maintenance. In order to negotiate a new place in the dominant structure, a fragment needs strategies to lower and renegotiate its boundaries, without necessarily removing them. These strategies bear on the crucial dilemma of all such groups, the contradiction between cultural maintenance and forms of accommodation. First generation migrants tend to emphasise cultural maintenance, while the second generation moves closer towards assimilation, thus creating a major fissure within the group across generations. But the split is in some respects a way of managing the fundamental contradiction, since the children are assigned the task of making links with the new on behalf of the group, while being required to maintain their allegiance to the old. The second generation has to live with a basic double message, to renounce purity while remaining true to the group.

We use 'multiculturalism' to refer to a kind of cultural map which acknowledges diversity without losing sight of the specific histories of the multicultural project. 19th century multiculturalism was differently constructed and had different effects—the metaphor of multiculturalism cannot be utilised sweepingly. It is also a strategy for coping with this diversity that characteristically lowers boundaries, allowing but not forcing cultural exogamy. The same attitudes applied to the international scene will value lower boundaries and reposition the nation more flexibly in relation to other nations and groups. The nationalist tradition understated the actual diversity of Australian society, and constructed an external world that seemed equally uniform, and overwhelmingly threatening. A multicultural perspective constructs a more complex but less hostile external world, with new allies to be invoked against the imperial centre and a more confident scepticism about its oppressive claims to universal truth. For many reasons it gives a special value to migrant writing, not simply for particular communities but also for the Australian community, which still attends insufficiently to these newly emerging cultural forms.

HIDDEN COUNTRIES

If the notion of Australia as a confident, fissureless monoculture has always been an illusion, an ideological stratagem, then we need to go back to moments when the illusion seemed at its most serene, to show how diversity was contained and elided from the cultural record. The most obvious such moment is the period around the turn of the century, when trenchant nationalism in literature and art coincided so precisely with the foundation of Australia. McQueen (1970) has criticised the racist paranoia in Henry Lawson and the *Bulletin* tradition, attitudes which were inscribed in the law and reinforced by major institutions in the state, including the trade union movement. These show the hysterical will to unity of the authoritarian personality as it existed amongst popular radicals, as the reflex of their nationalism. But there was always another strand in this movement, seemingly in contradiction with it. Richard White (1981) has noted that the small group of artists who were most responsible for the nationalist construction of Australian identity were middle-class 'bohemians', whose revolutionary nationalism drew polemical legitimacy from their appeal to the latest French models.

We can see this clearly in the first radical movement in Australian art, the Heidelberg School, who militantly invoked the French Impressionists in their battle against the then-dominant Anglophile and conservative art establishment. Apart from the famous 'Impressions' exhibition of 1890, where members of the group exhibited small scale loosely painted 'impressions' of various scenes, polemically repudiating the establishment's requirement that paintings should be carefully finished and polished, this group's most typical work showed a realist technique deployed on strongly Australian scenes and topics. Their ideology was considerably more nationalist than avant-garde, but their strategy of invoking a European tradition against the conservative British mainstream was highly effective and not at all unAustralian. Later artists were able to follow the same route, with artists like Nolan, Drysdale, Tucker and Dobell incorporating Australian themes in a modernist style that is now the orthodoxy.

In literature the exemplary instance is the poetry of Christopher Brennan. In histories of Australian literature Brennan's work is treated as an anomaly, a sport. During the two decades around the turn of the 20th century he proclaimed the French symbolist poets as models for his metaphysical, obscure and unAustralian verse, much of which was however published in the *Bulletin*, the bible of the nationalists (whose editor, J. F. Archibald was almost obsessive about his French cosmopolitanism). Since the 1970s his work has been revalued (Lawson 1983), as an ancestor of the modernist and cosmopolitan traditions that are now dominant, but this revaluation misses his ambiguous but by no means negligible reputation in his own time.

THE FRAGMENT SOCIETY

In our revaluation of the revaluation we want to draw attention to a crucial quality which linked Brennan to the nationalist tradition. In spite of the cosmopolitan erudition for which he was admired by his contemporaries, Brennan was also conscious of his Irish origins. 'While writing as an Australian, I cannot forget that I am Irish in blood and bone' he wrote in 1917, significantly at the point in his life when he was closest to repudiating that Irishness, briefly overwhelmed by the pro-British rhetoric of the first world war (McQueen 1970:43). Brennan became an associate professor of Comparative Literature at Sydney University in the early 1920s, but his father was an Irish publican, and his mother came from Cashel, in County Tipperary, perhaps the birthplace of Frank the Poet. He was an upwardly mobile second generation Irishman (though Sydney University interrupted that upwards trajectory abruptly in 1925 by sacking him for 'misconduct', i.e. for leaving his wife of 23 years and living openly with Another Woman, Mrs Violet Singer). In a suitably masked form, his poetry explored his dissident responses to his own personal but typical situation, expressing rebellion in a way that was still not quite covert enough for him to have got away with it.

In form his poetry was complex, allusive and difficult, but its subject matter was highly personal: essentially a 20 year meditation on the difficulties of his marriage, veiled in allegory as a universal myth of the human condition. Though there was much that was unique in detail in his marital woes, there was also much that was a common response to the problems of migrant exogamy. In 1897 in Australia he married Elisabeth Werth, a German woman to whom he had become engaged in Germany in 1893. The marriage started in difficult circumstances, against the opposition of both families. Frau Werth, Elisabeth's mother, disapproved of the match between the impecunious Irishman and her almost aristocratic daughter. Mrs Brennan disapproved of her beloved son's marriage outside the faith, to a Protestant. So Brennan had to wait for four years in Australia before his fiancé came out to marry him, and then another 23 years before he was able to unmarry her. For this scion of a working-class Irish family the marriage was exogamous in three dimensions, going across the boundaries of class, nationality and religion. In this respect it was therefore an ideal union for a second generation migrant with an unconscious mission to transgress the boundaries that enclosed his ethnic identity.

Brennan's unhappy marriage formed the provocation for the first two movements of his major work, *Poems* of 1913. The second section, the core of the book, was entitled 'The Forest of the Night'. The title recalls Blake not the French symbolists, and the strategy is greatly influenced by Blake. The section is organised through the figure of Lilith, who in Hebrew mythology was Adam's first lover, who 'did unite/ herself with Adam in unblest delight'. Adam, 'uncapacious of that dreadful love',

183

cannot enjoy Eden or Eve or paradisal innocence, and the repudiated Lilith takes a terrible revenge.

Like Blake, Brennan's use of mythology was able to produce many of the insights of psychoanalysis into the processes of the unconscious, in Brennan's case just before Freud's major works were published (not a negligible indicator of the interest of his poetry). Brennan used the opposition between Eve and Lilith to explore the double construction of women that Anne Summers argues is the classic image of the Australian patriarchal tradition. Brennan was aware of this pattern in his own sexual biography, where it provided the material for his mythology. Immediately after graduating Brennan taught at Goulburn, where his *Curriculum Vitae* written in 1930 hints at a double affair:

> Religion was gone, something else was now bound to follow: and at Goulburn I found someone to lose it along with me. It was a sweet initiation and a happy little secret affair—while it lasted. For what must I do but forsake it for a virtuous affection! This was for a well known Catholic girl of the town, who was simply amusing herself with me ... (Brennan 1984:181).

In the cryptic passage that follows this, Brennan claims to see a pattern that recurred, with Elisabeth as the successor to the well-known Catholic girl. In this text he does not mention that Elisabeth too had a double, a Berlin woman described by a 'friend' as 'a benevolent tart on the side' (Clark 1980:74). His love for Elisabeth was 'virtuous' and chaste, while he had a physical relationship with this other. But it should be noted that Brennan is repudiating this double image of woman at the same time as he is confessing that he has been its victim. The first sentence associates his first 'sweet initiation' with his intensely religious repudiation of religion, and he gently mocks his youthful capitulation to the ideology of 'virtuous affection'. Poems survive that recall these two women and his relationship with them as profound and positive experiences, by no means cynical sexual adventures. On the contrary, he saw his repudiation of them as a great betrayal, and the Lilith figure is the vehicle for exploring the terms of this catastrophic mistake.

That mistake was not simply his endorsement of a conventional middle-class marriage as against the values of a Blakean eroticism. Lilith is also definitively the first love, the love of the true paradise which was lost with the coming of Eden and Eve. The Elisabeth-Eve union was the fulfilment of one directive of the immigrant mother to her beloved son, that he marry out of and above the group. The Lilith union was the fulfilment of the contradictory command, that he marry within the group and be true to his ethnic affiliations and identity. In his life Brennan could not resolve the double message. Even his final satisfying union with Vie Singer could meet the conflicting demands only by combining a high status partner with personal catastrophe.

The French symbolists did not contribute much to the terms of his social theory of gender, but they were extremely useful in justifying his poetic enterprise. Brennan greatly valued the French connection. For instance, in a letter to Mallarmé accompanying his first published book of poems he wrote: 'this little book of verse is due to you & thro' you, to the literature of your race . . . as many an Irishman in other days found a new home in France, so I have found in her literature a spirit, in her writers a style, to which I feel myself instinctively drawn, as some are drawn towards home' (Brennan 1984:436).

There is no reason to doubt that this eulogy was sincere, and Brennan was certainly well read in contemporary French poetry. But what was much more important for Brennan than French influence was the belief that he and his contemporaries shared that this influence was there. The meaning of Frenchness was an important component of his significance for his first readers. The case is similar to that of the Heidelberg School of painters whom he admired: their own belief in their European up-to-dateness as shared by others helped to construct a cluster of potent meanings about their enterprise, which established a base for their successful attack on the artistic establishment. Axel Clark, Brennan's biographer, wryly notes that 'it was widely believed in Sydney that he was renowned as a scholar in Europe, though in fact his name was almost totally unknown there' (Clark 1980: 221-222).

Brennan's poetic enterprise was marked by two distinctive qualities, both of which have important if indirect roots in his ambiguous situation as a second generation Irish migrant. The most immediately striking quality for his contemporaries was a deliberate oddness, a protomodernist strangeness and difficulty. On the one hand he claimed, after the event, a kind of unity, along the lines of the French symbolist *livre composé* which Brennan explained was a 'book of verse conceived and executed as a whole, a single concerted poem' whose unity lay in its 'symphonic character'. In fact Brennan's book was composed over a long period of time, and retained all the discrepancies and fissures that marked his 20-year trajectory. In spite of predictable attempts by later critics to discover this unity, the book is crossed by innumerable markers of heterogeneity and disunity.

Brennan developed a number of devices whose common meaning was a fascinated equivocation with unity. On the one hand there are curious and seemingly arbitrary breaks—a puzzling excess of headings, and pages or half pages left blank. But more frequently there are also barriers not observed. Brennan often defied the convention that each new line of verse should begin with a capital letter, and he used run-on lines extensively, following the sense without a break from line to line and even stanza to stanza. Sometimes a single grammatical sentence flowed continuously over four or five stanzas, 16 to 20 lines. Although none of these tricks was as startling as the experimentation of later modernists such as Cummings or the Dadaists, it had a clear meaning which was seen clearly enough (and objected to) at the time. The message of Brennan's stylistic innovations was his repudiation of conventions that encode specious unity and pernicious barriers. Brennan's devices work primarily to destabilise confident assumptions that boundaries and divisions are natural.

The second part of Brennan's poetic program he referred to by the modish name of symbolism, but its roots were not exclusively in the French tradition. The key notion is that of correspondences, which he took from Baudelaire but used to make a basic link with forms of mysticism: 'Symbolism involves what may develop into a philosophical or mystical theory of the universe, as constituted by 'correspondences', analogies, spiritual kinships of significance'. In another place, developing this idea further, Brennan wrote: 'The law of correspondences .... is common to poetry and to mysticism, both of which are simply different aspects of symbolism' (Brennan 1984:259).

It is unusual to posit symbolism as the source and subsuming category for both poetry and mysticism, and his history of the term in practice gives primacy to a mystical tradition whose main exemplars were Swedenborg, Boehme and Blake. This tradition led to a view of the world which Brennan borrowed from Brahmanism, a view with which Joseph Furphy was familiar, a world where outer forms masked and mirrored an inexpressible deeper reality. This conception values silence as well as speech, its absolute claims challenging and evading the material world, its forms of language aiming to suggest everything and state nothing, equivocating with its most important meanings. It has the characteristics of antilanguage which are congenial to ambitious but threatened minorities, whose aspirations and resistances must be concealed but cannot be entirely suppressed. In this respect Brennan's poetry has much in common with genres that arise from colonised cultures, in spite of his apparently privileged position in AngloCeltic Australia.

Brennan described his form of 'symbolism' in some of his best-known lines, from the 'Epilogue' to his book of poems:

> *Deep in my hidden country stands a peak,*
> *and none hath known its name*
> *and none, save I, hath even skill to seek:*
> *thence my wild spirit came.*
>
> *Thither I turn, when the day's garish world*
> *too long hath vex'd my sight,*
> *and bare my limbs where the great winds are whirl'd*
> *and life's undreaded might.*

Brennan begins with the theory of correspondences in its simplest form, constructing an inner landscape that matches the outer. This is not only an inner world, but also a hidden world. The poet himself has only 'skill to seek', not clear knowledge to guide him on his odyssey. This is a place into which the poet retreats at moments of vexation in the stressful and unsatisfying 'garish world'. The purpose of this retreat is greater exposure to 'life's undreaded might', a confrontation that however is passive, a self-exposure ('bare my limbs') not an assault or examination of the topography of this landscape. The 'hidden country' is the source of his 'wild spirit', his origins (which in genealogical terms were in Ireland), but its function now, as inner world, is both solace and recuperation.

Brennan's poetry has two characteristics of the literature of oppressed peoples in a colonial context: a difficulty of language that functions like an antilanguage (in his case, for a society of one) and a quietist search for a 'paradise within' as a substitute for unattainable social aspirations. But Brennan was not always consistent, and his inconsistencies point to the divergent possibilities of this stance. This book of poems was published in 1913, at a low point in Brennan's career. He had produced a devastating critique of the conditions of his marriage but remained within it. Over this period he produced some jingoistic poems on behalf of Australian participation in the first world war, driven by his hostility to a very small number of German people much closer to home (his wife and mother-in-law). But earlier he had produced a series of poems condemning British imperialism in the Boer war, which he had originally intended to include as a separate section entitled 'The Burden of Tyre'. This would have given an explicit political dimension to his poetic vision: a denunciation of British colonialism that he was not able to articulate by 1913.

Brennan, then, should not be seen as an anomaly in Australian literary history. He was not a modernist before his time, so much as an Irishman after it. He does not fit into the opposition posed by Wilkes, between the 'Stockyard and the Croquet lawn', between crude nationalism and genteel cosmopolitanism. He represents a third tradition, closer to the first of these than to the second: the Celtic underground. This tradition includes Adam Lindsay Gordon before him, who entered the nationalist pantheon by celebrating horses, but who also wrote fascinated pastiches of classical Greek forms. Contemporary with Brennan were the different but related talents of Lindsay and McCrae, Neilson and O'Dowd, Gilmore and MacKellar. The tradition is still alive today in the work of Marion Campbell, whose first novel, *Lines of Flight*, (1985), deployed a coruscating variety of modernist experimental forms in following the trajectory of a young woman, Rita Finnerty, to France as the country of the Other. The Brennan tradition, which neither began nor ended with his work, has been a continuous occluded presence in Australian life and Australian culture.

THE ASSIMILATIONIST MUSE

In 1956 Melbourne hosted the Olympic Games. In 1957, John O'Grady published a best-seller *They're a Weird Mob*, under the pseudonym 'Nino Culotta', which purported to describe the bewildered but successful encounter between an Italian immigrant and the authentic Australian language. In 1958 Russel Ward published *The Australian Legend*, whose role we have already seen in the construction of a version of the Australian identity. Together these three events encapsulate some major changes that were underway at that moment in Australian society, challenging the previously dominant ideological structures.

The Australian media presented the Melbourne Olympics as a triumph of the Australian character. Dawn Fraser was a larrikin outside the pool but inside it she beat the world's best. The golden boys and girls of Australia (all White, and Anglo-Celtic in origin) showed the world the virtues of the true-blue, fair dinkum, no nonsense Aussie. What media coverage of the Melbourne Olympics did not highlight was the fact that many of the workers who built the stadium were descendents of the inventors of the original Olympics, the Greek hegemony that once spread from Turkey to Spain along the Mediterranean. These immigrants were the radical new element that entered Australia's demographic mix after the war, and slowly altered Australia's concept of its national identity. These people began to reach Australia under the Chifley Labor government's new immigration policy, whose architect was Arthur Caldwell. Throughout the period between 1947 and 1972 (until the return of the Whitlam Labor government) there was a clear order of preference: the British, followed by northern Europeans, with southern Europeans a poor third. But in good migrant years such as 1949–50 and 1955–56 a significant proportion of the 150 000 or so migrants per year were southern Europeans. The policy that underpinned Australian immigration was assimilation. To this end an Assimilation Unit was added to the Department of Immigration. This unit was renamed the Integration Unit in 1964 and is the precursor of the looser Multicultural Advisory Units which were to develop later on.

This post-war influx of southern Europeans forced a reappraisal of the original fragment society constructed out of the metropolitan British centre. Before 1947 a rigid and simplistic strategy had seemed adequate to the purpose: groups could be either 'assimilated' (similarities turned into perfect replication, as with the Irish) or discriminated against (turning differences of language and appearance into absolute barriers of racial difference, as with Aborigines). The resulting society could emphasise its fissureless unity as 'British' culture, and its crucial cultural symbols or artefacts—literature, law, art—were firmly monocultural and monolingual. The move to include large sections of non-British stock was made with the priorities of the dominant culture firmly in place. The 'new' Australians were to be assimilated and made more Australian than the Australians themselves. The official attitude of the Australian towards the darker-skinned southern European smacked of Macaulay's famous 'Minute on Education' of 1835, in which he had advocated the use of the English language in India to create a race who would be black only on the outside.

Southern Europeans presented many problems for this simplistic structure. They were darker than northern Europeans, but within the European range, and they spoke languages which were not English but came from a common European stock. The challenge that they represented was not just the practical problems they raised, but more importantly the crisis that they provoked in the previous ideological complex.

Race and class were important underlying issues, but for a variety of reasons it proved convenient to foreground language as the marker of difference and the target of the assimilationist programme. English is the language in common use in Australia, so it was not contentious to argue that all migrants should learn English in order to be able to participate fully in the life of the society. Language also carries potent cultural and ideological meanings, with decisive consequences for full membership of a group. But standard English in Australia as throughout the other former British colonies is also the carrier of the ideology of imperialism, and post-war Australia was strenuously declaring itself to be no longer a colony. It declared this difference through its construction of a radical egalitarian identity, which Russel Ward's *Australian Legend* neatly codified and legitimated in 1958, not when the 'legend' was at its most flourishing but just when it was needed most.

His oft-quoted catalogue of the 'typical Australian' (which we too have used extensively for our reading of this all-pervasive Australian myth) ends with a reference to the special vocabulary of this typical Australian: 'No epithet in his vocabulary is more completely damning than "scab", unless it be "pimp" used in its peculiarly Australasian slang meaning of "informer" ' (Ward 1958:2). Though this reference to language is included almost accidentally, as a rider so to speak, it is nevertheless the crucial pivot upon which the reconstructed typical Australian stands. This immediately seems to offer migrants a clear target in their search for a place in Australian society. All that they need in order to be able to draw upon the deeper psyche of the Australian, to be able to participate in the Australian legend (and its attendant features of jingoism, provincialism and so on) is simply a mastery of these Australianisms.

The text that brought these themes together in an exemplary form for the period was John O'Grady's *They're a Weird Mob* (1957). Neither the *Oxford History of Australian Literature* (Kramer, 1981) nor the *Macmillan History of Literature: A History of Australian Literature* (Goodwin, 1986) discusses this work, though Goodwin does include the text in his Chronological Table (p. 305). O'Grady's book was instantly popular (it went through 24 printings in the first three years after it was published, clearly touching a nerve in the Australian public and it was freely given to 'free-passage' migrants as they walked off the gangways) and in 1966 it was made into a successful film. But there were not enough earnest new migrants to explain its popularity: O'Grady's main target was old Australians, not the new.

O'Grady presents his narrator (and author, as the original editions pretended) as an Italian migrant, 'Nino Culotta'. Culotta is atypical in a number of ways. He is a journalist who apparently speaks perfect standard English. This allows O'Grady to pose a stark opposition between this standard English and the colloquial form that is to bewilder and fascinate him, and provide the focus for his satire. Unlike his Meridionali brethren who are short and dark-skinned and who form the vast bulk of Australian-Italians, Nino Culotta the character is a northerner, fair-skinned with blond hair. Already difference based upon looks (the difference which underlies racism) will not be one of his problems. The choice of a northern Italian by John O'Grady indicates a choice which would make Nino's transition from migrant to stereotypical Australian less difficult.

The process of assimilation is made explicit through Nino's initiation into the major institutions of the 'typical Australian's' existence: the pub, the work-place and the family. These stages are all marked by Nino's progressive and self-conscious mastery of a discourse which we have claimed has the same relationship to standard Australian English as anti-languages have to language proper. This alternative language is given an extraordinary primacy: 'Most Australians speak English like I speak Hindustani, which I don't. In general, they use English words, but in a way that makes no sense to anyone else' (p. 13).

Key expressions—'bloody' and three words associated with the argot of the pub—are immediately invoked to establish the dominance of this language. 'Bloody' is given a special place in the capitalised context of 'King's Bloody Cross' and endlessly repeated: 'Well bloody give ut to me before I call the bloody cops or do me block or some bloody thing. Give us me three bob' (p. 16). Within hours of reaching Kings Cross, Nino is initiated into the rituals of the pub. Situated in the very heart of the metropolis, the pub is a space in which the Australian myth and the outback slang are on display. In *They're a Weird Mob* the pub is not only the obvious context for words like 'schooner', 'middy' and 'shout', but also a site for the confirmation of (male) camaraderie or mateship which is one of the underlying themes of the Australian legend.

O'Grady's strategy in *They're a Weird Mob* is an instance of the class of strategies that make up 'Orientalism', since he has artificially constructed a European Other in the form of the northern Italian Nino in order to speak on his behalf: a classic device of colonialism. But

O'Grady gives this strategy a new twist, by confronting his pseudo-European with an equally alien pseudo-Australian, whose otherness must equally be appropriated and spoken for. His novel reworks a theme that goes back at least to Trollope, where a high-class Englishman comes to inspect the 'White Aborigines' but finishes up going native. The revelation that the author was no Italian immigrant but a 'native' Irish Australian adds a further twist. The Irish shared the same religion and the same schools as the now-despised 'wogs' and O'Grady becoming Culotta looking at O'Grady looking at Culotta plays with a buried identity between representatives of different waves of migration.

This level of meaning needs to be emphasised, though O'Grady foregrounds a simpler, less subversive message: constructing a migrant figure who endorses the assimilationist thrust of the White Australian immigration policy, and a work force which will present no problems. In his odyssey Nino discovers that a bloke in Australia must always do something for a 'crust' (16); he should enjoy 'hard yacker' (29); he rejects any concept of a hierarchical society ('None o' this sir an' mister stuff'); hates 'wowsers' and calls you a lucky bastard if he likes you. Thus Nino eulogises:

> So, you New Australians who think you can speak English, do not be discouraged. Keep listening, and you'll catch on in time. And if you are ever admitted to an Australian's friendship, thank your God for one of the finest things that can happen to you in this life. He will talk to anybody and everbody, this Australian, but his real mates are few. For them, he will die. Literally. (1957:157–58).

Nino's advice to 'keep listening' is absolutely crucial since only the mastery of 'their queer, abbreviated language', in other words their antilanguage, can guarantee entry into the psychology of the Australian. The vigour with which this line is maintained comes close to secular idolatry: without the legend the Australian doesn't exist. Since the legend becomes a stand-in for 'real' Australia, it must be emphatically endorsed.

Seen from the 1980s, *They're a Weird Mob* can look like a different, less complex text: crude propaganda for Australian monoculturalism and its oppressive assimilationist policy. This is in fact how it functions in relation to Professor Geoffrey Blainey's anti-immigration polemic *All For Australia* (1984) which is riddled with a nostalgia for Culotta's book and its film version (1966). Blainey's target was the more recent phase of Asian immigration, where the issue of race has become explicit. Against these recent migrants, many of whom look different and follow 'different customs' (Blainey, p.15), the immigrants of the 1950s and 1960s are given a resounding endorsement: 'No matter what nicknames the Old Australian had used then against the New Australian, he believed that immigrants in general were good for his country' (1984: 15–16).

But while Nino the northern Italian could marry a Catholic girl, the new non-White migrants, 'through no fault of their own', Blainey candidly admits, will find themselves rejected and relegated to 'front-line' suburbs like Cabramatta and Springvale. Blainey's work is more explicit about Australian racism than O'Grady's was, but paradoxically in order to sustain his myth of the 1950s he has to act as though the Australian anti-language did not mean what it said. O'Grady's tactic was less obvious: he does not give due space to the racist expressions which Wilkes (1978/1985) shows the Australian colloquial language is so well endowed with ('chow', 'reffo', 'blow-in', 'ding', 'spag', 'ethno', 'wog', 'boong' etc.) In spite of the prejudice so systematically encoded in colloquial Australian, these Australians were totally without prejudice, Blainey declares (without evidence beyond Culotta's successful fiction.) But O'Grady's reconciliation between the new migrant and the old Australian of the legend was a skilful ideological feat, not a social fact.

Assimilationist writing contemporary with O'Grady by 'real' (not Anglo-Celtic) migrants did not experiment with non-standard English or non-standard genres. Writers such as the Jewish Judah Waten wrote out their experience in fiction by appropriating standard generic forms. Waten's *Distant Land* (1964), which traces the history of a Jewish family in Australia from 1925 onwards, situates itself firmly into a body of earlier Australian writing which would include Alexander Harris's *The Emigrant Family* (1849) and Henry Handel Richardson's *The Fortunes of Richard Mahony* (1917–1929).

Polish Jews Joshua and Shoshanah Kuperschmidt migrate to Australia because Joshua, intelligent, imaginative but somewhat timid, wishes to break out of the 'straight-jacket' life he is leading in a culturally constrained Jewish ghetto. The choice of Australia is almost accidental. Shoshanah's cousin, Berel Singer, is already in Melbourne and she's heard from him that 'there's no anti-semitism in Australia' (1964:40). The story develops as a family saga interwoven into predictable narratives which seem to have become paradigmatic of the Jewish migrant experience. The holocaust has completely recast Jewish history itself. The writing out of migrant history as family saga, in the style of *Fiddler on the Roof*, is an alternative which White Australian writers have always taken up. The writing of this history duplicates the original moment of the fragment, representing another fragment as it begins to reconstruct its own culture removed from its own metropolitan centre. But faced by the coercive pressures of Australian nationalism the tendency towards cultural difference is suppressed. The pragmatic Berel Singer ('I sell glasses, NOT drinking glasses but eye glasses. I am a travelling optician', proclaims Berel the hawker) has no illusions about the power of assimilation: 'their children, certainly their grandchildren, will certainly be Christians' (1964: 45).

In Australia Josh and Susan Cooper's life (their names suitably anglicised) thus duplicates an unacknowledged narrative of assimilation. Their three children, Ezekiel, Ruth and Benjamin, represent the three alternative patterns of first generation Australians: the conservative Jew who will not touch non-kosher food and speaks of non-Jewish Australian women as 'shiksa', the accommodating and pragmatic daughter who recognises that times change, and the defiantly Australian Benjamin who emphasises 'I am an Australian ... Australia's my country': (p.167). But even Ezekiel will not be able to resist the pressures on his Jewish name. 'Eddie', the name Benjamin uses for his brother, might well become triumphant.

Like *They're a Weird Mob*, *Distant Land* demonstrates the ways in which political processes govern representation. Waten's assimilationist cast of mind can be seen in an autobiographical fragment, 'A Writer's Youth' (Skrzynecki 1985) in which he recounts the first eighteen years of his life. Even in his autobiography, Waten seems to be silent about his migrant experience. 'There was nothing about my migrant background' in his first novel, *Hunger*, he writes (p. 206). And when he overcomes the silence over this experience in *Distant Land*, he still conveys nothing of the traumatised response of multicultural writing proper.

As the example of Waten illustrates, genuinely multicultural writing could not get under way until very late. When it does, it does so in a 'postmulticultural' fashion. Like postmodernism it rears its head as the underside, as the unspeakable, as the authentic voices that Nino Culotta expropriated and Judah Waten suppressed. To speak from the experience of the Other, imperialist discourses themselves must be challenged. And it is only when the Other recognises the folly of an assimilationist literary practice that we get real challenges to the uncritical definitions of Australianness.

Judah Waten unobtrusively mastered standard English, the language of the powerful, while Nino Culotta was finally assimilated into the Australian legend itself. He learnt the antilanguage and effortlessly merged with the 'White' natives. This relatively straightforward process nostalgically outlined by O'Grady finds a counter fiction in a recent short story by Yasmine Gooneratne entitled 'How Barry Changed His Image' (1989). The crucial difference is that Gooneratne is not an Australian pretending to be ethnic who learns to be Australian. In the semi-autobiographical world that Gooneratne constructs, Navaranjini (Jeannie to her Australian friends) decides to improve her Australian vocabulary so that she can be of some positive use to her academic husband who has quickly become disillusioned with Australian society.

Navaranjini quickly gets pretty proficient at it, goaded as she is by the talk-back radio chats of a 'Mr. Casey', and a Professor 'Ronald Blackstone' who claim to speak for upwards of 95 per cent of all Australians. It doesn't take long to recognise that these names represent real people (the first name doesn't even undergo fictional disguise), and

Gooneratne's fiction becomes a political statement about the migrant whose colour will always be in the way of assimilation. But the Australian vocabulary that Navaranjini masters is mediated by G.A. Wilkes' *Australian Colloquialisms* (1978/1985), itself an essentially literary compendium of Australianisms based on what Germaine Greer called a 'monophone card index' (Greer 1978:17). Wilkes' work imposes an insular academic world-view upon a form of language which is vibrant and close to social realities. Much of what Jean masters lacks vitality since her source text (Wilkes) had emphasised that a distinctive Australianness may be found only in his chosen phrases (shit, fuck, fart and their many uses are conspicuously absent as a result). She masters the various meanings of 'bastard', refers to Ronald Blackstone's university as 'Woop-Woop', and in the tradition of the earlier Jewish and Mediterranean migrants hits upon the singular attractiveness of a name change. Bharat Wickramasingha becomes Barry Wicks; Navaranjini, Jean.

Jean's encounter at the University Lodge with Professor Blackstone, the author of many essays on the Asianisation of Australia and member of the pro-assimilation lobby (he had called a Sydney suburb 'Vietnamatta'), is the occasion to try out her recently acquired Australian vocabulary, which she does on the sociology professor, ending with the classic Australianism: 'may all your chooks turn into emus and kick your flaming dunny down' (1989:115). Gooneratne's short story is straightforward enough and reads like a roman à clef; its fictionality is shallow, its targets explicit, and its rancour is not concealed. Apart from the stilted appropriations of the antilanguage, she also explores the predicament of the colonial Sri Lankan in an Australian society which sees no difference between one Asian and another. This is something Barry recognises but Jean does not. Jean's awareness of her own race is played out as an act of showmanship, as a demonstration of linguistic skill without the re-socialisation which must also take place.

Gooneratne's short story stands as a critique of the simplistic assumptions of *They're a Weird Mob*. She shows that mastery of a 'defining' language can sharpen rejection and otherness, especially when race becomes an issue. Her story is one of a small number written by Asians who have already mastered the language of the coloniser, who explore the problems posed by 'assimilation' which can't be solved by linguistic feats like Nino's mastery of Australian English. In Chitra Fernando's 'The Other Country' in *Beyond the Echo*, edited by S. Gunew, & J. Mahyuddin, (1988) and Sue Chin's 'Sydney' (Modjeska 1989) it is the impossibility of a return to one's former cultural practices which problematises the individual's life in a new country. Rupa Gomez, heroine of Chitra Fernando's tale, begins to find the discourse of an arranged marriage unacceptably alien. In rejecting Dominic Perera, an English-educated researcher in a bank, Rupa recognises that just two years of teaching Vietnamese migrants in Sydney has changed her attitudes to life. Even while consoling her mother that she'll eventually 'come back home', she knows full well that a new cultural experience has irrevocably changed her—though whether for the better we never know.

Similarly Sue Chin's protagonist in 'Sydney' finds that the split is total: 'nine hours by plane, three hours difference in time' (p. 235). Though her mother's voice comes back to her from far away Malaysia, the past only exists as memories invoked by a ceiling fan or the sight of a goanna (ancestor of the Malay lizard or *cicak*). But the amnesia of the past is also a consequence of other Australian experiences. Australians do not want to know your past; 'just pretend you're from here' (p. 236) is the advice she gets. In the process she learns not to speak about her past and what was a device to avoid social tension takes a disturbing finality in a willed loss of memory of place. The loss, however, returns only as 'hypnosis', 'it affirms itself, over and over'. Origins are therefore repressed and the 'place called "home"' (p. 238) can occur only in inverted commas. The real home, through this forced amnesia, occurs only as a narrative fragment of the unconscious. And it is because of this that the old 'home', in inverted commas, is overtaken by a new 'home', here in Sydney, but also in inverted commas (p. 239). Like the 'sound of electricity' the mother's telephone call comes screeching back to her as the new 'home' seeks to reconcile itself with the old.

> How are you?
> I am good.
> Good? You mean fine. What is wrong with your English?
> I am fine, there is nothing wrong with my English. It is fine too.
> How strange you are.
> What do you mean, what are you talking about?
> Your English is strange. Is that how all Australians speak or are you being difficult?
> I am not being difficult. It is not strange English. Everyone speaks like this. If you rang less often you wouldn't have to hear any of it.
> (pp. 239–40).

'Fine', the colonial adjective for the well-to-do in Malaysia, accented in a sing-song Chinese tone, confronts the postcolonial, the defiant 'good'. The loss of 'fine' and the ascendancy of 'good' mark the conversion/transition from the old to the new. Yet the 'new' would still be stalked by the old. Even as she speaks to her mother on the phone she sees her reflection in the mirror. 'Her reflection surprises her, black eyes, pale skin, but the hair is purple, the accent so expert, so efficient' (240). This fissured object of her gaze carries the stigma of assimilation and its problems, as she is torn by conflicting allegiances and identities, poised between two instances of the colonial in such a way that there is no longer the possibility of a unitary 'home' or a unitary subject. Chin here is moving towards the themes and forms which were equally occluded by O'Grady's nationalism and by Waten's effacement, but which can be found in the recent multicultural writing that is able at last to challenge the dominant definitions of Australian identity.

FORMS OF MULTICULTURALISM

Not all migrant writing, present or past, adopts the same position in relation to the dominant society. On the contrary, writers have to negotiate the contradictory dimensions of a relationship with a dominant structure that is itself neither static nor homogeneous. We have advanced the thesis that Australian literature is the literature of a cultural fragment of the metropolitan centre, ossified at the moment of contact with the land under the weight of its own colonial mission, and largely reactionary as a consequence. It is precisely this paradoxical relationship with the centre, an urge towards radicalism grafted upon an inescapable conservatism (the paradox of all fragment societies) which makes theories of postcolonialism such an awkward hermeneutic for the study of Australian literature.

Ashcroft, Griffiths and Tiffin (1989) see a radical and subversive kind of postcolonialism in the new migrant writings in Canada and Australia. Situated within a postcolonial culture, migrant writings (and Aboriginal writing too) demonstrate much more acutely the underside of a cultural formation no longer willing to accept the myths of postcolonial homogeneity. 'Organised from within alternative language and cultural groupings, themselves marginalized within the [society] which ... produced them' (p. 145), Australian migrant writings are at the cutting edge of an emergent postcolonialism which Australia had hitherto silenced.

Other critics strip this writing of its radical voice by collapsing it into general tendencies of any cosmopolitan literature. Thus in a recent study of Australian fiction by Ken Gelder and Paul Salzman (1989), chapters entitled 'Voices of the Migrant Experience' and 'Aboriginality' comfortably sit alongside a host of other recent themes in Australian literature. Admirable as their work is—and their breadth of reading is impressive—it is regrettable that they do not recognise a different kind of dialectical tension. Not all 'migrant writing' is of a piece. The marginalisation that we write about rises from a radical cultural difference, which is not normally found among British migrants, who like White New Zealanders are very quickly absorbed into mainstream Australian culture.

Within this heterogeneous complex, we will distinguish two major strategies: reverse assimilationism, and radical multiculturalism. As an instance of the first we will look at the works of David Malouf. The son of a Lebanese Maronite Christian and a Protestant Englishwoman,

David Malouf's life situates itself between a Byzantine heritage on the one hand and an Edwardian decorum on the other. In his first novel, *Johnno*, this English 'style' is 'opposed to the emotionalism of my father's people'. (1975:3). The emotionalism is hinted at in his autobiographical piece, *12 Edmonstone Street* (1985), when he writes about his grandfather's skill at telling traditional Lebanese tales, a form of narration which had close parallels with oral poetics generally. There are also silent accusations directed against the Australian-born son of migrants. His father's Australianness ('My father was born here, had grown up "Australian" . . . ') is read as a betrayal, an enforced uprooting from his historic past as that past is genealogically confirmed. And yet David Malouf recognises in his father that special tension which arises out of a seeming displacement. No matter how Australian he might have become, there were still the 'Old Country' values, especially when it came to 'filial piety'. At some point the sons of migrants must come to terms with their adopted nation. In David Malouf's father's case this coming to terms took the form of an exogamous marriage. The son of the already assimilated father, David (named, ironically enough, after Dickens' David Copperfield) must rediscover the migrant voice in his father's ambiguous rejection of the fatherland.

David Malouf now lives outside Australia, an expatriate son of an assimilated migrant. This complex position gives a new twist to the theme of exile that has run throughout the mainstream literary tradition. The 'exile imperative' connects Brennan's Europeanism with Henry Handel Richardson's similar odyssey. One version of the exile imperative was the 'cultural cringe' and its logic: the exile must be complete so that Australia becomes no more than a reference point. Patrick White did negotiate a return while maintaining his Greek connection, but Christina Stead, Randolph Stow and Shirley Hazzard are among the many expatriates who no longer had or have a need to return for imaginative sustenance.

In contrast with these writers, for David Malouf Australia is *not* the place of exile; it is in fact the place of return. The examples of migrant writing we examine later reverse this problem in that Australia duplicates the initial moment of settlement to become a place of permanent exile. The structural dynamism of the exile imperative is typically disrupted in the case of migrant writing.

The double movement of exile—Australia as a site of exile and Australia as a country from which one exiles oneself—is at the heart of Malouf's celebration of Ovid's exile in *An Imaginary Life* (1978). The novel reconstructs the semi-barbarous Getae at Tomis on the western shores of the Black Sea and Ovid's discovery of the wild boy who reportedly grew up among wolves, and in this way develops a larger concern to define the experience of exile (its psychology) and to map out the terrain where the exile actually takes place. What Ovid discovers, finally, is the 'ordinariness' of the wild boy's life (wolves do not exist in that region) and his own composite identity ('I am three years old. I am sixty. I am six'). Malouf's fictional biography becomes an allegory of the nature of exile in which the narrative of exile duplicates the history of the country left behind. His style appears transparent, but this kind of historically remote and realist fiction resonates with meaning at every level. So much so that in a celebratory essay Harry Heseltine, who stakes the claim that 'the novel is nothing less than one of the classics of our literature', finds in Malouf's account of Ovid's exile a mirror image of a writer's reactions to the conservatism of Australian society in the post-Whitlam era (1989:27).

In Malouf's first novel, *Johnno* (1975), the exile actually returned to Australia upon the death of his father to discover a narrative which had been so far repressed. Going through his father's cupboards the protagonist (subsequently identified as Dante) stumbles upon a copy of the Brisbane Grammar School Magazine for 1949. Dante recognises a bespectacled member of the Stillwater Lifesaving Team in one of the photographs in the magazine, and this triggers a particular biography of Johnno, the larrikin whose antisocial behaviour was secretly admired by Dante and who had such a strong influence over him in later life. Like many of his other works, *Johnno* is a fictional autobiography written in the realist mode. Its significance lies in the way in which the photograph, with the clownish bifocals (perhaps the lens are missing), triggers a specific memory of place along precisely Wordsworthian lines. Australia needs authentication through the return of the exile, and like the story of Ovid in *An Imaginary Life*, and, later, like Roger Millis's *A Serpent's Tooth*, Johnno's tale is also an allegory about an ambiguous sense of attachment to Australia. As in all allegories, the specific instance, the microcosm, stands for the whole, the macrocosm. Thus Brisbane, 'the most ordinary place in the world' (1975: 52), in the context becomes Australia itself. Similarly, Dante's own existence in Australia is explained as a fluke of history, which sums up the situation of all non-native Australians: 'What an extraordinary thing it is, that I should be here rather than somewhere else. If my father's father hadn't packed up one day to escape military service under the Turks . . . .' (p. 52).

Johnno becomes, for Dante, both his uncanny mirror image and the shadow he always pursues. The retrospective narrative which is constructed through this procedure of 'mirroring' and pursuit becomes an intense representation of a kind of romantic-symbolist dilemma, an *ennui*, which can only end in an accidental or intentional death. The Johnno who is scathing in his reading of Australia ('this bitch of a country', 'the whole fucking continent') finds that there is no escape from Australia. In a way this is Dante's position too. His father's death (which is also Malouf the Elder's death) demonstrates the finality of displacement. The migrant dies in Australia, reconciled to it or not.

Malouf's work does not usually treat the original owners of the land, for whom the European exile and its attendant *angst* are alien concepts. In *Johnno*, there is some mention of the situation of Aborigines: we read that Queensland 'is a joke' and that 'Aborigines are herded on to reservations' (1975:52) but nothing more. However his play *Blood Relations* (1989), performed in the Bicentenary year, attempts to explore the two kinds of positions occupied by the Other, as represented by two of its main characters, Willy McGregor or La Farge (real name Spiros Kyriakou) and his part-Aboriginal son Dinny. On the North Queensland coast the dying Willy is confronted with the ghosts of his past during Christmas celebrations. The various postures/impostures he had adopted, the cheating, and denials of his origins, the abuse of women and friends haunt him on this day: 'You know, when I left that island I had to learn a whole new language. If I have to, I reckon I can do it again. [*Laughing*] If I'm lucky it'll be Greek' (p. 79).

This desire to repeat and improve upon the lost past is another version of the exile's dilemma we have isolated as David Malouf's central concern. But *Blood Relations* also has Dinny the part-Aborigine, through whose character the hidden text of the colonised surfaces. 'This island's mine, by Sycorax my mother . . . .' (p. 64) recites Dinny, opening up one of the central intertexts of colonisation, Shakespeare's *The Tempest*. He declaims Caliban's famous speech (*The Tempest* I, ii, 333–345), which however only angers and puzzles Willy ('That's enough, son. You've had enough'). This provokes Dinny to spell out the political agenda of *The Tempest* quotation:

> What's *that* got to do with it? Oh save your breath, Willy, you'll only tire yourself. I know this one too. I can do it by heart : '*Did I ever deny you anything? Didn't I send you to the best school money could buy?*' Yes you did, Willy. You sent me three thousand miles away, to fucking Brisbane. To be with white kids I never seen before. I missed you! You sent me away, to learn to think like a white boy. [*In a mixture of school war cry and aboriginal chant*]. Wangaratta, Wangaratta, Tarrangatta, ya, light blue, dark blue, ya, ya, ya. Maybe you should've just sent me down the creek, Willy, to me mother's people. I used to creep out there with the treefrogs, in the dark, and listen to them singing, swearing, getting pissed, and I'd be homesick. I learned what homesickness was before I even went away. I was homesick here' (p. 66).

It is consistent with Malouf's reverse assimilationist strategy that he can mobilise a text from the canon in order to critique the racism of his own community. Radical multiculturalism tends to be angrier, assaulting classic texts and confronting the official antilanguage, the 'Australian accent', with a more subversive form of antilanguage. As an example of this strategy we will look at the works of Ania Walwicz. Our starting point will be a comparison between A.D. Hope's 1939 classic 'Australia', which we have discussed earlier, and Ania Walwicz's recent prose-poem of the same name (1986). Hope wrote his poem as a disillusioned expatriate, returning bruised and hurt from the 'lush jungle of modern thought' (Oxford University, where the bright young colonial boy 'failed to distinguish himself' to quote Dame Leonie Kramer, 1979:7). He delivers his denunciation of 'this last of lands, the emptiest' with a magisterial air and old-fashioned poetic diction which draw their authority from the prestige of this very centre which had just found him wanting.

Walwicz's text begins like a disjointed meditation on Hope's classic: 'You big ugly. You too empty. You desert with your nothing nothing nothing. You scorched suntanned. Old too quickly' (Modjeska, 1989:241). Where Hope shows how close the notorious 'cultural cringe' is to the neocolonial lash, Walwicz composes from a migrant's position of linguistic and cultural alienation. Her discourse is fractured by the processes—linguistic, social and so on—which marginalise migrant women and postcolonialise their writing. Thus the declarative 'A nation of trees, drab green and desolate grey' with which Hope's poem begins is transformed in Walwicz's opening sentence into a defiant accusation: 'You big ugly'. This combines an excess (of feeling) and a deficiency (of standard English grammar) which Hope could not allow himself. Hope sees a desert, which he immediately fills with metaphors and allusions to prepare for the triumphant return of his colonial boy back to the centre ('From the deserts the prophets come'). Walwicz's repeated 'nothing' indicates that this emptiness is not organised by any system of differences that could project other synonyms. Her text continues with a shorthand that is more aberrant and extreme than Culotta's Australianese: 'You big ugly', 'Old too quickly', 'You nothing much', 'You copy', 'You too far everywhere', 'Road road tree tree', 'You too big sky', 'You laugh with your big healthy', 'You average average' signal the ambiguous relationship the migrant has with Australia, while delivering a precise and comprehensive critique with great economy.

'The disjointed format of the writing encompasses my experience', writes Ania Walwicz in a recent issue of *Mattoid* (13, p. 14). A work such as 'Wogs', which is essentially another version of 'Australia', continues the play on antilanguages and fractures the unproblematic representational assumptions of much of Australian writing.

> they're not us they're them they're them they are else
> what you don't know what you don't know
> what they think they got their own ways
> they stick together you don't know what
> they're up to you never know with them you just don't
> know with them . . . .
> (Mattoid 13, p. 16)

The antilanguage mechanism enables Walwicz to represent the paranoia that lies just under the surface of Australian racism in spite of the seeming certainties of a Bruce Ruxton. She voices the threat posed by the Other to the Australian legend, and at the same time the Other's own painful sense of exclusion. The marginalisation of the migrant is different in kind to that of Anglo-Celtic women generally. The question of identity and the difficulty of constructing a postmulticultural discourse surface dramatically in her 'Translate' (Gunew and Mahyuddin, 1988:34) where the construction of meaning through a gloss on Polish words leads to an endless deferral of the capacity to construct shared realities. The Polish words fissure the discourse and establish strings of associations which monolingual Australian culture can hardly accommodate:

> *Kraj country don't say same mean znaczy*
> *use same letters so can put sztuka play*
> *theatre bawimy ubaw zabawa play is not*
> *play like english child special word for*
> *play stage english relies few words*
> *say what neighbour relay on another polish*
> *describe exactly in but now i less fluent*
> *forget . . .*
> (p. 34)

The processes at work here recall the comment by Halliday on the Polish prison argot *grypserka*, in his classic study of antilanguages: 'Secrecy [is] a necessary strategic property of antilanguages' (Halliday 1978:166).

A similar strategy of critique can be seen in Incz Baranay's semi-fictional autobiographical piece entitled 'You Don't Whinge' (Gunew and Mahyuddin, 1988). This work is divided into two parts: 'How lucky you are' and 'Childhood was black salami'. 'How lucky you are' is a collection of ten statements about Australia, ranging from the new nation, the nation of the here and now, the lucky country ('You Australians don't know how lucky you are') to a nation without vigour and energy, a nation marked by an almost monotonous apathy. The final statement deserves quoting in full for its critique of the artificiality of Australian traditions: 'Australia has no traditions but images of a fantasy tradition: boomerangs, kangaroos, the outback. That's what people know: the fantasy images, the imagined traditions' (p. 26).

Through an autobiographical intercession Part II examines the implications of the fantasy images, the imagined tradition. In doing so what surfaces, once again, is another form of an antilanguage, an accent which incorporates the Australian antilanguage into its own semantic field only after trivialising or parodying it. The difference is given a material base, an anchor, in 'our smelly stinky reffowog lunches' at school. These lunches metonymically construct, for the Australian, the migrant as 'latvian bread polish sausage serbian pickle hungarian salami italian ham greek cheese . . . '. The food taboos exclude the Other, as well as reinforcing assumptions about 'real-Australians' and 'new-Australians, would-be-Australians, non-Australians' (p. 27). John

O'Grady's Nino clowned around this difference with jokes about his name 'Giovanni' and spaghetti, but was not allowed to affirm it as an inalienable possession, a defining characteristic. Writers like Inez Baranay and Ania Walwicz confront the deep attachment to differences in names and eating habits to split open the illusion of the comfortable, materially contented migrant, the sanitised Other as constructed by a failed assimilationist government policy.

Inez Baranay's persona suddenly recognises that Australian history is not the history of the migrant. It is 'their' history, the original colonisers', a history fraught with imperialistic assumptions and a nostalgic yearning for the metropolitan centre. The radical migrant writer thus constructs her own dark side of the dream, writes out over 40 years of institutional silence, constructs that silence into a vibrant fiction. The historical process which had silenced their language and had made their children into monolingual Australians surfaces as the unspeakable Other of Australian culture. Once articulated, the voice of the Other, as in a Gothic tale, challenges the discourse of its masters. Thus the monster tells Frankenstein, but I am you, I am indissolubly bound to you, I am both your destructive potential and your return of the repressed, I am the chaos you have artificially kept in check: 'Remember, that I am thy creature: I ought to be thy Adam; but I am rather the fallen angel, whom thou drivest from joy for no misdeed' (Shelley, 1974:95).

The migrant must now write down the initial moment, the original experience. The paradigmatic narrative of that moment is the 'black bread and salami' which metonymically encapsulates the migrant child's encounter with the White Australian. It is, as Inez Baranay says, 'the only way a migrant childhood story can start' (p. 30). But now that the story has been told, migrant writing too becomes postcolonial and postmulticultural. It transforms irrevocably the definition of Australian literature and makes that literature no longer a homogeneous entity (if it ever was one) but a heterogeneous practice marked by a variety of often contradictory tendencies. At the same time the migrant is also a fragment which embeds itself into the heterogeneous body of the original Australian fragment. Its postcolonialism is therefore marked by precisely the kind of ambiguities we found in Harpur and Brennan; and it is driven, ultimately, by precisely the same procedures of closure that sustained the earlier fragment. The nationalist myth, through the institutional endorsement of difference and diversity, might well duplicate the closed, autonomous worlds of the original fragment as coloniser, and the Aborigines as colonised. One must not overlook this capacity for a new recycling of the old themes and a radicalisation which is only spuriously represented in the literary texts. At the same time, if our analogy with the earlier moment holds, 'the authentic moment of an innovative present interrupts the continuum of history and breaks away from its homogeneous flow' (Habermas, 1987:11). An exhausted literary enterprise like 'Oz Lit' requires for its rejuvenation the intervention of the uncanonised.

10 Reading the dream

The dark side of a dream is the domain of repression. It is in that side—the forbidden, suppressed and 'unspeakable'—that another cultural history is played out. In this book we have read, symptomatically, texts which take us to the shifting meanings of a dream which has always been the Other of Australian culture. An unacknowledged secret that recurs throughout this 'dream', we have argued, is Australia's colonial history and the relations of domination formed within that history. It has seemed important to us to foreground this pervasive fact, because it helps to account for many otherwise inexplicable regularities of Australian cultural forms. These regularities provide the basis for delineating something that is characteristic and identifiable as 'Australian', at the same time as we recognise that this is no unique essence of Australianness, but a set of qualities which are found, in some form, in many other postcolonial societies.

That said, we do not want to go to the other extreme, reducing all other forces and differences to aspects or effects of colonialism. Colonialism is not a single, overwhelming force in Australian society, a universal metameaning lurking behind every text. But a postcolonial society like Australia does have three characteristics that seem to cut across different levels and structures of social life. One is the evolution of forms of language and culture that express and negotiate opposition: antilanguages and anticultures. Another is a typical pattern in family life, marked by double forms, double messages and double-think. The third is a form of consciousness, a characteristic way of constructing and interpreting meanings: a paranoiac mind. We do not claim that these qualities are inescapably linked, with each other or with a postcolonial society. Yet there is a logic that makes the association more than random. In this concluding chapter we want to sketch out, in a tentative way, a pattern we see; a pattern which links the dark side and the dream, and carries within itself its own way of reading.

ANTILANGUAGE, ANTICULTURE

Ashcroft, Griffiths and Tiffin (1989:38-77) have usefully foregrounded the problematic role of language that has emerged in the former colonies of Britain, focusing around an equivocation with English as the language of the centre. They propose a double movement, which they call 'abrogation' (denial of the monopolistic position of the standard language) and 'appropriation' (making over its forms to local uses and experiences). This double movement in relation to verbal language is emblematic of the cultural strategies of postcolonialism. Australia we have argued is primarily a settler society, but it also carries within it a range of other forms of postcolonialism, and its complex nested structure of groups is reflected and sustained by a repertoire of forms of postcolonial language.

Earlier we have used the term 'antilanguage' to describe this phenomenon. Here we will develop a more explicit account of antilanguage as it throws light on a range of cultural and linguistic processes in Australian life. The classic exposition of the concept is an article by Michael Halliday (1978) which examined how oppositional groups within a dominant society construct special languages to sustain difference and identity. In the cases that he studied (criminals, prisoners), this special language is opaque to outsiders, who are excluded from the group by being shut out from discourse. It also encodes the ideology of the group, foregrounding the world that sustains their identity, excluding other realities and other speakers that would challenge it. Other semiotic systems function in the same way as part of a complex, so that clothing codes, behavioural patterns etc. reinforce the construction of group identity through forms of speech. The development of antilanguage forms in postcolonial societies as reported by Ashcroft et al. is an exemplary form of the cultural strategies of subaltern groups.

The concept of 'antilanguage' usefully foregrounds the existence of antagonisms within a larger social formation. However we also need to recognise how varied and unstable are the forms of language and culture through which these complex relationships are expressed and lived. Antilanguages and other strategies of abrogation declare difference in a spectacular way, but spectacles of difference are not always or equally convenient for those engaged in struggle with powerful opponents. Antilanguages normally exist as a repertoire of possibilities, not as a single, stable language state. And it's equally important, if we are to understand how resistance and accommodation are managed by marginalised groups, to emphasise the strategies of decoding (ie. forms of antireading) which are indispensable for an antilanguage to function. When declarations of difference are dangerous, antigroups develop methods of hiding aberrant meanings behind a mask of normality, along with strategies for insiders to recover the hidden differences. Antigroups also develop reading practices to deploy on the texts of outsiders, to translate their meanings into the world of the group or to recover the occluded meanings of hostile others.

The relationship of colonisers and colonised is a strong instance of domination, and the richest development of antilanguage strategies in Australia is found amongst Aboriginal people. The intense attachment of Aboriginal communities to their traditional languages is an antilanguage strategy, excluding outsiders (White Australians, and even other Aboriginal groups) and bonding the community. At the other extreme, opposition can be managed by a strategy of 'appropriation', linked to a distinctive antireading strategy that is no less effective for being invisible. Bruce McGuinness and Denis Walker, two Aboriginal activists and writers, have this to say of the strategems of their people:

> It's important that people understand that Aboriginal lifestyles don't change a great deal when they are removed from a rural situation to an urban situation. It's just that they need to become less visible, because Aboriginal people are very visible within an urban situation ... With writing we find that the same situation also occurs. When Aboriginal people write they write in a style. They're able to adopt various styles of writing so that what they really want to write about is there. It's hidden. It's contained within their writing, if one can see through the subterfuge, the camouflage that they use when they're writing. (Davis and Hodge 1985:47)

McGuinness and Walker here draw attention to the balance a minority group must strike within a hostile society. Where the markers of Aboriginality are so visible in the colour of the skin then Aboriginality is displaced and concealed from the eyes of outsiders. But these writers insist that some people (the insiders) still must be able to see it in its covert form ('it's important that people understand', 'if one can see through the subterfuge'). And since the invisible meanings are more important than public markers of difference, it is the reading skills required to make them visible which mark core membership.

Most Aboriginal culture today operates with complex combinations of the two extremes of total abrogation and subversive antireading. As an example we will look at the work of Jack Davis. His plays are written in English but incorporate snatches of Nyungar as a central part of their strategy of mediation. *The Dreamers*, for instance, has characters who speak occasional words of Nyungar. Parallel to this is the intermittent appearance of a traditional Aboriginal figure, the Dancer, who can be seen by the mainly White audience of the plays but not by the Aboriginal characters, whose words, in Nyungar, are incomprehensible to the White audience but would be understood by some of the characters. In performance the program will often contain a word list, but this gives the nonNyungar speaking audience only the illusion that they are being given a code to enter into this world. In practice a word list is not enough to allow someone unfamiliar with a language to follow a speech. Those who buy the book have a glossary at the back and time on their hands, but even here there are different layers of entry.

As an instance of Davis's strategy we will look at a piece from the climax of the play, where the old man Worru, the family's strongest link with their Aboriginal past, has been taken off to hospital to die. Some younger members of the family occupy the main stage, a shabby kitchen looking like an impoverished parody of a European model and not at all 'Aboriginal'. Then the Dancer appears:

> *A narrow shaft of light reveals the DANCER sitting cross-legged on the escarpment against a night sky. He sings sorrowfully.*
>
> *Nitja Wetjala, warrah, warrah!*
> *Gnullarah dumbart noychwa.*
> *Noychwa, noychwa, noychwa.*
> *Wetjala kie-e-ny, kie-e-ny, kie-e-ny,*
> *Kie-e-ny.*
>
> ['The White man is evil, evil!
> My people are dead.
> Dead, dead, dead.
> The white man kill my people.
> Kill, kill, kill,
> Kill.']
> (Davis 1982:137)

For the audience, this figure is reassuringly recognisable but completely incomprehensible, signifying only Aboriginality (the old man Worru's pride in his race) and the 'universal' grief appropriate to a moment of death. The translation we have quoted is not part of the performance. Solitary readers can read a more angry message, a condemnation of what Whites have done to Worru's people.

But there are further levels of coding. If we consult Davis's glossary we will find that *gnullarah* means 'ours', not 'mine' as translated here. The difference is subtle but important: the difference between an individual possessing his people and a person incorporated into the collective at the moment of stating the relationship. If we go further into the language we will find that Nyungar like many other Aboriginal languages has more than one word for *we* and *our*, marking the distinction between inclusive and exclusive relationships (Von Brandenstein 1988). *Gnullarah* is the exclusive form, a 'we' that links the speaker to others as a collective ego but specifically excludes the people spoken to from that identity. So for those who understand this nuance of the language, the Dancer has divided the social world into two opposing groups, lumping the audience into the single category of 'Other'. But the audience, unless they are fluent speakers of Nyungar, will not know they have been constructed in this way. Only Nyungar speakers, who are included in an inner core group by their knowledge of the language, will know that they are being constructed as outsiders by the pronoun, or perhaps separated from the nonNyungars alongside them in the theatre and incorporated into a community with the Dancer. Meanwhile the White audience will have the illusion of having been welcomed without reservation into an inner centre of universal human feelings.

The notion that an antilanguage structure must be a simple opposition between two hostile groups is clearly inadequate. At every point the structures of opposition turn out to be relative and permeable, allowing continuous scope for negotiation and resistance as seems appropriate. Davis illustrates the deviousness that McGuinness and Walker indicated, the need to combine signifiers of difference (dramatic declarations of Aboriginality) with layers of camouflage to sustain the ambiguous relationship of Aborigines to the rest of the Australian community. The unity of Aborigines as a pan-Aboriginal identity opposed to the rest of Australia has a reality at some levels for some situations, but Aboriginal society is crossed by innumerable fissures and interconnections which are also crucial in maintaining their distinctive forms of social life.

The antilanguage strategies of recent migrant writing show a similar kind of complexity, deploying similar resources for equivocating with the desire to convey meaning. 'Picture', a short story by the Polish writer Ania Walwicz, begins:

> To have children. She said. If you did. That would calm down. You. What. We'll bring it up. If you don't want it. I thought I was pregnant. Shingles. You are a nervous girl. My mother. Has children. You got to. She said. I wanted to. I loved you. She. Mother. Woman. Children. That she was sick with me. That she was sick while waiting for me. That it was hard. So hard. (Gibbs and Tilson 1983:95)

Walwicz's mildly deviant antilanguage disrupts the decoding process but only briefly. Its subversion is not directed solely against the dominant English speaking community. It is positioned against two or perhaps three languages: standard English, the simple English of a child or someone learning English, and Polish, whose forms seem sometimes to have interfered with the English syntax. But the values expressed in the passage are the core values of a highly traditional Polish Catholic family. This meaning is fractured by the play of antilanguages, made less legible for mainstream speakers. But the mother's 'primitive' speech and conservative values are also caricatured by her daughter, and the role of ethnicity is ambiguous in the construction and decoding of this text.

Although the mother's discourse is constantly disrupted by Walwicz's demonic punctuation it continues inexorably, and Walwicz can be neither as indifferent to it as her English-speaking friends, nor as dutiful as her Polish family required. Antilanguage conceals this ambivalence towards her home group from the dominant society, and this is a typical feature of new migrant writings which adopt radical, antilanguage forms.

The Australian accent also functions as a kind of antilanguage, to mark and protect the secrets of Australian identity, but it has a rather different relationship to the dominant language and culture. Australian colloquialisms mostly came from low status groups, and they still carry some traces of these class origins. Ashcroft et al. use this to emphasise the affinity of this non-standard English with other forms of postcolonial English which refuse the metropolitan standard. But they now serve an integral function in the dominant construction of the national identity. This fact points to the complex function of this accent in Australian social life and literary culture. It is a marker of Australianness that is used in its full form by less than a third of Australians. The remainder construct their identity by their common repudiation of it. Its forms, as they are popularly understood, virtually exclude the possibility of complex thought or hidden levels of meaning. But insofar as the Australian accent is an antilanguage it conceals complex and hidden levels of meaning, hiding also (a common device for effective antilanguages) even the existence of these levels and this complexity. Indeed, Australian culture must periodically reproduce a non-existent community of speakers of 'pure Australian' to authenticate its own precarious existence.

This phenomenon illustrates how antilanguages arise from the subordinate as an instrument of resistance but can then be appropriated by the dominant, who use their forms to signify and control the threat of the Other. One way in which this happens is through such lexicographical works as G. A. Wilkes' *Australian Colloquialisms* (1978/1985) which assembles a set of examples of this strange form of speech as though it needs such codification and exemplification. Wilkes does not read his colloquialisms as an antilanguage. He prefers to speak in terms of 'a particular area of Australian English, not the whole field' which exists in 'familiar speech', as though he and all his readers are equally familiar with these forms, and know precisely where they fit in to the field of discourse as an indivisible whole. But the fact that he needs to write a book signals that this set of terms is not entirely familiar. This is the antilanguage of some other, who disconcertingly must still be called an Australian.

The language that he describes has the typical features of antilanguage, especially relexicalisation and oversemanticisation which reveal the ideology of the group. Antilanguages select themes and targets, and find endless variants to describe them. Sexual intercourse, for instance, gets a strong billing with expressions such as 'saddling', 'paddock', 'scrape', 'shoot between the posts'. As if to exclude any taint of homosexuality from the sacred concept of mateship, the terms here are highly derogatory: 'poofter', 'shirtlifter', 'tonk', 'wonk', 'triss', 'dike' and so on. Most of these terms, significantly, are no longer in common use.

Many of Wilkes's sources are literary, and this raises the issue of the relationship between literature and this form of Australian antilanguage. Some of the first literary references to Australianisms are unsurprisingly to be found in the literature of the nationalist period around the turn of the century. Henry Lawson and Tom Collins (Joseph Furphy) in particular gave these oral forms a written legitimacy which helped to construct a dichotomous portrayal of Australian life in terms of class and place, the 'bush' versus the 'city', or as Wilkes (1981) put it 'The Stockyard and the Croquet lawn'. But other writers have used this form of speech to explore divisions even within a single individual.

An instance of this can be seen in Patrick White's novel *The Twyborn Affair*. Eddie Twyborn is a bisexual, who makes a brief and traumatic return to Australia. One entry in Eddie Twyborn's diary dated 4 March 1920 (1979:141–46) describes a short stop-over in Fremantle. This text contains a catalogue of authentic Australian colloquialisms (those authorised by Wilkes) as well as others perhaps not so authentic: 'belly wobbles', 'wharfies', 'Pom', 'wonk', 'crypto-queen', 'schooner', 'O.S.' (for 'one old professional blue-nosed soak'), and 'poor bugger'. Here the antilanguage marks Eddie Twyborn's own return to his repressed origins—Australia as the place of his birth and as the origin of his own mother, Eadie. His fascinated use of the antilanguage draws him back into the world of the initiate; his otherness is effectively neutralised. This engagement with the language mirrors Eddie's later encounter with Don Prowse, when he is raped by this representative of the Australian legend. In this way White uses the antilanguage to signify the fascination and threat of the masculine ethos of the Typical Australian to Eddie's ambiguous sexual and national identity.

Antilanguages and related forms of anticulture have a close but complex relationship to the emergence of postcolonial cultures. In the extreme colonial situation, when domination is overt, the society is polarised into hostile groups who emphasise difference and use antilanguage mechanisms to express it. Even the culture of the coloniser is organised like an antilanguage, restricting access to the mysteries of the code, just as happens with the culture of the colonised. At the same time, the recognition of dependence is displaced by both into a fascination with the otherness of the Other.

From the Australian example we can see some modifications that must be made to this simple picture. Even in the colonial period a pattern of antilanguages precisely expressed and sustained antagonistic relations within the society as a whole. The colonisers as a fragment from the centre brought with them fragments of an earlier colonising process, along with a repertoire of antilanguage strategies that the new colony drew on to declare a new identity and a common repudiation of the centre. After independence, antagonisms continued that were masked by claims of a common language (standard Australian English) that was neither common nor standard. In this situation antilanguages acquire a new function: to express a continuing sense of otherness, which otherwise can exist only as a paranoiac projection outside the official version of the language and the nation. Antilanguages then become strangely reassuring to the majority, recognising and declaring difference and even antagonism in a safe (discursive) form. They become 'goods to think with' for a mainstream culture that needs to acknowledge these meanings. Aggressive forms of Australianism have similar forms and functions to markers of Aboriginal and multicultural difference to which they seem to be most opposed: and all of them play an integral role in the ongoing process of defining (and constructing) Australian culture today.

HAPPY FAMILIES

Theories of postcolonialism led us to rethink some of the assumptions of myopic nationalist histories of Australia, but our work has also been profoundly influenced by the work of women historians and social critics who have drawn attention to the key role of gender issues in the history of Australian society. In this section our discussion we will take as points of departure two books, both published in 1975, that helped to establish this new agenda: *Damned Whores and God's Police* by Anne Summers, and *The Real Matilda* by Miriam Dixson.

Both these books mounted a swinging attack on gender relations in contemporary Australia, and both tracked these patterns back to the foundation situation, the conditions prevailing in the first years of the colony. Anne Summers emphasised the motif of the split image of women, into 'Damned whores' and 'God's police', a split that we have argued is endemic in the construction of both men and women over the two hundred years since 1788. She associated the process with colonialism, specifically claiming that women were a 'colonised sex'. Miriam Dixson blamed these repressive structures on the social detritus from the early days, the lower class social inadequates who went on to form the ethos of the 'Australian legend'. Both books had the bold sweep of pioneering texts, adopting a polemic that was necessary for its time. Fifteen years later, there is still more work to be done before the connections are fully established between gender patterns and the history of relations between exploiters and exploited, colonisers and colonised, in Australia since 1788.

As a feminist, Dixson was concerned about the contemporary position of women and the possibilities of change:

> There's no doubt that Australian men and women are *supposed* to differ from each other in a quite weird way. The 'ideal' Australian male 'should' be insensitive and blockish, while his 'ideal' female counterpart should be so colourless that she seems mentally backward. Happily many of us ignore ideals like these. But still, by adopting such rigid ideal sex-role differences, Australian men and women deny one another too many of the human qualities which the sexes share. And so we short-change each other pathetically, stunting possibilities for fellowship and the kind of sexual joy that can only go with a rich sense of shared humanity. (Dixson 1976:12–13)

Her target here is the appalling and destructive gender models that are proffered as ideal forms, enshrined in the 'Australian legend' and deforming the experience of successive generations of Australian men and women. She notes that 'many of us ignore ideals like these' but the systematic policy of unofficial resistance it seems is not enough. The pattern that she diagnoses here is not simply a repressive ideology underpinning a repressive set of practices, but also a vigorous alternative ideal and set of practices, which are, however, seemingly neutralised and contained by a kind of double-think. There is a double pathology here: pathologically deformed women and men, pathologically unable to see that they are not as deformed as they think they ought to be.

As a historian, Dixson traced the origins of an explanation for these attitudes in the past, in the formative moments of the culture. Her title economically lays out the ground of her project. 'Waltzing Matilda' is Australia's unofficial national anthem, and it transmits a strongly gendered national stereotype from the 1890s. A 'Matilda' is slang for a swagman's swag. For Dixson this constructs woman as 'an item of property of a male who rejects women' (1976:11). But these Australian gender patterns are sustained from the present as well as the past. They respond to middle-class familial patterns, not just to the inadequacies of long-dead social isolates, lower-class convicts and pioneers who figure so large in explanatory schemes. But we should also recognise that the elimination of women and desire by the Australian gender stereotype was never uncontested, by both women and men, and one of the dark secrets of Australian society carried by its literary and cultural traditions has been the irrepressible if often distorted desire of men for women and women for men. To give just one instance, in Dixson's discussion of Australia's unofficial national anthem she does not quote the full chorus: 'Waltzing Matilda, waltzing Matilda, Who'll come a waltzing Matilda with me?' This chorus has no apparent connection with the plot of the ballad, which describes a swagman who suicided to escape from death at the hands of a squatter and the police. It is a fragment inserted into the narrative, where it asserts the pathetic longing of this social isolate for a woman, and for romantic love and gracious patterns of courtship ('waltzing'). The narrative of the swagman's desire is almost totally excluded from the song. It is now so compressed as to be incomprehensible ('Matilda' for 'swag' is an antilanguage code that would now be known to noone apart from this song) but it obdurately retains its place in the chorus and in the title of the song, a mystified but potent reminder to Australians of the horrendous consequences of the Australian way of life.

The hint of homosexuality in this narrative has not been unobserved, as a hidden quality of the Australian male's response to the Australian conditions of sexuality. Nor is it an accident that the writer who is officially Australia's greatest novelist, Patrick White, winner of the Nobel Prize for literature, sees his homosexuality as a precondition for his novelistic insights:

> ... ambivalence has given me insights into human nature, denied, I believe, to those who are unequivocally male or female—and Professor Leonie Kramer. (1981:154)

Here he announces the potency and centrality of his status as androgyne. But it is worth also noticing his ungenerous jibe at Professor Leonie Kramer, at that time arguably the most distinguished authority on Australian literature, whose criticism has helped to promote White's literary reputation. In this move White is opposing artist to critic, androgyne to antiandrogyne, the one incorporating both genders and mediating between them, the other excluding them and being excluded from human nature. But White's claimed transcendence of Australian gender roles does not leave him free of hostility towards a powerful and successful female, expressed in terms that would be applauded by male chauvinists throughout the land.

White's homosexuality lives out what has been called the latent homosexuality of Australian culture: female as well as male, we should add, because as Dixson points out a mirror structure links men and women in a frieze of frustrated desire. White's life therefore gives his work its unacknowledged but seemingly inexplicable authority as a quintessentially Australian phenomenon. His autobiography *Flaws in the Glass* therefore becomes an important source for the study of the set of meanings at issue. Its title points to one recurring motif. 'The Glass', a single definite glass, offers its taken-for-granted unity, a mirror that should construct a single double, the 'self', as in Lacan's theory of the 'mirror stage' in human development, the stage when the child sees his or her image in a mirror and is able to construct a unitary and external self. But White's mirror has its 'flaws' which disrupt the unity of the image, producing a multiplicity of defective doubles, so that his 'self' in these terms is never a unity, never complete without its shadow. We can extend the scope of the mirror-metaphor by drawing on an incident in

The Solid Mandala (1966) in which Waldo Brown, the 'normal' half of a pair of twins, discovers one of Mother's old dresses and puts it on in front of a mirror. The act of quasi-transvestitism is crucial as a metaphor for Patrick White's construction of doubles, revealing the Mother behind the androgyne, on both sides of the deceptive mirror.

The autobiography allows us to see some more ordinary manifestations of the split and its way of constructing doublets. One instance is White's notorious feud with the painter Sydney Nolan, once a close friend but now the subject of vitriolic abuse. Nolan's crime, the flaw which split his image into a before and after that was akin to God's police lapsing into whoredom, was his second marriage, which White castigated as adultery. The reason seems staggering in someone who defied social conventions so much more dramatically in his own homosexual 'marriage'. But we see here the role of a highly conventional 'bourgeois' view of marriage in the construction of such doublets. From this point of view an official marriage does not unite the man and woman, it divides the man from his desire, leaving the unsatisfied desire available for another more important (because more genuinely erotic) relationship. In this view the official (first) wife can be assumed to be the object of hatred and resentment, but this is not the case with the freely chosen second wife. The mutual repudiation of women, the withholding of desire from women as reinforced not counteracted by marriage, is the contract that allows for male bondings, close friendships as well as homosexual 'marriages'.

Behind the endless construction of unsatisfying doubles, then, is a murderous fascination with the Mother. The autobiography discusses his relationship with Ruth, his actual mother. In the novels, *The Eye of the Storm* deals most directly with this theme: significantly at the moment of the mother's death, not the formative stages when the patterns were first laid down. White's representative androgyne is driven by this ambivalence, internalised as a war with the self that can only end in death. This ambivalence is expressed intensely but it is not itself examined, and after a point we can ask: What has the Mother done so catastrophically wrong, and could she have done anything else?

White's status as androgyne is in fact a dangerous illusion. He does not have the experience of being a woman that he seems to claim, and it is necessary to turn to women writers to supply the products of that experience. Christina Stead's *The Man who Loved Children*, first published from the US without acclaim in 1940, provides a complementary perspective to White's novels. Stead's book deals with an American family, but it remains a classic study of the pathology of Australian families. It traces the process of disintegration of a marriage, Henny and Sam Pollitt's, until the death of Henny (poisoned with her mother's tacit complicity by Louie, the eldest daughter and the central character in the novel). At the end of the novel Louie departs, attempting to escape from the baleful influence of her father and the family pattern, which is still able to wreak havoc on the children after the death of Henny.

The formation of Louie is the theme of the novel: the eldest daughter of the family, an ugly duckling with a precocious literary talent, prematurely responsible for her parents but driven to the edge of schizophrenia, whose escape from the bosom of this schizogenic family at the age of 13 is about 12 years too late. Louie is the mother to her emotionally infantilised but inexorably rationalist father. He is 'the man who loved children', who constructed antilanguages that his children learned in order to become complicit in his fantasy world. Henny was his second wife, daughter of a wealthy father conditioned to be an object of desire (she painted beautifully, played the piano, and sewed, the only marital skills she brought into the marriage). But over the course of the novel she loses that decorative uselessness, and is unable or unwilling to learn how to fulfil the duties of the other half of the gender model. Louie is coerced into becoming useful, but she wants to be beautiful and desirable as well. Her development is skewed by the contradictory pressures on her from both parents, each constructing her to fulfil their needs while protecting themselves from satisfying their own.

Stead's study corrects the balance of White's by restoring the father to the centre of the eye of this storm, showing mercilessly how it can be the complex dynamic of the marriage that creates the distortions, not the Mother on her guilty own. It is the blockages to desire within the marriage that lead to the excessive and contradictory demands being made on both daughters and sons of the marriage (Ernie the son hung his dog just before his mother's death, self hatred linked to indiscriminate murderous impulses in both genders). Out of this pathological family comes the gifted woman artist, Louie, just as White the hero of *Flaws* is the product of his family background, but each could as well have joined the detritus of Australian social life, the itinerant 'casual poor' whom Dixson blames for the construction of Australian attitudes to gender.

Stead's work allows us to see the urgent need for a more even-handed attention to the roles of both women and men from all strata in Australian society in the formation of the national character. The Hartz thesis does not predict much about the fate of gender relations in colonial fragments, and nor should we expect it to. Whatever fragment went to the new land contained women and men, socialised into existing gender roles. The work of recent historians suggests that the new situation briefly skewed the previous balance between men and women, and gave some new opportunities and value to some women, but predictably the conservative tendencies of fragment societies often reasserted the older patterns in a more rigid form. Out of this situation arose the set of self-cancelling contradictions that we have seen: a polarisation into sharp oppositions, which generate endless doublets or fuse into dangerous ambiguities.

THE PARANOIAC CULTURE

Stead's work suggests a connection between antilanguage and the more individual processes of schizophrenic communication. It also raises the old issue of similarities between artistic and cultural production and what are elsewhere labelled by the culture as pathological symptoms. To begin tentatively to explore these issues, we will draw on some concepts in the work of Gregory Bateson (1973). Bateson was best known for his theories of schizophrenia, which showed the functional relations between textual forms (the typical qualities of schizophrenic 'thought' as found in symptomatic texts) and discursive strategies that make sense of the schizogenic family situation: particularly the role of double messages in organising relationships. But his early work dealt directly with what he called 'cultural contact' (a euphemism for the impact of colonial powers on the indigenous peoples of the Pacific region). He focused on the conflicts and tensions arising in these situations, and on the mechanisms that held these in check: 'schismogenesis', as he called the tendencies to fissure, and the 'steady state' when these forces were held in check. In this view stability is not natural and inevitable. Schismogenesis, fuelled by positive feedback, will escalate till the social order collapses, unless counteracting mechanisms, drawing on massive social resources, are adequate to contain it.

Bateson studied the nature of a steady state system most intensively in the case of Bali, at that time (the late 1930s) a Dutch dependency. The Balinese cult of beauty is part of Balinese culture, but Bateson saw the preconditions for this serenity in specific strategies of socialisation built on systematic double messages, starting within the family and determining gender roles and attitudes as well as attitudes to others in the hierarchical social order. The similarity of the terms 'schizophrenia' and 'schismogenesis' is misleading, since schizophrenia is a product of strategies designed to counteract schismogenesis. In Bateson's scheme the schizophrenic 'patient' is the site where the schismogenic forces within the family are contained and neutralised, as far as can be. Postcolonialism as the assertion of independence by a former dependent is a classic act of schismogenesis, insofar as that independence is effective. But as the example of Australia shows, when claims to independence are exaggerated and the exercise of power within the society in terms of class, race and gender continues in a masked form, pseudo-postcolonialism (PPC) becomes a kind of cultural pathology.

In making the point in these terms we need to avoid one misunderstanding. 'Pathological' carries a heavy negative charge, implying that the whole nation should be declared insane. Bateson's approach which we are following is more subtle than this. He sees important continuities between qualities that are considered 'normal' and what is declared 'pathological' in a given society, forcing us to recognise the 'normality' of the pathological as well as the pathology of the normal. In this spirit we will adapt two terms from the classic typology of schizophrenia, paranoia and hebephrenia, seeing them as two basic strategies for reading and producing meaning. Paranoiacs read deep and usually hostile messages in the texts of others, and construct messages which barely hint at their own almost irrecoverable meanings, in an antilanguage for a community of one. Hebephrenics adopt the opposite strategy, refusing to acknowledge any but the most superficial and literal meaning in the texts of others, and they produce texts of their own that seem banally innocent. But in spite of this apparent difference, Bateson sees both as a 'logical' response to the same basic situation, constituted by double messages of love and power so organised that they cannot be disambiguated. The paranoiac arbitrarily resolves the dilemma by always assuming that the real message is what is hidden, while the hebephrenic makes the opposite assumption, but because each strategy arises out of the same situation they each tacitly assume that the opposite is also the case.

The 'ideal' Australian male and female, as represented by the 'Australian legend' and criticised by Miriam Dixson, have the classic traits of a hebephrenic. In technical terms they show 'flattened affect'; they are relentlessly superficial, incapable of real relationships, so traumatised by the catastrophe of being Australian that they cannot think or feel. There seems to be nothing to read in their repetitious text. But the inexhaustible fascination of Australians with this cultural blank shows the presence of something rather different: the shadow of a deep and complex secret that conceals and in this way constructs the true identity of Australians. Australian readers attending obsessively to this text show all the signs of a paranoiac reading strategy. Popular Australian reading regimes, we can say, are built on the principle of hyper-reading, which is then managed and controlled by the discursive regimes of academic institutions (including the disciplines of English, history and sociology) or by the popular laconic tradition. Aboriginal reading strategies show this tendency taken to an extreme, based as they are on a more intense antagonism towards the mainstream society and a richer antilanguage tradition.

The 'Australian legend', then, is and has always been the after-image of the Australian nightmare, suppressing Australians' worst fears by representing them in glowing terms as an ideal. Those fears are by no means without their basis in social life. They are constituted by powerful forces that have been laid down early and are continuously reinforced by specific agents. Those forces are as pernicious as the critics of the Australian legend claim, and the legend has played a role in maintaining them by representing the nightmare as normal. But the real enemy is these forces and not the legend itself, which has also always been the exemplary text to be read through, in a rite of passage into a genuine Australian identity which is marked by endemic paranoia and a profound suspicion of all texts.

The various causes that have been offered for the construction of the Australian legend and the Australian cultural type have been convincing enough individually, but cumulatively they show a worrying excess. Convicts, the Irish, the casual poor, women, Aborigines, migrants—each successive cause fits with suspicious ease into the same predetermined slot. Each new incursion seems merely to reinforce the inexorable pattern of the old. We have used a version of the Hartz thesis to begin to theorise the pattern that we see, because this account at least attempts to explain the sequence of structures that link the past to the present. But on its own the Hartz thesis mystifies the historical process. By assuming that the child is father (or mother) to the man (or woman) it attributes an inexorable power to the foundation event and the initial state of the structure which then determine all that follows.

As we have tried to articulate the patterns that we have seen, we have wanted to show how the trick of continuity has been pulled off, against the grain of the forces that had to be contained by some specific means. The shadow of convictism, for instance, has a kind of continuity with the present because in the past it exemplified a strategy of control which still operates in current systems. The common pattern, we have argued, is a strategy for exercising power through a system of double messages, mingling the punitive with kinds of repressive tolerance in an indistinguishable mix. But after 200 years the spectacle of convictism has different meanings and functions, and it can be made available to make the process more visible precisely as a historical phenomenon, not as just a glib metaphor for the human condition.

The role of Aborigines in the construction of Australian social identity illustrates a different kind of tendency. NonAboriginal Australians' attitudes to Aboriginal people have been dominated from the beginning by a mixture of guilt and hypocrisy. With other instances of the characteristic Australian paranoia the majority are victims of double messages, but in relation to Aborigines this majority benefits from them. There are vested interests in not seeing through this set of double messages, in maintaining a rigorous policy of hebephrenia, which then serves to sustain hebephrenic strategies elsewhere in the culture. But this in fact is the greatest cost of White racism. To no small degree the chains of hebephrenia that still bind many Australians are held together by a wilful refusal to acknowledge the injustices inflicted on Aboriginal people in the past and the present, and to recognise the legitimacy of their aspirations for the future.

In this book we have tried to exemplify what is in some respects a paranoiac style of reading, which we claim is quintessentially Australian although its qualities are exactly opposite to those of the much better known 'typical Australian'. But we are not proposing to swap one pathology for another in our cultural diagnosis, and simply claim for ourselves a more acceptable or more fashionable form of the disease. Social life in Australia from the macro-level down to the level of individual interaction in families and other small groups is characterised by double-messages about power and identity. At times in Australia's history the tendencies to paranoia and hebephrenia have had catastrophic consequences, the two typically complementing each other. Australian war hysteria, for instance, has always deployed a paranoiac reading on the text of 'the Enemy', which itself is constructed out of the judiciously hebephrenic texts of simplistic demagogues. Sexism, racism and anti-Communism have been constructed in exactly the same way, sustained by the same discursive system that levels 'tall poppies' in the name of egalitarianism, and deploys a relentless scepticism against social and intellectual pretentiousness.

What we propose is in some respects a homoeopathic repetition of the pathology, in a form of hyper-reading that is oriented to criticism and change, while still recognising its roots in common cultural practices. It is precisely the Australian tendency to paranoia that we want to mobilise in a new kind of critical strategy. Australian culture has always been constituted by a rich and diverse but covert set of reading strategies, not all of them misdirected, and none of them the exclusive preserve of academics. Because these reading strategies have been so potent but invisible for so long it is time to focus attention on them now, and bring them to the centre of the debate about Australian society and its cultural forms. That debate has always been part of Australian culture, not an epiphenonemon that is outside and 'about' it. This book is a contribution to that debate, and as such it cannot pretend to be outside the culture that is its object. But then, outside and above is not where we wish to be.

Notes: sources and contexts

Chapter 1

As a general narrative history of Australia, Manning Clark's epic (1962–87) is still good value. The obsession with the founding moment was especially evident during the Bicentenary year (1988) when publishers vied with one another to get yet another version of Australia's past published. Some notable histories which were written in the shadow of the Bicentenary include Robert Hughes, *The Fatal Shore* (1987), *The Penguin Bicentennial History of Australia* by John Molony (1987) and the *Oxford History of Australia* under the general editorship of Geoffrey Bolton (1986–90). On the 'manufacture of Australian history' see Rob Pascoe's book with that title (1979) and Paul Carter's more recent critique of the imperial theme in Australian historiography (1987). For further discussion of other radical historians of Australia such as Humphrey McQueen, Richard White, Miriam Dixson and Anne Summers see especially chapters 8 and 10 of this volume, and notes thereon; for a fuller discussion of Bateson's theories, see especially chapter 10.

Hartz's *The Founding of New Societies* (1964) arose out of a symposium organised and influenced by his ideas. The idea of a partial and somewhat distorted duplication of the European 'ideological complex' (the 'fragment') was first developed some ten years before in his *The Liberal Tradition in America* (1955). For later critiques, see Bolton 'Louis Hartz' (1973) and J. Hirst 'Keeping Colonial History Colonial: the Hartz thesis revisited' (1984). On the nationalist tradition in both history and literature, see especially chapter 8 and notes.

Tiffin (1984) argued for a postcolonial perspective for the study of Australian literature, and Ashcroft, Griffiths and Tiffin (1989) is an important and helpful introduction to this approach.

A useful review article on Australian war studies is Robson (1988). On Australia's responses to the Vietnam war see Renouf (1976). For a good general account of literary responses see Peter Pierce, 'The Australian Literature of the Vietnam War' (1980). Alan Seymour's *The One Day of the Year* (1962) focused on emerging fissures in the Anzac legend. David Williamson's *Don's Party* (1973) captured the polyphonic essence of the instant cynicism that followed the Whitlam era. Outside literature, the film *The Odd Angry Shot* directed by Tom Jeffrey (1979) dealt with the Vietnam theme in a typically Australian laid-back style which contrasts with the more powerful treatment found in mainstream American cinema. Kennedy-Miller produced the highly acclaimed TV series *Vietnam* in 1987. In popular music, Redgum exploited the laconic, understated mode of the Australian accent in their highly charged anti-war ballad 'I was only 19'.

The first authoritative literary history was H.M. Green's *A History of Australian Literature* (1961), subsequently revised by Dorothy Green (1985). Its early, shorter, prototype (1930) laid down a critical methodology which condemned the vast bulk of Australian texts to mediocrity. Australian literature lacked, wrote Green, 'a directness . . . . sophistication . . . . intellectual content' when compared with 'work of a smilar level overseas' (p. 15). A.D. Hope's monograph (1963) was offered as a continuation of Green's *History*. Hope emphasised the continuity of Australian literature but the monograph is best known for its trenchant criticism of what Hope called Patrick White's 'pretentious poetic style' and his 'sometimes illiterate syntax' (p. 13). Geoffrey Dutton (ed) *The Literature of Australia* (1964) was an important contribution to the study of Australian literature as an object of inquiry in universities, especially since many of its contributors (Brian Elliott, Harry Heseltine, Leonie Kramer, James McAuley, Vincent Buckley, G.A. Wilkes, John Barnes, Chris Wallace-Crabbe and Judith Wright) were to influence a whole generation of critics. Two recent surveys are Goodwin (1986) and Hergenhan (1988). The latter, as the general editor comments in the Introduction, is not an exercise in pluralism but 'aims for flexibility rather than strict orderliness of organisation' (p. xv). In the process it loses its centre and becomes, as the cover suggests, another celebratory document to mark the Bicentennial, though some fine essays, notably those by Bruce Bennett and Peter Pierce, certainly stand out. For a feminist perspective, see Ferrier 1985. Graeme Turner's *National Fictions* (1986) adopts a cultural studies approach, comparing literary and filmic narrative traditions in a pioneering study. A provocative critique of both Kramer and the Australian critical establishment is John Docker's *In a Critical Condition* (1984). Docker divides *OHAL* into two distinct texts, *OHAL I* and *OHAL II* on the grounds that *OHAL I* offers a literary perspective (of Kramer, Mitchell and Smith) which is at odds with that of *OHAL II* (Terry Sturm's section). *OHAL* elicited some 20 major reviews in its first four years of publication, many largely hostile but often from a rather similar theoretical position.

In an exciting appropriation of Hayden White's theory of tropes (*Metahistory* 1973), Peter Pierce (1983) used the tropes of Metaphor, Metonymy, Synecdoche and Irony to categorise periods and/or tendencies in Australian literary studies. The *OHAL* is metaphorical in that it proposes to relate Xs (literary texts) to Ys (a certain implicit definition of reality) in respect of Z (some version of fictional mimesis). Case studies such as a study of the literature of the Depression which imply that they are 'symptomatic' of or a stand-in for the literature of other periods are metonymic. When the studies are 'integrative', 'regulative' or 'intrinsic' such as Phillips' *The Australian Tradition* (1958) and Ward's *The Australian Legend* (1958) and demonstrate how a particular characteristic (mateship, the democratic spirit, and so on) integrates literature and society, then they are synecdochic. The trope of irony does not accept the naive figurality of the other tropes, so that it both relativises prior modes of perception and negates what is affirmed positively on the literal level. In this way it can explore the ideological assumptions underlying all literary history. Peter Pierce endorses this model of literary history. Our own work has a similar tendency, aiming to relativise, to show how texts enter into multiple semiotic systems (historical, linguistic, ideological) and how texts, of necessity, demand a thorough examination of both the immediate contexts of their production and the quite 'heterogeneous ' or 'multiple' nature of their reception.

A useful collection of documents for a literary cultural history is John Barnes (1969). Among the texts anthologised there is one of the earliest versions of the 'Eternalist' thesis, Frederick Sinnett's essay 'The Fiction Fields of Australia' which appeared in 1856. Sinnett saw the literary text as an aesthetic object informed by two orders of influence. The first of these orders, and certainly the more important of the two, was universal 'value' such as an author's capacity to transcend the incidental, the outer, the 'other' of social forces through a concentration in fictional characters of those universal 'human feelings and human passions'. The second, and clearly inferior, order is 'social externals' or 'love, manners and customs'. The literary text is thus seen in terms of an implied humanist-Eternalist value system from which the social is largely excluded. The Eternalist model has been used by some of the major critics of Australian literature, including G.A. Wilkes, Vincent Buckley, Leonie Kramer, Leon Cantrell among others. In a curious fashion Brian Kiernan too endorsed this view in the final chapter of his book *Images of Society and Nature* (1971) by claiming that a version of the New Critical approach is to be valued over the 'socio-literary' approach. The former, so his argument went, is concerned with the 'text'; the latter with the 'extra-text'. The book is an Australian celebration of the 'affective fallacy' proposed by Wimsatt and Beardsley in 1949.

For a theoretical positioning of Bruce Dawe see Vijay Mishra 'The Formulaic text' (1987). Much Dawe criticism has attached a high value to the poet's 'voice' and 'diction'. The case put forward emphasises his use of a multiplicity of voices to eschew any equation of 'subject voice' with 'author voice': see John Wright (1974) and Mark Mcleod (1979, 1983). Chris Wallace-Crabbe (1976) uses the phrase 'one-shot poems' to describe Dawe's poems which we suggest are basically 'analogical' in design. On Judith Wright, see Hope (1975), Bennett (1976) and other essays by Donald Davie, Adrian Mitchell, R.F. Brissenden as well as an interview by John Thompson in Kiernan (1977a).

On Harpur, see chapters 6 and 7 below, and notes.

Chapter 2

C.D. Rowley's seminal three volume study of White Australian treatment of Aboriginal peoples (1970) still repays reading. This work provides the basis for his later more polemical works, notably *A Matter of Justice* (1978) and *Recovery: The Politics of Aboriginal Reform* (1986). Henry Reynolds' *The Other Side of the Frontier* (1978/82) contains the major argument that Aboriginal oral sources should be incorporated into any valid history of relations between the two peoples. His case that there was substantial resistance by Aboriginal people

NOTES

draws on the work of other historians, such as Bob Reece (1974). Reynolds (1989) argues polemically for some recognition of land rights. Anna Haebich compellingly documents the treatment of Aborigines during the late stages of paternalist policies of protection in Western Australia (1988). On racist attitudes in Australia see Colin Tatz (1979) and Broome (1982). The powerful documentary *Black Deaths*, produced by David Marr for the ABC in 1984, played a significant role in the establishment of a Royal Commission into Aboriginal deaths in custody which was still collecting evidence at the time of writing.

The Aboriginal activist Kevin Gilbert argues for a treaty in 'Black policies' (1985) while sharply distinguishing between real and spurious forms that such a treaty could take. As D.F. McKenzie shows in an admirable essay on the treaty of Waitangi (Te Tiriti o Waitangi), from the Maori point of view signatures themselves bear no absolute authority, no unproblematic transfer, through a mark on paper, of sovereignty. 'For us, the texts in context quickly deconstruct and lose their 'literal' authority—no book was ever bound by its covers', writes McKenzie (1984:363).

The argument about Orientalism in this chapter is adapted from an article previously published by Vijay Mishra, 'Aboriginal Representations in Australian Texts' (1988/89). Edward Said reviewed the concept in his 'Orientalism Reconsidered' (1985). On the dangers of binary oppositions in discourses of race see Abdul JanMohammed *Manichean Aesthetics* (1983).

Our argument about anthropological and romantic discourses was stimulated by Stephen Muecke's important article on 'available discourses' on Aborigines (1982) though our own typology differs significantly from his three categories, 'anthropological', 'romantic' and 'racist'. We see more in common between his first two categories, with the significant inflections of racism (or resistance) within each, rather than as distinct categories.

There are of course very many works on Aboriginal Australians and their (reconstructed) precontact culture produced by anthropologists. A standard work from this tradition is Ronald and Catherine Berndt's *The World of the First Australians* (1964). For a critique of the practices of traditional anthropology from the perspectives of the newer 'critical ethnography' see Patrick Sullivan (1986).

The argument against the traditional use of the category of 'the Dreaming' is presented at greater length in Hodge (1990b). It should be pointed out that the category plays a structural role in some important works which adopt a radical viewpoint, such as Eric Michaels' *The Aboriginal Invention of Television* (1986) and Diane Bell's feminist *Daughters of the Dreaming* (1983). We by no means wish to argue that use of this term always implies a conservative politics, or indeed any single political stance. Similarly, a version of the term (subtly different in ways that we have indicated) plays a role in the work of most of the important contemporary Aboriginal writers (Oodgeroo Noonuccal/Kath Walker, Kevin Gilbert, Jack Davis, Sally Morgan) and it is the cover term for the Western Desert art movement, used by the Aboriginal artists as well as by their White mediators (e.g. Bardon 1979, Michaels 1987, Sutton 1988). The history of this term is far from finished, and a summary judgment of its overall tendencies is at this stage entirely premature.

All major histories of Australia naturally give detailed treatment of the foundation moment. Paul Carter's *The Road to Botany Bay* (1987) uses a sophisticated analysis of discourse to distinguish between the unmediated events and the discourses that subsequently made sense of them. Bernard Smith's substantial *European Vision and the South Pacific 1768–1850* (1960) is the most influential statement of the proposition that the discourses of art and literature were preconditions for the Australian reality to be 'seen' and 'spoken'. This allows him to use artistic texts as evidence of the limits of perception, instead of (as we argue) as evidence of discursive norms and as a site of signs of the disruption of those norms by forces and experiences that they exist to control. Ian and Tamsin Donaldson's *Seeing the First Australians* (1983) is a useful collection of articles on the foundation moment and the responses of the colonisers. An excellent series of commentaries on the Bicentenary is Janson and Macintyre (eds) *Making the Bicentennial* (1988). On the Bicentennial itself as an occasion for the writing of fiction, see Kateryna Arthur, 'Recasting History: Australian Bicentennial Writing' (1990). The foundation moment is not a common theme for contemporary popular music. In television and film, convicts dominate the system of representations (see chapter 6) and Aborigines typically appear along with convicts and women (as in *Eliza Fraser*, or the more radical *Journey among Women*.)

Chapter 3

For a survey of treatments of Aborigines in literature see Healy (1978) and Shoemaker (1989). For a profound critical reading of the subject by an Aborigine see Mudrooroo Narogin (1990). Charles Harpur's 'The Creek at Four Graves' is an interestingly complex early work, reconstructing (in Miltonic blank verse) an early revenge killing by Aborigines from the point of view of a passive White man who managed to escape. This text shares in some of the early attitudes while also projecting some later positions. A popular and influential early Aboriginalist work was Dorothy Langloh Parker's *Australian Legendary Tales* (1896).

For influential theorisations of 'epic' and 'romance' see Georg Lukács, *The Theory of the Novel* (1971) and Northrop Frye, *Anatomy of Criticism* (1957). Two recent works that develop interesting new forms of the 'degraded epic' are David Ireland's *Burn* (1974) and Peter Mathers' *Trap* (1966). Of the two *Burn* offers a much tighter narrative partly because it had its origins in *Image in the Clay*, a play written by David Ireland in 1958 but published some six years later (1964). The narrative is centred on Gunner McAllister, his wife Mary, his sons Billy and Gordon, his adopted daughter Joy and his father, old McAllister. This world is infiltrated by a few other Aborigines, notably Gorooh, a couple of kids from the nearby township, and a policeman. When Gunner McAllister's land is 'purchased' for redevelopment in an ironic duplication of White (dis)possession of Aboriginal land, the original owners become squatters. The reaction takes the form of a symbolic rebellion in that Gunner McAllister uses the gun he had been given to fight against Japanese imperialism to defend himself against an imperialism from within. And yet the epic act, the act of epic defiance remains, for the Aborigine, an impossibility. What the Aborigine Jack Trap does in Mathers' *Trap* is to defy by refusing self-definition, and self-representation. So Mathers constructs a character who is amorphous and sprawling. He is a chameleon, ubiquitous and free like a spectre or a ghost. Thus the text that is written around him by David David, the diarist, must become fragmented and discontinuous. It is one fictional option available to the White writer—to represent the Other without finding an adequate means of doing so. A symbolic rendition of suppressed anxiety towards the stigma of genocide (through the character of the half-caste 'Touch of the Tar' Lily Perkins) is to be found in Dorothy Hewett's ritualistic *The Man from Mukinupin* (1979).

The use of Aborigines as 'goods to think with' in popular forms is very widespread. Aboriginality is a potent signifier in Peter Weir's film *The Last Wave* (1977), and less overtly in *Picnic at Hanging Rock* (1975). The abstract structural way it works can be seen from Weir's use of the 'Indian cave' as the place to which his American school boys retreat in order to construct their moment of rebellion in the internationally successful *Dead Poet's Society* (1989). In terms of this scheme it seems that girls can be boys and Aborigines can be Indians without disturbing the smooth operation of the trope. On the complex use of Aboriginality as a signifier in George Miller's apocalyptic *Mad Max 111* (1983), another international success, see Hodge (1986).

On Keneally's transformation of the Jimmy Governor narrative from a historical point of view, see Reynolds (1979). Terry Threadgold (1985) gives a definitively comprehensive study of the ideological and discursive processes constructing the 'truth' of the story, drawing on contemporary media accounts and later narratives, including Keneally's. Terry Sturm (1973) and John Frow (1983) offer excellent readings of *The Chant of Jimmie Blacksmith* as a text arising out of a complex interface between a European genre and the need for Aboriginal representation. On Prichard see Drake-Brockman (1967) and on Herbert see Heseltine (1973). On Chauvel's significance, see Cunningham (1986, 1987), and Routt (1989). On the controversy over 'The Last Tasmanian' see Tom O'Regan 'The Last Tasmanian Monday Conference' (1979) and also Bernard Smith, *The Spectre of Truganini* (1980).

Chapter 4

There are a large number of books and articles on Australian Aborigines by nonAboriginal writers. Useful summaries from the standard anthropological point of view are R. & C. Berndt (1964, 1982), K. Maddock (1982) and R. Broome (1982). Geoffrey Blainey's *Triumph of the Nomads* (1976) reads the anthropological literature through the lenses of his form of economic history, with interesting if not always uncontroversial results. In spite of later criticisms of this work, motivated by opposition to Blainey's position on Asian immigration, his discussion of Aboriginal society is mainly positive: a paradox that we argue is not unrepresentative (see our discussion of Stephensen in chapter 3).

Our discussion does not do justice to the position of Aboriginal women within the culture. The classic account here is Kaberry's *Aboriginal Women* (1939). See also Diane Bell *Daughters of the Dreaming* (1983). On sexuality see R. Berndt (1951).

On Aboriginal languages, the authoritative survey is Dixon (1980). Basil Sansom's *The Camp at Wallaby Cross* (1980) is a fascinating study of transformations of traditional discursive processes as they organise social life in a fringe-dweller camp near Darwin. Among the many collections of texts of Aboriginal languages, Jeffrey Heath's *Nunggubuyu Myths* (1980) is exemplary in its thoroughness though not user-friendly. Carl von Brandenstein and A. Thomas's *Tabi* (1974) is an elegantly presented set of song texts, including literal and free translations.

Our reading of myths as narratives built around opposites and a mediating factor or category follows the work of Claude Lévi-Strauss (1972 & 1963/68) which claimed that myths have a logical status as types of proto-histories and proto-philosophies, thus enabling us to understand the complex ideological systems which underpin Aboriginal myths which may otherwise be rejected as too simple. The systematic set of studies of Aboriginal mythology from this structuralist point of view is contained in Hiatt (1975). For an attempt to relate structuralist analysis of this kind to structural theories of language, see R. Hodge and W. McGregor (1989). W. Mcgregor has applied a range of contemporary theories of narrative to the study of Aboriginal oral texts: see e.g. 'The Structure of Gooniyandi Narratives' (1987).

The most useful general summary of the typical forms of oral cultures is Ong (1982). Margaret Clunies-Ross 'Australian Aboriginal Oral Traditions' (1986) is a valuable study of the relations between text and context in Aboriginal oral culture. Clunies-Ross and Wild *Djambidj* (1982) includes a record plus useful commentary: an appropriate solution to the problems of mediating oral texts. Tamsin Donaldson's 'Translating Oral Literature: Aboriginal Song Texts' (1979) is an exemplary and subtle discussion of the problems posed in translating Aboriginal song. Stephen Muecke's arguments for recognising oral qualities of Aboriginal narratives have been influential and controversial. Our analysis of his innovations is presented more fully in Hodge (1984). See also the widely praised Benterrak, Muecke and Roe *Reading the Country* (1984) and the less than enthusiastic review from an Aboriginal point of view by Colin Johnson (Mudrooroo Narogin) in 'Reading the Book' (1985) who sees Muecke's 'nomadology' as a form of tourism, another way of making the land safe for White intellectuals. Muecke draws on the work of Tedlock (1983) recognising the similar methodological demands posed by the oral cultures of American Indian peoples and Australian Aborigines.

On Aboriginal art, P. Sutton's *Dreamings* (1988) is the best introduction, combining a sophisticated approach to art with scholarly background on texts and contexts. The work of the Berndts integrates the study of visual and verbal art (see e.g. *The Speaking Land* 1989) which includes a large collection of narrative texts with commentary, plus relevant illustrations, and their *Aboriginal Australian Art* (1982). Nancy Munn's virtuoso *Walbiri Iconography* (1973) is a classic Aboriginalist study which is always suggestive if not always convincing. A collection edited by Peter Ucko *Form in Indigenous art* (1977) explores similarities between Aboriginal art and neolithic European cave paintings: the similarities are intriguingly close, though no more so than affinities with modern art.

Chapter 5

Aboriginal writing is still a new and growing area. Aboriginal perspectives were collected in an edition based on a conference of Aboriginal writers in Perth in 1984, Jack Davis and Bob Hodge *Aboriginal Writing Today* (1985). Mudrooroo Narogin's *Writing from the Fringe* (1990) is an important study by the leading

Aboriginal novelist, a book that is likely to be a definitive text for many years. Adam Shoemaker's *Black Words White Page* (1989) is a comprehensive survey of 20th century writing.

A short list of important Aboriginal writers and works would include Kath Walker's (Oodgeroo Noonuccal) *We are Going* (1964), the first book of poetry published by an Aborignal writer, which was reprinted six times in its first six months. She has continued to publish major work in a number of genres. Other important books of poetry include Jack Davis *The First Born* (1970) Kevin Gilbert *People are Legends* (1978) and Lionel Fogarty *Yoogum Yoogum* (1982). Colin Johnson (Mudrooroo Narogin)'s *Wild Cat Falling* (1965) was the first Aboriginal novel published, and as we have indicated, Narogin has continued to develop the range and scope of his work. Jack Davis has a similarly dominant position in Aboriginal theatre, although Bob Merritt's *The Cake Man* (1978) was also an important pioneering work.

Many Aboriginal texts cross the boundaries between history and literature. Kevin Gilbert's *Living Black* (1977) was a political intervention and a contribution to oral history. Robert Bropho's *Fringedweller* (1983) is an eloquent polemic as well as a 'lifestory', which Colin Johnson/Mudrooroo Narogin (in Davis & Hodge 1985) has argued is one of the major Aboriginal literary genres. There are many other 'lifestories' transmitted with varying degrees of fidelity to the Aboriginal voice of the speaker. A significant contribution to Aboriginal oral history has been the set of texts collected by L. Hercus and P. Sutton entitled *What Really Happened* (1988).

Geoffrey Bardon's *Aboriginal Art of the Western Desert* (1979) was a key text in launching the Papunya art movement. Eric Michaels *For a Cultural Future* (1987) links developments in art and video production to argue a radical case for the vitality of indigenous forms in using new technologies. For discussion of issues raised by Michaels' work, see the special issue of *Continuum* edited by Tom O'Regan (1990). The TV series *Women of the Sun* written by Hyllus Maris and Sonia Borg (1983) constructed an Aboriginal version of Australian history focused on four moments: the foundation event, dispossession, resistance, and the search for Aboriginal identity. Among Aboriginal documentaries, especially effective have been Gerry Bostock's *Lousy Little Sixpence*, (1980) and Robert Bropho's narration in *In the Name of the Crow* (1989).

The story of Jandamarra with its supernatural elements belongs to other mythic texts from antiquity which have been extensively documented in J.G. Frazer's classic study *The Golden Bough*, 13 vols (London: Macmillan, 1890-1936) and more recently in Joseph Campbell *The Masks of God*, 4 vols (New York: Viking Press, 1959-68).

For the complex ways in which the discourse of the colonised interacts with that of the coloniser—the double-bind which leads to the simultaneous appropriation and abrogation of the language of the imperial centre—see Homi Bhabha, 'The Other Question—the Stereotype and Colonial Discourse' (1983) and 'Signs Taken for Wonders: Questions of Ambivalence and Authority under a Tree Outside Delhi, May 1817' (1985). See also Gayatri Chakravorty Spivak (1987) and Henry Louis Gates Jr. (1984).

Chapter 6

In addition to Robert Hughes' popular and substantial history of convictism,

J. Hirst *Convict Society and its Enemies* (1983) is a useful study of the phenomenon. Humphrey McQueen makes a fierce case against romanticising convicts (1970). Paul Wilson and J. Braithwaite *Two Faces of Deviance* (1978) contains some important essays on the construction of criminality in Australia. Elizabeth Egglestone *Fear, Favour and Affection* (1976) is an authoritative study of the treatment of Aborigines in the legal system.

Foucault makes a very effective use of Bentham's Panopticon in *Discipline and Punish* (1975). 'Panopticism', for Foucault, was the mode of dissociating the seer from the seen. In the design of the Panopticon, which is formed around a central tower overlooking a semi-circle with cubicles which extend the whole breadth of the building, Foucault discovers an architectural form capable of sustaining domination and power by its mere design. Given such a design, he writes, 'in the peripheric ring, one is totally seen, without ever seeing; in the control tower, one sees everything without ever being seen' (p. 202).

Marcus Clarke's *His Natural Life* was first published in serial form in the *Australian Journal* between March 1870 and June 1872. The novel 'version' was published in 1874, having lost about one third of the original. For detailed examination of the two versions see Joan Poole, 'Maurice Frere's Wife: Marcus Clarke's Revision of *His Natural Life*' (1970). The title by which the novel is best known, *For the Term of His Natural Life*, was introduced in 1884, three years after the author's death. The complete serial version was not reissued until 1970 when Stephen Murray-Smith edited it for Penguin Books. See Michael Wilding, *Marcus Clarke* (1977), for a lucid essay on Marcus Clarke. In Marcus Clarke there is considerable equivocation between the laws of genre (romance) and social realism (the portrayal of the establishment of a penal colony). For an account of the literary uses of history in Clarke see L.L. Robson, 'The Historical Basis of *For the Term of His Natural Life*' (1963).

A more considerable equivocation with a correspondingly greater textual 'chaos' is to be found in James Tucker's *Ralph Rashleigh* (1845/1952), which is something of a literary curiosity. The manuscript surfaced in 1920 and appears to have been in the possession of the family of Mrs Margaret Baxter née Burnett. A garbled version of *Ralph Rashleigh* or *The Life of an Exile*, by Giacomo de Rosenberg appeared in 1929 as a literary memoir. Though historically it is not possible to give *Ralph Rashleigh* a 'precursor' status, nevertheless, Tucker's hero traversed the three major ingredients of early fiction: convictism, bushranging and Aboriginalism. Two more recent works should also be mentioned. The first is Thomas Keneally's *Bring Larks and Heroes* (1967) which reads the brutal history of convictism through a metaphysical mix of Melville's *Billy Budd* and Patrick White's *Voss*. The second is David Ireland's *The Unknown Industrial Prisoner* (1971) which is basically an allegorical rendition of industrial capitalism through the generic constraints of the Australian convict novel.

Rolf Boldrewood/Thomas Alexander Browne's *Robbery Under Arms* (1888) was originally published as a serial in the *Sydney Mail*, 1882-83. Earlier the bushranging theme had entered Henry Kingsley's *The Recollections of Geoffry Hamlyn* (1859) through the character of George Hawker who turns bushranger. The 'genteel' pretensions of Kingsley's style and his colonial preferences (he spent no more than four years in Australia) are parodied in Joseph Furphy/Tom Collins's *Such is Life* (1903).

NOTES

In art Sydney Nolan's *Ned Kelly* series established a dominant iconography of the Bushranger. He also painted a number of 'escaped convict' paintings. Convictism has proved a reliable staple in both film (e.g. *For the Term of His Natural Life* in 1927 (Dawn)) and TV (e.g. the televised version of *For the Term of His Natural Life* (1983) and the historical series *Against the Wind* (1983)). In the popular but controversial TV series *Prisoner* (1979–1986) prison functioned as a complex metaphor which viewers used to explore the role of institutions (including school and the work place) in everyday life; see Hodge & Tripp (1986). Graeme Turner (1986) analyses the connections between convictism and constructions of the self in Australian society in similar terms to ours, including an excellent discussion of Stephen Wallace's film *Stir* (1980).

Chapter 7

Fiske, Hodge and Turner *Myths of Oz* (1987) uses the basic structuralist opposition between nature and culture as the basis for their analysis of core meanings in Australian popular culture (in housing and urban design, and in sites and practices of everyday life such as tourism and the beach). Graeme Turner (1986) argues that this obsessive opposition is used to express and work out problems and conflicts that are primarily social: a position that we endorse. Geoffrey Blainey's *The Tyranny of Distance* (1966) has provoked much debate. Geoffrey Bolton's *Spoils and Spoilers* (1981) is a readable critical history of Australians' attitudes to the environment. Richard White's *Inventing Australia* (1981) describes some of the key moves in the Australian construction of 'the bush'. Humphrey McQueen (1970) points out the importance in Russel Ward's work of the image of 'the frontier' as originally formulated by Frederick Turner for the US: a connection which still awaits a detailed and critical exploration from a postcolonial perspective.

Two notable works which deal with the subject of Australian landscape are Brian Elliott, *The Landscape of Australian Poetry* (1967) and, in a more sprawling fashion, T. Inglis Moore, *Social Patterns in Australian Literature* (1971). G.A. Wilkes (1981) connects the new egalitarianism and democratic leanings arising out of a hitherto hierarchical 'social structure' with a shift in the way in which the landscape is represented. 'The aspects of the landscape which receive most emphasis are those with the least resemblance to English conditions—indeed the harsher features of Australian scenery may now be especially prized', writes Wilkes (p. 33).

The themes of 'the bush', 'the outback', and the role of landscape in both art and literature are too ubiquitous to need particular references here. For film see John Tulloch *Legends on the Screen* (1986) for the earlier period. See also Moran and O'Regan (1986) for a useful collection of readings in Australian cinema. For television, see Moran (1985). A persuasive analysis of the Heidelberg School and its ideological construction of the bush from an urban and class perspective is contained in Ian Burn 'Beating About the Bush' (1980).

Chapter 8

The major theoreticians of the 'radical nationalist' thesis were A.A. Phillips, Russel Ward, Vance Palmer and Geoffrey Serle. Their work exemplifies a basically historicist search for a distinctively Australian tradition in which values such as democracy, egalitarianism, mateship, and the bush ethos are enshrined. Underlying egalitarianism, democracy and so on is a certain utopianism, a wish to re-create in Australia, through a nationalist, 'postcolonial' ethos, the myth of a lost paradise. In essence it veers towards a folk culture fond of putting the 'industrial' clock back since it sees industrialisation as the sickness of 'advanced' societies. A crucial text here is Phillips' essay 'The Democratic Theme' (1958). The terms and Australian colloquialisms which recur in this essay are 'democratic spirit', 'spirit of mateship', 'scab', 'dinkum' etc. The dominance of these in the literature of the 1890s leads to a certain romantic formulation of literary history: 'Before the nineties there was no such thing as Australian writing, no continuous stream of creative work; there were only occasional books, standing like waterholes in a sandy bed of apathy. From the nineties, the creek has often run feebly, has never swelled to flood-level, but it has never run dry' (1958: 51).

The folk-basis of this utopianism helps Phillips to place the 1890s phenomenon in a 'proletarian' world, as opposed to the middle-class sympathies of the prevailing English fiction of the time. In contradistinction to English fiction, people like Lawson and Furphy, Phillips argued, 'wrote of the people, for the people, and from the people'. However, Phillips lacked both a theory of fiction and a definition of literariness. Consequently he often made the same kinds of comments about 'propitious' periods that Kramer, more subtly, raises in *OHAL*. For instance, Phillips regrets that Brennan's parents 'mated when they did' as in the 'interests of Australian literature, they should have delayed the consummation of their passions for twenty years' (p. 63).

For our critique of the Australian legend in this chapter we have drawn on a variety of sources who have already been listed: notably the work of McQueen, White, Summers and Dixson. For a fuller analysis of the 'Australian accent' that argues for its polysemic nature and its capacity to express a radical consciousness, see Fiske, Hodge and Turner (1987). That book emphasises the constitution of the 'accent' from below as always liable to fresh appropriations from above in a continuous dialectic: a model which underlies the present book.

Chapter 9

A useful history of migration in Australia is J. I. Martin, *The Migrant Presence* (1978). See also Lois Foster and David Stockley, *Australian Multiculturalism* (1988) for contemporary patterns and issues. For an account of the diversity of ethnic groups in Australia see S. Clyne, *Multilingual Australia* (1982). For comparative literary studies in other settler societies see William Walsh *Commonwealth Literature* (1973). For a controversial study of Indian culture in similar terms to our account see Mishra (1987): this article argued the 'heresy' (Bailey 1989) that Indian culture is radically de-centred, its binary oppositions continually reconstituted in an open transformational process.

In *Snow on the Saltbush*, Geoffrey Dutton concluded that though the 'Anglo-Saxon snow that kept falling on the Australian saltbush has long since melted . . . it will be a long time before some of the changes can be chronicled' (1985: 293). He added that it will be 'another twenty years before the impact of multiculturalism on the environment can begin to be defined'. Perhaps so, but the 'chronicling' Dutton has in mind belongs to a dated concept of incorpora-

NOTES

tion into what is really a version of the legend: Australian literature as a continuum defined by metaphors of stockyards, croquet lawns, saltbushes, etc. The 1970s and 1980s in fact witnessed a different kind of chronicling, one which emerged from the margins, and this took the form of essays and collections which appeared in magazines such as *Mattoid* or resource materials for courses in universities and colleges of advanced education.

One of the more important collections, *Displacements: migrant story-tellers*, was published by Deakin University in 1982. Edited with an introduction by Sneja Gunew, the collection brought together quite a galaxy of diverse writings by non-Anglo-Celtic Australian migrants. Three years before Gunew's selection Andrew Deszery edited an anthology which included works in 'community languages': *English and other than English Anthology in Community Languages* (1979). Other collections which have appeared since include Ron Holt's *The Strength of Tradition* (1983), Manfred Jurgensen's *Ethnic Australia* (1981), Sneja Gunew and Jan Mahyuddin's *Beyond the Echo* (1988), T. Spilias and S. Messinis' *Reflections: Selected Works from Greek Australian Literature* (1988), Peter Skrzynecki's *Joseph's Coat* (1985). Three collections of women's fiction which have combined the experience of migrant women and their Anglo-Celtic counterparts are Anna Gibbs and Alison Tilson's *Frictions* (1983), Anna Couani and Sneja Gunew's *Telling Ways: Australian Women's Experimental Writing* (1988) and Drusilla Modjeska's *Inner Cities* (1989). For useful, though dated, bibliographies of migrant writing see Lolo Houbein, *Ethnic Writing in English from Australia* (1984) and Peter Lamb and Anne Hazell, *Diversity and Diversion: An Annotated Bibliography of Australian Ethnic Minority Literature* (1983). Lolo Houbein also delivered a paper on ethnic and migrant writing in 1977 which showed the problems faced by a researcher in this area and the inadequacies of a form of classification and cataloguing which made the undertaking of such research in Australian universities and libraries so difficult (Tiffin, 1978).

Sneja Gunew has written the most exciting theoretical accounts of migrant writing. Her 'Migrant Women Writers: Who's on Whose Margins' (1983) was a path-breaking essay. She followed this up with an incisive reading of Rosa Cappiello's *Oh Lucky Country* (1985), as well as an essay on the ways in which migrant writing might be incorporated into a mainstream Australian literature curriculum (*English in Australia* 1987). In this paper she points out that writers such as 'Pi O and Ania Walwicz . . . . parody the various stereotypes attached to the non-English migrant condition' (p. 34). Gunew (1987) uses the writings of Ania Walwicz to connect Walwicz's conscious 'anti-homogenisation' tendencies with postmodernism. Pi O's own compilation of recent Australian writing with some fascinating poems on record published by Penguin in 1985 demonstrates the vitality of writing emerging out of the shadow of the high modern period of Kenneth Slessor, A.D. Hope and Douglas Stewart. On the question of black women's writing see Carole Ferrier's commentary and bibliography in *Hecate* (1987; 1988). Ferrier acknowledges the need for a thorough grasp of the source culture of writings by Black women.

Three varieties of migrant literature which have developed 'literary histories' of their own are Jewish, Greek, and Italian Australian literature. In 1984 L. & R. Kalechofsky edited *Jewish Writing from Down Under* while Nancy Keesing, seven years before, had published *Shalom: Australian Jewish Stories* (1978). Judah Waten's 'Discovering Migrant Literature' (1983) and his autobiographical piece referred to in this chapter explore the Jewish Australian experience further. As early as 1949 the *Australian Jewish Historical Society: Journal and Proceedings* published Judah Waten's 'Contemporary Jewish Literature in Australia' (vol. 3, part 2). The Bicentennial year also saw the publication of Suzanne D. Rutland's comprehensive history of two centuries of Jewish settlement, *Edge of the Diaspora* (1988). Con Castan, who also wrote the introduction to the Greek Australian anthology *Reflections*, has been in the forefront of research in Greek Australian literature having written a major paper for *AUMLA* in 1983. Ross King's essay on the Greeks in Australia appeared in *Meanjin* (1976) and the question of translating Australian migrant literature in Greek was taken up by John Vasilakakos in a recent issue of *Meanjin (1989)*. The text and translation of Dimitris Tsaloumas' *The Observatory* (1983) received the National Book Council Award. In reviewing it in *Quadrant* Bruce Beaver called Tsaloumas 'a poet comparable to the best poets of modern Greece' (1983:94). Gaetano Rando's essay on 'Italo-Australian Fiction' (1984) lays the groundwork for a more comprehensive account of that aspect of Australian migrant writing.

Ken Gelder and Paul Salzman *The New Diversity* (1989) devote an entire chapter to the literature of the migrants as well as using the works of Judah Waten and David Malouf elsewhere in their study. Bruce Bennett's essay 'Australian Perspectives on the Near North' (Tiffin, 1978) offers a lucid account of the imaginative transformation of the Near North by Australian writers, notably Hal Porter and Randolph Stow. For another account see Helen Tiffin's '*Tourmaline* and the Tao te Ching' in K.G. Hamilton (1978). Kateryna Arthur attempts a somewhat more radical reading of the migrant experience by comparing it to that of the Aborigines (Bennett, 1988). Colin Roderick's edition of Brennan's prose (1962) and G.A. Wilkes' facsimile reproduction of *Poems (1913)* (1972) are invaluable to any student of Brennan. Axel Clark wrote a fascinating critical biography (1980) which won the National Book Council Award for Australian Literature. A good short introduction to Patrick White is Alan Lawson's review essay on Patrick White (1979). Good historical readings of Patrick White are generally missing. Veronica Brady discovers in Patrick White an important interpretation of the religious experience (1980). The best collection of some of the crucial early essays on Patrick White is G.A. Wilkes' *Ten Essays on Patrick White* (1970). Vijay Mishra examines White's multiple perspectives and his use of European traditions, reading the novels through Mikhail Bakhtin (1984) and *Flaws in the Glass* through symbolist claims of androgyny (1982).

Chapter 10

To date no systematic attempt has been made to offer a theory of Australian colloquialisms with reference to Halliday's description of antilanguages. The first major compilation of Australian slang was undertaken by James Hardy Vaux and published as an appendix ('Vocabulary of the Flash Language') to his Memoirs (1812/1964). Vaux's Flash Language was not a record of the colony's unique vocabulary. Instead it reflected the antilanguage of the British/Australian convict underworld: 'black-slum', 'bender', 'Bastille', 'boned', 'old lag', 'slangs' belong to this general body of antilanguage. This general tradition is continued in the authoritative works of the Australian born Eric Partridge: *A Dictionary of the Underworld* (1961) and *A Dictionary of Slang and Unconventional English* (1970).

Earlier Australian English had been documented by Edward E. Morris (1898) and Sidney J. Baker (1941/43). For a critical review of research in Australian English, see W.S. Ramson (1965). The Australian Language Research Centre at the University of Sydney has published specialist vocabularies on a range of Australian subjects in their Occasional Papers Series (1964–).

The second important 'moment' in the lexicography of Australian slang (after Vaux) was the publication of G.A. Wilkes' *Australian Colloquialisms* (1978/1985). Wilkes offers the most comprehensive (though not critical or interpretive) account of the subject. He discusses some of the problems facing the lexicographer of colloquialisms in Wilkes (1982). Important reviews of Wilkes' book which, *inter alia*, also raise significant questions about the historical, social and linguistic ramifications of Australian colloquialisms are Arthur Delbridge (1978), W.S. Ramson (1978), Eric Partridge (1978), Germaine Greer (1978), G.W. Turner (1978), K.S. Inglis (1979), W.A. Krebs (1979) and John Hepworth (1980).

Fiske, Hodge and Turner (1987) develop the linguistic domain of Australian colloquialisms into a much more pervasive concept of the Australian accent with which they interpret a number of Australian semiotic systems. For a critique of Halliday's theory of antilanguages see Kress and Hodge (1979) and Roger Fowler (1981).

Contemporary Australian debates on gender and feminism may be examined best through the pages of Hecate (1975–). Carmel Shute (1975) argued persuasively that the myth of Gallipoli, the founding event of Australian 'manhood', effectively condemned Australian women to the state of second-rate citizens. Judith Godden (1979) reads the Pioneer Woman as a group constructed around the prevailing concept of women as the 'weaker sex' in the service of 'domesticity'. The literary evidence endorses this mythic 'role model' of the Pioneer Woman. See Jan Carter, *Nothing to Spare* (1981) for the recollections of fourteen women in the West Australian goldfields and Rhonda Wilson ed. (1984) *Good Talk* for the recollections of ten elderly women of Port Melbourne. On the question of Aboriginal economic and sexual exploitation, Ann McGrath draws a damning portrait of White settlers in the Northern Territory (1978). For the exploitation of Aboriginal women and their rape by a 'superior' race see Raymond Evans (1982). Carmel Harris in the same issue of *Hecate* shows how the summary deaths of Aborigines for real or attempted rape of White women was one way of confirming unqualified White supremacy. Jackie Huggins' essay (1987) concludes that for Black women gender distinction (women as women) cannot be seen apart from the overall struggle of Black people as a whole. The literary essays in *Hecate* range from Jane Sutherland's (1978) argument that Prichard eschews radical feminism in favour of a more general, and utopian, urge towards socialism while Dorothy Hewett (1979) points out how she self-consciously gave greater scope to heroines and anti-heroines in her own plays. Sneja Gunew and Louise Adler (1981) emphasise the quite bewildering variety of female discourse and the inadequacies of a feminist literary theory which continues to be based on a critique of women's writing as a reflection of an essentially male dominated or patriarchial discourse. For essays on the Australian Anti-Feminist Group see *Hecate*, Double Issue (1983). The reception of Australian women's writing is discussed by Bronwen Levy and others in *Hecate* (1985). The question of men appropriating the field of feminism generally is taken up by Julie Marcus (1988).

Two works which we have used quite extensively are Anne Summers, *Damned Whores and God's Police* (1975) and Drusilla Modjeska, *Exiles at Home* (1981). Whilst Summers work offers a valuable critique of power and the abuse of women in Australia, its underlying premise that white women constitute a 'colonized sex' collapses two very distinct forms of colonisation: the subjugation of race under imperialism and the exploitation of women, by the same race, in any given society. Modjeska fills in a major vacuum in our study of women writers by constructing a literary history which is not intimidated by two of Australia's best writers: Christina Stead and Henry Handel Richardson. Modjeska, however, is concerned more with literary archaeology than with comparative theory. For an unusual account of radical politics in Australia and nascent feminism see Jean Devanny, *Point of Departure* (1986).

Bateson's seminal articles are conveniently collected together in *Steps to an Ecology of Mind* (1973). See also his *Naven* (1936). For a more systematic development of the argument of this chapter, applying Batesonian concepts to the study of Australian culture, see Hodge (1989). For a suggestive use of these concepts to a study of Australian film, see Routt (1989).

Bibliography

Adorno, T.W. (1950) *The Authoritarian Personality* New York: Harper
Althusser, L. (1971) *Essays on Ideology* London: New Left Books
Argyle, B. (1967) *Patrick White* Edinburgh: Oliver and Boyd
Arthur, K. O. (1990) 'Recasting History: Australian Bicentennial Writing', Perth: Murdoch University External Studies Unit
Ashcroft, W.D., Griffiths, G., Tiffin, H. (1989) *The Empire Writes Back: Theory and Practice in Post-Colonial Literatures* London: Routledge
Australian Language Research Centre (1964–) Occasional papers, University of Sydney
Bailey, G. (1989) 'On the De-construction of Culture in Indian Literature: A Tentative Response to Vijay Mishra's Article' *South Asia* [New Series] Vol. XII, No. 1, June, pp. 85–102
Baker, S. J. (1941/1943) *A Popular Dictionary of Australian Slang* Melbourne: Robertson and Mullens
Baker, S. J. (1945/1966) *The Australian Language* Sydney: Angus and Robertson
Bardon, G. (1979) *Aboriginal Art of the Western Desert* Adelaide: Rigby
Barnes, J. ed. (1969) *The Writer in Australia 1856–1964* Melbourne: Oxford University Press
Bateson, G. (1936) *Naven* Cambridge: Cambridge University Press
Bateson, G. (1973) *Steps to an Ecology of Mind* Frogmore: Paladin
Baynton, B. (1980) *Barbara Baynton* [Portable Australian Authors] (eds. S. Krimmer and A. Lawson) St. Lucia: University of Queensland Press
Beatson, P. (1976) *The Eye of the Mandala. Patrick White: A Vision of Man and God* Sydney: A.H. & A.W. Reed
Beaver, B. (1983) 'A Greek Poet in Australia' [review of D. Tsaloumas] *Quadrant* Vol. 27, December, pp. 94–95
Beier, U. and Johnson, C. [Narogin, M.] (1985) 'The Aboriginal Who Found Buddha' *Quadrant* Vol. 29, No. 9, pp. 69–75
Bell, D. (1983) *Daughters of the Dreaming* Melbourne: Allen & Unwin

Bennett, B. (1976) 'Judith Wright, Moralist' *Westerly* No. 1, March, pp. 76-82
Bennett, B. ed. (1988) *A Sense of Exile* Perth, University of Western Australia: Centre for Studies in Australian Literature
Benterrak, K., Muecke, S. and Roe, P. (1984) *Reading the Country* Fremantle: Fremantle Arts Centre Press
Berndt, R. (1951) *Kunapipi* Melbourne: Cheshire
Berndt, R. (1976) *Love Songs of Arnhem Land* Melbourne: Nelson
Berndt, R and C. (1964) *The World of the First Australians* Adelaide: Rigby
Berndt, R. and C. (1982) *Aboriginal Australian Art: A Visual Perspective* Sydney: Methuen
Berndt, R. and C. (1989) *The Speaking Land* Ringwood and Harmondsworth: Penguin Books
Berzins, B. (1988) *The Coming of the Strangers: Life in Australia 1788-1822* Sydney: Collins
Bhabha, H.K. (1983) 'The Other Question—the Stereotype and Colonial Discourse' *Screen* Vol. 24, No. 6, pp. 18-36
Bhabha, H.K. (1985) 'Signs Taken for Wonders: Questions of Ambivalence and Authority under a Tree Outside Delhi, May 1817' *Critical Inquiry* Vol. 12, No. 1, pp. 144-65
Blainey, G. (1966) *The Tyranny of Distance* Melbourne: Sun Books
Blainey, G. (1976) *The Triumph of the Nomads* Melbourne: Sun Books
Blainey, G. (1984) *All for Australia* North Ryde: Methuen Haynes
Bliss, C (1986) *Patrick White's Fiction. The Paradox of Fortunate Failure* New York: St Martin's Press
Boldrewood, R. [Thomas Alexander Browne] (1888/1970) *Robbery Under Arms* Hawthorn, Victoria: Lloyd O'Neil
Bolton, G. (1973) 'Louis Hartz' *Australian Economic History Review* Vol. 13, No. 2, pp. 168-176
Bolton, G. (1981) *Spoils and Spoilers* Sydney: Allen & Unwin
Bolton, G. (gen. ed.) (1986-1990) *The Oxford History of Australia* Melbourne: Oxford University Press
Bourke, C. and White, I. (1980) *Before the Invasion: Aboriginal Life to 1788* Melbourne: Oxford University Press
Bowden, R. and Bunbury, W. (1989) *Being Aboriginal: Comments, Observations and Stories from Aboriginal Australians* Sydney: ABC Publications
Bradley, A. and Smith, T. (1980) *Australian Art and Architecture* Melbourne: Oxford University Press
Bradley, W. (1969) *A Voyage to New South Wales, 1786-1792* Sydney: Ure Smith (facsimile edition)
Brady, V. (1980) 'A single bone-clean button: the achievement of Patrick White' *The Literary Criterion* Vol. 15, Nos. 3-4, pp. 35-47
Brady, V. (1981) *A Crucible of Prophets. Australians and the Question of God* Sydney: Australia and New Zealand Studies in Theology and Religion
Brandenstein, C. Von (1986) *Nyungar Anew* Canberra: Pacific Linguistics
Brandenstein, C. Von and Thomas, A. (1974) *Tabi* Adelaide: Rigby
Brennan, C. (1914/1972) *Poems [1913]* (ed. G.A. Wilkes), Sydney: Sydney University Press
Brennan, C.J. (1962) *Prose* (eds. A.R. Chisholm and J.J. Quinn) Sydney: Angus and Robertson

BIBLIOGRAPHY

Brennan, C.J. (1984) *Christopher Brennan* [Portable Australian Authors] (ed. Terry Sturm) St Lucia: University of Queensland Press
Broome, R. (1982) *Aboriginal Australians* Sydney: Allen & Unwin
Bropho, R. (1983) *Fringedweller* Sydney: Alternative Publishing Cooperative Limited
Buckley, V. (1960) 'Capricornia' *Meanjin* Vol. 19, No. 4, pp. 13-30
Burn, I. (1980) 'Beating About the Bush: the Landscapes of the Heidelberg School' in Bradley, A. and Smith, T.
Butlin, N. (1983) *Our Original Aggression: Aboriginal Populations of Southeastern Australia 1788-1850* Sydney: George Allen & Unwin
Campbell, M. (1985) *Lines of Flight* Fremantle: Fremantle Arts Centre Press
Cantrell, L. (1977) *The 1890s* [Portable Australian Authors] St Lucia: University of Queensland Press
Carey, G. (1984) *Just Us* Ringwood: Penguin
Carey, G. and Lette, K. (1979) *Puberty Blues* Ringwood: Penguin
Carter, J. (1981) *Nothing to Spare* Ringwood and Harmondsworth: Penguin Books
Carter, P. (1987) *The Road to Botany Bay. An Essay in Spatial History* London: Faber and Faber
Castan, C. (1983) 'Greek Australian Literature' *AUMLA* No. 59, pp. 5-25
Césaire, A. (1955) *Discours sur le Colonialisme* Paris: Présence Africaine
Chisholm, A.R. (1961) 'Brennan and Mallarmé' *Southerly* Vol. 21, No. 4, pp. 2-11
Chisholm, A.R. (1967) 'Christopher Brennan and the Idea of Eden' *Meanjin* Vol. 26, No. 2, pp. 153-160
Chisholm, A.R. (1970) *A Study of Christopher Brennan's 'The Forest of the Night'* Melbourne: Melbourne University Press
Clark, Axel (1980) *Christopher Brennan* Melbourne: Melbourne University Press
Clark, Manning, *A History of Australia (1962-1987)* Melbourne: Melbourne University Press
Clarke, M. (1874/1969) *For the Term of His Natural Life* Sydney: Pacific Books
Clarke, M. (1929/1970) *His Natural Life* Ringwood and Harmondsworth: Penguin Books
Clarke, M. (1976) *Marcus Clarke* [Portable Australian Authors] (ed. Michael Wilding) St Lucia: University of Queensland Press
Clunies-Ross, M. (1986) 'Australian Aboriginal Oral Traditions' *Oral Traditions* Nos. 1/2, pp. 231-71
Clunies-Ross, M. and Wild, S. (1982) *Djambidj* Ringwood and Harmondsworth: Penguin Books
Clyne, S. (1982) *Multilingual Australia* Melbourne: River Seine
Couani, A. and Gunew, S. eds. (1988) *Telling Ways: Australian Women's Experimental Writing* Adelaide: Australian Feminist Studies Publications
Culotta, N. [O'Grady, J.] (1957/1974) *They're a Weird Mob* Sydney: Ure Smith
Cunningham, S. (1986) ' "The Sentimental Age": Chauvel, Melodrama, Nationality' *Framework* Vol. 30/31, pp. 40-59
Cunningham, S. (1987) 'Charles Chauvel: the Last Decade' *Continuum* Vol.1, No. 1. pp. 26-46
Daniel, H. (1988) *Liars: Australian New Novelists* Ringwood and Harmondsworth: Penguin Books

Dark, E. (1966) *The Timeless Land* Sydney: Collins
Davis, J. (1970) *The First Born* Sydney: Angus and Robertson
Davis, J. (1982) *Kullark/The Dreamers* Sydney: Currency
Davis, J. (1986) *No Sugar* Sydney: Currency
Davis, J. (1989) *Barungin* Sydney: Currency
Davis, J. and Hodge, R. (1985) *Aboriginal Writing Today* Canberra: Australian Instititute of Aboriginal Studies
Dawe, B. (1983) *Sometimes Gladness: Collected Poems 1954-1982* Melbourne: Longman Cheshire
Delbridge, A. (1978) [review of G.A. Wilkes, *Australian Colloquialisms*] *Australian Book Review* June, pp. 34-36
Derrida, J. (1985) 'Racism's last Word' *Critical Inquiry* Vol. 12, No. 1, pp. 290-99
Deszery, A. ed. (1979) *English and Other than English Anthology in Community Languages* Adelaide: Deszery Ethnic Publications
Devanny, J. (1986) *Point of Departure* (ed. Carole Ferrier) St. Lucia: University of Queensland Press
Dixon, R.M.W. (1980) *The Languages of Australia* Cambridge University Press
Dixon, R.M.W. ed. (1976) *Grammatical Categories in Australian Languages* Canberra: Australian Instititute of Aboriginal Studies
Dixson, M. (1976) *The Real Matilda: Women and Identity in Australia 1788-1975* Ringwood: Penguin
Docker, J. (1974) *Australian Cultural Elites: Intellectual Traditions in Sydney and Melbourne* Sydney: Angus and Robertson
Docker, J. (1984) *In A Critical Condition: Reading Australian Literature* Ringwood and Harmondsworth: Penguin Books
Donaldson, I. and T. (1983) *Seeing the First Australians* Sydney: Allen & Unwin
Donaldson, T. (1979) 'Translating Oral Literature: Aboriginal Song Texts' *Aboriginal History* No. 3, pp. 62-83
Drake-Brockman, H. (1967) *Katharine Susannah Prichard* Melbourne: Oxford University Press
Dransfield, M. (1970) *Streets of the Long Voyage* St Lucia: Queensland University Press
During, S. (1990) 'How Aboriginal is it?' [review of Mudrooroo Narogin, *Writing from the Fringe*] *Australian Book Review* 11, 8 February-March, pp. 21-23
Dutton, G. (1985) *Snow on the Saltbush* Ringwood and Harmondsworth: Penguin Books
Dutton, G. ed. (1964) *The Literature of Australia* Ringwood and Harmondsworth: Penguin Books
Dutton, G. ed. (1976) *Australian Verse from 1805: A Continuum* Adelaide: Rigby
Egglestone, E. (1976) *Fear, Favour and Affection* Canberra: Australian National University Press
Elliott, B. (1967) *The Landscape of Australian Poetry* Melbourne: Oxford University Press
Elliott, B. ed. (1979) *The Jindyworobaks* [Portable Australian Authors] St. Lucia: University of Queensland Press
Evans, R. (1982) ' "Don't You Remember Black Alice, Sam Holt?" Aboriginal Women in Queensland History' *Hecate* Vol. 8, No. 2, pp. 6-21
Fanon, F. (1967) *Black Skin, White Masks* New York: Grove Press

BIBLIOGRAPHY

Ferrier, C. ed. (1985) *Gender, Politics and Fiction: Twentieth Century Australian Women's Novels* St Lucia: University of Queensland Press
Ferrier, C. (1987/88) 'Teaching Courses in Black Women's Fiction in Australia: Some Observations' *Hecate* Vol. 13, No. 2, pp. 134-139
Ferrier, C. (1988) 'Bibliography of Black Women's Writing' *Hecate* Vol. 14, Nos. 1, 2, pp. 104-111; pp. 110-125
Fiedler, L. (1967) *Love and Death in the American Novel* New York: Jonathan Cape
Fiske, J., Hodge, B. and Turner, G. (1987) *Myths of Oz: Reading Australian Popular Culture* Sydney: Allen & Unwin
Fogarty, L. (1982) *Yoogum Yoogum* Ringwood and Harmondsworth: Penguin Books
Foster, L. and Stockley, D. (1988) *Australian Multiculturalism: A Documentary History and Critique* Clevedon and Philadelphia: Multilingual Matters Ltd
Foucault, M. (1966/1974) *The Order of Things: An Archaeology of the Human Sciences* London: Tavistock Publications
Foucault, M. (1969/1974) *The Archaeology of Knowledge* trans. A.M. Sheridan Smith, London: Tavistock Publications
Foucault, M. (1975/1979) *Discipline and Punish: The Birth of the Prison* trans. Alan Sheridan, Harmondsworth: Penguin Books
Fowler, R. (1981) *Literature as Social Discourse* Bloomington: Indiana University Press
Franklin, M. (1901/1974) *My Brilliant Career* Sydney: Angus and Robertson
Frow, J. (1983) 'The Chant of Thomas Keneally' *Australian Literary Studies* Vol. 10, No. 3, pp. 291-99
Frye, N. (1957) *Anatomy of Criticism* Princeton: Princeton University Press
Furphy, J. [Tom Collins] (1903/1970) *Such is Life* Hawthorn, Victoria: Lloyd O'Neill
Garton, S. (1988) 'The Dimensions of Dementia' in *Constructing a Culture* (eds. V. Burgmann and J. Lee), Ringwood: Penguin Books
Gates Jr. H.L. ed. (1984) *Black Literature and Literary Theory* London and New York: Methuen
Gelder, K. and Salzman, P. (1989) *The New Diversity: Australian Fiction 1970-88* Melbourne: McPhee Gribble
Gibbs, A. and Tilson, A. eds. (1982) *Frictions. An Anthology of Fiction by Women* Melbourne: Sybylla Cooperative Press and Publications Ltd.
Gilbert, K. (1977/1978) *Living Black* Ringwood and Harmondsworth: Penguin Books
Gilbert, K. (1978) *People are Legends* St Lucia: University of Queensland Press
Gilbert, K. (1985) 'Black policies' in Davis, J. and Hodge, B.
Gilbert, K. (1988) *The Cherry Pickers* Canberra: Burrambinga Books
Gilbert, K. ed. (1988) *Inside Black Australia: An Anthology of Aboriginal Poetry* Ringwood and Harmondsworth: Penguin Books
Godden, J. (1979) 'A New Look at the Pioneer Woman' *Hecate* Vol. 5, No. 2, pp. 7-21
Goodwin, K. (1986) *A History of Australian Literature* [Macmillan History of Literature], London: Macmillan
Gooneratne, Y. (1989) 'How Barry Changed His Image' *Meanjin* Vol. 48, No. 1, pp. 109-115

Gordon, A.L. (1946) *Poems* Melbourne: Oxford University Press
Green D. (1973) *Ulysses Bound: Henry Handel Richardson and Her Fiction* Canberra: Australian National University Press
Green, H.M. (1930) *An Outline of Australian Literature* Sydney and Melbourne: Whitcombe & Tombs
Green, H.M. (1961) *A History of Australian Literature* 2 vols., Sydney: Angus and Robertson
Greer, G. (1978) 'Cheechee and Bandicoot' [including review of G.A. Wilkes, *Australian Colloquialisms*] *Spectator* 12 August, pp. 17-18
Grey, G. (1841) *Journals of two expeditions of discovery in North-west and Western Australia* London: T. & W. Boone
Gunew, S. (1983) 'Migrant Women Writers. Who's on Whose Margins?' *Meanjin* Vol. 42, No. 1, pp. 16-26
Gunew, S. (1985) 'Rosa Cappiello's Oh Lucky Country: Multicultural Reading Strategies' *Meanjin* Vol. 44, No. 4, pp. 517-528
Gunew, S. (1987) 'Why and How Multi-Cultural Writing Should be Included in the English Curriculum' *English in Australia* No. 82, pp. 28-35
Gunew, S. and Adler, L. (1981) 'Method and Madness in Female Writing' *Hecate* Vol. 7, No. 2, pp. 20-33
Gunew, S. and Mahyuddin, J. eds. (1988) *Beyond the Echo: Multicultural Women's Writing* St Lucia: University of Queensland Press
Gunew, S. and Spivak, G.C. (1986) 'Questions of Multiculturalism' *Hecate* Vol. 12, Nos. 1 and 2, pp. 136-142
Gunew, S. ed. (1982) *Displacements: Migrant Story-tellers* Geelong: Deakin University
Habermas, J. (1987) *The Philosophical Discourse of Modernity* trans. F. Lawrence, Cambridge: Polity Press
Haebich, A. (1988) *For Their Own Good* Nedlands: University of Western Australia Press
Halliday, M.A.K. (1978) *Language as Social Semiotic* London: Edward Arnold
Hamilton, K.G. ed. (1978) *Studies in the Recent Australian Novel* St. Lucia: University of Queensland Press
Hancock, W.K. (1930/1961) *Australia* Brisbane: Jacaranda
Harpur, C. (1984) *The Poetical Works of Charles Harpur* (ed. Elizabeth Perkins) Sydney: Angus and Robertson
Harpur, C. (1986) *Selected Poetry and Prose* (ed. Michael Ackland) Ringwood and Harmondsworth: Penguin Books.
Harpur, C. (1987) *Stalwart the Bushranger with The Tragedy of Donohoe* (ed. Elizabeth Perkins) Sydney: Currency Press
Harris, A. (1849/1969) *The Emigrant Family* (ed. W.S. Ramson) Canberra: Australian National University Press
Harris, C. (1982) 'The "Terror of the Law" as applied to black rapists in colonial Queensland' *Hecate* Vol. 8, No. 2, pp. 22-48
Hartz, L. (1955) *The Liberal Tradition in America* New York: Harcourt Brace & World
Hartz, L. (1964) *The Founding of New Societies: Studies in the History of the United States, Latin America, South Africa, Canada and Australia* New York: Harcourt, Brace & World

Hasluck, A. (1955) *Portrait with Background* Melbourne: Oxford University Press
Hasluck, P. (1970) *Black Australians* Carlton: Melbourne University Press
Healy, J.J. (1978) *Literature and the Aborigine in Australia* St. Lucia: University of Queensland Press
Heath, J. (1980) *Nunggubuyu Myths* Canberra: Australian Institute of Aboriginal Studies
Hegel, G.W.F. (1975) *The Philosophy of Fine Art* New York: Hacker Art Books
Hepworth, J. (1980) [review of G.A. Wilkes, *Australian Colloquialisms*] *Australian Book Review* February-March, pp. 4-5
Herbert, X. (1937/1969) *Capricornia* Sydney: Pacific Books
Herbert, X. (1960) 'I Sinned Against Syntax' *Meanjin* Vol. 19, No. 1, pp. 31-35
Herbert, X. (1970) 'The Writing of "Capricornia"' *Australian Literary Studies* Vol. 4, No. 3, pp. 207-214
Herbert, X. (1975) *Poor Fellow My Country* Sydney: Collins
Hercus, L. and Sutton, P. (1986) *What Really Happened* Canberra: Australian Institute of Aboriginal Studies
Hergenhan, L. gen. ed. (1988) *The Penguin New Literary History of Australia* Ringwood and Harmondsworth: Penguin Books
Heseltine, H. (1973) *Xavier Herbert* Melbourne: Oxford University Press
Heseltine, H. (1989) 'An Imaginary Life—The Dimensions of Self' *Australian Literary Studies* Vol. 14, No. 1, pp. 26-40
Hewett, D. (1979) 'Creating Heroines in Australian Plays' *Hecate* Vol. 5, No. 2, pp. 73-80
Hewett, D. (1979) *The Man from Mukinupin* Fremantle: Fremantle Arts Centre Press; Sydney: Currency Press
Hiatt, L. (1975) *Australian Aboriginal Mythology* Canberra: Australian Institute of Aboriginal Studies
Hill, E. (1941) *My Love Must Wait* Sydney: Angus and Robertson
Hirst, J. (1983) *Convict Society and Its Enemies* Sydney: Allen & Unwin
Hirst, J. (1984) 'Keeping Colonial History Colonial: the Hartz thesis revisted' *Historical Studies* Vol. 21, No. 82, pp. 85-104
Hobsbawm, E. (1969) *Bandits* London: Weidenfeld & Nicolson
Hodge, B. (1984) 'A Case for Aboriginal Literature' *Meridian* No. 3, pp. 83-88
Hodge, B. (1989) 'National Character and the Discursive Process' *Journal of Pragmatics* Vol. 13, No. 3, pp. 422-444
Hodge, B. (1990a) *Literature as Discourse* Cambridge: Polity Press
Hodge, B. (1990b) 'Aboriginal truth and white media' *Continuum* Vol. 3, No. 2, pp. 201-225
Hodge, B. and Kress, G. (1988) *Social Semiotics* Cambridge: Polity Press
Hodge, B. and McGregor, W. (1989) 'Language and the Structures of Myth' *Oceania* Vol. 6, No. 1, pp. 17-36
Hodge, B. and Tripp D. (1986) *Children and Television* Cambridge: Polity Press
Holt, R. ed. (1983) *The Strength of Tradition* St Lucia: University of Queensland Press
Hope, A.D. (1963) *Australian Literature 1950-1962* Melbourne: Melbourne University Press
Hope, A.D. (1972) *Collected Poems 1930-1970* Sydney: Angus and Robertson
Hope, A.D. (1975) *Judith Wright* Melbourne: Oxford University Press

Horne, D. (1964) *The Lucky Country* Ringwood and Hardmondsworth: Penguin
Houbein, L. (1984) *Ethnic Writing in English from Australia* Adelaide University, English Working Papers
Hudson, J. (1978) *The Walmatjari* Darwin: Working Papers of the Summer Institute of Linguistics.
Huggins, J. (1987) 'Black Women and Women's Liberation' *Hecate* Vol. 13, No. 1, pp. 77-82
Hughes, R. (1987) *The Fatal Shore: A History of the Transportation of Convicts to Australia 1787-1868* London: Collins Harvill
Idriess, I.L. (1952/1957) *Outlaws of the Leopolds* Sydney: Angus and Robertson
Inglis, K.S. (1979) [review of G.A. Wilkes, *Australian Colloquialisms*] *Australian Literary Studies* Vol. 9, No. 1, pp. 131-138
Ireland, D. (1964) *Image in the Clay* St Lucia: University of Queensland Press
Ireland, D. (1971) *The Unknown Industrial Prisoner* Sydney: Angus and Robertson
Ireland, D. (1974) *Burn* Sydney: Angus and Robertson
JanMohammed, A.R. (1983) *Manichean Aesthetics: The Politics of Literature in Colonial Africa* Amherst, Mass.: University of Massachusetts Press
Janson, S. and Macintyre S. eds, (1988) *Making the Bicentenial (1988) Australian Historical Studies* special issue, Vol. 23, No. 19
Jefferis, B. (1980) 'The Drover's Wife' *Bulletin* December 23, 30, pp. 156-60
Jurgensen, M. ed. (1981) *Ethnic Australia* Brisbane: Phoenix Publications
Kalechofsky, R. & R. eds. (1984) *Jewish Writing from Down Under* Marblehead, Mass.: Micah Publications
Karberry, P. (1939) *Aboriginal Women: Sacred and Profane* London: Routledge & Kegan Paul
Keesing, N. ed. (1978/1983) *Shalom: Australian Jewish Stories* Ringwood and Harmondsworth: Penguin Books
Keneally, T. (1967/1968) *Bring Larks and Heroes* Melbourne: Sun Books
Keneally, T. (1972/1976) *The Chant of Jimmie Blacksmith* Ringwood and Harmondsworth: Penguin Books
Kermode, F. and Davies, M.B. (1961) 'The European View of Christopher Brennan' *Australian Letters* Vol. 3, No. 3, pp. 57-63
Kiernan, B. (1971), *Images of Society and Nature: Seven Essays on Australian Novels* Melbourne: Oxford University Press
Kiernan, B. ed. (1977a) *Considerations: New Essays on Kenneth Slessor, Judith Wright and Douglas Stewart* Sydney: Angus and Robertson
Kiernan, B. ed. (1977b) *The Most Beautiful Lies* Sydney: Angus and Robertson
King, R. (1976) 'The Dialectics of Culture: The Greeks in Australia' *Meanjin*, Vol. 35, No. 3. pp. 227-240
Kingsley, H. (1859/1970) *The Recollections of Geoffrey Hamlyn* Hawthorn, Victoria: Lloyd O'Neil
Kramer, L. (1973) 'Patrick White's Götterdämmerung' *Quadrant* Vol. 17, May/June, pp. 8-19
Kramer, L. (1979) *A.D. Hope* Melbourne: Oxford University Press
Kramer, L. ed. (1981) *The Oxford History of Australian Literature* Melbourne: Oxford University Press
Krebs, G.A. (1979) [review of G.A. Wilkes *Australian Colloquialisms*] *AUMLA* No. 51, May, pp. 179-180

Kress, G. and Hodge, R. (1979) *Language as Ideology* London: Routledge & Kegan Paul

Krupinski, J. and Stoller, A. (1974) *The Family in Australia* Rushcutters Bay: Pergamon

Lamb, P. and Hazell A. eds. (1983) *Diversity and Diversion: An Annotated Bibliography of Australian Minority Literature* Richmond, Victoria: Hodja

Lawler, R. (1957) *Summer of the Seventeenth Doll* Sydney: Angus and Robertson

Lawler, R. (1985) *The Doll Trilogy* Sydney: Currency Press

Lawson, A. (1979) 'Meaning and Experience: A Review-Essay on Some Recurrent Problems in Patrick White Criticism' *Texas Studies in Literature and Language* Vol. 21, No. 2, pp. 280-95

Lawson, H. (1972a) *Autobiographical and other Writings 1887-1922* (ed. C. Roderick), Sydney: Angus and Robertson

Lawson, H. (1972b) *Short Stories and Sketches 1888-1922* (ed. C. Roderick), Sydney: Angus and Robertson

Lawson, S. (1983) *The Archibald Paradox: A Strange Case of Authorship* Ringwood: Penguin

Lévi-Strauss, C. (1963/1968) 'The Story of Asdiwal' in Leach, E. ed. *The Structural Study of Myth and Totemism* London: Tavistock Publications

Lévi-Strauss, C. (1963/1972) *Structural Anthropology* trans. C. Jacobson and B.G. Schoepf, Harmondsworth: Penguin Books

Levy, B. (1985) 'Women and the Literary Pages: Some Recent Examples' *Hecate* Vol. 11, No. 1, pp. 5-11

Lucich, P. ed. (1969) *Children's Stories from the Worora* Canberra: Australian Institute of Aboriginal Studies

Lukács, G. (1971) *The Theory of the Novel* trans. Anna Bostock, London: Merlin Press

Lyotard, J-F. (1986) *The Postmodern Condition: A Report on Knowledge* trans. Geoff Bennington and Brian Massumi, Manchester: Manchester University Press

Macainsh, N. (1989) 'Steps into the Forest: Christopher Brennan's Fatal Attraction' *AUMLA* No. 72, November, pp. 229-51

Macartney, F.T. (1957) *Australian Literary Essays* Sydney: Angus and Robertson

Macaulay, B.T. (1953) 'Minute on Education' quoted in Cutts, Elmer H., 'The Background of Macaulay's Minute', *American Historical Review* Vol. 58, July, p. 839

McAuley, J. (1973) *Christopher Brennan* Melbourne: Oxford University Press

McGrath, A. (1978) 'Aboriginal Women Workers in the Northern Territory, 1911-1939' *Hecate* Vol. 4, No. 2, pp. 5-25

McGregor, W. (1987) 'The Structure of Gooniyandi Narratives' *Australian Aboriginal Studies* No. 2, pp. 20-28

McGuiness, D. and Walker, D. (1985) 'The politics of Aboriginal literature' in Davis, J. and Hodge, B.

MacKeller, D. (1982) *My Country and Other Poems* South Yarra: Lloyd O'Neil

McKenzie, D.F. (1984) 'The Sociology of a Text: Orality, Literacy and Print in Early New Zealand' *The Library* [Sixth Series] Vol. 6, No. 4, pp. 333-65

Mackenzie, M. (1965) 'Patrick White's Later Novels: A Generic Reading' *Southern Review* Vol. 1, No. 3, pp. 5-17

Macleod, M. (1979) 'Bruce Dawe and the Americans' *Australian Literary Studies* Vol. IX, No. 2, pp. 143–55
Macleod, M. (1983) 'Bruce Dawe and Frank Sargeson: Speaking in Other Voices' *Australian Literary Studies* Vol. XII, No. 1, pp. 3–13
McQueen, H. (1970/1975) *A New Britannia* Ringwood: Penguin
Maddock, K. (1982) *The Australian Aborigines* Ringwood and Harmondsworth: Penguin Books
Malouf, D. (1975) *Johnno* St. Lucia: University of Queensland Press
Malouf, D. (1978/1980) *An Imaginary Life* Sydney: Pan Books (Australia)
Malouf, D. (1984/1985) *Harland's Half Acre* Ringwood and Harmondsworth: Penguin Books
Malouf, D. (1985/1986) *12 Edmonstone Street* Ringwood and Harmondsworth: Penguin Books
Malouf, D. (1989) *Blood Relations* Sydney: Currency Press
Mannoni, D. (1964) *Prospero and Caliban: the psychology of colonization* New York: Praeger
Maris, H. and Berg, S. (1983) *Women of the Sun* Sydney: Currency Press
Martin, J.I. (1978) *The Migrant Presence* Sydney: George Allen & Unwin
Mathers, P. (1966) *Trap* London: Cassell
Maynard, M. (1983) 'Projections of Melancholy' in I. and T. Donaldson
Meredith, J. (1960) *The wild colonial boy: the life and times of Jack Donohoe* Sydney: Wentworth Press
Meredith, J. and Whalan, R. (1979) *Frank the Poet* Melbourne: Red Rooster
Merritt, R. (1978) *The Cake Man* Sydney: Currency Press
Metz, C. (1974) *Language and Cinema* trans. Donna Jean Umiker-Sebeok, The Hague: Mouton
Michaels, E. (1986) *The Aboriginal Invention of Television in Central Australia 1982–1986* Canberra: Australian Institute of Aboriginal Studies
Michaels, E. (1987) *For a Cultural Future: Francis Jupurrurla makes TV at Yuendumu* Sydney: Artspace
Mishra, V. (1977) 'Early Literary Responses to Charles Harpur' *Westerly* No. 4, pp. 88–93
Mishra, V. (1982) 'Negotiating an Autobiography: Patrick White's *Flaws in the Glass*' *Span* No. 14, May, pp. 25–32
Mishra, V. (1984) 'White's Poetics: Patrick White through Mikhail Bakhtin' *Span* No. 18, April, pp. 54–75
Mishra, V. (1987) 'David Shulman and the Laughter of South Indian Kings and Clowns' *South Asia* [New Series] Vol. 10, No. 1, pp. 83–88
Mishra, V. (1987) 'The Formulaic Text: The Poetry of Bruce Dawe' *English in Australia* No. 82, pp. 37–46
Mishra, V. (1988/9) 'Aboriginal Representations in Australian Texts' *Continuum* Vol. 2, No. 1, pp. 165–188
Modjeska, D. (1981) *Exiles at Home: Australian Women Writers, 1925–45* Sydney: Sirus, Angus and Robertson
Modjeska, D. ed. (1989) *Inner Cities. Australian Women's Memory of Place* Ringwood and Harmondsworth: Penguin Books
Molony, J. (1987) *The Penguin Bicentennial History of Australia* Ringwood and Harmondsworth: Penguin Books
Moore, C. and Muecke S. (1984) 'Racism and the Representation of Aborigines

BIBLIOGRAPHY

in Film' *Australian Journal of Cultural Studies* Vol. 2, No. 1, pp. 36–533
Moore, T.I. (1971) *Social Patterns in Australian Literature* Berkeley: University of California Press
Moran, A. (1985) *Images and Industry* Sydney: Currency Press
Moran, A. and O'Regan T. (1989) *The Australian Screen* Ringwood: Penguin
Moran, A. and O'Regan, T. eds. (1986) *An Australian Film Reader* Sydney: Currency Press
Morgan, S. (1987) *My Place* Fremantle: Fremantle Arts Centre Press
Morris, E. E. (1898/1972) *Austral English: A Dictionary of Australasian Words, Phrases and Usages* Sydney: Sydney University Press
Mountford, C. and Roberts, A. (1965) *The Dreamtime: Australian Aboriginal Myths in Painting* Adelaide: Rigby
Muecke, S. (1982) 'Available Discourses' in Botsman, P. ed. *Theoretical Strategies* Sydney: Local Consumption Publications
Muecke, S., Rumsey, A., Wirrunmarra, B. (1985) 'Pigeon the outlaw: history as texts' *Aboriginal History* Vol. 9, No. 1, pp. 81–92
Munn, N. (1973) *Walbiri Iconography* Ithaca: Cornell University Press
Narogin, M. [Johnson, C.] (1965/1984) *Wild Cat Falling* Sydney: Angus and Robertson
Narogin, M. [Johnson, C.] (1979) *Long Live Sandawara* Melbourne: Quartet Books
Narogin, M. [Johnson, C.] (1983) *Doctor Wooreddy's Prescription for Enduring the Ending of the World* Melbourne: Hyland House
Narogin, M. [Johnson, C.] (1985) 'Reading the Book' *Australian Journal of Cultural Studies* Vol. 3, No. 2, pp. 143–146
Narogin, M. [Johnson, C.] (1986) *Wildcat Falling: A Screenplay* (ed. Richard Guthrie), unpublished MS.
Narogin, M. [Johnson, C.] (1988) *Dalwurra, The Black Bittern: A Poem Cycle* Perth: Centre for Studies in Australian Literature, University of Western Australia
Narogin, M. [Johnson, C.] (1988) *Doin Wildcat. A Novel Koori Script*, Melbourne: Hyland House
Narogin, M. (1990) *Writing from the Fringe. A Study of Modern Aboriginal Literature* Melbourne: Hyland House
Noonuccal, O. [Walker K.] (1964) *We are Going* Brisbane: Jacaranda Press
O'Regan, T. (1979) 'The Last Tasmanian Monday Conference', video-crit, Brisbane: Griffith University
O'Regan, T. ed. (1990) 'Communication & Tradition: Essays after Eric Michaels' *Continuum* 3, 2
O. Pi (ed.) (1985) *Off the Record* Ringwood and Harmondsworth: Penguin Books
Ong, W. J. (1982) *Orality and Literacy* London: Methuen
Palmer, V. (1954) *The Legend of the Nineties* Melbourne: Melbourne University Press
Parker, D. L. (1896/1953) *Australian Legendary Tales* Sydney: Angus and Robertson
Partridge, E. (1961) *A Dictionary of the Underworld* London: Routledge and Kegan Paul

Partridge, E. (1970) *A Dictionary of Slang and Unconventional English* 2 vols., London: Routheldge and Kegan Paul
Partridge, E. (1978) 'As Australian as a Meat Pie' [review of G.A. Wilkes *Australian Colloquialisms*] TLS 18 August, pp. 933-34
Pascoe, R. (1979) *The Manufacture of Australian History* Melbourne: Oxford University Press
Paterson, A.B. (1921) *Collected Verse* Sydney: Angus and Robertson
Peterson, N. (1983) 'The Popular Image' in I. and T. Donaldson
Phillips, A.A. (1958/1966) *The Australian Tradition* Melbourne: Cheshire
Pierce, P. (1980) 'The Australian Literature of the Vietnam War' *Meanjin* Vol. 39, pp. 290-303
Pierce, P. (1983) 'How Australia's Literary History Might be Written' *Australian Literary Studies* Vol. 13, No. 1, pp. 67-79
Poole, J. (1970) 'Maurice Frere's Wife: Marcus Clarke's Revision of *His Natural Life*' *Australian Literary Studies* Vol. 4, No. 4, pp. 384-394
Praed, R. (1893/1988) *Outlaw and Lawmaker* London: Pandora
Price, C. (1985) 'The ethnic composition of the Australian population' in *Immigration and ethnicity in the 1980s* eds. Burnley, I., Encel, S. and McCall G. Melbourne: Longman Cheshire
Prichard, K.S. (1929/1956) *Coonardoo* Sydney: Angus and Robertson
Ramson, W. (1965) 'A Critical Review of Writings on the Vocabulary of Australian English' *Australian Literary Studies* Vol. 1, No. 1, pp. 89-103
Ramson, W. (1978) 'The Gentler Art Of Lexicography' [review of G.A. Wilkes, *Australian Colloquialisms*] *Quadrant* August, pp. 58-60
Ramson, W.S. ed. (1974) *The Australian Experience: Critical Essays on Australian Novels* Canberra : Australian National University Press
Rando, G. (1984) 'Italo-Australian Fiction' *Meanjin* Vol. 43, No. 3, pp. 341-349
Reece, R. (1974) *Aborigines and Colonists: Aborigines and Colonial Society in New South Wales in the 1830s and 1840s* Sydney: Sydney University Press
Renouf, A. (1976) *The Frightened Country* Melbourne: Macmillan
Reynolds, H. (1978/1982) *The Other Side of the Frontier: Aboriginal Resistance to the European Invasion of Australia* Ringwood: Penguin
Reynolds, H. (1979) 'Jimmy Governor and Jimmie Blacksmith' *Australian Literary Studies* Vol. 9, No. 1, pp. 14-25
Reynolds, H. (1984) *The Breaking of the Great Australian Silence: Aborigines in Australian Historiography* London: Australian Studies Centre
Reynolds, H. (1989) *Dispossession: Black Australians and White Invaders* Sydney: Allen & Unwin
Richardson, H.H. (1917-1929/1971) *The Fortunes of Richard Mahony* Ringwood and Harmondsworth: Penguin Books
Ricks, C. (1974) 'Gigantist', [review of P. White, *The Eye of the Storm*] *The New York Review of Books* 4 April, pp. 19-20
Riffaterre, M. (1980) *Semiotics of Poetry* London: Methuen
Robson, L.L. (1963) 'The Historical Basis of *For the Term of His Natural Life*' *Australian Literary Studies* Vol. 1, No. 2, pp. 104-121
Robson, L.L. (1988) 'Behold a pale horse: Australian war studies' *Australian Historical Studies* 23, pp. 115-126
Roe, P. (1983) *Gularabulu: Stories of the West Kimberley* (ed. Stephen Muecke) Fremantle: Fremantle Arts Centre Press

BIBLIOGRAPHY

Routt, W. (1989) 'The Fairest child of the motherland' in Moran, A. and O'Regan, T. eds.
Rowley, C.D. (1970) *The Destruction of Aboriginal Society* Canberra: Australian National University Press
Rowley, C.D. (1978) *A Matter of Justice* Canberra: Australian National University Press
Rowley, C.D. (1986) *Recovery: The Politics of Aboriginal Reform* Ringwood and Harmondsworth: Penguin Books
Rutland, S. D. (1988) *Edge of the Diaspora: Two Centuries of Jewish Settlement in Australia* Sydney: Collins Australia
Said, E. (1978) *Orientalism* London: Routledge and Kegan Paul
Said, E. (1985) 'Orientalism Reconsidered' *Race and Class* Vol. 27, No. 2, pp.1–15
Sansom, B. (1980) *The Camp at Wallaby Cross* Canberra: Australian Institute of Aboriginal Studies
Schaffer, K. (1987) 'Landscape representation and *Australian national identity*' *Australian Journal of Cultural Studies* Vol. 4, No. 2, pp. 47–60
Serle, G. (1973) *From Deserts the Prophets Come* Melbourne: Heinemann
Seymour, A. (1962) *The One Day of the Year* Sydney: Angus and Robertson
Shaw, B. (1981) *My Country of the Pelican Dreaming: The Life of an Australian Aborigine of the Gadjerong, Grant Ngabidj, 1904–1977* Canberra: Australian Institute of Aboriginal Studies
Shaw, B. (1983) *Banggaiyerri: The Story of Jack Sullivan* Canberra: Australian Institute of Aboriginal Studies
Shelley, M. (1818/1831/1974) *Frankenstein* (ed. James Rieger) Chicago: University of Chicago Press
Shoemaker, A. (1989) *Black Words, White Page: Aboriginal Literature 1929–1988* St Lucia: University of Queensland Press
Shute, C. (1975) 'Heroines and Heroes: Sexual Mythology in Australia 1914–1918' *Hecate* Vol. 1, No. 1, pp. 7–22
Skrzynecki, P. ed. (1985) *Joseph's Coat: An Anthology of Multicultural Writing* Sydney: Hale and Iremonger
Smith, B (1976) *The Antipodean Manifesto* Melbourne: Oxford University Press
Smith, B. (1960) *European Vision and the South Pacific, 1768–1850: A Study in the History of Art and Ideas* Melbourne: Oxford University Press
Smith, B. (1980) *The Spectre of Truganini* (1980 Boyer Lectures), Sydney: Australian Broadcasting Commission
Spencer, B. (1982) *The Aboriginal Photographs of Baldwin Spencer* (ed. R.Vanderwal) Melbourne: Currey O'Neil
Spilias, T. and Messinis, S. eds. (1988) *Reflections. Selected Works from Greek Australian Literature* Box Hill, Victoria: Elikia Books Publications
Spivak, G.C. (1987) *In Other Worlds* London and New York: Methuen
Stanner, W.E.H. (1979) *White Man Got No Dreaming* Canberra: Australian National University Press
Stead, C. (1965) *The Man Who Loved Children* New York: Holt, Rinehart and Winston
Steiner, G. (1974) 'Carnal Knowledge', [review of P. White *The Eye of the Storm*] *The New Yorker* 4 March, pp. 109–113
Stephensen, P.R. (1935) 'The Foundations of Culture in Australia: An Essay

Towards National Self-Respect' in Barnes, J. ed. (1969) *The Writer in Australia 1856-1964* Melbourne: Oxford University Press
Stewart, D. (1943) *Ned Kelly: a play* Sydney: Angus and Robertson
Storer, D. (1985) *Ethnic Family Values in Australia* Sydney: Prentice-Hall
Strehlow, T. (1971) *Songs of Central Australia* Sydney: Angus and Robertson
Sturm, T. (1973) 'Thomas Keneally and Australian Racism: *The Chant of Jimmie Blacksmith*' *Southerly* Vol. 33, No. 3, pp. 261-74
Sturm, T. (1976) 'The Structure of Brennan's *The Wanderers*' in Cantrell, L. ed. *Bards, Bohemians and Bookmen* St. Lucia: Queensland University Press
Sullivan, P. (1986) 'The generation of cultural trauma: what are anthropologists for?' *Australian Aboriginal Studies* No. 1, pp. 13-23
Summers, A. (1975) *Damned Whores and God's Police* Ringwood and Harmondsworth: Penguin Books
Sutherland, J. (1978) '"Lines Driven Deep": radical departures, or the same old story, for Prichard's women?' *Hecate* Vol. 4, No. 1, pp. 7-24
Sutton, P. ed. (1988) *Dreamings: The Art of Aboriginal Australia* Melbourne: Viking Books
Symons, A. (1899) *The Symbolist Movement in Literature* London: William Heinemann
Tacey, D.J. (1988) *Patrick White. Fiction and the Unconscious* Melbourne: Oxford University Press
Tatz, C. (1979) *Race Politics in Australia: Aborigines, Politics and Law* Armidale: University of New England Press
Tedlock, D. (1983) *The Spoken Word and the Work of Interpretation* Philadelphia: University of Pennsylvania Press
Threadgold, T. (1985) in O'Toole, M. and Birch, D. eds. *The Functions of Style* London: Frances Pinter
Tiffin, C. ed. (1978) *South Pacific Images* Brisbane, University of Queensland: South Pacific Association for Commonwealth Literature and Language Studies
Tiffin, H. (1984) 'Commonwealth Literature and Comparative Methodology' *WLWE* 23, 1 (Winter) pp.26-30
Treborlang, R. (1985) *How to Survive in Australia* Sydney: Major Mitchell Press
Tsaloumas, D. (1983) *The Observatory* (trans. Philip Grundy) St. Lucia: University of Queensland Press
Tucker, J. (1952) *Ralph Rashleigh* Sydney: Angus and Robertson
Tulloch, J. (1986) *Legends on the Screen* Sydney: Currency Press
Turner, G. (1986) *National Fictions* Sydney: Allen & Unwin
Turner, G.W. (1978) 'Australian Colloquialisms' [review of G.A. Wilkes *Australian Colloquialisms*] *Southerly* Vol. 38, No. 4, pp. 232-4
Ucko, P. (1977) *Form in Indigenous Art* Canberra: Australian Institute of Aboriginal Studies
Vasilakakos, J. (1989) 'Translating Australian Migrant Literature' *Meanjin* Vol. 48, No. 4, pp. 706-712
Vaux, J.H. (1812/1964) ed. N. McLachlan *The Memoires of James Hardy Vaux including his Vocabulary of the Flash Language* London: Heinemann
Wallace-Crabbe, C. (1976) 'Bruce Dawe's Inventiveness' *Meanjin* Vol. 25, pp. 94-101
Walsh, W. (1973) *Commonwealth Literature* Oxford: Oxford University Press

Ward, G. (1987) *Wandering Girl* Broome: Magabala Books
Ward, R. (1958) *The Australian Legend* Melbourne: Oxford University Press
Waten, J. 'A Writer's Youth' in Skrzynecki, P. ed. pp. 198-206
Waten, J. (1964/1978) *Distant Land* Sydney: Angus and Robertson
Waten, J. (1983) 'Discovering Migrant Literature' *Island Magazine* No. 16, pp. 26-9
White, H. (1973) *Metahistory. The Historical Imagination in Nineteenth-Century Europe* Baltimore: Johns Hopkins University Press
White, P. (1948/1969) *The Aunt's Story* Ringwood and Harmondsworth: Penguin Books
White, P. (1955/1970) *The Tree of Man* Ringwood and Harmondsworth: Penguin Books
White, P. (1957) *Voss* London: Eyre and Spottiswoode
White, P. (1961) *Riders in the Chariot* London: Eyre and Spottiswoode
White, P. (1966) *The Solid Mandala* London: Eyre and Spottiswoode
White, P. (1973) *The Eye of the Storm* London: Jonathan Cape
White, P. (1976) *A Fringe of Leaves* London: Jonathan Cape
White, P. (1979) *The Twyborn Affair* London: Jonathan Cape
White, P. (1981) *Flaws in the Glass: A Self-Portrait* London: Jonathan Cape
White, R. (1981) *Inventing Australia: Image and Identity 1688-1980* Sydney: Allen & Unwin
Wilding, M. (1977) *Marcus Clarke* Melbourne: Oxford University Press
Wilkes, G.A. (1962) 'The Eighteen Nineties' in Johnston, G. ed. *Australian Literary Criticism* Melbourne: Oxford University Press
Wilkes, G.A. (1969) *Australian Literature: A Conspectus* Sydney: Angus and Robertson
Wilkes, G.A. (1970) *Ten Essays on Patrick White* Sydney: Angus and Robertson
Wilkes, G.A. (1978/1985) *A Dictionary of Australian Colloquialisms* Sydney: Sydney University Press
Wilkes, G.A. (1981) *The Stockyard and the Croquet Lawn* Port Melbourne: Edward Arnold
Wilkes, G.A. (1982) 'Australian Colloquialisms and Colloquial Australianisms' *Southerly* Vol. 42, No. 4, pp. 436-444
Wilkes, G.A. ed. (1974) *The Colonial Poets* Sydney: Angus and Robertson
Williamson, D. (1973/1980) *Don's Party* Woollahra, NSW: Currency Press
Wilson, P. (1982) *Black Death, White Hands* Sydney: Allen & Unwin
Wilson, P. and Braithwaite, J. (1978) *Two Faces of Deviance* St. Lucia: Queensland University Press
Wilson, R. ed. (1984/1985) *Good Talk: The Extraordinary Lives of Ten Ordinary Australian Women* Fitzroy and Ringwood, Victoria: McPhee Gribble/ Penguin Books
Windows onto Worlds: Studying Australia at Tertiary Level Canberra: Government Print Office
Wright, J. (1971) *Collected Poems* Sydney: Angus and Robertson
Wright, J. (1974) 'Bruce Dawe's Poetry' *Westerly* No. 1, pp. 36-44

Index

Aboriginalism, 27–30, 32, 43, 60–61, 71–4, 77–8, 101–2, 107, 113
Adorno, Theodor W., 180
Africa, xii, 15, 25, 72
Althusser, Louis, 117
Archibald, J. F., 182
Art, Papunya (Western Desert) 75, 86, 92, 95, 110, 227
Ashcroft, Griffiths and Tiffin, x, xi, 196, 205, 209, 220
assimilation, 51, 114, 188
Aurukun, 87, 89, 115

Bail, Murray, 168, 170–71
Baker, Sidney, 233
Bakhtin, Mikhail, 232
Banks, Sir Joseph, 144, 152
Baranay, Inez, 201–2
Barthes, Roland, 158
Bateson, Gregory, xv, 137, 216–19, 220, 234
Baudelaire, Charles, 186
Baynton, Barbara, 168–70, 172, 175, 177
Beckett, Samuel, 110, 114, 154
Ben Hall, 136
Bentham, Jeremy, 119
Berndt, Ronald and Catherine, 77, 86, 223, 225, 226–7

Bicentenary, Australian, ix–x, 105, 220, 224, 232
Blainey, Geoffrey, xviii, 151–4, 191–2, 225, 229
Blake, William, 183, 184, 186
Boehme, Jacob, 186
Boldrewood, Rolf [Thomas Alexander Browne] 134, 228
Bradley, Lt. William, 34–6, 37, 39
Brahmanism, 186
Brennan, Christopher, 182–7, 197, 230, 232
Brockman, C. J., 158
Bropho, Robert, 93, 227
Brown, Maitland, 158
Buckley, Vincent, 58, 221, 222
Bulletin, 167, 170, 182
Bunaba, 105, 107

Caldwell, Arthur, 188
Campbell, Marion, 187
Canada, xii, 51
Carey, Gabrielle, 138, 139, 140
Carter, Paul, 20, 152, 220, 224
Cash, Martin, 122
Césaire, Aime, 29
Chauvel, Charles, 64–8, 225
Chifley, Ben, 188
Chin, Sue, 194–6

INDEX

Clark, Axel, 184, 185, 232
Clark, Manning, 162, 220
Clarke, Marcus, 121, 123, 125–30, 134, 137, 141, 150, 228
Cook, Captain James, 144, 152, 158
Country Practice, A, 140
Culotta, Nino [John O'Grady], 188–92, 193, 196, 200, 201, 202
Cummings, E. E., 186
Cunningham, Stuart, 65, 225
Cyprus, 122, 123, 128

Dark, Eleanor, 29–30
Darwin, Charles, 144
Davis, Jack, xviii, 59, 93, 103–4, 108, 114, 141–2, 206–7, 223, 227
Dawe, Bruce, 7–14, 20, 222
Derrida, Jacques, 109
Dixson, Miriam, xviii, 163, 211–13, 215, 217, 220, 230
Dobell, Sir William, 182
Douglas, M., 51
Drake-Brockman, H., 98, 100
Dransfield, Michael, 154–6
Dreamtime, 27–8, 95, 101, 111, 115
Drysdale, Sir Russell, 151, 168, 170–71, 182
During, Simon, 113
Dutton, Geoffrey, 42, 230

Eliot, T. S., 87
Elkin, A. P., 29, 30
Elliott, Brian, 58, 221, 229
Fanon, Frantz, 29
Fernando, Chitra, 194
Field, Barron, 39
Fiji, xiii
Fogarty, Lionel 227
Foucault, Michel, 118–20, 137, 140, 228
Frances, Raelene, 158
'Frank the Poet' [Francis MacNamara], 121–5, 127–9, 132–3, 139–40, 183
Fraser, Dawn, 188
French Symbolists, 183, 185
Freud, Sigmund, xvi, 137, 184
Fristrom, Oscar, 44, 47, 63
Furphy, Joseph [Tom Collins], 157, 186, 210, 228, 230

Gelder and Salzman, 196, 232
Gilbert, Kevin, 93, 108, 114, 223, 225, 227
Gilmore, Dame Mary, 30, 187
Godwin, William, 127
Goldsmith, Oliver, 41, 42
Goodwin, Ken, 189, 221
Gooneratne, Yasmine, 193–4
Gordon, A. L., 150, 187
Governor, Jimmy, 59, 105
Gray, Thomas, 41
Greer, Germaine, 194, 233
Grey, Sir George, 16–18, 20
Gunew, Sneja, 231, 233

Haley, Terry, 138, 139
Halliday, Michael, 201, 205, 232
Hancock, Sir Keith, 162, 164
Harpur, Charles, xviii, 19–22, 132–4, 136, 148–9, 150, 222, 224
Harris, Alexander, 192
Hartz, Louis, xii, xiii, xiv, 15–16, 18–19, 22, 31, 91, 116, 145, 179–80, 215, 218, 220
Hasluck, Sir Paul, 10–12, 14
Haydon, Tom, 69
Hazzard, Shirley, 197
Hegel, G. W. F., 27, 29, 103
Heidelberg School, the, 174, 182, 185
Herbert, Xavier, 3, 53, 56–8, 65, 157
Heseltine, Harry, 198, 221, 225
Hewett, Dorothy, 225
Heysen, Hans, 175–6
Hill, Ernestine, 159
Hobsbawm, E., 131
Hogan, Paul, 23, 151, 157, 172
Holt, Harold, 6
Holt, Joseph, 124
Homer, 60, 76, 79, 83, 107, 121
Hope, A. D., 164–6, 199–200, 221, 222, 231
Horne, Donald, xv
Hughes, Robert, 124, 136, 137, 220, 227
Hugo, Victor, 129
Humphries, Barry, 157

India, xii, xiii, 11, 27, 189, 230
Indian, American, 24, 25, 72

251

Indian, Mexican, 25, 52
Indonesia, 11
Ireland, David, 137, 224, 228
Irish, the, 116, 127, 133, 135, 142, 180, 188, 218

Jandamarra, 107
Jefferis, Barbara, 168, 171–2
'Jindyworobak', 30
Jones, Rhys, 69

Kelly, Ned, 123, 131, 132, 134, 136, 175
Keneally, Thomas, 59–62, 64, 67, 68, 225, 228
Kennedy, J. F., 107
Kiernan, Brian, 171, 222, 223
King, Philip Gidley, 32–5, 37, 39, 42
Kingsley, Henry, 228
Koori, 25, 112
Kramer, Leonie, 1–3, 156, 189, 200, 213, 221–2, 230

Lang, John Dunmore, 19–22
Lawler, Ray, 175–7
Lawson, Henry, 153–7, 160, 168–72, 175, 182, 210, 230
Leichhardt, Ludwig von, 159
Lester, Yami, 24, 50
Lévi-Strauss, Claude, 51, 52, 97, 226
Lindsay, Norman, 187
Lukács, Georg, 103, 224
Lyotard, J-F, ix,

Macartney, Frederick, T., 29, 30
Macaulay, T. B., 189
MacKeller, Dorothea, 165, 169, 171, 187
Macquarie, Governor Lachlan, 19
Mad Max III, 225
Mahabharata, The, 107
Malaysia, 11
Malouf, David, 196–9
Man from Snowy River, The, 148
Mansell, Michael, 69
Maori, 24, 25
Marvell, Andrew, 21
Mathers, Peter, 224
McGuiness, B., 206, 208
McKenzie, D. F., 223

McLuhan, Marshall, 76
McQueen, Humphrey, xviii, 136, 153, 162, 163, 168, 174, 180, 182, 183, 220, 228, 229, 230
Meredith and Whalan, 122, 123, 125, 132
Metz, Christian, 76
Mexico, 25
Michaels, Eric, 223
Mick, Minko, 105, 106
Millis, Roger, 198
Milton, John 21, 148
mode, eternalist, 2–5, 14, 19, 58, nationalist, 3–5, 19
Modjeska, Drusilla, 194, 200, 231, 234
Moffat, Tracey, 37
Molloy, Georgina, 145–8
Morgan, Sally, 93, 97–9, 100–1, 114–15, 223
Mountford and Roberts, 78, 79, 81, 82, 86, 87, 88
Muecke, Stephen, 83, 84, 108, 109, 223, 226

Narogin, Mudrooroo [Colin Johnson], xviii, 59, 61, 63, 66, 93, 97, 101, 105–6, 109–15, 136, 154, 224, 226, 227
Négritude, 28
Neilson, John Shaw, 187
New Zealand, 16, 18, 24, 25
Nolan, Sidney, 136, 151, 157, 159, 175, 182, 214, 229
Noongar/Nyungar, 25, 112, 206–8
Noonuccal, Oodgeroo [Kath Walker], 93, 114, 223, 227

O'Regan, Tom, xix, 225, 227, 229
Orientalism, xiii, 27, 29
Orwell, George, 137

Palmer, Vance, 3, 168, 229
Parkes, Henry, 20, 149, 150
Partridge, Eric, 233
Pat, John, 141
Paterson, A. B., (Banjo) 147, 150
Phillip, Governor Arthur, 32, 117, 119
Phillips, A. A., 3, 222, 229

INDEX

Picnic at Hanging Rock, 225
Pierce, Peter, 221
Praed, Rosa, 135–6
Prichard, Katharine Susannah, 53–4, 56–8, 61, 65, 157, 225
Prisoner, 140, 229
Propertius, 83

Ramayana, The, 76
Reynolds, Henry, xviii, 50, 59, 102, 222–3, 225
Richardson, Henry Handel, 155–7, 160, 165, 171, 192, 197, 234
Riffaterre, Michael, 113
Roberts, Tom, 45, 47, 54, 63, 157
Roe, Paddy, 83–5
Rowley, C. D., xviii, 30, 31, 38, 41, 44, 50, 53, 102, 140, 222
Rudd, Steele [Arthur Hoey Davis], 172
Ruxton, Bruce, 178–80

Said, Edward, xiii, 27, 223
Scates, Bruce, 158
Schepisi, Fred, 67
Scott, Sir Walter, 103
Senghor, Leopold, 29
Shaw, Bruce, 75, 76
Shelley, Mary, 202
Singer, Violet, 183–4
Sinnett, Frederick, 113, 148–9, 222
Skipper, Peter, 93–8, 101, 115
Smith, Bernard, 143, 224, 225
Solzhenitsyn, 30
South Africa, 51
Stanner, W. E. H., 32, 41
Stead, Christina, 197, 214–16, 234
Stephensen, P. R., 58, 225
Stewart, Douglas, 136
Story, Helen (Nelly), 145
Stow, Randolph, 197
Summers, Anne, xviii, 120, 163, 170, 184, 211, 220, 230, 234
Sutton, Peter, 79, 86–90, 95, 96, 223, 226
Swedenborg, Emanuel, 186

syntax, domino, 11–13, expatriate, 153, 157, 160, nomadic, 152–3, 156, 157, 160

tabi, 17
Tench, W., 32
Tiffin, Helen, 220, 232
Tompson, Charles, 39, 41–3
Treborlang, R., 137–8
Trollope, Anthony, 191
Tsaloumas, Dmitri, 232
Tucker, Albert, 175, 182
Tucker, James, 228
Tudewali, Robert, 65
Turner, Frederick, 147

United States, the, xii, 11, 16, 25, 51

Vaux, James Hardy, 232–3
Vietnam, 6, 7, 10, 11, 13

Walker, D., 206, 208
Walwicz, Ania, 199–201, 202, 208–9
Ward, Glenyse, 114
Ward, Russel, xviii, 3, 19, 136, 162–4, 168, 174, 188–9, 221, 229–30
Waten, Judah, 192–3, 196
Werth, Elizabeth, 183–4
White, Haydn, 221
White, Patrick, 59, 62, 63, 144, 159–61, 175, 177, 197, 210, 213–15, 232
White, Richard, xviii, 163, 168, 182, 220, 229–30
Whitlam, Gough, 188
Wilkes, G. A., 40, 187, 209, 221, 222, 229, 233
Williams, Frederick,151
Wirrunmarra, Banjo, 104–7
Wordsworth, William, 149, 198
Wright, Judith, 3, 13–14, 19, 146–9, 221–2

Yagan, 105, 141

253